CONTAINING ADDICTION

CONTAINING ADDICTION

The Federal Bureau of Narcotics

and the Origins of America's

Global Drug War

MATTHEW R. PEMBLETON

University of Massachusetts Press
Amherst and Boston

Copyright © 2017 by University of Massachusetts Press

ISBN 978-1-62534-316-1 (paper); 315-4 (hardcover)

Designed by Sally Nichols
Set in Adobe Minion Pro
Printed and bound by Maple Press, Inc.

Cover design by Jack Harrison

Library of Congress Cataloging-in-Publication Data
A catalog record for this book is available from the Library of Congress.

British Library Cataloguing-in-Publication Data
A catalog record for this book is available from the British Library.

For Bob, Dave, and Dan

CONTENTS

PREFACE

Historians like to say there is only one past but many histories, which is to say that our understanding of the past is under constant revision and shaped, inevitably and indelibly, by the context in which historians do their work.

This book is primarily about the Federal Bureau of Narcotics (FBN), the nation's first dedicated drug enforcement agency and the grandfather of the modern Drug Enforcement Administration (DEA). In terms of argument, this story pushes the framework of the war on drugs further into the past and reveals how, between 1930 and 1968, the Bureau built and elaborated upon the idea of a drug war while extending the reach and influence of American power at home and abroad. In the process, the FBN enlarged both the global footprint and the conceptual boundaries of U.S. national security. It also established many of the basic drug enforcement strategies and tactics still used today. Though we have moved—somewhat—beyond the image of rampaging dope fiends and marijuana-crazed ax murderers, we are still, in many respects, living in a world the FBN helped to create.

Because it took a while to research and write, the circumstances in which this book was conceived differ rather dramatically from those in which it was completed and in which it will be read. I began in the late George W. Bush era, trying to unravel the various ideological threads of U.S. national security doctrine. The book was composed during the Obama years, a time of ostensible rapprochement in both the Global War on Terror and the War on Drugs. The book was completed in the first days of the Trump era, in the same atmosphere of intense social and political conflict that bred earlier iterations of the drug war.

As someone who contemplates the challenges of governance over the grand sweep of American history, I'm drawn to subjects that explore the connection between citizen and state, the United States and the world, culture and politics. Soon after stumbling upon the story of the FBN, I realized the history of U.S. drug policy was a way to do all three. Plus, I'd get to write about the first international heroin investigations, which is pretty cool as far as history books go.

While thinking, teaching, and writing on the subject, I soon realized that the stakes go way beyond Depression-era drug busts or geopolitical intrigue in the Middle East. Those things are important, and they can teach us a lot about the development of state power, how the United States conducts itself on the world stage, and the strange ways that culture translates into policy. But at the heart of this story is the drug problem, one of the most vexing social and political issues in U.S. history. From the very beginning, Americans have used various drugs to cope with the struggles of modern life, and our political system has struggled to cope with all that drug use. Drug control has been a major challenge for every president since Kennedy, and, as a nation, we've been trying to solve the puzzle for well over one hundred years. Those struggles have exacerbated perennial tensions around race, class, and gender; expanded the boundaries of what society deems "criminal"; and resulted in some of the most momentous conflicts and events in U.S. history, from temperance and Prohibition to the articulation of public health and access to medical care, the rise of Big Pharma, the trials of Big Tobacco, and—most important for the tale you are about to read—the declaration of various drug wars.

Today, drug abuse is among the greatest public health threats facing the country. The National Institute on Drug Abuse calculates the economic costs associated with the abuse of alcohol, tobacco, and illicit drugs at over seven hundred billion dollars every year. In the past few years, the opioid crisis has emerged as the most acute aspect of the problem and one of the most serious challenges of the early twenty-first century. Since the start of the new millennium, the rate of opioid prescription and overdose has quadrupled, transforming and reinvigorating the heroin trade. Four out of five of the estimated six hundred thousand heroin users in the United States today began with a pre-scription painkiller. The dope menace can no longer be shrugged off as merely a problem of crime.

Together with the national movement to decriminalize marijuana and the growing backlash over the injustices of mass incarceration and punitive policing, the opioid crisis is prompting a long-overdue reassessment of how we approach the challenge of drug control. The story of the FBN takes us back to the founding of the modern drug control paradigm and offers at least a partial explanation for how we arrived at this point.

This is heavy stuff, but the history of the drug wars is cut with a big dose of absurdity, and I hope you read and enjoy with that attitude in mind. Above all, I hope this book makes you think: about the drug problem, the American style of governance, and the quirks of our national character. Let's make America smart again.

I accrued a great many debts writing this book—many in the form of student loans. Happily, the rest belong to the friends, family, and colleagues who supported me along the way. I can't name you all here, but know that I am grateful. The following people deserve special mention: Max Paul Friedman, Peter Kuznick, Ruth Schwartz Cowan, Aaron Bell, Kit Crawford, Michael Dambach, Nick Ercole, Alan Kraut, Jeremy Kuzmarov, Marge and Sue Maher, Jonathan Marshall, William McAllister, Alfred McCoy, Karen and Kelly Mills, Suzanna Reiss, Nathaniel Smith, Joseph Spillane, William O. Walker, Daniel Weimer, the UMass editorial team, and archivists everywhere—particularly those at the National Archives, the National Academies, and the libraries of American University, Stanford, and Penn State. Special thanks to my mom and dad and all my family for making me who I am. And, finally, I owe the greatest debt to my wife, Shannon, who has put up with me and this project for a very long time. Your patience and support made this book possible, and your achievements in the classroom are a constant source of inspiration and hope for a better tomorrow.

CONTAINING ADDICTION

INTRODUCTION
TOILING IN THE VINEYARDS

Opiate, n. An unlocked door in the prison of Identity.
It leads into the jail yard.
—AMBROSE BIERCE, *THE DEVIL'S DICTIONARY* (1911)

I toiled wholeheartedly in the vineyards because it was fun, fun, fun.
Where else could a red blooded American boy lie, kill and cheat,
steal, deceive, rape and pillage with the sanction and blessing
of the All-Highest?
—GEORGE H. WHITE (1970)

True-crime stories tell us there comes a time in most undercover drug busts when the masquerading agent must end the charade. This is always a moment of great peril; months—perhaps years—of painstaking work teeter on the precipice of sudden violence as the agent's true identity is finally revealed. Some prearranged gesture—a certain phrase, the tip of a hat, a lit cigarette—signals the distant cavalry and springs the trap. On June 4, 1948, on the second floor of a house in a bustling neighborhood of Istanbul, veteran U.S. narcotic agent George Hunter White sat across the table from two men: Irado-dos Terapyanos, a Western-educated Turk known as "Little Bob" to his friends, and Yasef Kariyo, a Spanish Jew who called himself "Joe." The atmosphere was tense as the undercover agent methodically examined several packages containing three kilos of crude heroin before counting out six thousand in Turkish lira and U.S. dollars. White's moment had arrived.

Turkish law specified that money and drugs must be exchanged to prosecute a narcotics violation in court. With the deal complete, the

American stood up, pulled a small revolver with one hand and his badge with the other, and announced that the two men were under arrest. As planned, White smashed a window to signal his Turkish reinforcements, but the noise was lost in the din outside as some forty officers disguised as laborers, sailors, and postmen continued their pantomime. Holding the two suspects at gunpoint amid mounting tensions and frenzied shouting, White finally hurled a chair through the window, showering the street with glass. That did the trick. The police stormed the house and took the traffickers into custody. It was a close call, but in his official report White was cavalier, as was his tendency. "The entire matter was like a comic opera, or maybe a keystone comedy," he remarked.[1]

For White, this was but one episode in a long and extraordinarily colorful career as a federal narcotic agent and undercover operative. He cheerfully moved on to the next city, the next case, the next target. For contemporary audiences, the scene offers a bit more to contemplate. How did this American police officer wind up halfway across the globe, well outside of his legal jurisdiction, flashing a U.S. government badge at Turkish citizens? Was this American imperialism? How did the episode look through Turkish eyes?

Subsequent Western accounts valorized the intrepid agent, and a *Reader's Digest* article published soon after described the bust as an early victory in "our global war on narcotics." Turkish reporters, however, wondered what White was doing there in the first place, noting that local police had busted several clandestine heroin labs prior to his arrival. The initial Associated Press story, they complained, was just another example of Western chauvinism—playing up White's heroics and ignoring the good work of Turkish police.[2]

Such episodes are gems for future historians, waiting to be unearthed, cut, polished, and set into the right framework. Turned one way, White's bust casts a light on differences in perception between the Turkish and American governments, where the case produced very different outcomes. With a slight shift, the incident uncovers noteworthy developments in the realm of international law enforcement. Held just so, the events of that June day and its many dramatic retellings illustrate how drugs and drug control were presented to the American public. In all, it was a telling prologue to America's global drug war.

Containing Addiction tells the story of the Federal Bureau of Narcotics and presents, for the first time, the origins of U.S. federal drug enforcement and the birth of the global drug war. This story provides new insights into the ideology of U.S. national security and the manner in which threats are perceived, shaped, and presented to the American people. Drugs were frequently portrayed as a foreign menace, while fears of unchecked narcotic addiction rampaging through the American underclass and threatening commonly held social values led the United States to develop a global police presence designed to cut off the foreign sources of the domestic market. In the final analysis, America's global drug war emerged from the persistent belief that security at home requires some form of hegemony abroad.

FBN agent George Hunter White is an important figure in this tale. His adventures in Istanbul presaged the creation of District 17, the FBN's internal designation for its first foreign office, opened in September 1951. From their headquarters in Rome, the agents of District 17 became directly involved in law enforcement operations throughout Europe, the Middle East, and North Africa. In 1962 the FBN expanded to Southeast Asia, Mexico, and South America and became a truly global American police force. But Agent White's role goes further still; as an important figure in an expansive true-crime literature, White's active mythmaking helped shape public perceptions of drugs, organized crime, law enforcement, and, in the end, American security.

The borders separating the realms of law enforcement, intelligence, and national security are often porous ones; the closer they are scrutinized, the more they seem to blur. White's career and story—and the history of American drug control more broadly—can help us understand what historian Alfred McCoy describes as the nation-state's "profane margins" and "shadowy interstices," where the prerogatives of security, secrecy, and democracy all collide.[3] Indeed, White surfaces in so many episodes of this history that he functions like a warped hybrid of Voltaire's Candide and Pangloss, cheerfully ushering readers through some of the most notable episodes in the development of the American national security state.

In short, White was a paragon of federal drug enforcement. He cut his teeth during the Great Depression with a yearlong undercover case against the Hip Sing Tong, a Chinese American fraternal association with a sideline in black-market opiates and other rackets. During World War II, he trained spies and paramilitary commandos for the Office of Strategic Services (OSS) and led counterintelligence operations in Calcutta (where, according to rumor, he personally dispatched two Japanese spies—gunning one down on a crowded city street and strangling another). He also did counterintelligence for the Manhattan Project and led a program to develop a potential "truth drug"—an OSS boondoggle resurrected as the infamous MK-ULTRA program under the Central Intelligence Agency (CIA). White's Istanbul case was the first time an American agent went abroad to disrupt the international drug traffic. Back home, a mobbed-up Dallas nightclub owner named Jack Ruby was rumored to be among his occasional criminal informants. In the late 1950s, White launched a sordid research initiative for the Company and used prostitutes to dope johns with LSD while he pounded gin martinis from behind a two-way mirror.[4]

Agent White reveled in both the limelight and the undercover ethos that characterized FBN operations, and he helped normalize aggressive counternarcotic tactics with the American public. While never a household name, White received one last burst of posthumous publicity in the 1970s when his role in the MK-ULTRA program became public and reporters rushed to examine his personal papers. Among those was a letter he wrote, near the end of his life, to Sidney Gottlieb, a scientist for the CIA and White's contact during the agency's mind-control experiments. With his customary wit, White wrote the following oft-quoted remark: "Of course I was a minor missionary, actually a heretic, but I toiled wholeheartedly in the vineyards because it was fun, fun, fun. Where else could a red blooded American boy lie, kill and cheat, steal, deceive, rape and pillage with the sanction and blessing of the All-Highest?"[5]

What were these "vineyards," and why was he a "heretic"? White's colorful embellishment illustrates many of the contradictions that have become emblematic of American national security and the American drug war. He describes himself as a "red blooded American boy" yet celebrates deviant behavior. A critical exception is implicit: White was "toiling in the vineyards." The Gospel of Matthew offers a parable comparing the "vineyards" to the "Kingdom of Heaven." White's vineyards were national security and drug control, and they too were hallowed ground; this was a battlefield of life and death, a privileged space wherein his fight against America's enemies—whether junkies, Japs, or commies—allowed him to step outside of the very same belief system he was sworn to uphold. This was a cognitive and behavioral trade-off of the highest order, and it was a pattern replicated at the national level throughout the twentieth century, as the United States tested drugs on unwitting citizens, initiated a drug war at home and abroad, supported dictators, fought wars of choice, and readily intruded upon the sovereignty of foreign nations—all while citing the imperatives of life, liberty, and the pursuit of happiness.

George White was one of many narcotics agents, and his story falls in the middle of this larger tale. The history of the Federal Bureau of Narcotics has yet to be fully told until now, and it has important implications for the drug war and U.S. foreign policy more broadly. Drug abuse (a more precise term than *addiction*) is primarily a domestic social problem and tangled up with a host of complicated issues like public health, mental illness, vice, morality, ethnicity, economic inequality, and social integration. But to a large degree, it is also simply the product of a basic human desire to experience altered states of consciousness, however fleetingly.[6] Officials like White's boss, Commissioner Harry J. Anslinger, tended to portray addiction as a kind of contagious lunacy that sprang inevitably from exposure to drugs and drug users. According to the Bureau, the temptation to indulge was irresistible to certain segments of the population. Demand was a constant. The only way to control drug use was to reduce global supply and prevent the exposure that created addiction. To reduce supply, however, the United States had to control or eliminate drugs at the site of production—often in locations where it lacked the power or focus to impose its will. This strategy began to coalesce during the 1930s, and by the end of World War II, the basic pattern was set, however flawed: the FBN would contain addiction by reducing global supply. The domestic response, a combination of harsh taboos and punitive incarceration, was mostly a holding pattern until the international situation was brought under control. In effect, the United States externalized a domestic problem, going abroad to solve a social crisis.

The FBN's tenure, from 1930 to 1968, coincides with one of the most important transformations in the history of American political culture.

We seldom speak of "the Republic" anymore, but at the dawn of the twentieth century, belief in limited government and opposition to the idea of a "garrison state" ran strong.[7] Over time, however, traditional fears of centralized power were eclipsed by the fear of crime and foreign enemies. Whereas Americans once emphasized the need for protection *from* the state, they began to seek the protection *of* the state. The history of the Federal Bureau of Narcotics helps us to understand the depth of this profound shift in American life and how it came to pass.

The FBN's logic of addiction and source control also conveniently mirrored a growing logic of American hegemony: to protect conditions at home, the United States must dictate or shape events abroad. On the world stage, the country posed as a victim rather than a consumer of drugs. Narcotics were a foreign problem requiring an extraterritorial response—in effect, America's early drug warriors claimed a global sovereignty, invoking their status as victims of the drug trade to effect a solution abroad and often trampling on the sovereignty of "producing" or "transit" nations in the process. "There are no national boundaries in our work," Commissioner Anslinger boldly declared in 1948. "*You can't afford national sovereignty when you're trying to break up the narcotics racket.*"[8]

As should be increasingly clear, the United States was battling drugs well before Richard Nixon declared war on them in 1971. The new crop of drug warriors and reformers who emerged in the late 1960s, Agent White groused to one colleague, had "just stumbled into a show that has been going on for ages with the naive notion it has just begun."[9]

The same is true for popular understanding of the drug war, which typically begins with President Richard Nixon or Ronald Reagan. Extending the interpretive framework of the drug war further into the past, however, offers valuable new insights. The fight against international traffickers presents a useful historical analogue to broaden the context of modern counterterrorism and international policing. Perhaps more cogently, the drug war (against a commodity) provides a critical analytical link between the Cold War (against communist ideology) and the war on terror (against a tactic of political violence). Each teaches us something of the American mind-set and the manner in which policymakers interpret the role of the United States in the world. All three blur the lines around conventional military conflict while using a strong metaphor to pit the United States in conflict with an intangible, and all three link domestic minorities and the socially marginalized to foreign enemies. These "wars" can never truly be won, yet each rallies the people to the flag. Each conflict rests on similar ideological assumptions, holds security as a central concern, and shares an elastic quality that encourages the cultivation of power and the suppression of critical voices. And none of them has made the American people feel much safer.

In other words, the history of the Federal Bureau of Narcotics is about much more than the struggle to implement an effective domestic or international counternarcotics strategy. At stake are fundamental questions about the character of the American government, the American social contract, and the role of the United States in the world.

American Drug Wars

Panic over drugs in the United States comes in waves. In *The American Disease* (1999), David F. Musto describes a rhythm in American attitudes, wherein early enthusiasm for various drugs tends to be followed by caution and prohibition and then fades back into tolerance. This pattern is clearly seen in the history of opiates and cocaine, each of which was initially hailed as a miracle drug by physicians, scientists, and consumers alike but became problematic as its hazardous qualities were realized and its use escaped the medical realm. Likewise, as the deficiencies of prohibition become pronounced, public attitudes soften, taboos weaken, drug use proliferates, and the pattern repeats.[10]

Nearly every decade of the twentieth century witnessed a spike in public anxiety over the danger of drugs. With its focus on controlling the behavior of the lower classes, Prohibition in the 1920s also closely aligns with the rhythm of American drug wars. Specific concern over narcotics (at times including cocaine) showed discernible peaks in the 1900s and 1910s, 1930s, early to mid-1950s, late 1960s and early 1970s, and mid-1980s, with noticeable valleys in the middle '60s and late '70s. There is, it seems, a cyclical or generational pattern at work, one that overlays periods of intense social crisis when fundamental values and competing notions of American identity are in conflict. These culture wars encourage an emotional style of thought that historian Richard

Hofstadter famously described as "the paranoid style" of American politics, in which emotional truths trump material reality.[11] Functioning as a stand-in for a host of intractable social, cultural, and economic problems, drugs are an issue that both ignite and are consumed in these maelstroms.

The result was a drug war—or, more precisely, a series of successive drug wars. Putting aside the possible inclusion of Prohibition, there were at least three major cycles of drug war during the twentieth century, perhaps more, and each with a distinct character, legacy, and undeniable parallels. Together they constitute what might be termed "the long drug war." Each cycle was sustained by a corresponding shift in popular opinion that I label the *drug war consensus*. Like the drug war itself, public support for a punitive response to addiction and recreational drug use has waxed and waned over time, driven in roughly equal measure by top-down political manipulation and bottom-up cultural attitudes.

The first drug war was the FBN's. Periodization is tricky, and—like the old aphorism that generals always fight the last war—the Bureau used ideas developed during the "prewar" of the 1920s and '30s to wage a campaign that lasted from the early 1950s into the mid-1960s, at least on the domestic side. The FBN established many of the basic tenets of federal enforcement, but the strategic focus was primarily on the international side, and officials like Commissioner Anslinger thought their only real hope was to isolate the American market from criminal sources abroad by launching a foreign drug war—a war that attained global scope and ultimately outlived the FBN.

Richard Nixon's drug war took shape between 1969 and 1971 and ended with his resignation in 1974. Forever suspended between pragmatism and paranoia, Nixon fought a surprisingly balanced drug war and split his attention between the foreign and domestic fronts, treatment and enforcement. Hungry for results and political gain, however, he lost patience with a balanced approach. The militarized tactics and direct White House involvement Nixon introduced to domestic law enforcement survived. The national treatment system he established did not.

Ronald Reagan's drug war began in 1982 and was fought with the greatest vigor. It lasts, arguably, into the present—despite the obvious collapse of the drug war consensus. Reagan's iteration was aimed primarily at the domestic front, but it had critical international implications—particularly for Latin America—and was the first to formally designate drugs a threat to U.S. national security. Whereas the FBN and Nixon fixated on heroin, Reagan confronted an old drug in a new guise: crack cocaine. A strongly bipartisan affair, Reagan's drug war proved incredibly durable, escalating through the subsequent presidencies of George H. W. Bush and Bill Clinton and unleashing the age of mass incarceration.

Although the drug war no longer occupies center stage in our political discourse, it continues to exert a persistent and malevolent influence on national affairs, facilitating the growth of the carceral state and fueling tensions over divisive issues like immigration, race, crime, and security. Donald Trump rose to political influence largely by exploiting white working-class anxiety around globalization and the threat of the "other," adopting a brand of rhetoric pioneered by figures like FBN veteran Joe Arpaio, who worked in Turkey roughly a decade after George White and made his name as "America's toughest sheriff" by fulminating against illegal immigration as the source of drugs, crime, and other social ills. After trading for years on doubts about the citizenship of America's first black president, Trump announced his own bid for office with the charge that Mexico actively exports drugs, crime, and rapists to the United States—and then took office with the pledge to end the "carnage" caused by drugs, crime, and general economic decline.[12] That mode of discourse has a long history.

At the same time, realization is dawning that the country is now in the grip of the worst drug crisis in living memory—and one catalyzed by legal industry rather than widespread criminality. The American Society of Addiction Medicine estimates that in 2015 around 2 million Americans—out of a total population of 320 million—suffered from a substance-abuse disorder involving opioids (a term used to describe both synthetic and organically derived opiates). That number includes nearly 600,000 active heroin users, and four out of five of them began with a prescription painkiller. Between 1999 and 2014, the rate of opioid prescription and overdose quadrupled in lockstep with one another. In 2015 the number of heroin deaths surpassed the number of deaths by gun violence, 12,989 to 12,979, and the number of total drug overdoses eclipsed, by a wide margin, the number of people killed in car crashes. Indeed, overdose is now a leading cause of death throughout the country and particularly concentrated in regions like the Rust Belt, Appalachia, and the Deep South. The numbers continue to climb, making the opioid crisis one of the greatest public health threats facing the nation.[13] With the national gaze fixed on foreign villains and criminals, we missed the real threat.

Collectively, the drug wars are widely regarded as one of the greatest policy failures in U.S. history. They have done demonstrably little to curtail crime, addiction, or the traffic in illicit drugs, which makes their persistence in the face of such profound failure difficult to fathom. So we must go deeper than a history of drug policy, enforcement, and control strategy. The secret to understanding the long history of American drug wars is this: *the drug wars are about more than drugs.* Each cycle has served larger American security interests, drawn greater authority into the hands of the state, extended the reach of U.S. power, and provided a rationale to discipline marginalized or suspect groups in American society.

More fundamentally, however, the drug wars are an expression of American identity. Addiction represents something that seems quintessentially un-American—despite the fact that Americans are among the more prolific drug consumers in the world. This paradox is the central dilemma and prime engine of America's many drug wars. Everything— the articulation of a punitive state apparatus, an interventionist global strategy, the inability to rein in Big Pharma, and all of those accumulated consequences—flows from this contradiction in the American character. And culture is where those conflicting impulses are reconciled. The central role of identity and culture is usually explicit, though somehow overlooked. On the day he declared war on narcotics, Nixon described addiction as "a problem which afflicts both the body and the soul of America." Reagan, as befitting the Great Communicator, said it best, remarking, "Drug abuse is a repudiation of everything America is."[14] The drug wars cannot be understood outside of this context. Drugs turned poverty, downward mobility, enslavement, and subversion into virulent contagions.

But justice is also part of American identity, and we stand poised at a moment of great potential change, prepared—perhaps—to bring our criminal justice system back into line with our social and cultural values. As we begin to renegotiate that future, it behooves us to heed the lessons of the past and the many lives of the American drug war.

Containing Addiction focuses primarily on the first of these cycles and events between World War II and the 1960s, when America's global drug war first took shape. It reveals how cultural attitudes shaped control policy and drove the FBN to insinuate itself into foreign lands across the globe. The agents and officials of the Federal Bureau of Narcotics were among the nation's earliest acolytes to the concept of national security, a holistic approach to national defense that relies on the outward projection of power to neutralize threats before they can fully develop.[15] In the Bureau's worldview, drugs were a harbinger; they signaled how the processes of globalization had fundamentally altered the nature of the threats facing the country. In one of the FBN's many true-crime adventure stories, a top official explained, "When you break a narcotics case you not only nab some of the nastiest specimens in existence but you save a lot of people from a lot of misery. An ounce of cocaine sold in New York may account for a hop-headed holdup man who kills a peaceful citizen in Dallas or a doped-up driver who rams a school bus in Ohio."[16]

The FBN was among the first federal agencies to recognize how this "butterfly effect" aspect of globalization had fundamentally changed the nature of threat in an increasingly interconnected world. That logic led the Bureau to look outward and center its counternarcotic strategy on source control, international policing, and preventing these dangerous commodities from reaching American shores in the first place. By initiating a global drug war, the FBN extended the boundaries of U.S. national security; blurred the lines between foreign and domestic, state and nonstate, military and nonmilitary; and set the stage for the drug war's subsequent escalation under Nixon and Reagan.

A few definitions are overdue. Terms like *drugs* and *narcotics* have inherited connotations at odds with their literal definitions—the sure sign of a complicated past. The term *narcotics,* for example, refers specifically to chemicals with pain-numbing and sleep-inducing qualities, but in popular usage it means an illegal drug. For much of the twentieth century, cocaine (a stimulant) and marijuana (a mild hallucinogen) were labeled narcotics to signify their illicit status. Likewise, the term *drug* usually means a prohibited intoxicant or medicine prescribed by a doctor, but its most basic definition refers to any chemical that has a physiological or psychoactive effect on the human body, including those in food items like alcohol, coffee, and sugar or popular commodities like tobacco. This conflation between biology and legality is a product of history; exposing that conflation is an important step in shedding the stigmas of the past. Addiction, too, is a moving target, and our understanding of it has changed substantially over time. All of that said, to simplify the text and reflect the way the term was understood by the relevant historical actors, I frequently use the word *drugs* rather than specify *narcotics* or *narcotic drugs*. As historian David Courtwright quips in *Forces of Habit* (2001), "For all its baggage, the word has one great virtue. It is short."[17]

How then to define a drug war? Or the War on Drugs? There is a difference. The *War on Drugs* has a specific historic meaning; though it is used in reference to both Nixon and Reagan and could describe the entire long drug war, it applies best to Reagan, who was the only one to actually use the term. A *drug war* is fuzzier. One concise definition might be a quasi-military conflict fought against drugs, drug traffickers, and drug users. That still leaves a lot to unpack. Three elements stand out in this history, all of which are examined in the pages to follow: the relationship between foreign and domestic aspects, prevailing views of addiction, and control strategy—which is to say enforcement strategy, since treatment is typically an afterthought.

One final dynamic to consider is a trend that Courtwright describes as the *psychoactive revolution:* the process by which ordinary people nearly everywhere have acquired "progressively more, and more potent, means of altering their ordinary waking consciousness."[18] This revolution began in the earliest days of oceanic commerce when the trade in tobacco, molasses, tea, and opium drove the growth of European empire and the American colonies. Psychoactive goods remain a cornerstone of global capitalism today, and modern science and technology have sped the pace of revolution. As any organic drug moves further from its agricultural roots, transformed from a semirefined plant product into a pill or a powder, its intoxicating and addictive potential grows exponentially. Consider, for example, the evolution of alcohol production from fermentation to distillation or the poppy's journey from flower to opium to morphine to heroin. Each step down this road increases potency as psychoactive qualities become concentrated and method of delivery more direct. The growing problem of synthetic drugs, erupting from crude laboratories faster than they can be outlawed, is a still more perfect illustration of our struggle to keep pace.

Addiction has a long history, but it's often been described as a problem of the modern world because modernity renders drug products cheaper, more potent, more plentiful, and more disruptive. That means that in an advanced industrial society, the psychoactive revolution will never end. In fact, the tempo will only increase as our ability to deliver ever more powerful drugs more cheaply will consistently outstrip our ability to evolve the social and cultural mechanisms to cope with their hazards. In other words, even if we pull back on enforcement, end the drug war, and develop new, better, and safer therapeutics, the psychoactive revolution and the American drug problem will remain. They must be confronted on new terrain.

Empire, the Deep State, and the New Drug History

Looking to the past won't unveil the future, but it can reveal the paths not taken. *Containing Addiction* adds to a growing field of scholarship that Paul Gootenberg, author of *Andean Cocaine: The Making of a Global Drug* (2008), has termed "a new drug history."[19] Strongly interdisciplinary, the new drug history draws insights and methodologies from biology, medicine, sociology, economics, political science, international relations, and so on, for just as drug use and the drug trade seem to touch on all aspects of human society, so too can its history. Recent high-profile works like Michelle Alexander's *The New Jim Crow: Mass Incarceration in the Age of Colorblindness* (2012) have attracted significant public attention, and the wealth of studies published in just the past few years indicates that the new drug history will remain a lively source of scholarship for years to come.[20]

Containing Addiction joins this broader effort by developing the connection between the new drug history and the study of U.S. foreign policy and the American state. The history of the FBN's global counternarcotics program challenges several camps of scholarship on U.S. foreign policy, particularly those dealing with the Cold War and questions of American empire. To those who portray the United States as a reluctant hegemon, the FBN demonstrates a proactive and outwardly reaching state. To critics who depict policymakers' frequent invocation of national security as an imperial ploy, the FBN demonstrates that appeals to national security were elastic but nevertheless sincere. And to those who portray the United States as a coolly realist superpower, the FBN demonstrates the remarkable and often unpredictable influence of culture on foreign policy.

One other thread needs mention: the connection between the drug wars and the American "deep state," which is to say the degree of conflict or collaboration between covert operations and counternarcotics. The deep state is, in short, the proverbial power behind the throne—unelected, accountable only to wealth, its influence veiled from the public and historians alike. The drug wars are sometimes framed as one of the machinations of the deep state, most of which, by necessity, unfold in secret. This is often the stuff of conspiracy theory: Illuminati, Bilderbergs, and brainwashing. Much of it is nonsense. But some conspiracies are real and some—like the CIA's MK-ULTRA program—are found in the pages that follow. And while a shadowy cabal of oligarchs pulling the secret levers of world government is likely only a figment of our collective imagination, scholars of the deep state have made several lasting contributions. In the larger sense, they draw attention to the fact that there are structural forces at work within the American government that supersede the influence of any one individual or agency. In a more immediate sense, they demonstrate the messiness of seemingly pat policy boundaries and the reality of unintended consequences.

Global intelligence services, spies, criminal traffickers, and undercover agents all swim in the same fetid waters, and it's often difficult to tell them apart in the muck. Historian Alfred McCoy was one of the first to reveal the overlap between these worlds with the 1972 publication of *The Politics of Heroin in Southeast Asia*. Now revised as *The Politics of Heroin: CIA Complicity in the Global Heroin Trade* (2003), the book describes how the CIA tolerated drug trafficking by select assets over time and throughout the world. These findings were so explosive when first published that they earned McCoy a congressional subpoena and, since then, have brought legitimacy to an important critique of U.S. foreign policy. Simply put, some covert operations require criminal actors whose entrepreneurial endeavors include drug trafficking that blows back on the American people—as in the six degrees of separation between Reagan's Contras and L.A. crack dealers chronicled in Gary Webb's *Dark Alliance* (1998). The problem for the historian is that skilled drug traffickers and secret agents leave few records. What we can say is that drug control occasionally serves ulterior goals. Channeling Clausewitz, Jonathan Marshall argues, "The 'war on drugs' has become an extension of foreign policy by other means." At various times, drug control has served as a front for traditional foreign intelligence operations, a complement to modernization and counterinsurgency programs, and a justification for police training programs that gird U.S. influence in foreign lands.[21]

All of which raises a few important questions: Expressing American identity is all well and good, but what is drug control really about when boots hit the ground? Is it truly intended to disrupt the global drug traffic or to serve larger imperial designs?

The history of the FBN and the origins of America's global drug war provide some definitive answers. The FBN's drug war was genuine. Agents serving abroad readily promoted American security by taking on extracurricular activities like investigating smuggling across the Iron Curtain or providing introductions to carefully cultivated police officials in foreign lands. Breaking up the Atlantic heroin trade, however, remained the FBN's foremost concern and priority number one. FBN agents were plenty cynical, and a certain gallows humor prevailed in the field. But they were deadly serious about the primary function of their job, and the records they left behind reveal few examples of conflict with other U.S. agencies (aside from Customs) and no clear-cut examples of the FBN providing cover for CIA operations (which is not to say it didn't happen).

The First Drug Cops

Containing Addiction is the first monograph to systematically employ the FBN's own official records—many of which are newly declassified—but it is not the first book on the FBN. Historian John C. McWilliams and journalist Douglas Valentine both deserve special mention, and this study would have been impossible without their trailblazing work.

Kathleen Frydl's *The Drug Wars in America, 1940–1973* (2013) offers a valuable look at the formal evolution of U.S. drug policy during this same period, and Elizabeth Hinton's *From the War on Poverty to the War on Crime: The Making of Mass Incarceration in America* (2016) similarly shifts the roots of the American carceral state backward through time. A number of journal-length treatments focusing on Anslinger's bureaucratic acumen and the FBN's role in the intelligence community also proved invaluable.[22] *Containing Addiction* takes the story a few steps further, making a concerted effort to move beyond both conspiracy theory and the "cult of Anslinger" to illustrate the relationship between drug control, American culture, and foreign policy.

In terms of sources, this study relies primarily on the records of the Federal Bureau of Narcotics—a virtue in that these sources remain unexploited, but also a potential danger in providing only one "voice." Multilingual and multiarchival histories have become the gold standard for scholars of U.S. foreign relations and for good reason. When it comes to police operations conducted on foreign soil, foreign-country sources would undoubtedly strengthen our understanding of international law enforcement. The scope and ambition of the U.S. counternarcotics agenda, however, pose significant challenges and suggest the use of sources from European countries like France, Italy, and Germany; Middle Eastern countries like Turkey, Lebanon, Syria, Iran, and Egypt; East Asian countries like China, Japan, Myanmar, Thailand, Cambodia, Laos, Vietnam, and the Philippines; and Latin American countries like Mexico, Nicaragua, Panama, Colombia, Ecuador, Peru, and Bolivia. Many of the necessary collections are closed or simply don't exist. An accurate account of global drug control and law enforcement will surely be a communal and ongoing project for the new drug historians.

The dilemma that animates this study, however, is a fundamentally American one, and if the goal is to study the American state and the interplay between drug addiction and national security, American sources will suffice. These, of course, must be treated with a healthy degree of skepticism, for the gaze of the federal officer produces a very specific view. The story of local law enforcement, often the front line in America's drug wars, is an important but challenging one that could not be incorporated here. Given the state of many municipal departments today, it's clearly a subject that merits attention. Another challenge in reproducing the history of any law enforcement program is the kind of sources that survive. While FBN records are rich with interactions between headquarters and the field and other police agencies, few investigative records survive or remain classified due to privacy concerns. What proved bountiful, however, were memoirs and true-crime stories—an early variant of the "infotainment" fare that remains popular today and illustrates the Bureau's success in shaping popular understandings of drugs and drug control.

Even if readers remain skeptical about the influence drug control had on American perceptions of national security or the value of pushing the drug war further into the past, the story of the FBN—and District 17 in particular—still has broader relevance and reveals the mechanisms by which even faulty policies become self-reinforcing when their central premise goes unexamined. This history tells us something of governmental processes and sheds light on the relationship between the American state and its people, the interplay between culture and politics, and the manner in which the United States conducts itself on the world stage.

Chapters 1 and 8 bookend this larger tale, summarizing the evolution of U.S. drug policy, the rise and fall of the FBN, and the drugs wars waged by Nixon and Reagan. The remaining chapters are largely biographical and organized around specific individuals whose stories illustrate particular facets of this complicated history. This was both an organic development reflecting the many colorful figures who animated the FBN and an effort to tell an interesting story. It's also an approach that raises useful questions about individual agency and the nature of causality—a particularly compelling issue when dealing with themes like addiction. The longevity of the drug war and the obstinacy of its essential paradigms speak to the importance of institutions and structural factors, like American ideology, political economy, and the prerogatives of the state. But as the following chapters demonstrate, individuals have played decisive roles at key moments. It's unlikely, for example, that the Bureau would have survived nearly forty years without a leader of Anslinger's political acumen and strange charisma. Would the CIA's MK-ULTRA program have gone so sideways without the perverse joy Agent White took in the research? Would the FBN's foreign program have survived in the absence of Agent Charles Siragusa's energetic zeal? The answers have important implications.

In *Heroin Century* (2002), Tom Carnwatch and Ian Smith argue, "Humans are not controlled by internal chemistry alone."[23] Historians ultimately believe in the primacy of individual agency. To paraphrase Karl Marx, people make their own history, but they do it in circumstances inherited from the past. The drug wars demonstrate a remarkable resiliency for reasons that supersede the contributions of any one person, yet they were built one piece at a time, often by individual men (and women), and they can be taken apart in precisely the same way.

CHAPTER 1
THE DISCOURSE OF THE DOPE MENACE

The opium poppy holds as much potential disaster as an atom bomb.
—HARRY J. ANSLINGER (1946)

Americans can take heart in the good news that we are defeating the
cruelest enemy we've ever faced: The murderous traffic in dope.
—HARRY J. ANSLINGER (1961)

When Commissioner of Narcotics Harry J. Anslinger testified on the merits of the 1937 Marihuana Tax Act, he described rising drug use as a "national menace" and brought a stack of gory crime-scene photos to illustrate the point. Marijuana, he claimed, was like a rattlesnake or a wildfire and directly responsible for an alarming number of gruesome crimes, images of which he displayed for the amazed legislators. The drug made people crazy and it was everywhere, he said, growing in ditches and vacant lots, so ubiquitous that schoolchildren could afford it even in the depths of the Depression. Not content with his oral testimony, Anslinger submitted several additional written statements into the record, including a report from a New Orleans district attorney (DA) that he called "one of the finest" he'd seen on the link between drugs and crime. The report described a marijuana-fueled crime wave that was as nefarious as it was violent, concluding, "The underworld has been quick to realize the value of this drug in subjugating the will of human derelicts to that of the master mind."[1]

Twenty years later, the Commissioner spun a similar tale, but now the stakes were even higher. The ability of drugs—be it marijuana or heroin—to erode human willpower and moral judgment remained intact; what had changed was the scope. According to the Federal Bureau of Narcotics, the dope trade began as a loosely directed criminal enterprise but had become increasingly organized and, in the case of communist China, a state-sponsored clandestine attack.

Like imperial Japan before them, Anslinger warned, the commies were using heroin as the vanguard of invasion, spreading addiction to soften their targets and fill their coffers. It wasn't just China's neighbors at risk; American troops in South Korea were exposed. "The communists have planned well," he told a UN audience in 1953, "and know a well-trained soldier becomes a liability and security risk from the moment he first takes a shot of heroin." Four years later, as American GIs patrolled the demilitarized zone, he repeated the charge to an audience of U.S. senators and reported that South Korean forces had intercepted thousands of communist agents entering the country "with heroin in one hand and gold in the other" on a mission "to corrupt our people there." The recent arrest of a gang of merchant seamen running drugs between Hong Kong and San Francisco, Anslinger argued, was proof that Red China was reaching across the Pacific. Closer to home, he warned that Fidel Castro had joined "the hammer and sickle—and the narcotic needle" by turning Cuba into a "privileged sanctuary" and "launching site" for communist drug traffickers to continue their assault on the free world.[2]

In other words, America's enemies—communists and criminals alike—were already waging a drug war against the red, white, and blue. This was a different kind of war, one without front lines or uniforms. In the closing pages of his 1961 book, *The Murderers*, the Commissioner urged Americans to "be on guard against the use of drugs as a political weapon" and speculated that communists might recruit fellow travelers or groups like the Mafia to "make narcotics a new 'sixth' column to weaken and destroy selected targets in the drive for world domination." Talk of "fifth" or "sixth" columns was a colorful way of linking drugs to the specter of foreign subversion or internal betrayal, and it positioned the dope menace as a transnational threat to freedom itself. "The greatest threat to America lies within her boundaries," Anslinger claimed; longtime FBN official Malachi Harney assured Americans, "Most of our danger is from without."[3] The danger, both would be quick to correct themselves, was everywhere, and it required a police force capable of meeting a truly global threat.

Creating Consensus

Anslinger could boast many accomplishments as commissioner, but his greatest legacy may have been framing the threat posed by drugs. During his thirty-two years in office, Anslinger wrote countless magazine and newspaper articles and discussed his work with an array of audiences. He even found time to indulge his literary aspirations and cowrote three full-length books: *The Traffic in Narcotics* (1953), *The Murderers* (1961), and *The Protectors* (1964)—all of which dramatized the FBN's fight against the dope menace. As the nation's top official on drugs, Anslinger's voice carried, and he never failed to press his message: drugs are a subversive foreign menace, the addicts who use them weaken the moral foundation of American society, and those who traffic in drugs are evil. The lurid appeal of this message with the press, the public, and U.S. policymakers helped prepare a cultural climate supportive of increasingly vigorous control measures.[4]

A pithy phrase with surprising depth, the "dope menace" or "narcotics evil," as officials typically abbreviated the complexities of the drug problem, had four central components: the actual drugs, the nature of addiction, drug users, and drug traffickers. Bureau officials weren't inventing this stuff out of thin air, but they saw the world through a particular lens—one shaped by the social, political, and cultural issues of their day—and then portrayed the dope menace in a manner sympathetic to their own institutional agenda. At times, the Bureau's depiction was cartoonishly overblown. At other times, it was almost subtle, as FBN officials linked drugs and addiction to festering cultural anxieties and long-standing problems in American life. The dope menace was, in short, a discourse and one packed with layers of meaning, each of which can be peeled away to reveal how deep-seated cultural beliefs shaped American policy.

This chapter sketches the dope menace's evolution from the first decades of the twentieth century into the 1960s and the rise and fall of the first drug war consensus. The dope menace represented the threat posed by drugs; the drug war consensus signaled broad support for a punitive, police-centered, and transnational response. To put it another way, the dope menace was the horse, and the drug war consensus was the cart. That's a mild oversimplification, as causal relationships could flow both ways, but what's important to appreciate is that the drug war was a response to a threat many thought was real and not merely a pretext for foreign intelligence operations or reinforcing racial segregation. Those are undoubtedly products of the drug war, but they are not its cause.

The dope menace took shape in the first decades of the twentieth century, before the FBN arrived on the scene. Bureau officials solidified the core concepts during the 1930s and elaborated minor variations into the 1950s. The drug war consensus was the response; its seeds were sown in the 1930s, germinated during World War II, and then cross-pollinated with the Cold War and bore fruit in the 1950s. Together, the dope menace and drug war consensus gave rise to the FBN's drug war and its subsequent escalation under Nixon and Reagan. And this is how it all began . . .

A Greater Evil than Human Slavery

Federal drug control began at the dawn of the twentieth century, an era of tumultuous change in American life. In the span of a single generation, from around 1890 to 1920, the country was radically transformed by the twin processes of industrialization and urbanization, turned from a rural agrarian nation into an urban industrial one. The ratio of people living in urban and rural settings drew even in 1920, and nearly all population growth took place in cities thereafter. The settlement of the western frontier closed an important chapter of U.S. history and raised questions about the future of America's "manifest destiny." It was a wrenching time for the nation's collective psyche and self-image. America's new industrial might turned the country into an economic powerhouse but seemed to change the national character and to create as many problems as it solved. Poverty, crime, and disease became issues on a scale as never before. Economic growth was explosive but unstable and its rewards uneven. A recurring cycle of boom and bust left many Americans looking to the future these changes had wrought with a typical but contradictory mixture of brio and unease. American elites responded in a number of ways. Some empowered the state to restore a sense of order; others turned their gaze to the horizon and exhorted the country to embrace a global role that might stabilize conditions at home.[5]

In 1926 Texas Democrat Tom Connally, still early in a long and distinguished political career, offered a folksy analogy that perfectly illustrated how American leaders made sense of their changing world. It was impossible, he argued, to untangle the political, economic, and moral relationships that geography had once kept separate. While explaining the need to engage with the League of Nations to a *New York Times* reporter—for reasons, we should note, that included drug control—Connally described the situation facing an anonymous farmer who rents a distant property to a fellow named Bill Jones. Prior to the farmer's financial stake, Connally explained, physical distance allowed a certain independence. "Bill Jones can get drunk, curse and swear and do anything he wants. . . . But when the farmer gets a mortgage on Bill Jones's property he becomes interested. If Bill Jones then gets drunk, curses, swears and shoots up the town the farmer will get mightily interested and will do something about it. So it is with nations." Connally concluded, "Now that we have large interests in Europe we are beginning to show a high moral interest in their affairs."[6] Fraught with symbolic meaning, drugs were an issue that crystallized such dilemmas and united the impulses toward reform, order, and global engagement.

At the turn of the century, however, the foreign and domestic aspects of the drug problem were largely separate matters. Opium was readily attainable by the early nineteenth century, and solutions like laudanum were a household item. An import, opium always had a foreign connotation that was most pronounced in the concern over Chinese-run opium dens, but these were more nuisance than threat. The real problem was that narcotic addiction was a frequent consequence of medical treatment, particularly after the trauma of the Civil War and introduction of the hypodermic needle. Medicine made rapid advances in the late nineteenth century, but it was primitive by modern standards and physicians relied on opiates like morphine—a potent but habit-forming alkaloid isolated from opium—to alleviate an assortment of ailments. Tuberculosis, for example, was a leading cause of death and essentially untreatable until the development of antibiotics, so the best doctors could do was administer various opiates—usually heroin after 1898—as a palliative to ease their patients' suffering. Opium's anti-diarrheal qualities were also valuable; germ theory was just taking hold, and many sources of drinking water were polluted. This array of ameliorating powers ensured opium's inclusion in a variety of patent medicines and mail-order cures at a time when roughly equal numbers of Americans preferred to self-medicate than face the expense and horror of the sawbones. By the end of the century, the single largest cohort of American opiate addicts was actually middle- and upper-class women, because they enjoyed the best access to medical care and the variety of snake-oil cures that usually packed a potent dose of opiates.[7]

The first federal drug laws addressed these two aspects of the domestic problem. The 1909 Opium Exclusion Act barred the import of smoking opium, but the real game changers were the Pure Food and Drug Act of 1906, which required proper labeling, and the 1914 Harrison Narcotic Act, which introduced federal oversight by requiring physicians and druggists to register with the government and pay a nominal tax. This power of taxation—rather than criminalization per se—formed the basis of U.S. drug enforcement for the next fifty-six years.

A new drug, however, challenged professional and legislative controls. Diacetylmorphine was developed under the brand name "Heroin" by the German company Bayer and brought to market in 1898. The name came from the Greek and German words *heros* and *heroisch;* both mean heroic or strong. Heroin is roughly twice as potent as morphine and works twice as fast. At a time when chemists were daily pushing the frontiers of their craft—Bayer introduced aspirin the following year—heroin was greeted as a miracle of modern science: praised for its ability to alleviate the suffering of tubercular patients and celebrated as less addictive than morphine. But troubling signs soon emerged. Doctors administering heroin reported crippling physiological dependence in their patients. Recreational users also developed a taste for the powerful narcotic, which could be sniffed rather than smoked or injected. With the hazards of addiction increasingly apparent, the American medical community abandoned the drug even before its import and manufacture were outlawed by the Heroin Act of 1924. Illicit use, however, continued. Odorless, low bulk, and incredibly strong, heroin was easy to smuggle and conceal as authorities clamped down on more notorious drugs like opium and cocaine, both of which all but vanished. The number of heroin users to emerge from the first decades of the twentieth century was small—and dwarfed by the much larger population of morphine users—but the psychoactive genie was out of the bottle, and it had dire consequences for the discourse of the dope menace.[8]

At roughly the same time, drug control became a major component of U.S. foreign policy due to events over the western horizon, where American reformers and missionaries were dismayed to find widespread opium addiction in China and the Philippines—one a coveted foreign market and the other a newly acquired colony. With the support of Presidents Roosevelt and Taft, Charles Henry Brent, an Episcopal bishop proselytizing in the Philippines, and Dr. Hamilton Wright, a tropical disease specialist, convened two diplomatic enclaves to address the world opium situation. The 1909 Shanghai Opium Commission accomplished little beyond a nonbinding statement expressing concern. The 1912 Hague Opium Convention, the world's first drug control treaty, was similarly constrained by imperial reluctance to abandon a lucrative colonial cash crop. It did, however, require each of its signatories to establish some kind of domestic control regime, a provision later incorporated into the Treaty of Versailles.

These were small steps, but they established lasting precedents on the American side. Leading the U.S. delegation, Hamilton Wright pressed the European powers to withdraw from the colonial opium economy and advocated strict agricultural caps as the best way to limit global supply. The Europeans thwarted this supply-side approach, but source control remained the foundation of U.S. counternarcotic strategy. America's special concern for Chinese addiction, meanwhile, revealed a curious blend of impulses: a kind of messianic humanitarianism reinforced the notion that a grateful, drug-free China would become an effective trade partner. This blend of American exceptionalism, economic interest, and geopolitics remained a defining feature of U.S. drug control—as did the period's rhetoric, with papers like the *Chicago Tribune* immediately proclaiming a "war on opium."[9]

The negotiations, however, also revealed the conflicted role played by the United States itself, which has historically been the primary impetus behind global control and a voracious consumer of both licit and illicit drugs—a revelation that horrified Hamilton Wright. After failing to broker a binding agreement at Shanghai, Wright launched an intensive study of global consumption in preparation for the Hague summit. In an interview titled "Uncle Sam Is the Worst Drug Fiend in the World," he explained that America had both the largest and the fastest-growing rate of per capita narcotic consumption in the world. Anticipating criticism, Wright argued that only tough domestic controls would restore U.S. credibility—which helped lead to the 1914 Harrison Act. In the meantime, Wright recognized that drug control exposed a glaring contradiction in the American worldview. "The history of the opium fight forms a queer illustration of our National blindness to our own faults," he lamented, "and emphasizes our National tendency to see, with amazing clarity, the sins of others, while remaining blind to our own viciousness."[10]

World War I—like the Civil War before it and World War II after it—was a watershed moment that had enormous impact on American drug habits. It also ignited a different sort of drug war as the nationalist and nativist sentiment stirred by the conflict tipped the scales toward Prohibition. Long a goal of the moralizing temperance movement, the campaign against demon rum had as much to do with disciplining the masses as it did with drink by the time the Eighteenth Amendment passed in 1919. In the context of industrial war, maintaining a sober, productive, and orderly society was a patriotic duty. Critics like Representative James R. Mann (R-IL), however, presciently warned that actual enforcement would require "government spies everywhere." Paradoxically, World War I also led to the abrupt social acceptance of cigarettes; previously disdained as a dirty habit and poor man's smoke, the "little white slaver" became associated with American soldiers and crossed into mainstream respectability, even as concerns began to surface that cigarettes might lead American youth to narcotics.[11]

The years around World War I witnessed the apparent high-water mark of American narcotic addiction. Statistics later compiled by the FBN indicate that from 1914 to 1919, the population of narcotic addicts hovered around two hundred thousand (out of a total population of one hundred million). Other estimates put it at roughly twice that number, but it seems evident that between the Harrison Narcotic Act, new pain therapies, and greater medical discretion, the tide of addiction began to recede.[12] With the incorporation of the Hague Opium Convention into the Treaty of Versailles, drug control became a near-universal obligation, and the country maintained active collaboration with the drug control bodies at the League of Nations, providing direct financial support even while eschewing formal membership.

By the 1920s, legal frameworks were in place at the national and international levels, and it became routine to see drug control described as a drug war in the press. Even a cursory search through period newspapers reveals the frequent use of terms like *war on opium* and *war on narcotics*. These early control efforts all fell short of a literal war, but the rhetoric used to describe them indicates just how long the idea of a drug war has been percolating.[13]

It remains something of an open question as to whether Prohibition should be considered the first of America's drug wars or the start of a longer conflict—which really boils down to what we mean by *the* drug war. It's certainly no stretch to describe Prohibition as *a* drug war, as Lisa McGirr ably demonstrates in *The War on Alcohol: Prohibition and the Rise of the American State* (2016). Prohibition legitimized the idea that public and private modes of consumption could be effectively managed through policing and, like the war on narcotics, provided a critical spur to state development. The credibility of a police-centered control model was diminished by Repeal but endured as a viable strategy in the realm of narcotics. The chief distinction between alcohol and narcotics, however, was and is in the scale of use—the difference of an order of magnitude or two—and that forced a cultural reconciliation still largely absent from narcotics. After the folly of Prohibition, the American people made their peace with "demon rum" by shifting the emphasis from drink to the drinker. The problem was alcohol*ism,* not alcohol. With narcotics, the picture is less clear, though something similar happened in the late 1990s, as pain specialists and Big Pharma promoted the liberal use of opioids and sought to shift the locus of addiction from the drug to individual patients. Culturally, however, the problematic aspects of narcotics have typically been split between the drug itself and the much smaller pool of individual users, who, as a rule, have been easily demonized. These critical differences make the respective "wars" waged on alcohol and narcotics distinct, if still largely congruent.[14]

The year 1930 marked the next major development with the creation of the Federal Bureau of Narcotics. The FBN was the brainchild

of Representative Stephen G. Porter (R-PA), chair of the House Committee on Foreign Affairs and an enthusiastic participant in the drug
control talks at the League of Nations. Porter was fiercely proud of
America's success at reducing opium addiction in the Philippines and
considered the drug traffic "a greater evil than human slavery." Van-
quishing it was part of America's historic mission and complemented
the nation's messianic identity. Domestic enforcement, however, was
entrusted to a subdivision of the notoriously corrupt Bureau of Prohibition, and Porter complained that the country was suffering billions in
economic loss to addiction while drugs were treated as "a sort of step-
son of prohibition." To raise drug control's profile and rescue it from the
sagging fortunes of the Noble Experiment, Porter introduced a series of
bills in early 1930 to create an independent Bureau of Narcotics. After
a few minor amendments, H.R. 11143 passed both houses of Congress
and was signed into law in June. Porter died shortly thereafter, but a
new generation of professional bureaucrats led by Anslinger quickly
replaced the missionaries and private interest groups who animated the
first attempts at drug control.[15]

Although Hamilton Wright had earlier anguished over the connection between American consumption and the global traffic, it was the
FBN that most effectively elaborated the links between the domestic
and international drug trade. Yet whereas Wright was dismayed to find
American consumers driving global demand, the Bureau and its allies
began to twist the narrative in a manner that simultaneously absolved
the country for its insatiable appetite and empowered the state to seek
solutions abroad. The need for international action was widely acknowledged during debate over the future Bureau, and Porter argued that
"one nation, standing alone, can not control this traffic." Anslinger, then
supervising drug enforcement at the Bureau of Prohibition, agreed that
the foreign dimension was paramount. "We feel our domestic situation
is pretty well under control," he testified. "Our trouble is with smuggled goods almost entirely." Over time, the FBN's focus on smuggling,
criminality, and foreign adversaries would shear away any ambiguity
about U.S. culpability. In *The Murderers*, Anslinger later wrote, "There
are growing nations and manufacturing nations and 'target' or victim
nations where the stuff is sold finally. The United States has always been
in the latter category."[16] This was partly a willful misrepresentation, but

the belief that America was a victim reflected both the task with which the FBN was charged—enforcing the Harrison Act and investigating the illicit traffic—and notable demographic shifts in the ranks of American drug users.

The Birth of the Dope Menace

Anslinger liked to begin speeches in grand fashion. "Opium," he would intone, "is like the finger of God." By invoking the divine, the Commissioner was trying to capture something of the drug's remarkable power and duality; the same chemicals that banished pain and comforted the sick could also induce catastrophic addiction. Narcotics could smite or they could heal. When in a literary mood, he would compare them to "the two-faced god Janus" or the "kindly Dr. Jekyll" and the "cruel monster, Mr. Hyde." (Marijuana, he testified to Congress, was all Hyde and no Jekyll.)[17] He rarely strayed from this framework of good and evil and once delivered the following verse to a group of med students:

> Halting speech and trembling lips
> Tell the tale of life's eclipse.
> Men and women marked as prey
> By the wolves of modern day
> Waked at last from fancied bliss
> Doomed to hear the serpent's hiss
> Hell can match no hell with this.[18]

References in Anslinger's remarks indicate the poem was delivered in the mid-1950s but not when it was composed. Whether that was during the Depression, World War II, or the early Cold War, however, it's worth noting that Anslinger judged the hell of drug addiction worse than crushing poverty, Nazis, nuclear annihilation, or literal hell. As the nation's top drug cop, Anslinger felt compelled to emphasize the bad over the good; he never waxed poetic on the benefits of opiates.

Heroin was the FBN's public enemy number one and, like morphine, is a derivative of the opium poppy. Known by its scientific name as *Papaver somniferum*, poppy was one of the first domesticated plants, and its seeds have been found amid the ruins of many ancient civilizations.

Opium poppies grow particularly well in semiarid climates or on the sloping hillsides of mountainous jungle regions, with flowers blooming in a palette of vivid hues. When the brightly colored petals fall, they leave behind a bulb, swollen with seeds. When lanced with a special knife, the wound oozes a milky white sap that dries and darkens to a deep brown or black and is later scraped away with a wide, flat blade. This dried sap is raw opium. Boiled down into a sticky paste and cured, the opium can be eaten or smoked or treated with various acids to create morphine and heroin.[19]

Anslinger was well aware of this ancient heritage. "The poppy, the symbol of sleep and death," he wrote in one book, "is age-old in the lore of antiquity." The implication was not that mankind has a long, complicated, and coevolutionary relationship with the poppy but that opium was primordial, a vestige of our savage past. He pulled the same trick with marijuana—which played a minor role in enforcement but a major one in antidrug sentiment—and linked cannabis to tribal Malay berserkers and the ancient sect of Persian warrior-priests known as the Assassins.[20] Unlike marijuana, however, opium was a necessary evil. And so long as there was opium, there would be heroin and heroin addicts.

In the eyes of the enforcement community, drugs like heroin possessed an almost mystical ability to attract users, and FBN officials often reflected a kind of *narcotic determinism*. How else, they asked themselves, could you explain the junkie's decision to plunge a dirty needle into a rotten arm or a teen's choice to hazard the pull of addiction? What if the choice wasn't actually theirs? The Commissioner once explained, "Opium, wherever produced, will always seek a consumer."[21] Here, in a nutshell, was the Bureau's dilemma. In a sense, Anslinger imbued opiates with agency all their own—inanimate yet acting upon the world independent of the people who used them. The implications of this style of thought were legion, but three stand out: narcotics usurped the free will of their users, addiction was a nigh-inevitable consequence of exposure, and the only way to curb addiction was to prevent that initial exposure. These ideas became central to FBN counternarcotic strategy, which began to fully cohere after a series of important shifts in the 1920s and 1930s.

One of the more pronounced trends in the history of the dope menace is that when drugs and addiction move into disadvantaged communities or take root among marginalized people, the consequences are more devastating in the absence of a social safety net and the actual drugs become more ominous to mainstream society. This happened with narcotics in the early twentieth century and with cocaine in the 1980s. Drugs were a catalyst, and when heroin first hit the streets, it seemed to operate on a level unto itself. It took a long time for a morphine addict to become a burden on society, Representative Porter observed during the FBN debate, but "the heroin addict loses all sense of moral responsibility."[22] Heroin (and marijuana, according to the FBN) threatened to snatch away the thin veneer of civilization that governed everyday life, giving free rein to the masses' bestial urges to fight and fornicate. Drugs would turn American cities into bubbling cauldrons of violence and decay.

The dope menace was born when narcotic addiction first slid down the socioeconomic ladder. In the years that followed the Harrison Narcotic Act, the overall number of narcotic users declined, and a bifurcated view of addiction emerged to separate addicts into "medical" or "recreational" categories. Any drug use that took place outside of a rapidly shrinking medical context was attributed to vice, deviance, and mental illness as the lasting image of the "junkie" began to coalesce around urban underclass men, who were now assumed to be recreational users. The reality, of course, was more textured. Some were unrepentant hedonists, and others were hooked by their doctors; some lived in the city, many lived in the country, addiction readily broached class lines, and some were not truly addicts at all.[23] Cut off from legal sources (save for a brief experiment with clinical treatment), many turned to the black market. Criminal traffickers importing narcotics from abroad began to supplant doctors and pharmacists as the primary suppliers of the American market, and heroin became the underworld's drug of choice. The purity of street heroin, however, diminished as the quality of manufacture declined and enterprising traffickers cut the product— and this had further negative consequences, as hardened users turned from sniffing to injection and introduced a whole new set of problems like festering sores and a host of infectious diseases. The growth of the criminal market and differentiation between categories of use and user justified still further government intervention. Even President Herbert Hoover, with his dogged belief in limited government, supported the expansion of federal law enforcement and what he described as the FBN's "steadfast campaign" to "destroy [the] illicit traffic in narcotics."[24]

The growing emphasis on criminality was reinforced by events at the diplomatic level. In 1931 Anslinger led a delegation to Geneva to negotiate the Convention for Limiting the Manufacture and Regulating the Distribution of Narcotic Drugs. Better known as the 1931 Limitation Convention, the treaty was designed to funnel unrefined narcotics into licit channels and cap global output. The Americans were again frustrated in their attempt to introduce strict agricultural limits, but the treaty did establish a system of production quotas, instituted new supervisory bodies at the League of Nations, and reiterated the obligation to maintain special domestic control agencies (based explicitly on the FBN). For the next thirty years, Anslinger and his allies at the State Department used that provision to shield the agency from a series of bureaucratic challenges.[25] In the short term, the limitation treaty closed the loop on the drugs-crime connection. Thereafter, any drug use or sale that took place outside of sharply circumscribed channels was proof of criminality and deviance.

Control thus came with a price. As the world's industrial powers tightened their grip on the global opium market, some of it inevitably slipped through their fingers. Like a snake eating its own tail, prohibition created a black market and affirmed the connection between drugs and crime that drove further intervention. Each step toward tighter control pushed elements of illicit manufacture further into the criminal realm. This is an important argument, as critics of the drug war often contend that the illicit traffic is a direct consequence of prohibition. The correlation is indisputable, but causation is less clear. In the case of cocaine, for example, a gray or "shadow market" clearly preceded legal prohibition as medical practitioners grew more discerning.[26] But it's evident that one consequence of U.S. drug control was the rise of heroin—a drug perfectly engineered to survive in the face of its legal prohibition. And heroin's emergence as the ultimate street drug had further consequences of its own. As narcotic addiction slipped down the socioeconomic ladder, it transformed from a medical problem into a criminal one, deeply prejudicing public and professional attitudes and slowing the growth of addiction research until well into the 1960s.[27]

An Inexorable Master

The retreat of the scientific community and weak medical consensus on the nature of addiction allowed the FBN to impose law enforcement prerogatives with little opposition. The Bureau had several things going for it, including a unique vantage astride regulatory, investigative, and domestic and foreign policy channels and a period of general intolerance that narrowed perceptions of legitimate drug use. As a result, the FBN enjoyed almost total dominion over public discourse from the 1930s until the early 1960s. Anslinger was frequently lauded as "the greatest living authority" on dope and eclipsed the influence of any other individual. Having worked on Prohibition prior to helming the FBN, the Commissioner was convinced that America's Noble Experiment failed not because of its inherent absurdities and inequalities, but because it lost public support.[28] To keep drug control from the same fate, FBN officials built up strong social taboos by emphasizing the threat that addiction posed to public welfare and cultural values. The FBN had important regulatory functions, but it was first and foremost a police agency and that, too, shaped how it saw the drug problem. In short, the FBN was a hammer, so everything looked like a nail.

The Bureau's ability to normalize a simplistic and largely moral view of addiction constrained popular and scientific understanding for a long time. Addiction is already a difficult concept to nail down and is forever caught between medical and moral interpretations. Many of its mysteries are locked up with those of the human brain. The modern tendency is to treat addiction as a disease and a problem of psychological and physiological dependence.[29] Anslinger and others, however, clung to views that evolved around the time of the Harrison Act. Right up until the Bureau's demise in 1968, officials stubbornly depicted addiction as an outright moral failure or a contagious form of madness leading to crime, violence, and social decay.

Anslinger's 1953 book, *The Traffic in Narcotics,* represents the FBN's most detailed exposition on the problem of addiction; the cover sells it as the "long-awaited reliable survey of the malignant and growing evil of narcotics." The Commissioner was especially taken with the work of Dr. Lawrence Kolb, a noted psychiatrist who ran the Division of Mental Hygiene at the U.S. Public Health Service from 1938 to 1944 and helped create the National Institute of Mental Health. Early in his career, Kolb theorized that addiction was a symptom of underlying personality disorders. He became a sharp critic of the police approach later in life, but Kolb's theory that addiction was the result of deviance and mental illness gained a wide following at a time when "psychopathy" was a favored catchall diagnosis to label individuals unable to cope with the demands of modern life.[30] Anslinger liked this interpretation because it left little need for further explanation. Addiction was a cause and consequence of madness.

While leaning heavily on explanations that featured mental illness, the FBN did recognize the physiological side of addiction, and Anslinger referred to "habituation, tolerance and dependency" as the "tripod of addiction."[31] The psychology of addiction might be subject to debate, but the acute withdrawal symptoms caused by physical dependency were irrefutable evidence of abuse, no matter the cause. Beat writer William S. Burroughs described his own experience with heroin withdrawal in *Junky* (1953), a quasi-anthropological memoir of addiction: "My nose and eyes began to run, sweat soaked through my clothes. Hot and cold flashes hit me as though a furnace door was swinging open and shut. I lay down on the bunk, too weak to move." These symptoms were well known to FBN agents, many of whom claimed a knack for spotting addicts simply by their general carriage and demeanor. Experienced agents undoubtedly were able to pick out individuals who fit their expectations, but there was no single addict experience and not all users matched the profile of a "dope fiend."[32]

FBN agents acknowledged the social causes of addiction on occasion. While supervising operations on the West Coast in the 1950s, Agent George White wrote an editorial for the *San Francisco Chronicle* that described addiction as "a symptom of social delinquency" to be remedied through general social and economic reform. "Clear the slums, improve our schools, churches and playgrounds," he urged, "and drug addiction, along with many other 'crimes,' will be effectively controlled in the years to come." Anslinger, too, recognized that for some, "narcotics block out the sights and sounds of poverty and inequality, the rapid pace at which we move in today's world, the constant trembling on the brink of disaster." But for the most part, he was dismissive, concluding, "The reason for taking drugs has been forgotten; narcotics has become their way of life."[33]

Anslinger's comment exemplifies how the FBN elaborated on old debates about nature versus nurture and drew on distinctions between the "worthy and unworthy poor" that date to the Gilded Age. In keeping with the American tradition of self-reliance, Anslinger ultimately believed that "disregard for personal responsibility" was "the very touchstone of narcotic addiction." On that point, the FBN and disaffected Beats were in rare agreement, and Burroughs claimed, "You become a narcotics addict because you do not have strong motivations in any other direction. Junk wins by default."[34]

Race, class, and gender combined with these notions about personal responsibility, heredity, and environment to reinforce the implicit classification system. Well-heeled users (already better equipped to manage their addiction) were generally seen and treated as victims and medical cases, while less privileged addicts were judged recreational users and therefore deviant. Addicts who lacked resources were dismissed as criminals and psychopaths, and, because their numbers were typically larger, addiction took on a more menacing character, becoming something to be contained rather than treated.

In the end, most agents would have shrugged if asked why people use drugs. Mental illness and hard living might play a role, but few agents thought it was their job to worry about that. Nor did they make much effort to reconcile the belief that addiction was a moral failure with the conflicting notion that it could be caught like a disease. "Innocence and guilt crop up in unexpected corners," Anslinger conceded at the end of *The Traffic in Narcotics.* "There is room for compassion, for pity, for help and for common sense in carrying out our responsibilities. But before all else is the safeguarding of the government and its laws and its people." (Note the order he lists those in!) The agents had a popular saying: you don't have to be a veterinarian to clean up shit.[35] It was their job to enforce the law and protect the American people. The rest was academic.

In keeping with this bifurcated view of addiction, FBN personnel frequently toggled back and forth between moral and medical language and appropriated scientific idiom whenever convenient to describe drug addiction as a fever, cancer, or outbreak. The epidemiological slant emphasized addiction's contagious potential and was a strong argument for the FBN's proactive, preventative approach. In one 1942 radio address, Anslinger warned that the mere presence of an addict in any community is "a causative factor in increasing addiction." In *The Traffic in Narcotics*, he elaborated, "Drug addiction springs from association with drugs and addicts," who should be "plucked out of the community and quarantined."[36] Eventually, this led the FBN to endorse a policy of incarceration, and by the late 1930s officials were pushing for mandatory sentencing as a way to arrest the spread of addiction.[37]

In the short term, the "addiction as contagion" idea solidified a core concept in FBN strategy: limiting exposure. In the Bureau's often fatalistic view, abuse and addiction were inevitable consequences of exposure. Doctors, the Commissioner noted from time to time, were disproportionately troubled by addiction due simply to their daily proximity to narcotics. FBN officials reasoned that there wasn't much they could do about the mental illness or poverty that created an underlying demand for drugs—aside from not adding more fuel to the fire—but maybe they could keep the sparks from the tinder and disrupt the vectors by which addiction was transmitted. Without drugs, they reasoned, there could be no addiction. "There are many more addiction-prone individuals running around in the world who have not yet had contact with drugs," Anslinger warned. "That is reason enough . . . for the existence of the Commissioner and the whole control program."[38]

Indeed, at times the FBN thought drugs so addictive and addiction so contagious that physical contact wasn't even necessary, encouraging a policy of censorship—albeit a deeply conflicted one, given the Bureau's own expert use of propaganda. The Commissioner scoffed at the idea that prohibition increased the allure of drugs, but he also worried that candid portrayals might arouse curiosity, so the Bureau was a strong proponent of the "Hays Code" that sharply limited depictions of drug use on film. In effect, the Bureau imbued addiction with Medusa-like qualities and worried it might be *visually* contagious, able to leap from screen to bloodstream. Clearly, however, the FBN pursued whatever course was expedient, and Anslinger complained about the sensationalism of detective stories built around drugs, even as he used the

FBN's true-crime adventures to buttress support for the drug war.[39] The trick was to keep the level of discourse carefully calibrated: the pitch had to be cranked high enough to ensure everyone agreed drugs were dangerous but short of exposing the internal contradictions embedded within antidrug rhetoric.

To elide such dilemmas, Anslinger and other Bureau officials came up with a variety of colorful ways to express the danger of addiction. One of Anslinger's favorites was "murder on the installment plan." At times he argued, "Drug addiction is a cold, calculated, ruthless, systematic plan to undermine by creating new addicts while sustaining the old." Field agents echoed the boss and described addiction as a "living" or "slow death" and "the greatest evil in the world today." These formulations had two purposes: they established the threat and insinuated conspiracies against the American people. Using even more illustrative language, Bureau officials frequently evoked monsters or vermin by describing "tentacles of addiction" or "parasitic addicts" and mobsters. In *Dope, Inc.,* a book written with FBN cooperation, journalist Joachim Joesten described addiction as a "maelstrom" and the drug traffic as the "hydra of our times: every time one of its ugly heads is chopped off, two new ones seem to sprout."[40]

The Bureau didn't invent this way of thinking, but it did more than any other individual or group, before or since, to elaborate those dangers for the American people. One of the most famous antidrug tracts of the interwar period was Richmond P. Hobson's 1928 pamphlet, *Mankind's Greatest Affliction and Gravest Menace.* Hobson—a war hero, two-term congressman, and veteran of the temperance movement— described addicts as "abject slaves," "destructive parasites," and, most evocatively, "the living dead." A kind of feedback loop passed these modes of language back and forth between the Bureau and its allies, creating an echo chamber that reinforced the FBN worldview. Riffing on Hobson's take, the Bureau issued its own series of pamphlets over the years titled *Living Death: The Truth about Drug Addiction.*[41]

While the "living dead" conjures images of addicts as zombies, both Hobson and the Bureau were driving at an adjacent point: addiction was slavery; addicts were technically alive but lived only for their next fix. Anslinger frequently described addiction as "enslavement" and addicts as "slaves to heroin." Dipping back into literary allusions, one radio script prepared by the Bureau proclaimed, "Simon Legree was not as cruel a slave master as opium when it clutches a victim."[42] As with other elements of the dope menace, the addiction-as-slavery idea seeped into the broader culture. Publications like *True Detective* and *Actual Romances* catered to very different audiences but reached common ground on drugs, as boys learned that "no slave ever cringed before a more inexorable master," and girls read how heroin "enslaves a human being—makes him a craven, beaten, degraded thing."[43]

Slavery was the only metaphor that captured the terrible compulsion of addiction and was a particularly charged element of discourse at a time when the country was grappling with the legacy of *actual* human slavery—almost as if drug control could atone for America's original sin while turning national attention away from the existence of Jim Crow. The tragic irony, of course, is that police-style drug control has ultimately done more harm to African Americans than any other community. But the age of mass incarceration still lay in the distant future, and in the years surrounding World War II, the addiction-as-slavery metaphor provided a stirring call to arms. "If drug addiction is an evil habit—and who will say that it is not," Anslinger challenged in the final pages of *The Traffic in Narcotic Drugs*, "it should be rooted out and destroyed."[44]

These cultural narratives of addiction may well be the most important theme in the history of drugs in America, the fulcrum on which public policy and counternarcotic strategy actually turn. Drug statistics are notoriously unreliable: reporting is inconsistent, results are manipulated, and the lines between use, abuse, and addiction are inherently subjective.[45] Nevertheless, the data indicates that the number of American drug addicts (excluding alcohol, tobacco, and—perhaps most important—pharmaceuticals) is small in relation to the total population. Historically, the number of regular heroin users is tiny, generally less than 1 percent of the population.[46] Though surely underreported, these numbers suggest the threat posed by drugs and addiction is as much symbolic as actual—which is not to dismiss the suffering of addicts or the dire social problems exacerbated by drugs. The loss of agency represented by addiction stirs something deep within American culture. Addiction was something inflicted upon America and Americans, from outside our borders and outside our bodies, and it could rob the nation of its fundamental liberty. And worse, some seemed to will-fully surrender. This narrative was firmly established by the mid-1930s, and it has played a central role ever since. Throughout the long history of American drug wars, casting drug control as a fundamental defense of freedom has reconciled an otherwise intrusive policy with America's libertarian ideology and, in the minds of early drug warriors, reversed black-market forces: the United States was not a consumer of drugs; it was a victim of the global drug traffic.

An Effective and Subtle Tool of War

Before World War II, however, talk of a drug war was largely aspiration-al. The country lacked the geopolitical clout to go beyond troubled dip-lomatic initiatives, and it was not quite warring on its own drug-using citizens. Yet the rough outlines of the first drug war consensus were there. The threat posed by addiction, the moral and security imperative of control, intolerance for drug use outside of medical channels, fixa-tion on criminality, a global view of the American drug problem, re-flexive martial rhetoric, and a preference for policing over treatment—all of these components were in place by 1940 and then galvanized by another global conflict.

World War II was a turning point; it broadened American hori-zons and irrevocably changed the concept of U.S. national security. It also strengthened the rationale supporting the incipient drug war and gave American policymakers the influence necessary to finally pursue aggressive counternarcotic measures abroad. The irony was that Amer-ican narcotic addiction had dropped to an all-time low. According to FBN estimates, by 1942 the population of known addicts had dwindled to around 20,000 (out of a total population of 135 million), driven down by the disruption of international trade and improved medical atten-tion to the hazards of addiction.[47]

Yet even as addiction waned, World War II added new dimensions to the dope menace, as narcotics became both a strategic commodity and, the Commissioner warned, "an effective and subtle tool of war."[48] Anticipating global conflict in the late 1930s, Anslinger began pulling strings to corner the global opium market and build a strategic reserve to ensure adequate medical supplies for the United States and its allies.

In public, however, he was far more likely to emphasize the threat, most dramatically in the weeks following Pearl Harbor when the Treasury Department described Japanese narcotic production over the previous decade as "an offensive in which the weapons were narcotic drugs." Seizing the moment, Anslinger added, "We have experienced Pearl Harbors many times in the past in the nature of dangerous drugs from Japan which were meant to poison the blood of the American people."[49]

It took a few years, but the geopolitical reshuffling and American ascendance that followed World War II set the stage for the birth of the global drug war. During the war, U.S. policymakers scored an important victory by tying the liberation of former British, Dutch, French, and Portuguese colonies in the Pacific to the end of state-sponsored opium industries. Germany and Japan, both pharmaceutical and manufacturing powerhouses, came under military occupation and installed control systems under American supervision. The supervisory bodies at the defunct League of Nations received a new home at the United Nations, and source control was fixed as a legal—though still contested—international norm. Between the low rate of U.S. addiction and favorable geopolitical developments, the postwar period initially looked quite promising for America's early drug warriors.

Yet Anslinger was vexed. As 1946 dawned, readers of *True Detective* magazine found an ominous warning emblazoned with the Commissioner's grim visage and byline: "With the coming of peace our country faces a foe that can be just as deadly as the enemy on the field of battle." *True Detective,* of course, was no policy journal. It was, however, one of the many reliable "infotainment" outlets through which the FBN built popular support for a new kind of aggressive international policing. As the Commissioner explained, the postwar offered a chance to renew global controls, but traffickers would soon reemerge to target U.S. citizens and their "high-income standards." Making matters worse, he continued, thousands of troops had been stationed in drug-producing areas and exposed to narcotics, and there would inevitably be some "whose moral fiber cannot resist the temptation to experiment"—a fear that resurfaced during the Vietnam War and profoundly shaped Nixon's war on drugs. It was this sense of foreboding that led Anslinger to conclude, "The opium poppy holds as much potential disaster as an atom bomb."[50]

The postwar environment raised the stakes, even as it seemed to offer the chance to finally implement a truly global strategy. The compulsive allure of opiates, Anslinger told *True Detective*'s readers, meant that "effective control of the drug traffic must begin at the source." But that meant going abroad, and here Anslinger captured the wider geopolitical dilemma faced by American policymakers contemplating the postwar world. As the Commissioner put it, "The United States will always have to lead—if for no other reason than self-protection."[51] In an increasingly interdependent and vulnerable world, security could be found only in leadership. To protect conditions at home, the United States had to shape events abroad.

And so the drug war and the Cold War grew up together—like brothers from other mothers. One was born of international political, economic, and ideological competition, the other of domestic social and cultural anxieties. Both sprang from the loins of American identity and, as a result, were shaped by certain notions of American exceptionalism—which is to say that how Americans saw and thought about themselves shaped the way the country confronted communist expansion and the specter of a global dope menace. Though the Cold War was clearly the favored son, both conflicts drew on a rich legacy of defining American identity against its enemies, of seeing the United States as the vanguard of human progress, and a transgressive sense of manifest destiny that linked security and prosperity to expansion.[52]

This common heritage shaped the respective strategies used to fight both communism and drugs and imparted the logic of containment and source control with striking similarities. Early Cold War policy papers like Kennan's Long Telegram, the Truman Doctrine, and NSC-68 all demonstrate a specific understanding of America's role in the world and made direct connections between global leadership, individual liberty, and American security. In his November 1946 missive, George Kennan described international communism as "a malignant parasite which feeds only on diseased tissue" and warned that America's ability to withstand it would depend on the "health and vigor of our own society." President Truman's March 1947 speech—the unofficial start of the Cold War—justified military aid to Greece and Turkey on the grounds that the United States was obligated to protect the "freedom-loving peoples of the world" from outside aggression. The top-secret 1950 strategy paper NSC-68 similarly argued that it was America's duty to shoulder the burden of global leadership and "assure the integrity and vitality of our free society" by opposing the "slavery" of Soviet communism.[53]

America's early drug warriors saw the world in the same terms. They, too, thought globally, believed that national security required international leadership, and invoked a compelling dichotomy between freedom and slavery—well before the Cold War had become a reality. "We must realize that a terrifying responsibility confronts the human race in battling the awful tyranny of drug addiction," Anslinger claimed in a 1936 radio broadcast. A few months later, he told another audience, "The narcotic evil is never wholly national in its incidence, and can never be solved by one nation alone"—a fact Anslinger used to coerce support for American policy. By 1940 the Commissioner boasted that such cooperation allowed the FBN to "reach around the world."[54]

In other words, by dividing the globe between freedom and slavery and then claiming the duty of leading the free world, U.S. security policy followed an ideological and rhetorical path that was already well trod by America's first drug warriors. The drug war and the Cold War had independent origins, but each drew from the same ideological well and each contributed to the rise of national security thinking; as policymakers came to perceive a shrinking and increasingly dangerous world, many concluded that security and stability at home required hegemony abroad.

Hegemony is a loaded term, but the American version differed from European empire or Marxist depictions of unchallenged dominion. Instead, the United States relied on the ostensible power of its example and influence over institutions rather than direct territorial control or outright imperialism, nor was American authority ever close to complete. The key element was leadership of a cooperative alliance system, what some historians describe as an "empire of invitation."[55] *Leadership* and *hegemony* are, of course, not entirely synonymous, but American assistance has a way of becoming American intervention and drugs were an issue that consistently blurred the line.

Diplomacy was the first choice for accomplishing U.S. drug control objectives, but continued agricultural overproduction and excess manufacture in the postwar era quickly revealed the limits of international accord. Every nation involved was fiercely protective of its own exports, whether crude opium or advanced pharmaceuticals. Conflict over the intractable issue of agricultural limits finally came to a head during the battle between two rival UN frameworks. The 1953 Opium Protocol featured strict agricultural controls backed by tough oversight and sanctions. But those provisions were so unpopular that they were scrapped in favor of the milder 1961 Single Convention—a major setback for the FBN that nearly led Anslinger to repudiate the new treaty.[56]

With drug diplomacy hamstrung by basic conflicts of interest, the FBN turned to international policing to carry out its objectives and assert U.S. leadership. To the Bureau, however, leadership meant the physical presence of American cops. Agent Charles Siragusa, a protégé of George White, was chosen to lead efforts in the Mediterranean and immediately reported back, "It is necessary for one of us to direct operations, give orders, see that things get done."[57] U.S. Treasury and State Department officials agreed and authorized the FBN to establish its first foreign office under Siragusa's leadership at the Rome embassy in September 1951. The FBN called that office District 17, a designation that covered all of Europe and the Middle East. From their headquarters in Rome, the agents became directly involved in police operations in France, Holland, West Germany, Italy, Greece, Turkey, Lebanon, Syria, and even communist Yugoslavia. Soon thereafter, the Bureau began to tout the success of District 17 with a lively body of true-crime stories boasting titles such as "Our Global War on Narcotics" and "The World War against Narcotics."[58]

The creation of District 17 marked the start of the FBN's foreign drug war. As with the Cold War, this drug war was formally undeclared but widely understood, and it looked a lot more like modern counterterrorism than conventional military conflict. For the first time, drug war rhetoric began to match reality, and the FBN put ever more strategic emphasis on foreign counternarcotic operations. From their new outpost abroad, the agents began to study and target criminal networks in a manner akin to a global counterinsurgency campaign, styling drug enforcement as a low-grade but high-stakes quasi-military conflict fought in the shadows. As it broadened the scope of its operations, the FBN turned drug control into a drug war and then sold the concept to the public through tales of heroic undercover agents battling evildoers and patrolling the changing frontiers of American society.

Consensus Hardens

The arrival of the drug war in the 1950s was driven by the convergence of several trends, including momentum gathering since the 1930s, fortuitous international developments, and further shifts in the composition of American drug users.

World War II essentially reset the demographics of addiction. Freed from the constraints of depression and war, the American people embarked on a prolific era of consumption while basking in the postwar boom. Overall drug use soared and cut across racial, class, and gender lines. The use of tobacco was truly epic and peaked around 1960, at which point the average American was consuming around ten pounds of tobacco a year and the nation was collectively smoking four hundred billion cigarettes per annum, creating a cancer epidemic that has yet to fully abate. New classes of drugs like barbiturates, amphetamines, benzodiazepines, and minor tranquilizers like Miltown emerged or gained widespread use for the first time and became subject to abuse. After a celebratory spike in 1945, alcohol consumption dipped and then swiftly returned to the pre-Prohibition yearly average of two to two and a half gallons of pure ethanol per person.[59] Both alcohol and tobacco caused significant harm, yet it was heroin that attracted a drug war.

By war's end, the cohort of Harrison and Depression-era addicts had mostly died off. But according to FBN estimates, between 1946 and 1951 the population of American narcotic addicts tripled, growing from twenty to sixty thousand.[60] The outward character of this new cohort was younger, urban, and predominantly black and Puerto Rican—though most of the renewed antidrug hysteria centered on their white suburban counterparts. Explanations for this vary. The FBN was partial to the theory that organized crime outfits like the Mafia were dumping narcotics into poor neighborhoods. Some historians point to the influence of "hepster" role models like jazz musicians or early counterculture icons like the Beats who glamorized drug use. The most persuasive explanation actually boils down to one of the FBN's core tenants: exposure. Drug markets typically exist in the shadow of large commercial and population centers and migrate to economically depressed areas where enforcement is poor. The return of the drug traffic was inevitable, and as the demographics of the inner city changed, so did the composition of the addict population.[61]

The FBN always claimed to be more interested in traffickers than users, but this had critical implications for antidrug discourse. In the 1930s, the FBN concentrated on the Chinese, Jews, and Italians. Each group remained important as potential traffickers in the postwar years, but the FBN's focus on actual use soon shifted to the African American community, which grew in major northern cities throughout the mid-century. "The increase in young heroin addicts is centered around large metropolitan areas, notably New York, Detroit and Chicago," Anslinger told his colleagues on a National Academy of Sciences committee. "It is mainly among young hoodlums and about 80 percent of them are colored. Usually the story is the same, indulgence in marihuana and then trial of heroin." In public, *urban* was soon code for *black,* and the Bureau encouraged the conflation by insisting that drugs were mostly an urban problem—a view that complemented the notion that addiction was a distinctly modern issue, exemplified by busy city life, much as habitual drunkenness and nervous disorders like neurasthenia were seen as symptoms of modern civilization in the nineteenth century. Elsewhere, the Commissioner elaborated, "The big addiction centers are large cities: New York, Philadelphia, Washington, Baltimore ... Chicago, Cleveland, Detroit, Los Angeles."[62]

Each of those cities was, of course, home to large black communities that were subject to active discrimination and confined to poor neighborhoods where they were exposed to drugs and drug markets at a much higher rate than other Americans. The exposure theory has its limits and fails to account for individual choice or explain when contact becomes use, but it does suggest that addiction has as much do with *where* drugs are used and sold as with *who* is actually using them.

As the dope menace developed an ostensibly darker complexion, the medical-versus-recreational classification system—complete with all of its inherent racial, class, and gender biases—became more pronounced. And this, in turn, reinforced a myopic view of narcotic addiction as FBN agents found ample evidence to reinforce discriminatory stereotypes and overlooked or discarded trends that might have complicated antidrug discourse. Take, for instance, Anslinger's discussion of drugs in the nation's capital. "We have a bad addiction problem in Washington, D.C.," he wrote in 1953. "If you go across the bridge into Alexandria or Arlington, you don't find addiction."[63] In fact, the agents almost certainly would have found addiction had they crossed the Potomac with any regularity—it just would have looked different, with different people, different drugs, and different types of use.

There is ample evidence to support a more nuanced view within the Bureau's own files and experience, and officials were well aware that addiction troubled small towns and white rural areas. In 1962, for example, an agent named Jack Kelly was banished to a one-man outpost in Albuquerque after crossing one of the suits. The area, he later recalled, was considered "the sticks." But, he quickly realized, the region had been "entirely overlooked as a narcotics center," and the city climbed from a rank of thirty-five to nine in the FBN's estimated addict population simply because Kelly ensured the relevant paperwork was filed. It's these kinds of structural deficiencies that make most drug statistics, including those offered by the Bureau, somewhat dubious. As Agent Kelly observed, "One can conclude from drug statistics what one wishes!"[64]

More important, this selective official view indicates that drug abuse could be found wherever the Bureau cared to look. Fiercely protective of its institutional agenda and a product of the cultural prejudices of its day, however, the FBN really only cared to look for drugs among people and places that were already suspect in the eyes of mainstream America. This structural bias gave the dope menace much of its particular shape.

By the end of the 1950s, Anslinger had turned the suspicion that some people were genetically predisposed to addiction into a racial argument and was publicly claiming that African Americans were biologically more susceptible than other races on the grounds that they represented about 60 percent of the addict population but only 13 percent of the total U.S. population. Occasionally, he was pressed on the issue, at which point the Commissioner would acknowledge that low socioeconomic status was a factor but insist that blacks were simply more prone to addiction than others. Sometimes he tried to preempt accusations of racism by citing the number of black agents employed by the FBN—more than all other federal agencies combined. The demands of undercover work meant that the diversity among narcotic agents was indeed unique, but pointing to black agents while defending such a claim was the equivalent of saying, I'm not racist—some of my best employees are black.[65]

Despite its reputation, the FBN was actually quite sensitive to being seen as racist. In 1934 Anslinger's tenure nearly came to an abrupt end when he casually used a racial slur in an agency-wide memo and was sternly rebuked by the Senate and White House. Following this incident, the Bureau took pains to avoid overt racial prejudice. One speech on marijuana, for example, was edited: "The clientele was principally ~~colored~~ men of the racketeer type and white prostitutes."[66] Many of the outlandishly racist Anslinger quotes found on the Internet, particularly those associated with his testimony on the Marihuana Tax Act, are apocryphal. Anslinger could be fanatical in his views, but he had strong instincts for self-preservation. Coded language thus became a critical part of FBN discourse. The Bureau, for example, was notorious for hounding jazz musicians; attacking jazz as a carrier of addiction was an indirect way of addressing black drug use. In FBN publications, Anslinger played up the arrests and overdoses of jazz legends Billie Holiday and Charlie Parker. The Bureau even made containing jazz a component of its foreign policy and sought to restrict musicians from international travel. In France agents provoked the arrest of Milton Mezzrow, a Jewish saxophonist famous for introducing musicians like Louis Armstrong to marijuana, on the grounds that he "exerts a harmful influence and is a discredit to the United States." Ironically, only a few years later, the State Department sent Armstrong and his band around the world as exemplars of American culture.[67]

While race formed the most overt line of discrimination, class also deeply influenced how drug use was perceived and discussed. To give the dope menace sufficient scope, the Bureau stressed that addiction threatened all Americans, regardless of standing. Elizabeth Bass, a hard-nosed political operator and Chicago supervisor in the 1930s, told reporters, "The problem is not entirely an urban one. It is not confined to any class of society or race." Anslinger, too, pointed out, "Actors, lawyers, engineers, surgeons and even diplomats have come to this office for help."[68] The critical distinction was in how addicts from different social strata were treated. One 1949 memo urged agents to drop charges against addicts "of previous good reputation" who agreed to seek treatment. White middle- or upper-class users were almost always coded medical addicts and spared criminal charges. Lower-class or otherwise marginalized users faced the full force of the law.[69]

Some of the best examples of this preferential treatment come directly from Anslinger, who liked to highlight examples of FBN magnanimity. In *The Murderers,* Anslinger recounts his acquaintance with a "beautiful, gracious" woman of Washington society who was hooked on Demerol. Despite his strident opposition to ambulatory treatment, the Commissioner secretly contacted her physician and had her supply gradually replaced with placebos until one day Anslinger took her aside and told her, *abracadabra,* you're cured and haven't had narcotics for a month. This lady received the benefit of the doubt because she was part of Anslinger's social circle and conformed to widespread gender expectations. A more disturbing example comes from Anslinger's account of the treatment afforded a powerful congressman who was addicted to morphine but unwilling to seek care. Rationalizing that this was "one of the most influential members" of Congress at a time of geopolitical peril, Anslinger kept a lid on the scandal by providing the legislator with a direct supply of morphine, thus averting a Soviet propaganda victory. Historian John C. McWilliams speculates that the unidentified congressman was none other than Senator Joseph McCarthy, who may have used morphine to temper his alcoholism.[70]

It was easy for someone in Anslinger's position to treat the individual addicts who came to his attention with compassion, but when the addict-as-victim view came into conflict with the addict-as-carrier view, the FBN came down firmly on the side of containment. In the American context, drugs and addiction represented downward mobility, and many FBN accounts emphasized the addict's loss of station. One 1950 radio program described the fall of a former judge, who mourned the loss of his practice and family. "That's the way it is with dope," the narrator solemnly intoned. "It doesn't matter who you are . . . or what side of the tracks you live on."[71] In the Bureau's estimation, addicts were totally incapable of holding down a regular job or living a normal life—thus cutting off access to any kind of social mobility. This, Reagan would later observe, is the antithesis of what it means to be American. Addiction kept the poor poor and threatened to pull everyone else down with them.

Like race and class, gender also served to code worthy and unworthy addiction and shape public perception. Here the critical question was: Did the individual user confirm or threaten commonly accepted cultural norms? When the person in question appeared as a damsel in distress, as with Anslinger's "beautiful, gracious lady" of Washington society, gender norms ensured she was coded a medical addict. If the addict in question threatened traditional norms—like promiscuous women or homosexual men—they were rolled into the construct of the dope menace. In *The Murderers,* Anslinger described the predations of "effeminate Teddy," a homosexual who targeted young boys and traded drugs for sex. "There are a thousand of these sub-strata vermiforms crawling in the shadows of any major city," the Commissioner warned. A more common device was to describe the plight of nice "white girls from good families" who experiment with drugs and fall into sexual degradation. In the early years, when the FBN was focused on the Chinese, Anslinger claimed that white women were particularly vulnerable to "a special Oriental ruthlessness" that spread "incense-flavored depravity" across the country. That remained a useful trope at midcentury, and in the opening pages of the same book, Anslinger painted the lurid image of a "flaxen-haired eighteen-year-old girl sprawled nude and unconscious on a Harlem tenement floor after selling herself to a collection of customers . . . in exchange for a shot in her arm." The Harlem backdrop was no afterthought, layering miscegenation atop promiscuity, drug use, and the dangerous urban setting. In another book Anslinger remarked, "Violation of the puritan codes regarding sex in America could stir the greatest public outrage," a fact the Bureau consistently used to its advantage.[72]

The descent of white teenagers into addiction was a familiar story line in 1950s popular culture. Widely read magazines like *Actual Romances, Woman's Home Companion, True Story,* and the *Saturday Evening Post* frequently received FBN assistance and ran boilerplate accounts of teens falling in with the wrong crowd, experimenting with drugs, and plunging into a life of addiction and crime. Serving as an outlet for the growing concern over teenage rebellion and stresses on the American family, these stories were larded with moral lessons: troubled teens came from broken or dysfunctional households with confused gender roles; some could be redeemed through compulsory institutionalization or fervent prayer, but most were doomed.[73]

The critical point is that race, class, and gender were not just categories used to describe addicts and drug use; they shaped how addiction was seen and understood. Anyone who transgressed social norms was coded deviant and therefore deserving of their addiction. They needed to be quarantined, not rehabilitated. A cynical reading suggests that drugs were a way of branding entire classes of people already on the outskirts of mainstream society—and there's something to this view. But it's also true that it was difficult for the "square" world to parse the socioeconomic problems that created a stratified society and made the disenfranchised seem so threatening. A predilection for drug abuse merely confirmed their marginal social and political status. In *The Traffic in Narcotics,* Anslinger reminded readers, "We are in the main not dealing with average citizens . . . but in fact with people who had unpleasant and troublesome tendencies before drug addiction was superimposed."[74] He was talking about personality disorders, but it's not hard to see how "troublesome tendencies" might include being poor, black, Asian, Latino, gay, young, or culturally rebellious.

The FBN's depiction of drug trafficking underwent similar shifts. Although users tended to crowd public discourse, the Bureau spent most of its time working against traffickers—preferably those operating at the wholesale level but more often against those on the retail end. In the early years, the FBN concentrated on Chinese, Jewish, and Italian gangs and then on the Japanese as the interwar networks began to break up under the pressure of police action and global conflict. After World War II, the Bureau refocused on organized crime and became one of the first law enforcement organizations to identify and go after the Mafia. And although it played a minimal role in actual enforcement, communist China also became a major feature of FBN presentations following Mao's 1949 victory in the Chinese Civil War.

Each adversary brought a different flavor to the discourse of the dope menace, but there were some common denominators. Whatever drug ring the FBN was investigating on any given day was almost always described at *the* most dangerous and *the* greatest supplier to the American market. Bureau officials consistently emphasized that drug traffickers were a breed apart from even the worst of the criminal milieu, distinguished by their ruthlessness and ingenuity. But most troubling was how the immense profit of the drug traffic encouraged criminals to get organized.

The landscape of the drug world tends to be more horizontal than usually depicted, and trafficking networks, then and now, come in all shapes, sizes, ethnicities, and nationalities. Yet as the Bureau cycled through various targets over the years—particularly the Mafia and communist Chinese—it became increasingly monolithic in its thinking and portrayed the drug trade as rigidly hierarchical and tightly controlled. A more unified enemy was ultimately more threatening and subversive. Mining a deep vein of American anxiety about secret societies and enemies within, the Bureau and its allies described organizations like the Mafia as a secret "government of crime" that undermined the sovereignty of the American state.[75]

Against villains such as this, a drug war seemed justified. Support for the Bureau's police-centered approach was significant and widespread, and it led to a general clampdown on the domestic front. The FBN's focus on the Mafia gave the agents a starring role in several high-profile investigations and led to the first federal mandatory minimum sentencing laws in the Boggs Act of 1951 (signed just two months after the establishment of District 17). As the estimated number of addicts rebounded from its World War II nadir, President Eisenhower also took note and, in November 1954, ordered his cabinet to "minimize and stamp out narcotic addiction." Papers like the *New York Times* announced the start of yet another "war on drugs," while Secretary of State John Foster Dulles formally reiterated the U.S. commitment to source control. Eisenhower's cabinet report, delivered two years later, was surprisingly mild in its conclusions, but Eisenhower ignored it and instead signed the 1956 Narcotic Control Act, a law that increased mandatory sentencing and authorized the death penalty for the sale of heroin to a minor.[76]

The punitive framework enshrined in these laws represented the crest of the drug war consensus under the Bureau. Skepticism toward treatment and rehabilitation ran high, and FBN views went mostly unchallenged. "Never in the history of our country has a heroin addict been cured," one senator claimed.[77] To the FBN, this was all to the good. Any softening of public attitudes represented a threat to drug war orthodoxy and the FBN's bureaucratic turf. But the domestic front was, to some degree, a secondary concern—a quality that distinguishes the FBN's drug war from those of Nixon and Reagan. In the Bureau's view, lengthy prison sentences were necessary to quarantine addicts and pressure low-ranking peddlers into snitching, but the FBN recognized that imprisonment alone would not solve the drug problem.

Wherever there were drugs, there would be addicts, so source control remained the guiding principle and the only apparent means of winning the drug war.

The Rise of the Global Drug War

With its domestic flank secure, the FBN embarked on a period of steady expansion that escalated into the 1960s and gave the modern DEA much of its global footprint. Yet one of the most remarkable qualities of the drug war's expansion was its tenuous quality—beginning with the FBN's inability to identify the real source of the American market.

Year after year, the FBN issued contradictory statements about the origin of American street drugs. In 1942 it estimated that three-quarters of the opiates seized in the country came from Iran but also described Japan as the source of "90% of all the illicit 'white drugs'" in the world. The following year, the Bureau identified Mexico as the main source of American narcotics, which was true until the end of the war. By 1948 the Bureau had shifted its attention to Europe and identified Italy as the newest and greatest source of heroin. But in 1951 the Bureau was telling reporters that Mexico was again responsible for 85 percent of the opiates entering the country. Eventually, the Bureau narrowed its focus to the Mediterranean, where the Turkey-to-France-to-America route, known as the "French Connection," was responsible for much of the Atlantic heroin trade. When France was designated as the latest major source country in 1961, an exasperated Agent Siragusa finally asked headquarters if that was consistent with the repeated and conflicting claims that "the principal sources of supply for heroin are Communist China, Syria, Turkey and Lebanon."[78] With source control serving as the basis of U.S. counternarcotic policy and the agents unable to identify—let alone cut off—the origins of the American market, the drug war was destined to falter.

Making matters worse, the presence of American cops on foreign soil was frequently contested. Law enforcement is a closely held sovereign right and jealously guarded by most states. Although the United States had sent police forces abroad to facilitate domestic law enforcement before, the drug war was something altogether new, as the FBN agents inserted themselves into actual investigations and participated in arrests. With few precedents, the details were left to each agent to negotiate as best they could, and informal cop-to-cop diplomacy dictated the success of every case. As Siragusa characterized his time abroad, "We functioned somewhat as roving ambassadors of the Federal Bureau of Narcotics."[79] That lent the growth of the foreign drug war a tentative but ultimately revealing quality, as the agents struggled to navigate the politics, bureaucracy, and criminal milieu of each successive country.

Although drug enforcement and the military and intelligence operations associated with the Cold War remained mostly distinct, the connective tissues between them deepened over time. This was most acute with communist China, which the FBN spent a great deal of time, effort, and ink trying to implicate as the "dope-vending dragon of the East" and principal source of the Pacific heroin trade. Any tie-in between the communists and heroin would have been political gold, and the Bureau was hypervigilant for signs of ideologically motivated or government-backed traffickers—to little avail. But that was almost beside the point. The drug war reinforced the image of a besieged and beleaguered America tenaciously leading the free world.

Much of Anslinger's posturing can be chalked up to politics, but the assumptions that guided U.S. strategy rested on much deeper foundations. As they looked to the global landscape, both drug warriors and cold warriors saw the world in unsurprisingly similar terms. Poor social and economic conditions created fertile ground for addiction and communism alike, and officials described both as contagious epidemics that would spread and subvert traditional Western values if left unchecked. Modernization in the American mold would inoculate against both radicalism and drug abuse.[80] As they argued for the importance of preventative measures in the drug war and the Cold War, respectively, both Anslinger and Secretary of State Dean Acheson independently relied on the same "rotten apple" analogy to make sense of the world and describe how the contagions of radicalism, addiction, and crime spread across borders. This logic informed the "domino theory" in Vietnam, and it was the same calculus the Bureau applied to the dope menace.[81] "The fester of these narcotic-financed criminal organizations has infected other nations," one FBN official complained of the French Connection. While the defense establishment held the line against communism, the

Bureau sought to contain addiction. "Prevention here is worth a million times the cure," Anslinger argued in one book. "Our view is that prevention *is* the cure."[82]

Just as NSC-68 globalized U.S. national security by describing the "defeat of free institutions anywhere" as "a defeat everywhere," by the early 1960s the Bureau had translated the moral imperative of drug control and the geographic reach of the dope menace into demands for international cooperation and, ultimately, claims on a kind of universal jurisdiction. "If you want to control this traffic," Anslinger warned in 1957, "you have got to surrender some sovereign rights."[83] In a telling passage from *The Murderers,* the Commissioner muses, "Evil is of one cloth whether in Shanghai or Istanbul, the Middle Eastern deserts or the western plains. To me the change is only in coloration. The hole-in-the-wall barrooms of East Harlem become the adobe dives of Laredo, Jimenez or Tijuana; the night club circuits of Rome or Algiers become the chrome-plated gambling joints and fancy houses of Vegas, Reno, or Phoenix. Or Mexico City." Note how easily he slides along the geography of the drug trade, deliberately conflating locations foreign and domestic. With the dope menace posing a global threat, Anslinger argued, "We need a cop at the crossroads of the world. We need the fellow with the nightstick to root out the rats, to blow the whistle on evil."[84] That cop, of course, was the United States.

Driven by what it saw as the genuine threat posed by the global drug trade, the Bureau cajoled, snuck, or bluffed its way into other countries and turned drug enforcement into an issue that circumvented the usual diplomatic legalities. The ultimate effect of this was to turn the nation's gaze outward, toward foreign gangsters and foreign drugs and away from the economic and social conditions that ultimately fostered drug abuse in the United States.

The FBN's drug war went global in 1962. Following the creation of District 17 in September 1951, jurisdiction over foreign enforcement was split between the FBN and Customs, with the FBN taking the lead in Europe and the Middle East and Customs retaining its authority in Latin America and East Asia. But in August 1962, the Bureau used a series of covert investigations in Bangkok to engineer Customs' ouster. Treasury officials rewarded the FBN with jurisdiction over all foreign drug enforcement, and Districts 16 and 18 (covering Latin America and

the Far East) were added to the Bureau's domain. The official announcement was made at the highest level, by President John F. Kennedy, at the
opening of a high-profile White House conference in September. Kennedy specifically cited the work of agents in District 17, whose "efforts
have been so successful," he announced, "that the activity of the Bureau
of Narcotics is being expanded to other parts of the world, a program
which will be implemented before the end of the year."[85]

Yet here lies another irony, for the drug war went global at the very
same time that the drug war consensus was coming apart, lending the
White House conference an oddly discordant tone. Only a few months
earlier, the U.S. Supreme Court announced in *Robinson v. California*
that addiction was an illness and not a crime. Part of the FBN's problem was a turnover in leadership. At age seventy, Anslinger was forced
into mandatory retirement, and his replacement, longtime FBN official Henry Giordano, was unable to navigate the shifting tides of public opinion. Even as Kennedy announced the expansion of the foreign
drug war, his frustration with drug control at home was evident, and he
complained of a field torn by "divided opinion" and "a dearth of hard,
factual data." The following day, Attorney General Robert Kennedy
remarked, "We have somehow assumed that the narcotics problem is
so intensely dangerous and vicious that the solution is principally punitive." Both Kennedy brothers acknowledged the need for policing and
specifically thanked the outgoing Commissioner for his service. "But,"
Bobby continued, "law enforcement is only one aspect. The root of the
problem remains." Just what that root was or where it might lie, neither
Kennedy could say. The conference basically signaled growing disillu-
sionment with the FBN's martial approach without offering any viable
alternatives.[86]

Drug policy drifted for the next six years, lost in the tumult of the JFK
assassination, civil rights, and escalation in Vietnam. New classes of
drugs like barbiturates, amphetamines, and LSD complicated the enforcement situation and led to a welter of overlapping jurisdictions and
agencies. Public attitudes softened and polarized as drug use became
a central feature of the counterculture and began leaking into mainstream, middle-class America. In the last year of his own troubled presidency, Lyndon B. Johnson ordered the consolidation all federal drug

enforcement within the Department of Justice (DOJ), and the FBN was absorbed by the newly created Bureau of Narcotics and Dangerous Drugs (BNDD). And all the while, the global drug war marched on, surviving the death of the agency that launched it, its fundamental premise left largely unexamined.

Just how, exactly, did the drug war become unmoored from the consensus that spawned it? And how has it continued in the face of clear failure? Why was demand never seriously addressed? The ancient Greeks wrote of a mythic king named Sisyphus who was greedy and deceitful and doomed by the gods to spend the rest of eternity pushing a immense bolder up a hill, only to watch it plummet back down. There's a similar quality to the history of American drug policy—one in which failure seems to encourage perseverance and stubbornness rather than reexamination. The roots of this quality and the answers to some—but not all—of these questions lie in the bureaucratic politics of the FBN and Anslinger's unique managerial style.

CHAPTER 2

THE WORLD'S GREATEST LIVING AUTHORITY ON DOPE

Anslinger never rests in his ceaseless fight against dope.
—*TRUE DETECTIVE* (1939)

Compulsory cure is the only way to abolish slavery to the drug habit.
—HARRY J. ANSLINGER (1947)

Harry J. Anslinger was an imposing man. The Commissioner—or the Old Man, as the agents liked to call him, though never to his face—was a big fellow, more thick than fat and built like a wrestler. He had a gleaming bald head and a penetrating gaze that was said to catalog everything, all at once. His friends teased him that he looked like Mussolini. His manner was reserved and straight to the point, a quality that unnerved more than one agent. Anslinger was a study in contrasts: he was both diplomat and cop, the studied decorum of a high government official tempered by the Pennsylvania coal fields where he was born and raised. One reporter tried to convey the odd tenor of an audience with Anslinger: "Listening to the commissioner, one gets the strange impression of being in two worlds at once. He is an educated, cultured gentleman. . . . But as he gets into the swing of a story, something happens to his polished phrases. 'Trade terms' begin to creep in. Soon he is speaking an underworld patois in a Harvard accent."[1]

The Old Man's office was the same way. "His paper littered desk is that of the typical Washington executive," the reporter continued, "but the rest of his office is a luxuriously furnished narcotics den, hung with scores of engraved and inlaid opium pipes. . . . One shelf has a half a hundred hypodermic syringes. Another is laden with homemade gadgets—needles, syringes, pipes, and applicators of all sorts, including some that even Anslinger can't explain." For a while, the Commissioner's office was in the Tower Building on K Street. Eventually, FBN headquarters moved to 1300 E Street, a few blocks from the Treasury Department. "How come your bureau doesn't rate an office in the Main Building?" another reporter ventured. "Because our work is nobody's business," came the growled reply.[2]

Anslinger was like that in his public life. He was in but not of official Washington and took pains to keep it that way. Despite thirty-two years as a federal bureaucrat, he never made the city home and stayed at the Shoreham Hotel in Northwest D.C. whenever he was in town.[3] Behind closed doors, he was a loyal friend and a touchingly devoted husband.[4] Every now and then, he even betrayed a sense of humor. Right after likening addiction to the devastation of nuclear war with one audience, Anslinger launched into an anecdote about a Chinese woman who was discovered smuggling heroin in a pair of fake breasts. The Old Man wasn't sure how his agent had uncovered the "set of falsies" but confided that applications for screening positions had subsequently jumped by 50 percent. "I think that's the first time that we ever saw that kind of a communist front," he quipped.[5]

Jokes from the Commissioner were rare, however, and as America's top drug cop, Anslinger was usually rather brusque. One agent remembered, "If you got a 'well done' out of him it was like getting a citation from some one else." The Commissioner was a distant figure for most agents, and few were eager to face his measured stare. "A call from the director was comparable to a call from the President," recalled another agent, or "the Wizard of Oz." And woe unto the unfortunate soul who angered the Commissioner. One reporter described the spectacle: "He plants both of his size-twelve feet on the ground. His ham-like hands turn to fists and he pounds his desk until the ash trays jump. His barrel chest swells till you fear for his shirt buttons. His bow tie shifts up and down over his Adam's apple and his beetle-bald scalp reddens in righteous wrath."[6]

As the U.S. commissioner of narcotics from 1930 to 1962, Anslinger set American drug control policy for three critical decades—almost unilaterally. The term *drug czar* carries a certain autocratic air and didn't come into fashion until Richard Nixon brought drug policy into the White House. But Anslinger, more than any other figure before or since, is the one who best fits the image. For thirty-two years, his influence in the field of drug control was unrivaled, and U.S. policy bore his unmistakable imprint. He was often referred to as "the world's greatest living authority on dope," an expertise that saw him nominated for a Nobel Prize and put him on Adlai Stevenson's short list of VP candidates in 1952. (A registered Republican, he declined.)[7]

Anslinger, however, has left a conflicted legacy. Many scholars give him short shrift.[8] To the extent that he is remembered today, it is generally not with warm regard. In contrast to studies that ignore the Commissioner is a field of literature that might be termed the "cult of Anslinger"—often harshly critical but positioning him at the absolute center of American drug prohibition. In *The Drug Hang-up: America's Fifty-Year Folly* (1972), Rufus King calls him "one of the most tyrannical oppressors of his fellow citizens ever to be sustained in public office." Indeed, the Commissioner's wide influence, penchant for grandstanding, and overheated rhetoric on marijuana have left a one-dimensional image of Anslinger as a moralizing zealot whose narrow views established a legacy of failure in the drug war—a valid interpretation, to some degree.[9] But Anslinger was also much more. Fortunately, the cult of Anslinger has also drawn careful practitioners, who find much to learn in the Commissioner's bureaucratic style and lengthy political career. As John C. McWilliams points out in *The Protectors: Harry J. Anslinger and the Federal Bureau of Narcotics, 1930–1962* (1990), Anslinger's remarkable stint of thirty-two years in office is rivaled only by J. Edgar Hoover, a singular feat that alone "merits a full-scale investigation of his career."[10]

Overlooked in most accounts is the extent to which Anslinger turned drug control into a drug war—a framework that reflected the Commissioner's genuine belief in the threat of the dope menace and sheltered the FBN from outside interference. But in any war, there are casualties: in this case a rehabilitative model of drug control, which Anslinger worked tirelessly to destroy as a viable policy option. This chapter demonstrates how Anslinger applied lessons learned early in his career, as an intelligence operative in post–World War I Europe and an official with the Bureau of Prohibition, to the task of shaping and fighting a drug war while navigating the Washington bureaucracy for three decades. By establishing the threat of drugs, Anslinger positioned the FBN as a bulwark of American values and security, thus ensuring its survival throughout his tenure. Maintaining the discourse of the dope menace, however, also meant silencing critical voices who threatened the basic preventative and punitive framework of the drug war.

The Young Mr. Anslinger

Anslinger's personal and professional background had a profound influence on the way he approached the job of the nation's top drug cop. From boyhood encounters with addiction to hunting communists in post–World War I Europe and taking on rumrunners as the assistant commissioner of Prohibition, Anslinger was primed to see the drug problem in a light that melded diplomacy, law enforcement, and cloak-and-dagger tactics.

Anslinger's first encounter with what he would later call "the narcotics evil" came at the tender age of twelve. Born to John Anslinger and Christina (née) Fladtt in 1892, little Harry grew up in the outskirts of Altoona, Pennsylvania, at a time when middle- and upper-class women comprised the majority of American addicts. In *The Murderers* (1961), Anslinger recalled that about one in ten of the locals were regular opiate users and how one night he heard the screams of a neighbor enduring the agony of withdrawal. The tormented woman's husband soon appeared and urged young Harry to rush into town and purchase morphine from the local pharmacist. "I recall driving those horses, lashing at them," he wrote, "convinced that the woman would die if I did not get back in time." Anslinger returned with the morphine to soothe his distressed neighbor, but, he later wrote, "I never forgot those screams. Nor did I forget that the morphine she had required was sold to a twelve-year-old boy, no questions asked."[11] Anslinger is surprisingly unique here; among the memoirs left by agents, only he cites such a formative childhood experience.

As a young man, Anslinger earned an associate degree from Penn State. He then went to work as a construction supervisor and investigator for the Pennsylvania Railroad, where he had his "first brush with Mafia violence in America." One day Anslinger found a member of his mostly Sicilian work crew laying in a ditch, gunshot and near death. Anslinger discovered that the man had refused to pay off a local "Black Hand" thug running a protection racket, so he tracked the gangster down and threatened to kill him. His crew was thereafter left in peace, and Anslinger learned that crime could be checked with the threat of force.[12]

When the United States entered World War I, Anslinger rushed to enlist. He was denied combat duty due to a childhood eye injury but earned the rank of second lieutenant in the Army Ordnance Division. In 1918 he joined the State Department and was assigned to the consular staff of the U.S. Embassy at The Hague. Already fluent in German, Anslinger quickly learned Dutch and was tasked with, in his words, "behind-the-scenes intelligence reports and investigations." His mentors in the early intelligence community were Julius A. Van Hee and Charles "the Sphinx" Dyar, both of whom cut rather dashing figures and increased the allure of espionage. Anslinger received the sensitive assignment of infiltrating the entourage of Kaiser Wilhelm II, then taking asylum in the Netherlands, and convincing him to reclaim the German throne. Posing as a representative of Dutch intelligence, Anslinger warned that Germany's Social Democrats would "bring on revolution, strikes and chaos." The kaiser, of course, abdicated, leading Anslinger to speculate that success might have prevented the rise of Hitler.[13]

The devastation of war-torn Europe made a deep impression on young Anslinger. "The sight of a large city in ruins, without a house seen standing," he wrote while traveling through Belgium, "creates a feeling that is difficult to describe." But the large piles of captured guns he saw laying about were proof that "civilization has won against barbarism, that spirit has triumphed over the brute in man." This contrast between civilization and barbarism became a central theme in the Commissioner's repeated calls for international drug control, as would the antagonists he encountered among the ruins. Throughout his travels, Anslinger saw despondent GIs who turned to drugs in despair or became addicted in the course of medical treatment, describing "young fellows whose faces bore the stamp of the opium smoker, the user of morphine or the new 'kick' called heroin." A more immediate concern, however, was bolshevism, and Anslinger was charged with monitoring and investigating communist agitation. He took the job seriously and exposed a few communist

agents en route to the United States, along with an American in Rotter-
dam who provided fraudulent visas, but reported great distress with the
passive attitude displayed back in Washington.[14]

Anslinger's career ambitions were temporarily frustrated when
he was transferred to the Venezuelan port city of La Guaira in 1923.
Compared to the intrigue of Europe, there was little for Anslinger to
do in Venezuela, and he feared the backwater posting was a dead end.
"I cannot even find a little Communist about," he complained to one
colleague. In 1926, however, he was transferred to the Bahamas, a critical transshipment point for bootleg liquor, and Anslinger's efforts to
secure British cooperation on U.S. interdiction quickly drew him into
the foreign policy of Prohibition. Anslinger so impressed his superiors
at a London meeting that summer that he was asked to organize the
Division of Foreign Control for the Prohibition Unit of the Treasury
Department. Shortly thereafter, Treasury requested Anslinger's formal
transfer from State, and, in 1929, he was appointed assistant commissioner of Prohibition.[15]

Anslinger came late to the Noble Experiment, when public opinion
had already turned firmly against it. Anslinger, too, quickly soured on
the project. "The Law must fit the facts," he wrote. Prohibition failed,
he felt, because "the American people regard it as obnoxious. Temperance by choice is far better than the present condition of temperance
by force." The future drug warrior learned a key lesson here: not to be
wary of efforts to legislate morality "by force," but to ensure that policy
retained broad public support. In a series of strategy papers, Anslinger
began to develop arguments he would later apply to narcotics. Believing
that a poorly informed public was Prohibition's biggest flaw, he thought
educational campaigns were the best way forward. He was also critical of
the disproportionate federal role in street-level enforcement. "The Federal function should be primarily *investigative* rather than that of policing," he argued, and concentrate on large-scale criminal operations or
instances of official collusion but otherwise avoid a frontline role. Ultimately, however, Anslinger recognized that Prohibition was doomed
and later complained, "It was becoming obvious that this was a thank-
less and impossible assignment. The people of the nation had rejected
Prohibition. . . . Liquor poured across the borders not in a trickle but in
a flood."[16]

Meanwhile, the moral reformers behind Prohibition had pivoted to a new intoxicant: narcotics. Pushed by private citizens like Elizabeth Washburn Wright (widow of Dr. Hamilton Wright) and politicians like Representative Stephen G. Porter (R-PA), Congress was also ready for a new target. In addition to providing the policing mechanisms for Prohibition, the 1919 Volstead Act transferred drug enforcement from the Bureau of Internal Revenue to the Bureau of Prohibition. Control of alcohol and narcotics, however, suffered in the notoriously corrupt agency. In 1929 a federal grand jury uncovered rampant corruption in the New York office of the Narcotics Division. Padded expense accounts, falsified arrest records, agents consorting with dealers—the list of offenses was damning. Still worse was the discovery that the son and son-in-law of division chief Colonel Levi Nutt were attorneys for the notorious (and recently murdered) gangster Arnold Rothstein. It was clear a shake-up was in order. Anslinger briefly took over the Narcotics Division but was ambivalent on the need for a new agency. Drug enforcement, he told Congress, "is pretty well divorced from Prohibition," and he described smuggling as a bigger problem than corruption. Congress, however, was eager to separate drugs from booze. "We were all convinced of the wisdom of separating narcotics from prohibition, for the very simple reason that there is absolutely no relationship between the two," Representative Porter testified. "The latter is highly controversial and the former is not."[17]

Anslinger wasn't the first choice for commissioner of the new Bureau of Narcotics. The bill that created the FBN (H.R. 11143) was signed in June 1930, and both Porter and Elizabeth Wright initially lobbied for Admiral Mark Bristol. Anslinger, however, was named acting commissioner in a July recess appointment and confirmed in December after taking down a network of Chinatown traffickers and leading a national roundup of Italian gangsters—an operation the media dubbed a "War on Drug Rings." Given his experience at the State Department and Bureau of Prohibition, Anslinger was a natural choice to lead the FBN. But it probably didn't hurt that his wife, Martha Dennison, whom he married around 1923, was a relative of Treasury Secretary Andrew Mellon. Anslinger was actually hesitant about the appointment and still harbored ambitions of becoming a diplomat, but it was his internationalist bent that secured him the job given the strong emphasis on diplomatic accord and cooperation among international police forces.[18]

Taking the helm of an unproven federal agency must have been daunting to the thirty-eight-year-old Anslinger, particularly after the spectacular failure of Prohibition. The position of commissioner of narcotics was something of a novelty in American government, with responsibilities divided between foreign and domestic policy, regulating the medical and pharmaceutical industries, and leading federal police. Ultimately, few people, Anslinger least of all, could have foreseen that he would become one of the longest-tenured government officials in U.S. history, a vantage from which he dominated the discourse around drugs for the next thirty years.

Defending the Bureau

Drugs, both then and now, are an enticing political target, and the FBN's early years were marked by constant trial and tribulation. The FBN's uncompromising attitude attracted only a handful of serious critics in the early years; most of Anslinger's challengers came on his flanks, in the form of rivals or budget hawks looking to shrink the bureaucracy. With his agency under steady fire, Anslinger took some early lumps and apparently even suffered a nervous breakdown that caused most of his hair to fall out. Over the course of his long career, however, the Old Man proved adept at defending the FBN and its prerogatives.[19]

In a pattern that became all too familiar, Anslinger hadn't even settled into office before he was criticized on the floor of Congress, where Senator Cole Blease (D-SC) brandished a tin of opium that, he complained, was "sold within the shadow of the United States Capitol." Anslinger realized he had to act fast to legitimize the new agency. While Congress debated the merits of an independent Bureau, Anslinger threw all of his resources into an assault on the District's Chinese-run opium dens, culminating in a series of flashy raids that brought national headlines against the backdrop of an impending gang war. Promising to smash the dens "into a teakwood pulp" if they reopened, Anslinger claimed his "first victory at close quarters with the narcotic underworld," the glory of a big bust washing away the sting of criticism.[20]

The episode displayed Anslinger's penchant for using a good publicity stunt to galvanize support and counter attacks on the Bureau. Social problems in the District have a way of being magnified as symptomatic of national trends. To meet the political (if not criminal) challenge, the Bureau had to act and take responsibility for a situation that was largely beyond its control. Right from the start, controlling the narrative was a way to compensate for the impossible task of eliminating drug use in America. Anslinger's well-publicized raids in Chinatown countered Senator Blease's criticism by making a show of arresting a handful of foreigners to absorb the blame while the actual traffic just went further underground. By the 1950s, the Bureau was once again forced to deal with the local traffic when Washington's Chinatown opium market reemerged. By then, however, the FBN was better established and could blame the problem on foreign enemies like Red China, blending drug control into a familiar Cold War narrative. As *Official Detective Stories* reported, "Washington, the heart of the free world, had been chosen as the first point of saturation."[21] This was a consistent trend under Anslinger's leadership: depicting his agency as a frontline protector of American values was an effective way of defending the Bureau's prerogatives.

Over the years, the Commissioner developed an extensive network of supporters to spread the Bureau's message and extend his influence. From 1931 to 1959, Anslinger was a member of several committees on addiction organized by the National Academy of Sciences and actively pushed the national research agenda in the direction of pharmacology rather than rehabilitation.[22] Interested journalists were reliable allies, and Anslinger was close to reporters like Victor Riesel, Frederick Sondern Jr., and Jack Lait and Lee Mortimer of the Hearst syndicate. Even a cursory look at Anslinger's personal papers reveals a web of contacts scattered across Hollywood and the media, Congress and the federal bureaucracy, foreign governments, the pharmaceutical and medical communities, and a host of influential special interest groups. Through phone calls, favors, and salutations, the Commissioner kept this network primed. Anslinger biographer John C. McWilliams dubs the group "Anslinger's Army," and it was capable of wielding serious political firepower.[23] When trouble appeared on the horizon, the Commissioner could generally count on a outpouring of support to carry the Bureau through its many crises.

One good example is Elizabeth Washburn Wright, who, despite lobbying against Anslinger's appointment, became a critical ally. Independently wealthy and something of a firebrand, Wright enthusiastically took up her late husband's crusade and was the first woman granted plenipotentiary powers by the U.S. government. "It was good to have her on the team," Anslinger wrote. She could "lift a telephone and secure an immediate audience with any Cabinet officer. She had the ear of the President himself." This made Wright a useful ally when the time came to rally support for various Bureau initiatives. Anslinger, for example, credited Helen Moorhead, an activist at the Foreign Policy Association in the mold of Elizabeth Wright, with helping to secure the appropriations to send agents on their first overseas tours after World War II.[24]

Anslinger's Army was essential to maintaining the Commissioner in his post. As a political appointee, Anslinger served under five different presidents but was unsure of his position with each incoming administration. When President Franklin D. Roosevelt took office in 1933, Anslinger assumed that he, like most Hoover appointees, would be dismissed. But allies from across the political spectrum lobbied FDR to keep Anslinger. Richmond P. Hobson, president of the World Narcotic Defense Association, was an active FBN booster and implored Roosevelt to "preserve the integrity and efficiency" of U.S. drug policy in the person of Anslinger. Similar missives came from allies at the State Department and pharma executives. Roosevelt even heard from the legendary British colonial officer Sir Thomas Russell Wentworth Pasha, head of Egypt's Central Narcotics Intelligence Bureau, who called Anslinger "a live wire" and predicted that if he was replaced, "our work would suffer very much indeed; and the enemy would rejoice."[25] Anslinger was unique in that regard, and it was unusual for a political appointee to have such a diverse constituency.

As 1952 turned to 1953 and President-Elect Eisenhower began to install his own people after twenty years of Democratic governance, Anslinger's allies again rallied around him. The president of Sterling Drug wrote the incoming Treasury secretary to describe Anslinger as "extremely fair (I might say strict) to those of us in the Industry who deal in legitimate narcotics. In fact, were his control over any product other than narcotics, this letter might well be one of complaint because of too strict regulation." The Sterling executive urged other industry leaders to do the same and argued that Anslinger represented the best hope for effective drug control "not only in the United States but in other countries as well." R. R. Reed of Wyeth Laboratories similarly reported that Anslinger "commands the respect of the entire drug industry. . . . The world is better today as a result of his many accomplishments."[26]

Even the executives of America's favorite beverage company pledged support. In *Andean Cocaine: The Making of a Global Drug* (2008), Paul Gootenberg explains that "a political pact reigned between Coca-Cola and the FBN on coca and related cocaine issues," a relationship similar to the one between the U.S. government and United Fruit. Alone outside of the pharmaceutical industry, Coca-Cola was allowed to import raw coca leaf (the basis of Coke's secret flavoring syrup) through intermediary Maywood Chemical Works. The FBN–Coca-Cola relationship rewarded both parties: Coca-Cola and Maywood received an exclusive right to import bulk coca leaves, while the Bureau got a compliant industry partner to help manage the legal cocaine trade. Maywood could place employees in locations otherwise inaccessible to Bureau agents, particularly in South American countries like Peru, where executives functioned as the FBN's eyes and ears. Anslinger developed personal friendships with executives at all of these companies over the years. Ralph Hayes, director of Coca-Cola International from 1948 to 1967, was among his most ardent supporters and readily joined the lobbying effort to keep Anslinger ensconced in the commissioner's office.[27]

The enthusiastic support of industry executives does, of course, raise the question of whether Anslinger's Army was actually *cultivating him* and maintaining a sympathetic figure within the federal bureaucracy. The reality is that this was a two-way street, and Anslinger was careful to return minor favors to his supporters and friends.

Threats to the Bureau, however, were not always so overt as broadsides delivered from the Senate floor or changes in presidential administrations. The FBN was under constant duress from the federal bureaucracy itself, as budget hawks sought to trim expenses and consolidate federal policing. One of Anslinger's greatest priorities was autonomy, and he fought hard to protect his fiefdom. A key strategy was to keep Bureau appropriations modest; big budgets made big targets.[28] Fortunately for Anslinger, the FBN could supplement its resources with asset forfeitures—a major issue in contemporary critiques of the drug war.[29] Civil forfeiture laws basically allow law enforcement to seize any property or vehicle associated with drug trafficking, even outside of a trial setting and almost irrespective of guilt.

Confiscation of private property has long been central to U.S. drug control. The federal government authorized the confiscation of ships used to evade Customs revenues during the very first Congress of 1789. The Bureau began lobbying for the power to claim vehicles associated with the drug traffic in 1933 and received it in 1939.[30] This was a real boon to the perennially cash-strapped agency. One friendly journalist wrote, "Testimony to the Bureau's shoestring achievements is the fact that it has never purchased a single car." Even then, the ability to somewhat arbitrarily seize cars was a pernicious influence, and one agent described taking "expensive autos as both a game and legal booty." FBN records from the late 1950s indicate that seized vehicles netted the Bureau roughly five hundred thousand dollars each year. One memo instructed agents to proceed with caution, while another directive ordered agents to seize cars whenever possible as a matter of policy. This served a dual purpose: it punished suspected traffickers and transferred resources to the Bureau outside of the appropriations process.[31]

Keeping FBN overhead low wasn't always sufficient to keep the agency off the chopping block, and several plans to consolidate federal law enforcement threatened the Bureau's autonomy. The first came in 1933, when FDR's budget director proposed recombining the FBN and Bureau of Prohibition and transferring them to Justice. Both the commissioner of Prohibition and the attorney general supported the plan, but Anslinger, of course, did not. The inevitability of Repeal made it a moot point, but Anslinger and Stuart J. Fuller, head of the Far East Desk at the State Department, made sure everyone knew such a plan would violate the recently enacted 1931 Limitation Convention—a treaty negotiated by Anslinger!—which required the government to maintain an independent drug control agency. This, too, was a recurring pattern, and Anslinger frequently parlayed treaty obligations into valuable internal leverage and to protect his bureaucratic turf.[32]

A second reorganization attempt was launched in 1936, this time by Anslinger's own boss, Treasury Secretary Henry Morgenthau Jr., who proposed consolidating all Treasury Department law enforcement (including Customs, the Alcohol Tax Unit, the Intelligence Unit of the Internal Revenue Service [IRS], and the FBN) into a single agency led by a shaken-up Secret Service. The Secret Service Reorganization Act, as it became known, was an effort to streamline costs and keep

Treasury's police arm even with the growing Federal Bureau of Investigation (FBI). Anslinger again feared for his job, but this time the Commissioner had stock memos on hand explaining the importance of an independent FBN.[33]

Sometimes, however, bureaucratic challenges required greater strategic shifts. The 1937 Marihuana Tax Act is a contentious case in point and often portrayed as a power grab by Anslinger. In many ways, the Marihuana Tax Act is a microcosm of the myriad controversies surrounding the Bureau. More ink has been spilled over marijuana than any other aspect of FBN history, narrowing popular understanding of both the Bureau and drug prohibition in America. Given his hyperbolic claims on the dangers of cannabis, Anslinger is treated rather contemptuously in such accounts, portrayed as the creature of a reactionary and socially conservative corporate America. One popular canard is that business titans like William Randolph Hearst and the Du Ponts pressured an acquiescent Anslinger to ban marijuana in order to protect extensive timber holdings and the synthetic fiber industry from competition from hemp. The library and Internet are awash with conspiratorial accounts attributing marijuana prohibition solely to the machinations of Anslinger and his corporate overlords.[34] Even serious treatments depict the FBN's support for marijuana prohibition as a Depression-era tactic to keep the Bureau relevant in the face of tightening expenditures or to undercut the planned Secret Service Reorganization Act.[35]

Far from a conspiratorial power grab, however, expanding the FBN's mandate to include marijuana without additional agents or appropriations was actually a setback and, had it been taken seriously, would have stretched the chronically understaffed agency even thinner. Anslinger was candid with his superiors that "it would be almost hopeless to expect any kind of adequate control" over a wild-growing plant through the same tax and revenue system used to police manufactured drugs like heroin and morphine. Marijuana was useful for cultural purposes like maligning jazz musicians and strengthening antidrug sentiment, but policing its sale and use led to only a modest increase in overall arrests and was a distraction from more pressing heroin cases.[36]

As late as the 1920s, marijuana was considered only a minor nuisance, and even narcotics reformers paid it little mind. But public sentiment tracked a familiar arc, and pressure for marijuana prohibition built as the drug became associated with Mexican migrants in the Southwest and jazz musicians traveling up the Mississippi. For the first several years of the Bureau's existence, Anslinger maintained that marijuana was best left to local police and began linking it to violent crime and issuing his notorious "assassin of youth" claims only when there was already a substantial movement to criminalize the drug. By the time the Marihuana Tax Act passed in late 1937, twenty-four states already had some form of marijuana prohibition or control on the books, and Anslinger got on board to boost the chances for a set of Uniform State Narcotic Laws.[37]

How and why the Marihuana Tax Act passed raises important questions about causality in the history of American drug control and the reach of FBN influence. Was drug prohibition an organic bottom-up development? Or was it foisted on the American people by the likes of Anslinger and Hearst? The answer sheds light on the triangular relationship between the FBN, public sentiment, and actual policy. Though Anslinger scholars differ on the specific paths leading to marijuana prohibition, most portray it as a largely top-down affair, dictated to the public by bureaucrats and policymakers.[38] But Anslinger's fearmongering was effective only because it resonated with a public whose negative views on drugs and minorities made it receptive to such extravagant claims. The FBN had great influence, but it still had to navigate the currents of American culture—plus the federal bureaucracy and Congress—and this had critical implications for the manner in which the Bureau conducted itself.

In practical terms, the history of the Marihuana Tax Act demonstrates the error of looking to the past for "bad guys" like Anslinger to scapegoat for failed policy, in much the same way the FBN tried to pin blame for the heroin trade on kingpins like Charles "Lucky" Luciano or Red China. The reality of drug trafficking is complicated, as is the relationship between policymakers and the public, and the drug wars were built on deep cultural anxieties that predisposed the state to a militant and punitive response. Anslinger was not a passive player and did impart American drug control with much of its particular shape and form, but it's important to heed the institutional and historical contexts in which these developments took place. It is telling, for example, that Anslinger's first instinct after coming around in support of federal marijuana prohibition was to introduce a clause into a treaty that would have obligated a federal law rather than going right to Congress.[39] Adding marijuana to the FBN's portfolio likely did not, as several authors contend, guarantee its survival or thwart the Bureau's absorption into a consolidated law enforcement agency. Instead, the FBN's survival was tied to the American people's readiness to see drugs as a transnational problem that required federal action.

But that was a two-way street, and Anslinger was sensitive to public suspicion of sprawling police agencies. The Secret Service Reorganization Act and subsequent attempts at police consolidation all failed because they aggravated American anxiety about centralizing too much power. Even as he sought to extend the Bureau's reach, Anslinger remained cautious about tipping that balance and explained, "Our staff, in order to avoid accusations of being like the Gestapo, has remained the same size as it was when the Bureau was established." Morgenthau's plan was dropped because it smacked of a European-style "secret police." Sentiment for a powerful federal government arguably reached ascendancy with the establishment of the national security state in 1947, but in the 1930s it was not yet sufficient to overcome the reluctance to create a garrison state.[40]

FBN leadership got better at dealing with such challenges over time. Well-maintained files of arrest figures and modest appropriations were always close at hand, and stock memos rarely failed to mention the Bureau's compliance with treaty obligations or its effective working relationship with the medical and pharmaceutical professions.[41] Anslinger was particularly fond of citing FBN arrests against other federal agencies. In one book, he pointed out that during the 1930s, the FBN was responsible for 12 percent of the federal prison population while constituting only 2 percent of federal law enforcement. By the 1950s, the Bureau remained at only 2 percent of federal police, yet was responsible for nearly 18 percent of federal incarcerations. The average agent, Anslinger calculated, "was making 300 per cent more criminal cases" than their colleagues outside of drug enforcement.[42] These figures were intended to demonstrate the Bureau's outsize ability, but they also reveal how a policy of incarceration is partly rooted in bureaucratic competition. Further galvanized by the structural racism woven into the American criminal justice system, this pressure to quantify success—much like body counts in Vietnam—set the stage for the era of mass incarceration and the escalation of the drug war.

Defeating the Clinics

The old adage "The best defense is a good offense" captures much of the Bureau's essence, in terms of both enforcement strategy and the manner in which it patrolled the borders of its institutional domain. Unfortunately for American addicts, that meant eliminating any alternative to prohibition. Criminalization (via backdoor revenue measures until 1970) underwrote the entire law enforcement paradigm, and the Bureau responded forcefully to any softening of policy or taboos. Drugs, Bureau officials felt, were a problem for cops rather than doctors, who had already demonstrated their inability to contain addiction. Any movement toward public health strategies meant backsliding on the drug problem and undermined FBN autonomy. Anslinger's strident opposition to an outpatient, clinic-based treatment system shows how the stubborn categorization of drugs as a moral issue and security threat is also partly rooted in a bureaucratic context.

In many ways, the Bureau had an impossible task. Charged with breaking up the illicit traffic and regulating the legal industry, the FBN risked being held responsible for eliminating drug abuse entirely; any uptick in use could be construed as a failure of enforcement. This exacerbated the Bureau's already uncompromising attitude and made officials sharply sensitive to criticism. FBN strategy revolved around aggressive undercover investigations to disrupt the traffic coupled with long prison sentences to isolate and deter users. The Boggs Act of 1951 and the Narcotic Control Act of 1956, which introduced and increased mandatory sentencing, were major victories for the Bureau and represented the ascendancy of a punitive framework. But the FBN's police-first approach was not the only proposed method of combating the dope menace.

For a brief moment in the years leading up to 1920, on the heels of the Harrison Act and before the FBN's time, narcotic clinics sprang up in cities all across the country. Most were connected to state health departments and reflected the Progressive Era belief that public health problems like mental illness or venereal disease could be ameliorated through careful study and government aid. The clinics practiced an outpatient approach described as "maintenance" or "ambulatory treatment." Confirmed addicts could register with a local clinic and present themselves daily for a dose of morphine sufficient to prevent withdrawal but not so large as to send them into ecstasy or off on a bender. This remains the strategy behind methadone and other maintenance programs, which began in earnest in the late 1960s. The intention was to stabilize the individual user and separate them from the illicit trade. The theoretical goal was to gradually reduce the dosage until the patient was freed of addiction. Wealthier addicts found more private ways to manage their condition, so most clinics had small clienteles of poor and working-class men of middle age—often white and native born—and, though imperfect and unpopular, the clinics found a rough degree of success with those users willing to seek treatment.[43]

Their existence, however, was immediately challenged by the Treasury Department, resulting in a series of Supreme Court cases on the constitutionality of the Harrison Narcotic Act and legality of the maintenance approach. In the 1916 *U.S. v. Jin Fuey Moy* decision, the Court interpreted the Harrison Act narrowly as a revenue measure that did not preclude ambulatory treatment. But in 1919, Treasury capitalized on the increasingly conservative political climate wrought by World War I, Prohibition, and the Red Scare to bring two new challenges before the Court. The *U.S. v. Doremus* and *Web et al. v. U.S.* decisions effectively reversed *Jin Fuey Moy* when the Court ruled (by narrow five-to-four margins) that it was illegal, in either private practice or a clinical setting, to prescribe narcotics for the sole purpose of maintaining addiction. Under threat of indictment, all of the clinics closed their doors, and by the mid-1920s American addicts were left with few alternatives to the black market.[44] Combined with the crackdown of Prohibition, the shuttering of the clinics marked a critical step in the development of the drug war and forestalled progress on public health strategies for roughly forty years.

Both federal and state governments made a faltering attempt to close the breach with the creation of a few prison hospitals, or "narcotics farms," where addicts were forcibly detoxed in an institutional setting. Prompted by complaints about the number of addicts swelling federal prisons and his own belief in the need for specialized facilities,

Representative Porter introduced a bill in 1928 to create a pair of federal prison hospitals designed specifically for addicts. It took another year for the bill to pass Congress and seven more before the first flagship "farm" opened its doors in Lexington, Kentucky, in the summer of 1935. (A second, smaller, facility opened three years later in Fort Worth, Texas.) Operating under the direction of psychiatrist Lawrence Kolb, one of the country's few experts on addiction, the Farm at Lexington offered a more humane environment than a typical jail and combined the often strange welter of influences characteristic of the late Progressive Era: it was part hospital, part prison, part work camp, part research facility—and the only such institution in all the world.[45]

The clinical research wing, dubbed the Addiction Research Center in 1948, represented the cutting edge of addiction science, but it was still a blunt instrument, and all of the research was conducted on the captive population. Tasked with studying—and hopefully solving—the riddle of addiction, the researchers were more interested in the pharmacology of opiates than the psychology of addiction, misled by the belief that science would offer a technological fix (in the form of nonaddictive synthetics) and absolve the need to confront the drug problem head-on. Over time, the Addiction Research Center developed a close working relationship with pharma and took on the responsibility of testing new drugs for their addictive liability before they went to market. Many of the Farm's research practices now seem barbaric—such as repeatedly administering and withdrawing opiates from patients or testing hallucinogens like LSD with escalating doses over prolonged periods—but it remained a unique and important source of basic scientific data that was otherwise unavailable. It even developed useful therapeutics, like opioid antagonists capable of reversing an overdose. The Farm was also an important cultural touchstone: a trip to Lexington was a rite of passage for many American addicts, and, in addition to some killer jazz bands, its halls nurtured a generation of scientists and clinicians who later challenged the police paradigm. Right up until it was decommissioned in 1974, however, the Narcotic Farm was unable to escape its split personality or the suspicion that addiction was ultimately the product of a damaged mind.[46]

On taking up his post in 1930, Anslinger vigilantly opposed any return to the clinic system and cooperated with the staff at Lexington so long as they remained committed to forcible institutionalization and interpreting addiction as a form of mental illness. Busting Chinese traffickers made good headlines in the early years, but much of the Bureau's initial attention went to medical practitioners, who had been the primary cause of American addiction until only a few years previous. To monitor the licit trade, the FBN created a headquarters division to administer a system of certificates and licenses designed to ensure that doctors, pharmacists, and drug manufacturers were treating illness and not feeding addiction. Over time, the medical and pharma communities became more aware of opiates' addictive properties and voluntarily curbed their use, leading to an increasingly cordial relationship with the Bureau. By 1964 Anslinger estimated that the FBN spent about 20 percent of its time monitoring legal industry.[47]

In the meantime, the FBN used all of the creative rhetoric at its disposal to malign the idea of maintenance treatment, driven by the belief that addiction was contagious and every addict a carrier. Providing a secret and controlled supply to a few Washington insiders was one thing, but underwriting the addiction of the masses was quite another. Because addicts were contagious, the Bureau argued they must be isolated from the general population, reinforcing the tendency to treat them like criminals rather than patients or victims. Anslinger also sharply refuted the idea that clinics separated addicts from the criminal underworld; in essence, he argued, they *were* the underworld, and he claimed that "a large proportion" of small-time crooks like thieves, prostitutes, gamblers, and con men were confirmed drug users. Pointing to spikes in local crime rates, Anslinger characterized the clinics as "nothing more than supply stations" for roving bands of criminals.[48]

More fundamentally, FBN officials believed the clinic system simply failed to address the compulsive nature of addiction. Once again toggling in and out of the disease concept of addiction, Anslinger argued in a 1939 radio broadcast, "You cannot cure a disease by injecting more germs, any more than you can cure morphinism by giving a patient more poison." It would be the equivalent, he later claimed, of "establishing infection centers during a smallpox epidemic." (In fact, that's almost exactly how inoculation works, demonstrating the FBN's tenuous grip on the complexities of epidemiology.) FBN official Malachi Harney likewise tried to highlight the impracticality of the clinic system, arguing, "If we were told that the way to stop drunkenness was to send the drunk to a doctor who would supply him with enough whisky to keep him drunk, we would consider it a joke." While such facile comparisons convey the Bureau's dismissive attitude, the conviction that addiction represented a symptom of underlying mental illness made officials doubt that even those addicts stabilized in a clinical setting possessed the fortitude to repair their broken lives. After all, Anslinger pointed out, addicts demonstrably lacked "the physical willpower and mental stamina necessary to solve the problems which led them to drug addiction in the first place."[49] He wasn't alone in that belief. At a 1960 meeting of one of the National Academy of Sciences' committees on addiction, Herbert Raskin (a Wayne State University psychiatrist who favored public health strategies) described the addict as "a person who is helpless to make an adequate adjustment by himself. Pervading his entire clinical picture is an insidious, insinuating, inexorable helplessness to deal with his addiction by himself."[50]

Blaming the victim was a viable strategy so long as images of the dope fiend dominated public understanding, which made Anslinger's frequent invocation of the moral dimension all the more critical. At other times, Bureau officials claimed their hands were tied. It was their duty to enforce the laws, they argued, never mind their own considerable lobbying efforts. The FBN believed it had a legal obligation to oppose any departure from prohibition; that criminalization failed to stem the drug traffic was no reason to abandon the entire enforcement structure. The Bureau also frequently invoked its reliable fallback position of international leadership and treaty obligations. Accepting the reestablishment of a clinic system, at any level of government—and therefore sanctioning addiction—officials argued, meant abandoning a hard-fought position of leadership on the world stage. Any return to a clinic plan, Anslinger charged, represented "abject surrender" to "the evil of drug addiction." When the Nixon administration began putting federal dollars into methadone treatment, the Old Man was horrified and called it a "monstrous" development.[51]

The only real solution, according to the Bureau, was abstinence, an uncompromising belief echoed in the Reagan-era campaign to "Just say no." "The best cure for addiction?" Anslinger postulated, "Never let it happen!"[52]

Sometimes the Old Man took more direct action against the potential of the clinic system. In a confidential 1940 letter to his Canadian counterpart, a close personal friend, Anslinger reported that public health officials in Mexico City had begun experimenting with ambulatory treatment and that he had withheld all drug exports in retaliation. After exhausting their stocks, Mexican health authorities begged for additional time and offered to appoint a special committee to study the issue if the United States resumed exports—a proposition Anslinger gleefully denied. "Evidently the shoe is pinching the health authorities," he gloated. "They appear to be somewhat shaken over the whole thing."[53] It was not the last time Anslinger leveraged U.S. drug exports to coerce foreign nations into compliance with FBN objectives.

The aggressive manner in which the Bureau attacked all public health proposals and strategies led critics like Rufus King, lead author on a joint American Bar Association (ABA) and American Medical Association (AMA) report issued in the late 1950s, to accuse the FBN of a decades-long campaign of intimidation intended to bully medical professionals into supporting drug prohibition. In his 1972 book, *The Drug Hang-up*, King alleged that, beginning in the 1920s and continuing under the FBN, "doctors were hounded and bullied . . . [in] a relentless attack upon the medical community, carried on by police authorities whose leadership and direction came directly from Treasury officials in Washington."[54]

This is an important complaint that speaks directly to contests over the central premise of American drug policy. King points to the example of Dr. Thomas Ratigan Jr., a Seattle physician who provided maintenance treatment to roughly seven thousand addicts a year in the early 1930s, roughly a decade after the Supreme Court struck down the clinic system. In 1934 the FBN brought charges against Ratigan, but a jury found the doctor not guilty. Seven months later, Ratigan was arrested again on what King describes as manufactured assault charges. They were dropped, but Ratigan was arrested a third time in October 1935 after one of his patients turned informant. At trial federal prosecutors revealed that Ratigan had dispensed more narcotics than all other physicians in Seattle and Portland combined. This time the jury found him guilty of violating the Harrison Act. Ratigan, however, was unrepentant. "The present enforcement of laws by narcotics agents is wrong," he said, and "the solution to the narcotics problem" lay in maintenance-based treatment. Increasing the stakes, Ratigan announced that he intended to run for Congress but was sentenced to prison after the circuit court and U.S. Supreme Court both declined his appeal. King cites Ratigan as an example of the Bureau's intimidation of doctors, contending, "A menacing call from the federal agents, coupled if necessary with open threats of prosecution, would usually prevail when a doctor dared minister to an addict."[55]

Ratigan surely suffered from FBN persecution, but as a vocal proponent of addiction maintenance, his example was not typical. At the helm of a police agency, Anslinger refused to tolerate such open dissent from the notion that drugs were a police problem. The tactics ordinarily used to investigate most doctors were as routine as they were simple. When ordering wholesale narcotics from a manufacturer, physicians and druggists filled out a specific order form in triplicate. One copy went to the retailer, one to the Bureau, and one to the practitioner's files.[56] This allowed the FBN to monitor for signs of diversion into the black market—a legitimate concern. Anslinger recognized that retaining the support of the medical and pharmaceutical professions was key to the Bureau's success. Soon after taking office, he circulated orders prohibiting investigations against physicians or pharmacists without explicit instruction, and reports coming in from the field supported a cautious approach. It was easy to get an informant to purchase a small amount of narcotics from a physician or pharmacist, the district supervisor in Seattle warned, but that did not always indicate "the bad faith of the physician," and the Bureau had to avoid interfering with medical and state-level health practices. The supervisor in Jacksonville explicitly ordered his agents to treat all medical professionals with the utmost courtesy and "not go out at random" making cases on doctors.[57]

World War II nearly accomplished what the FBN could not: with international shipping in disarray, the foreign sources of the black market were temporarily cut off, and Anslinger was optimistic that American addiction was approaching its "irreducible minimum." Although some heroin began to arrive by way of Mexico, investigations of malpractice and legal diversions took on greater urgency as FBN leadership urged field agents to press their advantage.[58] The manner in which these investigations were carried out, however, was inconsistent. One veteran supervisor in Minneapolis complained, "There has been a policy of sending informers in on doctors and making cases regardless of the circumstances," but his office had closed several cases with a quick chat. Anslinger, ever mindful of the optics, wrote back in agreement that "it would be good policy to continue handling minor infractions" in this manner. Not all of these conversations went smoothly, and much depended on the personality of the individual agent. Obtuse agents and scared doctors, aware their careers were at risk, made for a volatile mix that did little to allay criticisms of FBN bullying. Occasionally, the Bureau did encounter clear-cut examples of physicians engaged in the illicit traffic, but, Anslinger acknowledged, these cases were "few and far between."[59]

Most agents simply felt little urgency about registrant cases, and even during the war many languished for years. In 1946 Anslinger reminded Agent George White, then supervising the Chicago office, "You must be keenly aware of the importance of closely following up on any information on excessive purchases by registrants." White, however, well known as an agent's agent, didn't care for the paper-trail style of investigation required to check on medical professionals and explained that a backlog had grown because the secretary who normally handled this function was ill.[60]

In short, there is not much evidence in FBN records to suggest registrant cases were used to intimidate or coerce cooperation that was not already forthcoming. Anslinger, admittedly not the most reliable narrator, told Congress that when dealing with physicians, an FBN agent does "not act like a policeman. . . . He is more in the nature of a fatherly advisor." Monitoring the licit trade was an important function, but standing orders were to approach these investigations with the utmost caution and act only on clear evidence of criminal intent. Moreover, in the absence of any real action—the kind of cases that advanced careers—street-level agents were bored by such cases. By 1965 the backlogs had become lengthy enough to prompt FBN headquarters to complain of the neglect. If this was an FBN-led "reign of terror," it was an awfully lackadaisical one.[61]

There were, however, two factors outside of the paperwork system guaranteed to trigger FBN action: complaints from important people or vocal criticism of the Bureau. Ratigan is a good example of the latter; his vocal support for ambulatory treatment made him an obvious target. In *On the Street* (1974), Agent Jack Kelly recalled an example of the former.

Sometime in the mid-1950s, Anslinger received a complaint from Senator Harley Kilgore (D-WV) that addicts had gathered in the bucolic Appalachian town of Bluefield, West Virginia, leading to a rash of petty crime. The Old Man sent Kelly to check it out. After visiting the sheriff and springing a local addict named Tom Patterson to use as an informant, Kelly called on the physician suspected as the source. By Kelly's own account, Dr. Horton was a typical country doctor. At age seventy-five, he was a fixture in town and often bartered treatment for goods or services. When Patterson went to see the doctor and requested a shot of Dolophine (a synthetic opioid), Dr. Horton obliged and politely offered one to Kelly as well. Kelly declined but requested a prescription, which Dr. Horton wrote while admonishing Patterson to quit doping. Incredulous, Kelly brought in another agent to pose as a down-on-his-luck horse jockey and buy from local peddlers allegedly supplied by the accommodating Dr. Horton. After rounding up several small-time dealers, Kelly arrested Dr. Horton. At trial Horton's lawyers pleaded insanity; the judge found him guilty and stripped his medical license but suspended the elderly doctor's prison sentence. In Kelly's recollection, this was an open-and-shut case; a handful of local peddlers supplied by the doctor's negligence went to jail, Horton was no longer practicing, and Anslinger banked a favor with a senator.[62]

In the context of the Bureau's confrontation with a maintenance-based approach to addiction, however, Kelly's investigation takes on additional overtones. Dolophine, the drug Horton readily provided to the confirmed addict Patterson, is today better known as methadone, a synthetic opioid that works more gradually and lacks the euphoric "high" of quickly metabolized narcotics like morphine or heroin. In the late 1960s, clinical researchers Marie Nyswander and Vincent Dole began to use methadone in an experimental program at Rockefeller University and, as in the clinic era, found that patients addicted to heroin could be stabilized on a carefully calibrated methadone regimen. Freed from the dramatic highs and lows and acute withdrawal symptoms of heroin use, many patients were able to resume the rhythms of their old lives, hold down jobs, meet family obligations, and function as otherwise normal citizens.[63] Today, methadone has been largely supplanted by newer therapeutics like Suboxone, a blend of a semisynthetic opioid and antagonist/blocker.

By prescribing the slow-acting Dolophine to patients suffering from withdrawal back in the 1950s, Dr. Horton, whether intentionally or not, had stumbled into an addiction maintenance program roughly ten years too soon or forty years too late. Agent Kelly recalled that Horton "really believed he was helping suffering mankind." Patterson, the addict-informant, also defended the doctor and told Kelly, "Doc Horton doesn't ordinarily give fixes unless he thinks folks need one . . . doesn't like to see them hurting, you know."[64] For the Bureau, the question of criminal intent was paramount, and a country doctor who took old appliances or home repair as payment was clearly not enriching himself by peddling dope to all comers. But the interest of a U.S. senator and suspicion that Horton's narcotics reached the street ensured an FBN response.

Preventing the return of any sort of clinical maintenance system was just one of the ways the Bureau policed drugs in America. It was the FBN's steadfast position that ambulatory treatment only encouraged the spread of addiction, and because it would vest power with physicians rather than police, such public health approaches were a real threat to FBN autonomy. Anslinger was fending off attacks on the Bureau from its very first days, hard-wiring an institutional protectionism into the agency that was on full display in its confrontation with maintenance treatment. Much of the Bureau's public relations strategy relied on the taboos of criminalization, and it refused to tolerate any softening of American attitudes. Defending FBN orthodoxy required discrediting the clinics or any other threat to the discourse and beliefs supporting prohibition.

Silencing the Critics

While the Bureau's control over public discourse was never absolute, the manner in which it confronted its detractors reveals that Anslinger and his fellow drug warriors were not content with controlling drugs—they wanted to control how Americans thought about the entire drug problem and moved forcefully against their most vocal critics.

Examples of the FBN suppressing critical voices are scattered throughout its history, but several of the more illustrative incidents date to the late 1930s, when Anslinger became more confident about asserting Bureau prerogatives. Anslinger's Army was again a critical partner. In April 1938, freshman representative John M. Coffee (D-WA) complained that the federal government had strayed from the intent of the Harrison Narcotic Act and introduced a resolution ordering the U.S. Public Health Service to audit domestic controls in the hope that enforcement would wind up back in the medical realm. The Commissioner apparently didn't even feel compelled to respond directly, and Coffee's resolution died a lonely death by committee after failing to attract a cosponsor. Anslinger probably did some unrecorded private lobbying, but this demonstrates that the Bureau was operating in a favorable climate and Congress had little interest in challenging the basic law enforcement posture of drug policy.[65]

At other times, the Bureau took more direct action. In the early 1930s, a prominent Los Angeles physician named Dr. E. H. Williams agreed to help city health authorities treat a small group of addicts, most of whom were visibly or terminally ill. As with Ratigan, the inclusion of a federal informant among his patients led to a swift indictment. Williams avoided prison but abandoned his practice and created a nonprofit organization called the World Narcotics Research Foundation, which the Bureau promptly labeled a "criminal organization," since Williams technically had a conviction on the books. The irony was that Williams was actually a moderate and advocated maintenance only for special or terminal cases; the World Narcotics Research Foundation seems to have been founded as an alternative to organizations like the White Cross, which favored a broader application of maintenance treatment. A few years after discrediting E. H. Williams, agents discovered that his brother Henry, a retired physician and science writer, had published a book provocatively titled *Drug Addicts Are Human Beings* (1938), and they immediately dug into this Dr. Williams's background as well—only to find that he had no criminal record, an upstanding reputation, and a serious bird nest–collecting habit. Undeterred, the investigating agent suggested that Anslinger ask the Intelligence Unit of the IRS (the same outfit that toppled Al Capone) to investigate the recent sale of his 130-acre Connecticut farm. Meanwhile, Anslinger prepared for future confrontations by collecting statements from the editors of the *Journal of the American Medical Association* (*JAMA*) labeling Henry Williams a "quack."[66] The Bureau may not have set out to intimidate the profession at large, but as the example of the Williams brothers clearly demonstrates, any doctors who publicly challenged the basic premise of American drug control were quickly maligned.

The Bureau was even willing to take on prominent politicians when they deviated from drug war orthodoxy. Although the Marihuana Tax Act passed Congress with little debate, New York City mayor Fiorello La Guardia was skeptical. As a congressman, the "Little Flower" had praised Anslinger as "an exceptionally able, alert and competent official" but was an outspoken opponent of Prohibition and openly critical of criminalization. In 1939 he commissioned a panel of decorated physicians and public officials to study marijuana use in collaboration with the New York Academy of Medicine. The committee moved at a deliberate pace and did not publish its final report until 1944, but it challenged several FBN positions. Blending sociology, physiology, and psychology, the La Guardia Report found that marijuana use was largely contained and its effects fairly banal. Anslinger launched a counterattack before the report was even published. When some of the initial findings were aired in a 1942 issue of the *American Journal of Psychiatry*, Anslinger attacked from the pages of the *JAMA* and continued to use the journal as a platform to discredit the La Guardia Report thereafter, leading to the report's almost total marginalization.[67]

One of the Bureau's most well-known confrontations was with the sociologist Alfred Lindesmith, who studied addiction from a psychological, rather than physiological, perspective. Lindesmith first came to the FBN's attention while conducting field research on drug users during his graduate studies at the University of Chicago in the late 1930s. Lindesmith's essential argument was that the self-perception of the user is just as important as a drug's pharmacological properties—in short, addicts had to perceive themselves as addicts in order to actually become addicts. Over the years, he authored a number of books elaborating on this theme, including *Opiate Addiction* (1947, republished as *Addiction and Opiates* in 1968), *Drug Addiction: Crime or Disease?* (1962), and *The Addict and the Law* (1965). In all of his writing, Lindesmith was sharply critical of U.S. drug policy and attacked the reductionist view of addiction as an untreatable mental illness. Lindesmith was largely on the periphery of addiction research, but his work marked the start of an important critique and opened up new fields of inquiry.[68]

The Bureau repeatedly tried to discredit Lindesmith. When Lindesmith was offered a tenure-track position at Indiana University in 1939, agents from the Chicago office dropped by to warn university officials that he consorted with a "criminal organization" run by a "collection of racketeers"—the Williams brothers' World Narcotics Research Foundation. The university was undeterred, and Lindesmith remained on the faculty for most of his career. The following year, he published a brief article titled "'Dope Fiend' Mythology" that refuted many FBN positions. Anslinger was loathe to respond directly, so the Bureau recruited Twain Michelsen, a San Francisco circuit court judge and personal friend of the Old Man, to issue a vitriolic rebuttal titled "Lindesmith's Mythology." Running in the same journal three months later at three times the length, Michelsen's article rehashed familiar orthodox positions and tarred Lindesmith as a "pseudo-scientist." Undeniably in FBN crosshairs, Lindesmith came to fear that agents would plant narcotics and have him arrested on drug charges. One internal memo suggests the FBN may have utilized an illegal wiretap, and at one point Anslinger even asked J. Edgar Hoover for any intelligence linking Lindesmith to "Communist-Front organizations."[69]

Ironically, the Bureau may have taken Lindesmith more seriously than did his professional colleagues, and the FBN's sustained effort to discredit him did little to alter the overall direction of addiction research. Over at the National Academy of Sciences, for example, most of the committees working on the drug problem, along with the scientists at the Farm in Lexington, remained focused on developing synthetic alternatives to opiates and better understanding morphine's analgesic qualities.[70] The tide didn't begin to turn against the police approach until the late 1950s, and Lindesmith had little to do with it, despite his role as harbinger. Clearly, however, the FBN felt compelled to respond aggressively to any public challenges.

One final example demonstrates how the FBN's refusal to tolerate dissent, even behind closed doors, carried over into actual operations. From 1960 to 1962, the Bureau carried out a discrete investigation of State Department Foreign Service officer Elwyn F. Chase, who, seemingly out of pique at FBN prominence on the diplomatic circuit, reportedly "expressed hostility" toward the Bureau in general and Agent Charles Siragusa in particular. In response, the Bureau assigned a surveillance team to monitor Chase, check out his medical prescriptions, and collect evidence of his purported alcoholism or anything else that could be used to discredit him.[71]

The forceful manner in which the Bureau responded to critics shows how important it deemed public perceptions to the efficacy of drug control. Any breakdown in the taboos supporting prohibition undermined the FBN objective of deterring all drug use, while examples like the investigation of Chase reveal how obsession with such criticism sometimes distracted from the Bureau's core mission of actual counternarcotic investigations.

Cops versus Docs: Consensus Fractures

In the late 1950s, the proxy war between cops and doctors finally broke into the open. Two rival frameworks jockeyed for power. On one side was the prevailing law enforcement paradigm championed by the FBN, in which addiction was a moral issue and addicts were dangerous deviants. On the other side was the medical paradigm, in which addiction was a disease and addicts victims in need of care. The medical paradigm was slow to develop, constrained by the frontiers of science and public revulsion toward the stereotypical dope fiend. There was considerable overlap between the two; everyone agreed that drugs were dangerous, that addiction was contagious, and (for the most part) that addicts required institutionalization. But the essential conflict between the moral and medical emphasis of each side hollowed out that common ground, leading to a series of increasingly contentious clashes and ultimately the fracturing of the drug war consensus.

This conflict played out on a number of levels: in popular culture, the halls of Congress, and the corridors of the National Institutes of Health (NIH). The 1955 film *The Man with the Golden Arm*, based on the award-winning 1949 book of the same name, starred Frank Sinatra as jazz drummer and recovering heroin addict Frankie Machine and offered a sympathetic portrayal of addiction that broke new cultural ground.[72] The pressure for reform—in one direction or the other—generated rival legislative packages during the Eighty-Fourth Congress. In early 1955, Senator Frederick G. Payne (R-ME) introduced a bill that drew forty-two cosponsors and proposed increasing penalties,

transferring the FBN to Justice (a perennial threat), *and* reestablish-
ing a national clinic system—but it failed to get out of committee. Just
over a year later, Congress instead passed the 1956 Narcotic Control
Act. Dropping any pretense toward rehabilitation, the new law established two- and five-year minimum sentences for first-time offenses
and authorized the death penalty for the sale of heroin to a minor. It
was the most draconian drug law in the U.S. history until the passage of
the Anti–Drug Abuse Act thirty years later.[73]

This was a moment of triumph for the FBN, but events were starting to outpace Anslinger and company. Congress had developed an
enthusiasm for punitive enforcement all its own, and the Bureau was
actually not wild about bringing in the death penalty. "That seems a
little drastic even to us," FBN counsel remarked. The Commissioner's
once formidable command over national discourse was beginning to
weaken as additional players took an interest and the increasingly strident direction of national policy sparked a slow-growing critique of the
police approach. Roused from their complacency, the country's legal
and medical professions began to reassert their own claims on the drug
problem. In February 1955, the American Bar Association and American Medical Association launched an ambitious joint study of national
drug policy—the same month that Senator Price Daniel (D-TX), a
staunch FBN ally and noted segregationist, began the series of hearings
that would culminate in the Narcotic Control Act. The ABA-AMA Joint
Committee was led by counsel Rufus King (future author of *The Drug
Hang-up*) and included some genuine luminaries, like future Supreme
Court justice Abe Fortas and Dr. Robert Fenix, head of the National
Institute of Mental Health. In theory, the rebellion of the country's legal
and medical professionals represented a profound threat to FBN orthodoxy. Marginalizing the committee—and clearing the field of challengers at the FBN's moment of triumph—was one of the Old Man's last
great battles in office.[74]

Fortunately for the Bureau, the ABA-AMA Joint Committee found
little support from either parent organization, and by the time it published its first "interim report" in 1958, President Eisenhower had
already signed the Narcotic Control Act into law. The initial ABA-AMA
report's most controversial recommendation was to establish some kind

of experimental outpatient treatment system, an idea that gained some grudging support but generally fell outside of the consensus view that addiction could be handled only in an institutional setting.

The realization was growing, however, that the nation's medical community had failed to meet the challenges posed by addiction. "Most addicts know of no place they can go for help without being locked up," explained Dr. Isaac Starr, a decorated cardiologist, member of the ABA-AMA team, and chair of a National Academy of Sciences committee on addiction. "The time is ripe to explore other methods of helping them." Outpatient treatment was problematic for any number of reasons, he conceded, but it was better than warehousing addicts in prison. "Even if it failed we would not be worse off," he argued at a meeting convened by the Academy. To the Bureau, however, outpatient treatment was tantamount to maintenance and therefore anathema. With the recidivism rate running high even at specialized institutions like the Farm, FBN officials agreed with the need for follow-up psychiatric care but refused to accept that addicts would stop using without coercion. "Voluntary patients never remain voluntary," FBN counsel countered, and the lengthy prison sentences sought by the Bureau were intended to target traffickers, not addicts. If the individual in question happened to be both, he argued, they shouldn't get a pass on dealing just because they were also an addict. Incensed by Starr's increasingly public comments, Anslinger resigned his own committee membership in 1959 when the Academy didn't move fast enough to distance itself from the ABA-AMA report or Starr's personal views.[75]

The battle was already won at the legislative level, but Anslinger did everything he could to prevent the proposed outpatient experiment from gaining additional traction. As soon as the ABA-AMA interim report came out, the Old Man hastily convened his own "Advisory Committee" chaired by Representative Hale Boggs (D-LA) and stocked with Bureau stalwarts. The group existed on letterhead only and never actually met but quickly issued a rehash of FBN talking points packaged in a deliberate facsimile of the ABA-AMA report. Copies of the FBN advisory group's "Comments on Narcotic Drugs" soon outnumbered—and were often mistaken for—the actual ABA-AMA report. With few sponsors willing to fund it, the ABA-AMA Joint Committee limped along for a few more years until Lindesmith arranged to have its final report published by the University of Indiana in 1961.[76]

The two camps had what turned out to be one final exchange at a conference held at the National Institutes of Health in March 1958, before the lines between cops and doctors hardened to such an extent that dialogue became difficult. Over the course of two days, almost every major participant in this ongoing debate gathered in the Washington suburbs to once again stake out their respective positions. The group included members of the ABA-AMA Joint Committee, staff from the Narcotics Farms in Kentucky and Texas, and personnel from an array of U.S. health organizations. Complaining that the conference was stacked with "experts who wished to turn over all drug addiction to the doctors," Anslinger refused to attend but was well represented by longtime FBN official Malachi Harney and other allies.[77] Although the debate was often heated, it remained cordial, and for a brief moment it seemed like real progress was possible.

One of the most telling exchanges came between Harney and Dr. Lawrence Kolb, former director of the Farm at Lexington and now a gray eminence in the field. Kolb's early work on addiction and mental illness informed much of the FBN's own concept of addiction. Now retired from public service, however, Kolb freely voiced his qualms about the direction of U.S. drug policy and the "enormous mass of misinformation" that plagued the public sphere. He was especially troubled by the demonization of addiction and the conflation between drugs and foreign enemies. The notion that narcotics were a tool of subversion and war, he argued, could gain credence only "in an atmosphere already clouded by propaganda and permeated with fear." Kolb also sharply disputed the idea that addiction was a sign or cause of moral decline. Importantly, however, Kolb recognized that such misconceptions were not the product of government conspiracy or federal power grabs but were created by "sincere laymen and law enforcement officers" and "otherwise competent physicians." The problem, he argued, was that the campaign for drug control had generated "enthusiasm and zeal for the suppression of vice rather than the desire to obtain and spread proper knowledge of drug addiction." The promulgation of increasingly punitive drug laws was "a tragic thing," he charged, "that must eventually end just as witch burning eventually ended"—an analogy first made by Lindesmith.[78]

It fell to Harney to defend the status quo. "The question of whether or not narcotic addiction is a sin is something perhaps for the Pope to pass on," he mused, and its legality was a question for the courts. But the FBN was a police agency, and "when a program is laid down," he insisted, "we ought to carry it out in the best conscience, and see that it is carried out." Harney readily acknowledged that doctors had a different view of the problem, "but I will still say as a simple policeman," he continued, "who has walked the streets with these addicts that this stuff is a poison." As Harney defended the criminal paradigm, Kolb pressed him, asking if drug use or even trafficking was really "as serious a crime as murder, kidnapping or rape." Harney was evasive, replying, "You and I see a little different type, of course, doctor." He was not wrong. Although at times they dealt with some of the same unfortunates, federal narcotics agents and public health physicians faced vastly different scenarios in their professional lives and had very different formative experiences. Some addicts might deserve sympathy, Harney conceded, but traffickers were a different story, and anyone who sold a fellow human into the bondage of addiction, he insisted, was "worse than a great many murderers."[79]

Although the conference featured some of the toughest criticism yet leveled against the police approach, it is also striking how much common ground still existed. Kolb, for all of his criticism, maintained his belief that drug control was necessary. He, too, equated addiction with slavery and agreed it was "such a fearful thing that it does demand control measures." The country needed drug control, Kolb argued; it just needed a *different kind,* conducted by different personnel.[80] The problem was that American policy had drifted in the course of its confrontation with such a complex, multifaceted, and difficult problem.

The NIH symposium now seems like a missed opportunity. Each camp identified common ground as well as bottom-line institutional priorities, thus establishing a potential foundation on which to build a more effective policy. But when the participants broke up and dispersed to their respective agencies, *nothing happened.* Rufus King, smarting from Anslinger's successful outmaneuvering of the ABA-AMA Joint Committee, contends a "bulldozing campaign" ensued to suppress the findings of the symposium, which weren't published until 1963. Some, like Kolb, had stature sufficient to place them beyond reproach. But other officials who criticized the status quo, he claims, were quietly reprimanded by their agencies, each according to his station.[81]

By the end of the 1950s, law enforcement and medicine had reached an impasse. The FBN and police approach still carried the day, but the nation's physicians were no longer passive accomplices. In the wake of the NIH conference and the debate over an outpatient system, Dr. Harris Isbell, director of the Addiction Research Center at Lexington, voiced his distress over the "rapidly widening rift" between the two camps and thought both were "guilty of inflammatory statements and the use of propaganda." But he remarked wistfully that he "would do anything he could to heal the breach." What little goodwill remained, however, was quickly drying up in the face of FBN shenanigans and Anslinger's stubborn refusal to compromise on national strategy. Only a few years later, Isbell's patience, like that of a growing number of critics, had run out, and he confided to a colleague, "I have reached the point where I do not lose much sleep over the attitude of the Bureau of Narcotics."[82]

The FBN held the ideological high ground for most of its existence. But the debate over the clinic system and basic enforcement posture, one-sided though it often was, reveals how the fundamental question of whether drugs should be controlled through law enforcement or medicine was under constant negotiation. Even with the successful countermeasures it routinely deployed against its critics, there was little the FBN could do about the broader cultural shifts that shaped the 1960s and changed the relationship between drugs and the American public.

With each passing year, FBN officials found themselves increasingly behind the times. By 1962 Anslinger was living up to his Old Man nickname and forced to retire. At age seventy, he had become something of a dinosaur and, facing mandatory retirement, was out of tricks. Though he retained his international portfolio until 1970, his departure from the Bureau proved to be a loss of leadership rather than a changing of the guard.[83] His successor, Henry Giordano, shared none of the Old Man's bureaucratic talents or forceful personality but inherited all of Anslinger's stubbornly antiquated views on the science and morality of the drug problem.

And so the drug war consensus began to unravel even as the drug war itself achieved global scope. Anslinger winds up a Moses-like figure in the grand narrative of American drug wars, successfully holding off alternatives to prohibition and shepherding the FBN's quest to battle drugs at the source into a new global era but denied his own entry to the promised land.

Through a combination of political skill, astute networking, and rhetorical mastery, Anslinger proved remarkably adept at defending his bureaucratic domain and put his personal stamp on U.S. drug control for more than thirty years. As he learned during the waning days of Prohibition, maintaining public support was paramount, and that required silencing critical voices and ensuring that drugs were seen as a problem for law enforcement. But there was more at stake here than the survival of a federal agency—namely, the treatment afforded to tens of thousands of American citizens struggling with addiction. Anslinger, however, eager to simplify public narratives and retain support for his agency, clearly felt compelled to meet any and all challenges to a punitive police approach.

Over the course of his thirty-two years as the commissioner of narcotics, Anslinger sheltered the drug war and its supporting ideology through a tumultuous infancy and adolescence—to a stage where the drug war survived not only the void left by his departure but also the collapse of the consensus that spawned it. Yet in his effort to nurture the drug war and protect the FBN from institutional challenges, Anslinger made drug war ideology brittle and injected it with a reactionary quality that was slow to dissipate—to the point where any compromise risked undermining the basic moral and security framework of drug policy and therefore the Bureau's continued existence. Upholding the dope menace as a means of protecting the FBN worked for a long time. Yet when the Old Man finally left office, all that remained of the consensus was the acknowledgment that both law enforcement and medicine were necessary—and no agreement on the proper balance between the two.

So how did the drug war achieve a life of its own and survive the collapse of the drug war consensus? The key to the drug war's success was not in its actual efficacy—it demonstrably did not keep drugs from reaching American shores or American users, as Anslinger knew all too

well. Rather, the key to its success was in turning the nation's gaze outward and focusing attention on evil foreigners and depraved junkies. To
understand how and why the drug war was so successful as a normative
and operational reality, we must turn our attention to the drug war itself
as it slouched toward its Bethlehem in the 1930s and '40s.

CHAPTER 3

ON THE STREET AND BEHIND ENEMY LINES

The principle is the same whether it is in Turkey or New York.
—GARLAND WILLIAMS (1950)

The criminal must always move in the shadows, in the underworld.
It is our job to follow him there.
—HARRY J. ANSLINGER, *THE PROTECTORS* (1964)

arland Williams was kind of spooky. Some of the stories about him went back to Prohibition, when he used to haunt the bays and inlets of the Gulf of Mexico. A lanky fellow with a soft Mississippi drawl, Williams would sit alone for hours in a small boat, bobbing gently with the waves, scanning the horizon and waiting for the rumrunners to come ashore laden with booze from Mexico, Honduras, and Cuba. The smugglers, Williams knew, had to put in somewhere, and when they did, he would radio the Coast Guard to hit the exchange. If the hooch made it off the beach, it was as good as gone. Catching the traffickers as their precious cargo changed hands was the best chance to make a big seizure, roll up the smuggling networks, and prevent the black-market alcohol from reaching American consumers. It was a good tactic but required patience. As Williams saw it, this was the narrowest point of the contraband booze trade and the most vulnerable place to strike.[1]

Years later, Williams applied a similar strategy to narcotics. The drug traffic, much like the underground booze market, was a tricky thing to nail down. Populated by a disparate, ever-shifting coalition of smugglers, hijackers, financiers, con men, temporary entrepreneurs, small-time hoods, and some genuine villains, the black market was built to evade detection. But the moment when the wholesalers brought their product in from overseas was a perfect chance, Williams thought, to finally impose some authority.

"Our narcotic control system should be in the shape of an hour glass," he once wrote to Harry Anslinger, his on-again, off-again boss. At one end, out in the world, the U.S. government should work to cut foreign production and prevent the unrefined narcotics from escaping their place of origin. The other half of the hourglass was the retail side, where the drugs were sold to their ultimate consumers. There, Williams argued, the dope menace should be met by "a hard-driving investigative and police group" that would "give the roughest sort of treatment" to peddlers and users alike. But source control and street enforcement both presented serious challenges: source countries rarely shared the Bureau's enthusiasm, and the increasingly stiff penalties leveled against the array of dealers, petty criminals, and users populating the domestic market had only a limited effect. The "narrow waist" where real weight and paper changed hands, however, might be vulnerable.[2] There was some debate over just where that "narrow waist" was located. Having cut his teeth as a Customs agent, Williams thought it was the borders. Agents who worked overseas pointed to the manufacturing stage, where opium was converted into heroin in a relatively limited number of clandestine labs.[3] As ever, law enforcement was aiming at a moving target.

Throughout the thirty-eight years of the FBN's existence, street agents and supervisors continually refined their craft, pioneering innovative strategies and techniques that had an impact well beyond the world of drug control. Due to the unique challenges of counter-narcotics, many FBN tactics centered around the use of informants and undercover work. As supervisor of the critical Manhattan office during the drug war's gestation in the 1930s, Garland Williams played an outsize role in the development of FBN operations and then applied that experience to the job of training American spies, saboteurs, and commandos during World War II and beyond. While Anslinger worked at the national and diplomatic level to shape public perceptions, Williams was in the trenches shaping the way the drug war was actually fought.

From Hooch to Heroin

When Harry Anslinger took the job of FBN commissioner, he discovered an agency in total disarray. The situation in Manhattan was particularly bad; the squad there was known as the "Forty Thieves" for its expertise in graft. As the largest city in the world's largest consumer market, New York played an organizing role in the global heroin trade and functioned as something of a clearinghouse for the domestic market. That made it a critical battleground in the early drug war.[4]

In the early 1930s, the Manhattan office struggled to police the city's drug trade. Beset with corruption, the office was in constant turmoil, and few cases were being made. Anslinger had his own problems back in Washington and little time to spare for the Bureau's flagship field office. Exasperated with the trickle of cases reaching his desk, the local U.S. attorney complained to Secretary Henry Morgenthau that "no serious effort" was being made "to prosecute the wholesale importers and principal distributors who ultimately are the real menace." Already irritated with Anslinger's early missteps, Morgenthau sent in a team of Treasury officials to clean house. In a fortuitous turn of events for the embattled Commissioner, the delegation was led by Garland Williams.[5]

Williams was a man on the rise during the waning days of Prohibition. Born in Prentiss, Mississippi, in 1903, Williams joined the U.S. Army Reserve at the age of twenty-one while studying civil engineering at the University of Mississippi. He distinguished himself when, five years later, he was given command of a National Guard company stationed in New Orleans. Upon his arrival, Williams found the company "highly disorganized and broken in morale," but he earned the rank of captain after quickly reorganizing and invigorating the unit. In 1929 he was recruited by U.S. Customs. While Prohibition agents were responsible for hunting bootleggers and raiding speakeasies, Customs was tasked with preventing smuggled liquor from reaching the United States in the first place. Williams took to the work and accelerated through the ranks as part of a "Flying Squad" assigned to Anslinger's various interdiction projects. In 1933 he was elevated to the top post in Galveston, Texas, an important Gulf port. Williams even led an official delegation to Mexico to persuade the government to raise export taxes on Mexican booze and assist on cross-border investigations. Three years later, he was promoted again and asked to create and organize the new Southwest Patrol District, an administrative feat accomplished in only six weeks that left Williams in charge of 160 men and the entire southern border.[6]

Treasury officials had big plans for Williams, and in November 1936 he was formally transferred to the Bureau of Narcotics and given reign over the New York office as part of a department-wide shift toward drug control. Just as he had throughout his Customs career, Williams imposed a new sense of order and discipline on the unruly New York office. Together with representatives of the U.S. Attorney's office and the IRS, Williams went after any signs of overt corruption. Eleven of the eighteen agents stationed in New York were demoted and shipped out, including Williams's predecessor.[7]

Younger generations recall Williams with a touch of reverence. Howard Chappell was recruited by Williams into the World War II–era intelligence services and from there into the Bureau. He remembered Williams and Malachi Harney as "two of the most wildly acclaimed Agents of the old Prohibition unit" to come over to the FBN, providing a direct link between Prohibition and drug enforcement and bringing a wealth of experience into the agency. Like Williams, Harney had one foot in law enforcement and the other in military service. A former marine, Harney was described by one colleague as "gung-ho as all hell" and often professed "to think of the Bureau as a little Marine Corps." Rare among the personnel associated with Prohibition, both Williams and Harney were noted for their integrity and served as Anslinger's main field marshals. Both men later advanced to several higher offices, increasing the Bureau's political clout and influence as they rose.[8]

As the new supervisor in Manhattan, Williams was intent on targeting high-level traffickers, but he faced a challenging police environment. New York in the 1930s was a patchwork of ethnic enclaves. Since well before the turn of the century, wave after wave of immigrants looking for a new life had crashed and broken on the city. With few resources beyond distant kin, new arrivals tended to cluster in specific neighborhoods and slums, giving each a distinct ethnic character. That made New York one of the most international cities in all the world— and some areas nearly impenetrable to law enforcement.

Foremost among Williams's targets were the Jewish and Italian gangs suspected to run the burgeoning international heroin trade. Just like Anslinger, Harney, and Williams, many of these groups got their start in Prohibition. Anslinger later explained, "Dope had always been part of their operation," but after Repeal, "it took on a bigger role." With a criminal infrastructure already in place, Anslinger recalled, it was an easy transition: "They had the organization, the contacts, the personnel." The gangs also proved stubbornly resistant to law enforcement, as rank-and-file soldiers were easily replenished from New York's working poor.[9] The trick was to go after the leadership, but that required new tactics and a fundamental shift in the way the Bureau did business.

Making Cases

The challenges inherent in drug investigations are legion. Underlying all of them is the fact that drug use, like most vice, is usually a consensual crime. "Narcotic police work differs from nearly all other police work in that there is no complainant involved in the transaction," the Commissioner explained in a 1942 radio address. "The seller is satisfied and so is the purchaser."[10] Although many agents claimed a knack for spotting drug users, the consensual nature of the crime made drug use and trafficking difficult to detect. Prohibition may have been where most of the FBN's senior staff learned their craft, but drugs and alcohol produced very different consumption and trafficking patterns, and, contrary to Anslinger's overblown tales of rampaging dope fiends, most addicts carried out their drug use in private. That meant narcotic agents had to go looking for their quarry.

There were also, Williams learned, unresolved questions about strategy and targeting. Drug control, like Prohibition before it, was a clear-cut attempt at social control that disproportionately affected the poor and the marginalized. The ultimate objective was to eliminate an intoxicating habit deemed inimical to American values and society. In contrast to crimes like theft or murder, which are investigated after the fact, the Bureau's task was preventive rather than purely investigative. This suggested targeting users, and over the years the Bureau pushed for increasingly punitive drug laws to deter use and isolate addicts. But FBN agents and officials were well aware that the compulsive nature of addiction limited any strategy to police the traffic from the ground up. The Bureau also knew it could not vanquish addiction head-on, so from the very first days, the strategy was to focus on supply. One of Anslinger's first orders as the acting commissioner directed all agents to pursue only "worthwhile cases involving actual peddlers and dealers in narcotic drugs in an attempt to strike at the source of supply." Cases involving "petty addicts" should be turned over to local authorities.[11]

Most suppliers, however, were canny enough not to expose themselves to arrest, and serious trafficking organizations were layered to protect the principals. The degree of separation between top and bottom varied with each organization, but every agent knew, Agent James Mulgannon explained in his memoir, that "a multiple-ounce dealer of heroin can very well be one step removed from the actual smuggler."[12] The cell-like structure of most organizations, however, meant the moneymen and wholesalers rarely interacted with the street-level dealers or addicts encountered by police, necessitating a delicate and time-consuming style of investigation as the agents worked their way up the supply chain and hierarchy.

The agents also faced serious countervailing pressures. Impatient to be seen making an impact, many offices resorted to general roundups aimed at known addicts or drug markets, a strategy Anslinger thought would have a "salutary effect on the criminal element" but was the modern equivalent of "clearing the corners." Over in Chicago, district supervisor Elizabeth Bass—an anomaly in the otherwise all-male world of the Bureau—favored a blunt strategy of leveling maximum charges against the largest number of offenders possible. After leading a series of raids in December 1934 that took in approximately 250 known addicts and peddlers and disrupted a gang estimated to move $3.6 million worth of narcotics each year, Bass told reporters, "Our purpose is a general round-up of all known addicts and peddlers in this area. We aim to exterminate all the handlers and minimize the effects of this absolutely devastating business." The use of the term *exterminate* is particularly striking—an indication that she considered the suspects vermin rather than people.[13]

In New York, however, even this roundup style of enforcement had fallen by the wayside during the era of the "Forty Thieves," and it was up to Garland Williams to get the Bureau's most important office on track. Following his arrival in November 1936, Williams returned the FBN's attention to international and regional suppliers rather than users and small-time dealers. Within a year, the Bureau's tightened focus led to a series of big seizures, dramatic raids, and national headlines.

The revised strategy began to pay off in the autumn of 1937. In October FBN agents launched simultaneous raids in New York, Houston, Galveston, and New Orleans against a network suspected of distributing between $5 and $25 million worth of narcotics, which the *Washington Post* described as part of the Bureau's "war" on dope smugglers. Williams and Manhattan DA Lamar Hardy received national praise for bringing in 74 suspects and ringleader Nicola Gentile, an early Mafia figure who jumped bail and resurfaced as a lieutenant in Lucky Luciano's suspected postwar transatlantic drug empire.[14]

The Mafia was still only a glimmer in the eyes of enforcement officials, and, at the time, there was much more excitement about the conclusion of the Hip Sing Tong case, one of the true-crime adventures routinely featured in FBN literature. Any news about the Chinese fraternal associations known as tongs made for big headlines in the 1930s, and, in late November, Williams announced that "one of the biggest dope rings in the country" had been destroyed with the arrest of some 38 suspects nationwide, including the Hip Sing Tong's national president. As the *New York Times* summarized, in language likely provided by Williams, "The round-up . . . was in keeping with the smashing blows dealt to narcotic traffickers since the shake-up a year ago when Major Garland Williams took charge of the Treasury Department's Narcotic Bureau here."[15]

The heavily Orientalist portrayals and exotic nature of the tongs immediately turned the Hip Sing Tong case into a popular police adventure story—one that highlighted the FBN's unique brand of undercover work. Although Williams refused to identify the agents involved, the case was initiated by George White sometime in early 1937 with the arrest of an elderly Chinese addict in Seattle. Threatened with deportation, the addict agreed to set up a meeting between Agent White and his dealer, a former tong "hatchet man" identified as Charlie Lum (a.k.a. Lum Git, Charlie Lee). Given the same choice between cooperation or prosecution, Lum turned informant. Posing as representatives of a West Coast organization—White joked they worked for his rich uncle Sam—the two traveled the country making purchases and setting up cases along the tong's national distribution network and managed to rope in some of Lucky Luciano's known associates in Manhattan. Given the ostensible business he was generating, White was even formally initiated into the tong, an unprecedented honor for a white man and the first time the Bureau managed to infiltrate an ethnic Chinese gang. The number of suspects tended to grow with each retelling, but the investigation led to several indictments, prison sentences, and deportations.[16]

The case was a textbook example of working up the supply chain. Agent Tom Tripodi, who worked for the FBN, CIA, and BNDD in the 1960s and '70s, explains, "Given the time, effort, motivation, and energy, you can start with a junkie and go all the way back to the source of supply." This was basically the end goal of any narcotic investigation. The Bureau was willing to drop the charges against the Seattle addict and White's "hatchet man" informant for access to tong leadership and a case against a major distributor. Contemporaneous media reports immediately seized on the romanticism of the case, describing how Agent White "furnished courage and brains," while tong members were rendered in reliable caricature—all of which helped define the growing narrative of a drug war at a time when most Americans remained leery of spies and secret police.[17]

One month later, the feds unveiled indictments against noted Jewish mobsters Louis "Lepke" Buchalter and Jacob "Yasha" Katzenberg. Buchalter was notorious for his involvement in New York's labor and garment rackets and (somewhat after the fact) his command of the Mafia hit squad "Murder, Inc." FBN literature variously attributes the case to a jilted lover, an aggrieved rival, and an undercover agent. Through one or all of these sources, the Bureau learned that Buchalter was supplied by sources in Japanese-occupied China and ran the drugs past corrupt Customs inspectors in Manhattan. Both Buchalter and Katzenberg fled the country when the indictment was issued, but their drug ring was finished. Estimating that the gang moved roughly ten million dollars in narcotics every year, Anslinger immediately announced that the FBN had "crushed" a "drug smuggling conspiracy of world-wide ramifications" and cited the case as proof of the need for tougher controls in the Far East. Katzenberg was arrested in Greece less than a year later and extradited to the States, where he was sentenced to ten years after testifying against his partner. Buchalter famously remained on the lam until August 1939, when he turned himself in to columnist Walter Winchell and FBI director J. Edgar Hoover. That was a sore point for the FBN, where Anslinger credited Andy Koehn—an agent so adept at surveillance and misdirection that the Old Man called him "a one-man counterintelligence corps"—with turning up the heat on Buchalter to the point where his only option was surrender.[18]

Like Hoover, Anslinger knew the power of headlines and occasionally took to the field to make them. In April 1939, the Commissioner led a series of raids in Kansas City to cap an eighteen-month investigation into what the he called "the capital of narcotics distribution in the mid-West." Agents seized or confiscated some five hundred thousand grains (equivalent to approximately one hundred pounds) of narcotics valued at over one million dollars, implicated at least one local police officer, and fueled the ongoing battle between political boss Tom Pendergast and Governor Lloyd C. Stark.[19]

The drive against major distributors continued in January 1940 when the FBN issued charges against the "Newman Brothers," a trio of international traffickers who eluded authorities for twenty years and were periodic colleagues and competitors to Manhattan's most notorious gangsters. As Williams explained to the *New York Times,* under the Americanized moniker "Newman," brothers Henry, George, and Charles Neiditch were suspected as one of "the underworld's principal source of supply for narcotics," a network worth an estimated fifteen million dollars. In 1937 Williams assigned a team of agents to drop everything and go after the Newmans. Though the case files were likely destroyed, FBN records indicate an expansive approach. Anslinger invited agents from the Immigration and Naturalization Service (INS) to join the hunt after the FBN turned up multiple birth certificates for Charles. In January 1940, the agents delivered a lengthy dossier, leading to indictments on tax fraud and conspiracy to violate the Harrison Narcotic Act. With multiple agencies closing in, the brothers turned themselves in a few months later and pleaded down to face lenient sentences and nominal fines.[20]

The Newmans got off easy, but the case highlighted the benefits of interagency cooperation and the often central role of immigration. The FBN had frequent occasion to work with Customs, and every now and then the FBI, but both relationships were characterized by competition and institutional rivalry. The FBN and INS, however, were fast friends, given the number of suspects who were first- or second-generation immigrants and the considerable overlap between human and drug trafficking. The two agencies developed an effective partnership over the years and were, for quite some time, the only police forces legally permitted to conduct search and seizures without a warrant. Several years after the Newman case, Anslinger circulated an agency-wide order to invite the participation of INS agents whenever agents encountered undocumented migrants. Another agency-wide memo from 1951 pointed out that the Chinese were particularly vulnerable and that "fear of deportation is often greater than fear of imprisonment for narcotic violations," helping agents to coerce confessions and flip informants.[21]

Between Garland Williams's arrival in 1936 and the close of 1940, the Bureau leveled an impressive series of blows against major distribution networks operating in and out of New York and even took out a few suppliers of genuine international stature. Many of the FBN's initial targets in the 1930s were Chinese and Jewish; ironically, the elimination of those networks (along with Hitler's impending Final Solution) may have inadvertently paved the way for the Mafia's postwar domination of the narcotics trade. Despite big cases against the Hip Sing Tong, the Buchalter-Katzenberg ring, and the Newman brothers—each of which was variously identified as *the* biggest source of supply—still the drug traffic persisted. Bureau officials were getting their first look at the incredible malleability and resilience of the illicit drug trade. Years later, Williams complained, "No matter how hard we hit it, it seems to keep springing up again." The agents knew they could not arrest the problem away: "The prisons will not hold them all," Williams conceded, but "we must keep on trying."[22] As 1939 edged into 1940, and the shadow of war loomed over both shores, the underworld's ability to absorb the Bureau's attack and expose American vulnerability raised pressing concerns.

Battlefields

With several of the wholesale operations out of business, Williams turned his attention to the specific neighborhoods that seemed to keep breathing new life into the dope menace. In many respects, this was a return to the "roundup" style of investigation. But Williams knew that if the FBN was going to make any kind of headway, it would have to confront the criminal infrastructures that turned places like the Lower East Side, Harlem, and San Juan Hill into veritable open-air drug markets and talent pools for future traffickers. "We have learned that to arrest the petty passers of narcotics is futile," he told reporters after a bust in Harlem. "It merely creates a job for another criminal. So we extended our investigation over a period of many months to get the higher-ups—and I believe we finally caught up with them."[23]

When agents began looking into Harlem, they professed astonishment. Williams described conditions in the largely black and Spanish neighborhood as "atrocious" and an "eye-opener" for the agents. "Dealers fairly swarmed over a few poolrooms and restaurants with their wares, and they sold to men, women and children of all descriptions," he said. "Some of the narcotics were paid for in pennies begged on the streets." One unnamed Treasury official claimed that children were selling narcotics "as openly as though they were selling apples, and with a good deal more success."[24] For what it's worth, that's *not* how many former residents remembered their neighborhood. Many of the subjects interviewed in David Courtwright's oral history compendium *Addicts Who Survived* (1989) recall a vibrant community that resisted urban blight until the 1960s and '70s. Drugs could certainly be found; one addict acknowledged, "In Harlem you can buy anything—you just have to know where to buy it." But most sharply refuted the image offered by Williams. "You didn't see no kids selling or using drugs," countered Arthur, an addict and resident of Depression-era Harlem.[25] The difference was almost surely one of perspective: the gaze of a lawman differs from that of a neighbor.

Targeting specific neighborhoods was one way of undermining the structure of the drug traffic, but the ethnic and racial character of these areas required greater sophistication from the Bureau. Cases like the Hip Sing Tong investigation, where a white agent infiltrated an ethnic gang, were exceedingly rare. Sometimes the Bureau compensated with simple ruses. In one 1937 investigation of Manhattan's Chinatown, FBN agents donned shabby clothing and wandered around pretending to sell discount eggs. More often, however, the Bureau needed informants—or, better yet, actual agents—who fit the necessary racial profile. "Most of our agents in the Chinese districts are of Oriental extraction," Anslinger wrote in *The Murderers*. "They speak Chinese fluently, know the idiom and the slang and can merge in the Chinese community. Similarly in the investigation of Sicilian mobs here or abroad, we frequently use our agents of Italian—preferably Sicilian—backgrounds, steeped in the ancient culture of Sicily, aware of the obscure customs, meanings, intonations, idioms and oaths."[26]

One FBN target in Harlem was a ring of smugglers who crewed the cruise ships and ocean liners plying the waters between New York, Cuba, and South America. To infiltrate the gang, the FBN needed a Latino agent, who later explained, "I had to pretend I was Spanish—which I am by birth—and 'on the lam' from the law. I had to dress in infested second-hand clothes to play my part, eat filthy food and mingle with people who'd turn an ordinary stomach." He was also repeatedly forced to prove his criminal bona fides, at one point "stealing" a government car and initiating a "street brawl" when rivals accused him of being a "stool pigeon." Ultimately, the Bureau arrested ten people in connection with the case, and the U.S. Attorney's Office estimated the ring was responsible for smuggling at least sixty thousand dollars' worth of (unspecified) illicit drugs into New York.[27]

Although consistently excluded from FBN leadership, African American agents were in particular demand. In 1958 one supervisor complained about the difficulty of conducting investigations in Denver's predominantly black Five Points neighborhood, where "the presence of a white person . . . causes some alarm among the Negroes." This complaint was common throughout FBN history. In 1933, for example, another supervisor requested a black agent for a series of cases in Louisville, Kentucky. "Most of the dealers are negroes," local supervisor G. W. Cunningham observed, and "there is not much opportunity for putting the fear of God into them." Anslinger arranged to have a black agent sent from Chicago, prompting immediate protests about the loss of a critical investigative asset.[28] In time, Anslinger would cite the number of black agents employed by the Bureau to refute charges of institutional racism.[29] That the Bureau hired black and other minority agents in an era when few were employed by the federal government is indeed commendable, but their hiring was driven by investigative need and Cunningham's privately expressed desire to "put the fear of God into the Negros" exposes a clear limit to any genuinely progressive ethos.

Indeed, the focus on neighborhoods like Harlem throughout 1939 and 1940 demonstrated that the Bureau's emphasis on suppliers did not mean the abandonment of a more bare-fisted approach. The area once known as San Juan Hill was, by almost all accounts, a rough place. Situated on Manhattan's West Side along Amsterdam Avenue, the tightly packed tenement houses were home to one of the city's oldest and largest black communities. By the 1940s, it was among the city's most notorious slums. Williams called it one of "the wildest streets in America" and claimed that no fewer than seven policemen had been killed by bricks and debris thrown from rooftops—a perfect hideout for what he identified as the "most notorious, vicious gang of narcotic peddlers in America." Curtis, a former small-time dealer, recalled, "There were more drugs sold in the San Juan Hill than anywhere in the world." Williams explained to reporters, "For more than 25 years this section has resisted every effort of enforcement agencies to clean it up. My men have made more than 100 arrests in one block in the last two years, but the narcotics trade, along with almost every other conceivable vice and racket, has gone on unimpaired."[30]

On February 2, 1939, Williams led some forty federal agents on a dramatic raid, cordoning off the block and then plunging into the densely populated tenements of San Juan Hill. The ostensible purpose of the raid was to capture a ring reportedly supplying a "white surgeon and ten of his Negro followers" who sold heroin to "poor white addicts" in Asheville, North Carolina. (As a surgeon, it's doubtful the alleged distributor would have been interested in the highly adulterated product coming out of San Juan Hill, which had an estimated purity of only 3 percent.) Inside, the agents discovered a warren of secret tunnels and passages connecting the dilapidated buildings, delighting reporters who gleefully described how "prisoners scurried through tunnels they had laboriously dug through stone walls." Exploiting intelligence gleaned from subsequent interrogations, the Bureau staged a series of follow-up raids four days later that brought in an additional thirty suspects, twenty-six ounces of heroin, and "large quantities" of marijuana.[31]

Given the diluted product coming out of San Juan Hill, an astute analyst like Williams would know this was a relatively unimportant and low-ranking branch of the traffic. The real purpose was simply to hit a disreputable neighborhood known for spawning minor drug offenders while publicly demonstrating the FBN's commitment to law and order—the police equivalent of showing the flag. Race surely contributed to the Bureau's aggression, but Williams was also trying to attack the criminal infrastructure that continued to replenish the drug trade. Years later, Anslinger claimed that Williams "succeeded, so great were his powers of persuasion, in getting the indomitable and much loved Fiorello La Guardia to raze the block of houses." Following World War II, San Juan Hill was indeed torn down, not because of any FBN involvement, but to make way for the Lincoln Center and Opera House and a housing project known as the Amsterdam House.[32]

The Right Stuff

For Garland Williams and the New York office, the late 1930s were a formative period in which the agents refined their techniques, field craft, and institutional culture. Building on that seminal time, the FBN developed an array of different tactics for combating the dope menace. In *The Corner: A Year in the Life of an Inner-City Neighborhood* (1997), a frontline chronicle of the 1990s-era drug war, David Simon and Ed Burns observe, "Stupid criminals make for stupid police." The reverse is also mostly true: savvy criminals require sharp police, and drug trafficking is a tricky enterprise. In *The Traffic in Narcotics* (1953), Anslinger wrote, "Drug trafficking is a very ingenious and resourceful business. All the tricks and ruses of the professional magician, all the devices and inventions of Houdini himself seem tame and unimaginative beside the innumerable dodges and disguises thought up by the tribe of international drug traffickers."[33] That left federal agents and traffickers locked in an adversarial embrace, where advances or innovations made by one side led the other to develop countermeasures, spurring continual evolution on both sides of the law.

The Bureau was always on the lookout for new investigative aides and tactics to counter the increasing sophistication of traffickers, but much depended on the personal style of the agents. Some preferred to just kick in suspicious doors or find an addict or immigrant to intimidate. Rough-and-tumble agents like Jack Kelly professed to "come from the old school . . . where the basic tool was a size twelve pair of shoes" and collecting intelligence meant roughing up perps in secluded alleyways.

Other agents settled into a more deliberate style and the use of technical aids like bugs and wiretaps to chart the structure of a criminal organization. Wiretaps were particularly controversial during the early days of FBN history due to the excesses of the Bureau of Prohibition and were deemed unconstitutional by the 1928 *Olmstead v. United States* decision. Secretary Morgenthau, however, favored the use of wiretaps or any other available tool in the fight against the dope menace, telling reporters, "We do not propose to be sissies." Wiretaps became a consistent feature of FBN surveillance and operations over time, even before their use was revalidated in the 1967 *Katz v. United States* decision.[34]

Some of the Bureau's more creative (and unrealized) proposals included using a Geiger counter to track people, vehicles, money, or contraband tagged with radioactive powders or inserting a chemical marker into the raw ingredients used in heroin manufacture that would allow seized dope to be traced to its point of origin.[35] Not every technique was successful, but by the mid-1960s the Bureau was sufficiently advanced in its use of technical equipment that it acted as a covert purchasing agent for what one briefing paper elliptically referred to as "other Top Secret Government agencies"—most likely the CIA or a State Department agency providing aid to foreign police.[36]

One of the more notable innovations Williams introduced in the 1930s was the use of drug dogs, a practice now synonymous with drug control. There's a bit of jockeying in the historical record between different agents and agencies claiming to be the first to use dogs in the field. Most accounts agree the practice was initially met with great skepticism. Agent Siragusa recalled setting out for the first time in a creaky station wagon with a fellow agent and two dogs (a German shepherd named Daro and an Irish terrier named Wolf) peering out the back window while his squad "stood on the sidewalk convulsed with laughter." Anslinger similarly recorded the reaction of two Customs officials who politely declined to take part in the experiment and departed his office "shaking with laughter interspersed with simulated barks."[37]

The Bureau's greatest asset, however, was its highly developed use of undercover operations. Though it was hardly the first organization to employ the technique, it quickly became one of the most effective. In the nineteenth century, the Pinkerton Detective Agency frequently went undercover to undermine various labor movements or pursue private investigations on behalf of corporate America. Under J. Edgar Hoover, the FBI generally avoided undercover tactics to support law enforcement objectives but readily used them to collect political intelligence or sow discord among American leftists, civil rights activists, and antiwar protesters.[38] No other police agency at the time employed undercover operatives to fulfill basic law enforcement goals as consistently as the FBN, a fact that came to define the Bureau's institutional culture—so much so that successful undercover work became an unspoken requirement for advancement. Each agent's reputation revolved almost entirely around his purported "street smarts" and ability to make cases.

Anslinger, no surprise, put a romantic spin on the FBN's undercover work. "In order to smash criminal combines and bring gangsters to justice," he wrote, "we've had to step out of familiar uniforms into theirs—plain clothes. The criminal must always move in the shadows, in the underworld. It is our job to follow him there."[39] This was more than self-aggrandizement; the romanticism suffusing FBN literature smoothed the rough edges from drug enforcement and normalized exploitative and invasive techniques reminiscent of secret police.

But it wasn't quite as simple as chasing criminals into the underworld. In *The Investigators: Managing FBI and Narcotics Agents* (1978), Harvard criminologist James Q. Wilson offered a more clinical take on undercover drug enforcement. Instead of intrepid adventurers, Wilson characterized narcotic agents as "instigators" whose task was to provoke a criminal act under controlled circumstances rather than investigate one after the fact.[40] This proactive style of policing—in which FBN agents instigated criminal acts that *might* not have otherwise occurred—created a moral ambiguity that true-crime stories actively worked to resolve. In tales like George White's Hip Sing Tong case or the Bureau's pursuit of the Mafia, the end always justified the means.

This element of moral ambiguity lent FBN operations a swashbuckling air that was a point of pride for the agents and one, they felt, that separated narcotics from all other branches of federal law enforcement—particularly their clean-cut, lily-white cousins at the FBI. Drug enforcement was unique and it took a special type. "A narcotics agent," Wilson observed, "like a big-city patrolmen, is always on his guard, suspicious and wary. His authority does not depend, as with an FBI agent, on his office or, as with the patrolmen, on his uniform, but rather on his demeanor: he must personally take control of situations by his manner and bearing." As the Old Man put it, "An agent must be a better actor than an Academy Award winner, quick on his feet, even faster with his hands, and ten times as fast with his mind." Most agents seemed to feel either you had *it* or you didn't—that ineffable quality, that edge required of undercover work. An author like Tom Wolfe might describe the blend of bravado, ingenuity, and cavalier machismo shared by the Bureau's undercover agents as *the right stuff.*[41]

For the agents, it was all part of the job, and living their professional lives out near the edge had its perils and its rewards. Danger, wrote decorated undercover agent Sal Vizzini, was "as routine as a morning cup of coffee." The physical hazard was a big part of the FBN's swagger, and over the course of its thirty-eight year history, seventeen FBN agents were killed in the line of duty—a significantly higher ratio than at the much larger FBI. But the rewards were sweet, and the FBN accounted for a wildly disproportionate number of federal arrests—statistics that Anslinger and his agents credited to the Bureau's daring institutional culture.[42] Looking back from the present of a failed drug war and overcrowded prisons, it often sounds as if the Bureau was proud of its dedication to a flawed strategy of incarceration. At the time, however, the prison population remained relatively small, and the agents took the tally of FBN arrests as proof that they were part of an elite club.

The reasons for choosing this line of work varied as widely as the agents' individual backgrounds, but it is noteworthy how few cite personal experience with drug abuse or addiction as a motivating factor. Most were lured by the sense of power and adventure. Jack Kelly professed to be drawn by "tales of adventure, of million-dollar busts in exotic lands, of shootouts and intrigue in high places," as well as the "curious prestige" of the job and a "feeling of absolute power." James Mulgannon wrote reverently of his "brilliantly-shined gold badge of authority." Tom Tripodi, an agent who toggled between the FBN and CIA, found the secrecy intoxicating. "I was a U.S. narcotics agent," he wrote. "I knew it, they didn't. There was a sense of power in that. Invigoration. Control."[43]

The Bureau's techniques and attitudes, however, were not without controversy. The secretive nature of the job and abundance of cash in the drug world fostered a level of corruption that irrevocably damaged the FBN's reputation by the mid-1960s. The Bureau's reliance on surveillance, wiretaps, and informants led to frequent complaints about violations of privacy and entrapment, and the cavalier attitude that made some agents successful in undercover work led others into recklessness and a casual resort to violence—a tendency that's doubly alarming given that, in the glory days of the late 1930s, the FBN ranked near the bottom in Treasury Department marksmanship contests, besting only the accountants at Internal Revenue.[44]

Perhaps the most contentious aspect of FBN operations was the extensive use of criminal informants. The FBN's field manual, a compendium of official policy and standard operating procedures kept in every office, made it clear that an agent's ability to recruit and handle informants was considered a "reflection on his professional ability," and the agents received a great deal of specialized training on the subject. Most agents saw informants as a necessary evil. The relationship between agent and informant was unavoidably coercive and ideally based on fear and respect in equal measure. Many informants had to work off charges and, in addition to providing intel, were pressed into direct service as buyers in undercover operations or members of surveillance teams.[45]

One common practice was to send agents and informants on the road for "special endeavor assignments," during which the pair would travel through a designated region, making buys and setting up cases. There were strict rules governing the use of addicts as informants, but few agents balked at using addiction to compel cooperation. Agent Vizzini, for example, recalled using "a strung-out junkie . . . turned stoolie" early in his career. "He was my bird-dog," Vizzini wrote, "the necessary evil that would lead me to the pushers and suppliers who peddled the stuff." It was technically against the rules to use access to drugs as a cudgel, but, one senior agent coached the young Vizzini, "sometimes we go by the book and sometime we write the book as we go along." It was this kind of rule bending that made the FBN an effective police force (depending on the measure) and got it into trouble on more than one occasion. And, of course, the agents' cavalier attitude rarely benefited the informants caught in their snare.[46]

In public accounts, all but the most exceptional informants were stripped of their humanity in much the same manner as traffickers or junkies. Despite rules to the contrary, several agents admit to providing their informants with drugs and observing their use. Vizzini character-ized his informant Arthur Bee as a "poor devil" and a "bird-dog" on a "leash." Mulgannon similarly described one Chinese informant as "a walking pincushion," distinguished only by "ghastly festering sores." Even Anslinger wrote about a regular addict-informant nicknamed "Oozy," because "he oozed dope from every pore of his body." The Old Man thought Oozy was "repulsive" and "beguiling" but wrote with grudging respect, "I do not know how he stayed alive. He could take heroin, mor-phine and cocaine all mixed together in one colossal dose, shoot it into any part of his body and show no ill effects whatsoever."[47]

Faced with the realities of the global drug traffic and criminal milieu, the Bureau was forced to make constant trade-offs: between short- and long-term goals, patience versus punishment, and the fact that agents had to become a part of the world they were meant to police. Above all else, the FBN's reliance on criminal informants exemplified the inevita-bility of compromise—a fact that stands in stark contrast to the Bureau's militant public defense of drug war orthodoxy, where compromise was fatal. In his memoir, *The Trail of the Poppy* (1966), Agent Charles Sir-agusa readily admitted that he would "work with the devil" to break a big case. An often explicit—and deeply ironic—acknowledgment that the systematic use of criminal informants represented a kind of Faus-tian bargain runs throughout FBN literature. In the foreword to Vizz-ini's memoir, Anslinger echoes Siragusa's sentiment that if "it meant making a case, he would grow a tail and dance with the devil."[48]

Ultimately, the real problem with the reliance on informants was that it created a structural and procedural dependency on the very traf-fic the Bureau was sworn to stamp out and on a class of people the Bureau deemed fundamentally unreliable. FBN officials, however, saw it as a necessary and unavoidable evil, even at the expense of allow-ing informants to continue their criminal activities—be it using or dealing. During Treasury's internal debates about the best approach to drug control, Anslinger dismissed Customs' search-based strategy and argued, "The seizure of narcotics in New York City as well as in other places depends upon information obtained either from inside this country or from sources abroad," usually furnished by paid infor-mants. In his study of federal investigators, James Q. Wilson identified the same tendency in the early Drug Enforcement Administration, the FBN's ultimate successor, writing, "DEA agents see no practical way of finding informants other than by arresting street-level dealers after making undercover drug buys. This belief leads DEA agents to define their central task as one of making buys."[49]

Put another way, working up the supply chain was the gold standard of counternarcotics work and seen as the only effective way to disrupt the traffic and get to the source. But the Bureau could crack those kinds of cases only by first making as many retail-level arrests as possible, which introduced a problematic tension between short- and long-term investigations. The pressure to make cases inevitably pushed the agents toward the line where investigating criminal intentions ran up against entrapment. By the 1960s, FBN officials had compiled a file thick with formal complaints. Anslinger's successor, Henry Giordano, summarized, "The common denominator in all of the allegations is that the defendant was framed by the informant," many of whom were actual dealers and, detractors charged, essentially had "a license to sell narcotics" by virtue of their association with the FBN.[50]

The secretive and consensual nature of the drug trade made the use of criminal informants a necessity, but it remained suspect in the eyes of the public—particularly following the backlash against McCarthyism and the second Red Scare—and a significant volume of FBN literature was given over to defending their use. In *The Murderers,* Anslinger claimed that informants resolved 95 percent of all crime. Williams's successor in Manhattan, supervisor James Ryan, defended informants as "brave citizens," often "former addicts" who worked for the Bureau at "great personal risk." In 1960 Malachi Harney published *The Informer in Law Enforcement,* which was half apologia and half narrative adaptation of FBN training curricula developed by Williams.[51] Even official FBN policy reflected a schizophrenic view of informants. In an effort to shake the stigma associated with the term, in June 1950 the Bureau ordered all agents to drop the word *informant* in favor of the phrase *special employee* or the abbreviation *SE* but then reversed the policy twelve years later.[52]

Despite all the problems inherent in both practices, undercover work and the systematic use of criminal informants provided the operational foundation of the FBN's drug war. By the time the first agents went abroad in the late 1940s and early '50s, the actual methods used to fight the dope menace, both at home and abroad, were deeply entrenched and further solidified with the establishment of the Treasury Law Enforcement Officers Training School, another product of the 1956 Narcotic Control Act. Run by Agent Patrick O'Carroll, the training school formalized techniques developed over the previous decades and cemented the FBN's influence with the local and foreign police services that trained there.[53]

The training school helped the Bureau achieve many of its postwar objectives by disseminating the basic blueprint for fighting a drug war. Garland Williams had moved on from the Bureau by then, but he left a deep imprint on FBN procedures, techniques, and basic investigative strategies—and his unique expertise did not go unnoticed. By 1940 Williams possessed a rare blend of talents and experience that had become necessary to prepare America for a new style of combat.

Good Wars

On September 1, 1939, Nazi Germany invaded Poland. It took several months for the fighting to engulf Europe, but World War II had begun. The impact on the dope traffic was immediate. With East Asia already embroiled in war and Nazi subs prowling the Atlantic, global commerce was thrown into total disarray, and U.S. Treasury officials reported an immediate 75 percent drop in the volume of smuggled goods. "I can't recall ever having seen things quieter on the smuggling front," a top Customs officer remarked. In New York, the sudden shortage combined with the FBN assault on distributors to touch off a prolonged heroin panic. Street prices soared, and Williams happily reported that addicts all over the city were "having themselves committed to hospitals for the cure as fast as they can be taken in."[54]

The dope menace was momentarily vanquished, but a new menace awaited. With American involvement looking increasingly inevitable, the U.S. government called on individuals like Williams to prepare for war. Secretary Morgenthau had been burned once already by public skepticism toward large national police forces, but he knew that changes were needed to meet the challenges ahead and pushed coordination (instead of consolidation) to boost the efficiency of Treasury law enforcement. Morgenthau appointed a high-ranking IRS official named Hugh McQuillan as the "coordinator" of all mid-Atlantic Treasury enforcement and asked Williams to serve as second. Williams then took over in October 1940. It was still a year prior to Pearl Harbor, but Treasury was on war footing. The *New York Times* described Williams's promotion as "an intensification of efforts to guard against sabotage, to locate Fifth Columnists and to push the preparedness program." In his remarks to reporters, Williams stressed the importance of government revenue to Uncle Sam's war chest.[55]

Anslinger, meanwhile, prepared for war by building a massive opiate stockpile. In a 1935 meeting with Morgenthau, the Commissioner pointed out that the country's entire stock of medicinal opiates was in private hands and sufficient for only one year. The federal government, he noted, had no supply of its own—a precarious situation given Nazi Germany's expansionist intentions. Morgenthau recognized the vulnerability and immediately authorized U.S. pharmaceutical companies to increase their stock by 130,000 pounds of cured opium, with another 50,000 pounds to be held by the Treasury Department itself.[56]

Taking advantage of his position astride regulatory and diplomatic channels, Anslinger and industry allies bought up nearly all available opium stocks in Turkey, Iran, Yugoslavia, Bulgaria, India, and Afghanistan. The details of this arrangement are unclear. The FBN had a modest budget, so Anslinger likely arranged loans or direct subsidies from defense mobilization agencies to cooperative pharmaceutical firms—while making it clear to industry that anyone trading with the enemy would face reprisals. By 1940 the FBN had 300 tons of opium packed into chests and stored in the same vaults that once held the nation's gold reserves, only recently moved to Fort Knox. One of Anslinger's literary collaborators later claimed the FBN's "stockpile of mercy" was "more precious than any gold" and saved thousands of lives. At war's end, the stockpile was rumored to be mostly intact, with tons of opium tucked away in anonymous crates.[57]

The stockpile formally drew the FBN into the war effort, and in May 1941 it was officially designated a "defense agency." The Commissioner made it clear to other Washington policymakers that he considered the FBN's opium cache an integral part of America's "arsenal of democracy" and testified to the House Appropriations Committee that the Bureau was providing for the "medical needs of a lot of our friends."[58]

In the context of global war, opium—and the morphine derived from it—suddenly became a strategic war asset rather than a pernicious foreign scourge. The FBN opium stockpile not only guaranteed the war needs of the Western Allies but also denied critical war matériel to the Axis powers.

At least one congressman challenged Anslinger's involvement in war planning and sought to differentiate drug enforcement from the war effort, asserting that FBN activities related to the national welfare but not the war. Anslinger saw no such distinction, retorting, "They are related to both. Our work with respect to critical and strategic materials all ties into the war effort."[59]

While Anslinger was squirreling away crates of opium, the remaining agents found themselves left with few traffickers to hunt. In keeping with the Commissioner's effort to make the Bureau indispensable to the growing defense establishment, the FBN began to vet enlistees and investigate recreational drug use among soldiers. Bureau records indicate that hundreds, perhaps thousands, of enlistees were rejected by the military for suspected drug use and their names quietly turned over to the FBN for investigation and inclusion in a patchy registry of known addicts. Much of this correspondence was emblazoned with the following warning:

> Discreet investigations should be made as may be indicated. UNDER NO CIRCUMSTANCES SHOULD ANY REFERENCE BE MADE TO REJECTIONS BY THE MILITARY SERVICES AND YOUR INQUIRIES SHOULD BE CONDUCTED IN SUCH A MANNER THAT THERE WILL BE NO INFERENCE THAT THE INFORMATION CAME FROM MILITARY AUTHORITIES AS IT WAS OBTAINED QUITE CONFIDENTIALLY.[60]

In effect, the draft became a giant drug screening program, a development usually associated with Vietnam. Anslinger was encouraged that only one in every ten thousand soldiers screened by military doctors was a drug user, a vast improvement from the one-in-three-thousand ratio reported during World War I. Maintaining a drug-free military wasn't as sexy as hunting international drug lords, but it was an important function and Anslinger later estimated that around a quarter of the FBN's wartime personnel were "engaged in keeping army and other military camps free of narcotic peddlers and drug addicts." With heroin in short supply, the Bureau concentrated on stamping out marijuana use among American servicemen, and Anslinger reported "complete cooperation from the Army in this regard."[61]

Top agents like Garland Williams, however, had more important assignments. In the closing months of 1940, Williams was summoned to Washington to meet with General Sherman Miles, chief of U.S. Army Intelligence. "I've been told that you know something about secret operations and that you'd be a good man to organize some sort of plain-clothes unit for the Army," Miles reportedly told him. "You might as well know, we'll be at war before long and General Marshall says that we'll need a lot of trained people to fight spies and that type of thing."[62]

With the outbreak of war, the United States found itself in the unfor-tunate position of having to build an espionage and intelligence appara-tus from scratch. In the hunt for radicals and other subversives during and after the First World War, those roles were filled by the Army Corps of Intelligence Police (CIP) and the FBI. Most Americans continued to look askance at the idea of secret or political police, and many policy-makers felt, as Henry Stimson famously said, that "gentlemen do not read each other's mail."[63] The result, however, was that the country was ill-prepared to run its own intelligence operations or disrupt those of the Axis powers. It fell to people like Garland Williams, with his military background and unique expertise, to build a crash course in intelligence and special operations. Who better to hunt enemy spy networks than someone who had made a career out of directing the investigation and infiltration of criminal networks of all shapes, sizes, and ethnicities?

General Miles initially put Williams in charge of the Corps of Intelli-gence Police, a military intelligence unit that languished after its World War I glory days. Williams reported for duty in January 1941 and imme-diately organized a four-week training course to prepare agents for the dual role of police investigator and counterintelligence officer. A post-war report by the army described the school's curriculum: "Students were taught the principles of observation and description, espionage and counterespionage, bombs and 'infernal machines,' undercover work, and numerous other topics that the well-trained investigator should know." Williams drew on his federal law enforcement background when designing the course and even required students to spend time with local detective squads to reinforce lessons in undercover work, surveillance, handling informants, and interrogation.[64]

Once again, Williams forged order from chaos. In July he requested greater centralization of CIP efforts, complaining that there were "14 different policies, 14 different practices, 14 different methods of work and in general, 14 separate and distinctive units." His assignment ended in August 1941, but Williams had already graduated nearly three hundred agents and set the organization on a path from police force to intelligence agency. On January 1, 1942, the Corps of Intelligence Police was officially renamed the Counter Intelligence Corps (CIC) in recognition of its shift in mission.[65]

Around the time that Williams was overhauling army intelligence, influential Wall Street lawyer "Wild Bill" Donovan was trying to convince President Roosevelt that he needed a dedicated intelligence agency. At the urging of Donovan and British intelligence, FDR created the Office of the Coordinator of Intelligence in June 1941. One year later, he split the office's two functions: wartime propaganda would be conducted by the Office of War Information, while the Office of Strategic Services would handle espionage, intelligence, and special operations under Donovan's leadership. He and Anslinger were longtime acquaintances who shared an interest in all things cloak-and-dagger. The Commissioner eagerly recommended Williams for the new agency and secured Secretary Morgenthau's permission to serve as an outside consultant to the OSS.[66]

Following his assignment with CIC, Williams briefly served as an instructor at the Infantry School in Fort Benning, Georgia, and the Chemical Warfare School at Aberdeen, Maryland. In January 1942, he was hired by Preston Goodfellow, one of Donovan's top aides. Together, Williams and Goodfellow created a series of camps to prepare OSS operatives for assignment behind enemy lines.[67]

But first they needed a little training of their own. Much of the impetus to build a U.S. intelligence and special operations capacity came from the British, who were under siege in Europe and eager to get the Yanks into action. In February 1942, Williams attended a four-week training course at an outpost run by British special forces, situated on the shore of Lake Ontario, near the Canadian hamlet of Oshawa.

Designated "Camp X," the facility was established to impart Britain's expertise in asymmetric warfare and train OSS instructors. Williams was one of the first students. The subsequent training session in March was attended by fellow FBN agent George H. White, who immediately dubbed the place "the Oshawa School of Mayhem and Murder." (White reportedly "got drunk and shot up the camp" one night—the kind of rumor that followed him everywhere.)[68]

Upon his return, Williams immediately set about establishing similar camps in the capital region. The first was an old Civilian Conservation Corps site in the Catoctin Mountains. Dubbed "Area B" (for basic training), the camp became an important training site for OSS operatives, many of whom were dropped into occupied Europe or went on to play prominent roles in U.S. national security, like future CIA director William Casey and counterintelligence czar James Jesus Angleton. Late in the war, Roosevelt went up to inspect the school and was reportedly so impressed that he took over part of the camp as a weekend retreat and dubbed it "Shangri-La." Years later, President Eisenhower expanded the facilities and changed the name to Camp David, after his grandson.[69]

Williams recruited heavily from the ranks of federal law enforcement to staff the camps and chose George White as chief instructor for "Area A" (for advanced training), a second converted Civilian Conservation Corps camp located near Quantico, Virginia, and the primary training facility for long-term paramilitary operations and counterintelligence. As befitting a school dedicated to unconventional warfare, the atmosphere was kept informal, and the training seminars given by White, now at the rank of captain, were described in a subsequent report as "well planned and well given."[70]

Williams created six camps in all, dubbed Areas A through F. The final one was situated on the grounds of the Congressional Country Club in Bethesda, where a C-47 fuselage was parked in front of the clubhouse for parachute training and students were known to dabble with demolitions on the sand and water hazards. A total of around thirty-six hundred American operatives were trained at the camps, including the widely celebrated "Jedburgh" commandos and the infamous Detachment 101 that led indigenous resistance to the Japanese in occupied Burma. Williams also set up an additional facility at Lothian Farm near Clinton, Maryland, for instruction in human intelligence collection.

The site's formal designation was RTU-11, but everyone called it "the Farm," a name that caught on when the CIA set up its own version in Williamsburg, Virginia, after the war.[71]

Combining his own law enforcement background and undercover expertise with the training received from British commandos at Camp X, Williams designed a curriculum to instruct students in the clandestine arts. "The guerilla concept of warfare will be the guiding principle," he wrote in a detailed training guide. The first sessions served as a critical "weeding out" process to see which students lacked the necessary edge. A postwar report described the ideal recruit as "a complete individualist," and the organization quickly acquired a reputation for producing, as one of Williams's trainees put it, "a different breed of cats." Like the Bureau, OSS recruited with an eye toward language and ethnicity and sought individuals—including foreign nationals—who could pass in target countries. The main point, Williams wrote, was to condition the students, both physically and mentally, "for the aggressive and ruthless action which they will be called upon to perform at later dates."[72]

As with undercover work, mental attitudes were just as important as technical skills. Special operations required a special blend of mental and moral flexibility not be readily apparent in all trainees. Williams wrote: "In some cases the mental attitude of the individual will have to be changed from that of an intellectual and cultured man with high ethical standards to the practical ideas and reactions of a 'thug.' While in other instances the thoughts and ideals of the individual may have to be raised from the level he previously possessed. In all instances there must be a continuing development of the individual's power of memory as well as his power of understanding and utilization of a fellow man."

In the later stages of training, Williams and the OSS instructors sought to further refine and test the recruits' capacity for leadership and independent action by sending them out on exercises, like infiltrating actual industrial sites or planting fake explosives in nearby cities. The students came from a variety of backgrounds and would receive wildly different assignments, so the emphasis was on producing operatives who were flexible and resourceful. On any given day, the students might be trained in hand-to-hand combat, use of technical equipment, the recruitment and handling of informants, demolitions and small-arms fire, or selecting targets for sabotage. A postwar assessment by the OSS wryly observed, "It has been jokingly said that the E courses produced about two thousand potential post-war house breakers, forgers, thieves, and murderers, and it has been suggested (it is hoped without justification) that another Schools and Training program will be needed to untrain these men and their unAmerican ways."[73]

Some of the most advanced training took place at "finishing schools" held at the camps or in service with police agencies like the FBN. One OSS memo from November 1943 indicates that a number of trainees were sent to the FBN's New York office to "gain actual investigative experience in surveillance, interrogation, search, etc." While the pace had slowed during the war, the office still gave ample opportunity for OSS trainees to practice their new skills, and the New York agents were uniquely qualified to teach the fledgling spies tradecraft like wiretapping, surreptitious entry, and clandestine investigations.[74]

Now commissioned as a major, George White eventually returned to New York City to supervise the later stages of training from a safe house on West Sixty-Seventh Street. Most of his students were slated for X-2, the OSS's secretive counterintelligence branch, so White spent a lot of time on subjects like interrogation and surreptitious entry—even designing a set of lock picks mounted in a standard pocketknife frame and bragging that his students could "open almost any lock within two or three minutes time." This was an important stage for the trainees, and the OSS put a lot of confidence into White's instruction, who was given wide latitude and the freedom to apprentice students with fellow federal agents. This was also the last chance to discretely monitor the newly commissioned operatives for signs of misconduct or personal vulnerabilities that might jeopardize their missions. White recommended that at least one student, an open and flamboyant homosexual, be removed from service—further evidence that FBN agents policed both drugs and American social norms.[75]

Not everyone was impressed with the swift but slapdash manner in which the OSS cranked out operatives. Donovan answered directly to Roosevelt, but tensions quickly emerged between the upper ranks of the OSS and the Joint Chiefs. The military was hungry for useful intelligence but highly skeptical of the OSS operatives. There was also significant resentment for the "direct commissions" given to civilians like

White, who finished the war a colonel with no actual military training. A history of the OSS training program produced after the war admitted that in the early years, "the same over-all policy which dictated a tremendous drive for speed, mass production, and mass results, at times gave the OSS an impression of hopeless confusion and indecisive direction." Making matters worse, the military was slow to assign the new OSS commandos, who began to stack up at holding camps.[76]

Under pressure from the military, the OSS reorganized the entire training program in August 1942 and created a separate Schools and Training Branch. Preston Goodfellow and Garland Williams, responsible for most of the training to date, were sidelined as military brass took greater interest in the program. Goodfellow was put in charge of the new Strategic Services Command, and Williams was forced out of the OSS entirely. Although Donovan's vision of a multiethnic global commando force eventually found supporters in the military, Williams pushed too far too fast with the paramilitary training program. The OSS's in-house report later summarized: "In many ways Williams revealed great talent and a genuine zeal for the work but his impatience with routine and his tendency to cut corners was beginning to hamper his efforts to improve his own program. . . . [H]e was one of the early sacrifices to the order which was deemed necessary for an ultimately successful organization. *Certainly it can be said that he was a year and a half ahead of his time.*"

Professional soldiers began to replace the FBN agents chosen by Williams as instructors, but as these men returned to their civilian agencies (or, like White, took their talents overseas), the OSS lost the very unconventional expertise it wanted to instill in its operatives. One student complained, "With the exception of Capt. White, no single instructor had any major experience with undercover work. . . . As a graduate of this course, I still have no idea of how to deal with 'black market' operations, false entry, financial operations, or any of the present day operational problems."[77] In other words, in the absence of sustained instruction at the hands of agents like Williams and White, many trainees wound up lacking a true grounding in the clandestine arts they would soon be called upon to practice.

Although booted from the OSS, Williams was quickly appointed as the commanding officer of the paratrooper school back at Fort Benning, where he worked as a talent spotter. From this perch, Williams recruited men who went on to successful careers not only in the OSS but also in the FBN and CIA. Howard Chappell was one of the students recruited by Williams, first into the OSS and later the FBN, where he worked under George White as the supervisor in Los Angeles. It's likely that Bill Colby, another future director of central intelligence, was also among the students Williams recruited into the OSS. Chappell's wartime service leading Italian partisans seemed to validate the potential of the OSS commandos and earned him both a Purple Heart and a Silver Star.[78]

A number of active FBN agents followed Williams and White into the intelligence services, largely on the strength of their special blend of language skills, undercover expertise, and investigative experience. Charles Siragusa served with the OSS in North Africa and Italy. FBN agent Angelo Zurlo was recruited to organize resistance in Italy. Melvyn Hanks, a Customs agent specializing in narcotics, served in a counterintelligence post with the Coast Guard. Agents J. Ray Oliveira and Francis X. Di Lucia worked for the FBN and Customs and were both sent to Europe with cover as financial attachés, as was Charles Dyar, a close friend of Anslinger's and a veteran of the FBN and Customs. An expert on European finance, Dyar served under Allen Dulles in Berne and was later appointed the top drug enforcement official with occupation forces in postwar Germany.[79]

The always colorful George White also served abroad, leaving OSS officials in despair over the loss of such an effective instructor.[80] White was a high-level X-2 operative, but records held in FBN files and his own papers indicate that he served two masters: the OSS and Anslinger. White occasionally traveled to various parts of the Middle East on counterintelligence missions throughout 1943 and 1944 and used the opportunity to survey the narcotic situation in each country he visited. In Iran White found the "opium situation" bleak. Despite the fact that Anslinger had bought up huge quantities for the Allied reserve, opium and morphine were readily available and sold openly. Iranian officials told White that at least half of the population were regular opium users, and Colonel Herbert Norman Schwarzkopf, a decorated former police commander in country to train Iranian forces, reported that 75 percent of the Iranian gendarmerie were addicts. White also learned that Basra, an Iraqi border town and key terminus for Soviet lend-lease supplies, had become a lively smuggling hub. "The Iranian Government will sell raw or prepared opium to all comers," he complained. "Apparently no one is bothering their heads over this possibility at present and smuggling may well be going on at a good rate now." For White and Anslinger, the lack of hard intelligence was just as upsetting as the abundance of opium. The situation was somewhat better in Palestine, White reported, where the British maintained "law and order" and allowed him to inspect a warehouse filled with fifteen tons of seized opium, which, he suggested, could be added to the Allied stockpile. Anslinger followed White's reports closely and asked him to follow up on legal drug shipments and prices while abroad.[81]

In 1944 White was commissioned a colonel (much to his delight) and went to India to support OSS and Allied forces engaged in China and the Pacific. White's principal task was to root out a Japanese spy network based in Calcutta. According to legend, after a bit of sleuthing White identified his target and one day approached an elderly Chinese lady shuffling down the street with the aid of a walking stick. White seized the figure, yanked off her wig and upper garments to reveal a Japanese man, and then shot him dead before an astonished crowd. Other versions have him throttling the spy with his bare hands and then taking a photograph, which he later displayed on the wall of his apartment.[82]

For the Commissioner, the opportunities afforded by having a trusted subordinate traveling through strategic locations abroad were too good to pass up, and Anslinger made semiformal arrangements to cover White's extracurricular activities.[83] In addition to surveying the opium situation in India, as he had in Iran and elsewhere, White also investigated rumors that the Allies were paying indigenous resistance groups in opium. In fact, both British and American forces (including Detachment 101, an OSS group assembled and trained by White and Williams) had made it a common practice. Anslinger strongly disapproved and complained to the rest of the Washington bureaucracy. Secretary of War Henry Stimson eventually acknowledged the issue and explained to Morgenthau that he had been unaware of the practice and put a stop to it.[84]

White, meanwhile, found the opium situation in India *complicated*. In a lengthy October 1944 report, White warned that drug control in India was a diplomatic nightmare, with numerous competing interests at play. The main problem was that lax control measures allowed opium to be "regularly be sold to all comers, including U.S. troops." Anticipating fears that became especially pronounced during the Vietnam War, White remarked to another colleague, "We know addiction occurs through association and is, in a sense, as 'infectious' as any other communicable disease." If American servicemen were exposed to opium, they would become addicted and spread the vice to other troops. "This is particularly true," he pointedly added, "in the case of negro soldiers." Worse still, these soldier-junkies would bring their addiction home. "I have little doubt," he continued, "that in my future peace time work, as an agent of the Narcotics Bureau . . . I will have occasion to interrogate drug addicts who will state they first became addicted in India while serving in the United States Army."[85]

Still more aggravating was the fact that no one would take responsibility for the situation. White consulted a lot of people but admitted, "Not many cases of drug addiction had come to the official attention of either the police or medical authorities." U.S. officials throughout the region unanimously refused to discuss it. No stranger to bureaucratic politics, White knew this was to be expected. Military authorities shrugged it off as a diplomatic problem. State Department officials worried about offending the British. Ultimately, White concluded that if American policymakers were serious about drug control, they would have to step on some toes.[86]

White's experience overseas led him to the same conclusion as Anslinger: the only real solution to illicit drug use was to reduce global supply. The halfhearted control measures implemented by colonial authorities in countries like India, White argued, "can be of little avail in combating the illicit diversion of narcotic drugs. The only practicable method of restricting the traffic, lies in restricting the growth of the poppy itself." With attention focused solely on point of sale—thus avoiding strict controls on actual production—the temptation to divert legal opium into black-market channels would remain.[87]

With White in India, Anslinger saw the investigative possibilities that would open up with a few key men overseas. Within about a year, White's network of informants began generating tips that led to seizures half a world away. In February 1945, a tip gleaned from White's contacts led to the discovery of 220 pounds of opium aboard the SS *Teucer* in

Glasgow. "Even though this was seized in England we have every reason to believe it was coming to the United States," Anslinger assured him. In September and October 1945, another tip from White led to seizures aboard the SS *Chung Shan* in Baltimore and Galveston. With the war drawing to a close, cases were beginning to pile up at the FBN, and Anslinger promised White, "We are saving some big ones for your early attention." As he prepared to leave India, White leaned on colleagues in the U.S. Army's Criminal Investigation Command (CID) to maintain his network and, together with Williams, even planned a few discrete investigations to be conducted in his absence.[88]

New Horizons

World War II was a turning point for the United States and no less so for the Federal Bureau of Narcotics. White's investigations in India paved the way for Anslinger's renewed emphasis on foreign enforcement and demonstrated the benefits of having people on both sides of the traffic. Many of the Bureau's most dynamic agents served in an intelligence capacity that seemed to validate the skill sets and attitudes they had developed while fighting the dope menace—skills and attitudes widely considered un-American only a few years earlier. Having made important contributions to the war effort at both the individual and the institutional levels, the FBN greeted the postwar period with elevated stature and a commitment to leveraging this new influence in the fight against drugs.

Both the FBN and the discourse of the dope menace were irrevocably changed by World War II—as was the career of Garland Williams. Although he briefly returned to the helm of the Manhattan office, Williams had ascended to a higher level of government service. Ironically, given the fact that it was military brass that forced Williams from the OSS training program, he finished the war on the planning staff of the Joint Chiefs after his stint at Fort Benning. As the Cold War threatened to turn hot a few years later, Williams's experience with training, intelligence, and asymmetric warfare made him a sought-after commodity in high government circles.

When the Korean War began in June 1950, Williams was once again tapped by military intelligence. This time he was asked to create and command a new division, the 525th Military Intelligence Service Group. Existing records indicate the military was pleased with this new outfit and that Williams's influence was considerable. A letter of commendation from Major General R. C. Partridge thanked him for his "outstanding contributions" to the development of intelligence in general and combat intelligence specifically, which he attributed to "the imagination, initiative and unceasing drive which you, as Commanding Officer of the 525th, have imparted."[89]

Williams, however, disliked military routine. In March 1951, he wrote to Anslinger from Fort Bragg, North Carolina, where the unit was stationed and trained. "I have gotten a reputation for organizing and training and it is being rumored that my unit will remain here and keep a flow of trained people going over. I will be thoroughly disgusted if this turns out true," he groused. When Anslinger sent him some case files to look over, Williams relished the chance to get back to his first love—the nascent drug war. The reports, he confided, "took me completely out of this world here and for awhile I was back in my office in New York concentrating on my real work." Later that year, Williams again checked in with Anslinger and reported that he had been shuttled around for training in a variety of functions and commands. "Maybe they are fattening me up for something," he speculated. But Williams was weary of the constant travel and uncertainty of his military career. Both he and Anslinger recognized that the postwar had opened new possibilities for global drug control.[90]

Williams got a brief taste of foreign enforcement when Anslinger recruited him to serve as a United Nations (UN) envoy for a 1949 diplomatic tour through the Middle East—and he was awarded the Treasury Department's Exceptional Civilian Service Award on his return— but Williams never did make it back to the FBN after his second stint with military intelligence.[91] In early 1953, Williams was designated the new assistant commissioner of the IRS, in charge of the department's intelligence division, but he was forced out a few months later when "discrepancies" were found in his own tax returns. It's not clear from existing records what happened, but the general impression seems to be that he was on the losing end of some political game; as one of his FBN colleagues observed, "One lives by the sword and dies by the sword."[92] Momentarily defeated, Williams technically returned to the Bureau but went on immediate sick leave and officially retired in March 1954.

Little is known about the next three years of his life. In February 1957, Williams resurfaced to embark on yet another remarkable career as a narcotics specialist with the State Department's International Cooperation Agency. In 1961 President Kennedy reorganized the ICA into the U.S. Agency for International Development (USAID), and Williams became an important official in the Office of Public Safety, a shop dedicated to training foreign police forces. Williams played an influential role in training police forces in Iran, Ethiopia, and the Ivory Coast, bringing their police structures—and, when possible, their drug control policy—into alignment with U.S. interests. Howard Chappell later remarked that Williams "was involved in so many things much of which was in sub-rosa activity not as an Agent or operator, but as an organizer or administrative position. This is probably true of all of his activity subsequent to 1941."[93]

Stepping back from the wide arc of Williams's career reveals the practical influence of counternarcotic operations and—to some extent—the ideology and culture of the early drug war on U.S. intelligence operations, displaying an obsession with fieldwork and the importance of secrecy and deception as investigative tools. Moreover, Williams's latter-day career in the State Department shows how the FBN contributed its expertise not only to the American intelligence services but also to national police forces in strategic locations all over the world.

CHAPTER 4

A RED-BLOODED AMERICAN BOY AND TRUE-CRIME ACTION HERO

One thing worse than no publicity is bad publicity. If you can't call the
tune, you had better hang up your fiddle and stay out of the orchestra.
—G. W. CUNNINGHAM (1949)

For our side—this aint cricket. For the enemy, it's all in a day's work.
—GEORGE H. WHITE (1955)

George Hunter White was a living legend—at least in certain circles. Fellow agents spoke of him with something between awe and
exasperation. Journalists embellished his exploits with gusto. Famous
actors portrayed him on the silver screen and narrated his adventures
on the radio. Jazz singer Billie Holiday reportedly took his song requests
during shows—even after White collared her for heroin possession. He
counted judges, congressmen, attorneys, writers, cops, mobsters, diplomats, spies, and a few scumbags among his close personal friends. In
short, everyone seemed to know George White.

Maybe it was because he cut such a memorable figure. White per-
sonified a tough street cop, almost like he was sent from central casting.
Journalist James Phelan did a whole series on White's adventures in
True: The Man's Magazine and described him as "built on the general
lines of a beer keg, with a thick neck, balding head, and cold blue eyes
that met the appraising stares head on." He showed up in the *New York
Times* as a "stocky, barrel-chested, two-fisted agent." Even the Old Man
remarked, "As round as he was tall, White looked like Buddha."[1]

Much was also said of the stocky agent's talents and personality. "The ubiquitous White," Anslinger called him, "always ready to shake hands with trouble." Garland Williams considered him "the greatest investigator in the world." To James Mulgannon of the San Francisco office, White was simply "the Boss." Jack Kelly recalled him "as a god-like figure." Charlie Siragusa, White's onetime apprentice, called him "one of the finest agents the Bureau ever had." Howard Chappell ran the Los Angeles office under White's watch and remembered him fondly as "a liar and a B.S. artist without parallel." OSS colleague Stanley Lovell described him more extravagantly as a "half-legendary, half flesh-and-blood hero of the Morte D'Arthur day of Roland and Roncesvalles."[2]

The press poured on similar plaudits. Frederic Sondern Jr. of *Reader's Digest* described White as "well educated, articulate, charming, imaginative and very fast." Derek Agnew dedicated his 1959 book, *Undercover Agent—Narcotics,* to White's escapades, calling him "Agent Extraordinary" and blessed with an understanding of "the frailties of his fellowmen" more common to "a philosopher rather than a policeman." Phelan called him "the shrewdest dope-buster in the world today."[3]

In short, White was something of a role model. He was an example to his fellow agents and represented the Bureau's undercover ethos to the American public. Today, George White is hardly a household name, but his mythic image lives on in a fascinating—though sensationalist—body of literature, due mostly to his role in the CIA's MK-ULTRA program. With a character as colorful as White, it's hard not to seize on the wilder aspects of his story, and contemporary accounts have created a figure just as exaggerated as his living-legend image. *San Francisco Bizarro: A Guide to Notorious Sights, Lusty Pursuits, and Downright Freakiness in the City by the Bay* (2000) describes White paying prostitutes to dope johns with LSD, then perching "atop a toilet, sipping at a pitcher of martinis" to watch the action unfold from behind a two-way mirror. In *Acid Dreams: The Complete Social History of LSD: The CIA, the Sixties, and Beyond* (1994), Martin Lee and Bruce Shlain depict a man tormented by demons, gin-drunk and "slumped in front of a full-length mirror . . . shooting wax slugs at his own reflection." In *The Strength of the Wolf* (2004), Douglas Valentine locates White within a kinky Greenwich Village swinger scene and explains his purported sadomasochistic streak and leather fetish as "overcompensating for poor body image."[4]

The result is a distorted picture of a real person, a genuine historical actor. But there's more to White's story than colorful antics. The deplorable nature of the CIA's experiments with mind control and White's participation in this real-life conspiracy highlights the overlap between law enforcement and counterintelligence but overshadows other facets of his career that are just as important. White, more than any other member of the FBN aside from the Old Man himself, shaped public perceptions of the Bureau and counternarcotics work more generally. One of White's most important roles was as a pioneer of foreign enforcement. His 1948 foreign tour directly presaged the genesis of the foreign drug war. Public accounts of White's many adventures, meanwhile—conveyed in print, radio, and film—helped prepare the American people for the new obligations and tactics required in the increasingly global threat environment exemplified by the dope menace.

Though FBN agents rarely used it, the term *narc* was originally short for narcotics officer. Today it's an epithet frequently tossed around playgrounds and street corners, synonymous with *tattletale, traitor,* or *rat.*[5] The negative connotation reflects the broad libertarian streak running through American political culture and animosity toward duplicity. The vast majority of narcotic cases, however, depended largely on deception. Given the periodic exposure of corrupt agents and public ambivalence about undercover policing, it was critical for the FBN to maintain a positive image as daring soldiers in a just war. Agent White's story exemplifies the dilemmas, trade-offs, and nuance involved in the making of a law enforcement legend.

A Hero's Fate

George Hunter White was born on June 22, 1908, and raised in a comfortably middle-class home in Alhambra, California, where his father was a city manager. After graduating from Oregon State College (now University) in 1928, White worked as a reporter for the *San Francisco Bulletin* and *Los Angeles Daily News.* The future agent was a talented writer but chafed at the role of passive observer. "Newspapering is all right," he explained, "but it makes a bystander out of you. I want to get out on the field where the game is going on." Looking for adventure, White joined the Border Patrol in 1933 but quickly tired of desert patrols and locking up desperate migrants. He had enjoyed covering the Los Angeles narcotics squad while on the police beat, so he resolved to find a job in the burgeoning field of drug enforcement.[6]

After less than a year, White transferred into the Federal Bureau of Narcotics and was assigned to his adopted hometown of San Francisco. "I'd like to say that dedication to law enforcement lay at the bottom of my first candidacy for a hero's fate but it wasn't," he later wrote. "True, the eradication of malefactors was semi-involved but a certain strange stubbornness about the truth, a nagging sense-of-humor and the official record of the moment forces me to admit that my own personal economy was predominantly involved."[7]

White wanted action and rushed out to find it, but his first bust was a disaster. When a local dealer known as Albert "Toughy" Jackson tried to cheat White during an undercover deal (in those days, buy money often came out of pocket), the agent drew his gun and was immediately jumped by Jackson's bodyguards. In the ensuing melee, White's gun was taken by one of his assailants and pressed to his ear but failed to fire with the safety engaged. By the time local police arrived to end the scuffle, White had been stabbed but managed to shoot Jackson twice at point-blank range with a derringer—with one shot hitting Jackson directly between the eyes and scraping along his skull to exit behind his ear. White's first investigation thus resulted in gunshots on a city street, a wounded suspect, a wounded agent, and no incriminating evidence. White's supervisors were unimpressed and banished him to a dead-end post in Seattle, where, he recalled, most of the men were "former prohibition agents, thicker than thieves with a corrupt police department." Fortunately for the Bureau, White stayed clean and soon encountered the elderly Chinese addict who launched the Hip Sing Tong investigation and punched White's ticket to the big show in New York.[8]

Under the guidance of Garland Williams, White proved a gifted investigator and became one of the FBN's most effective agents. During the critical period of the late 1930s, White led a squad that included Charles Siragusa, and he helped break cases against major traffickers like Lepke Buchalter and Eli Eliopoulos.[9] But this idyllic situation, with much of the FBN's talent gathered in New York, did not last long. The approach of World War II necessitated the expertise of agents like Williams and White be turned to new tasks and new enemies. At war's end, the Bureau's erstwhile agents and part-time spies began to trickle back to the home front and return to civilian duty. In recognition for his experience and a reward for the extracurricular activities carried out with the OSS, White was promoted to district supervisor and put in charge of the critical Chicago office. The assignment, however, was short-lived, and the postwar years proved turbulent ones for George White.

Mobsters and Crooked Politicians

Chicago in the late 1940s was something of a mob town, and White's penchant for confrontation made a conflagration only a matter of time. Anslinger later observed that White "had an obsessive hatred . . . for trusted officials who abused public responsibility," and when he "started riding the behinds of some of those people, they could forget about getting off or away."[10] These were admirable qualities in a federal agent, but they also made White a political liability.

White reported for duty in Chicago on October 1, 1945. With the international traffic still in disarray, there were few heroin cases to be made in the Windy City, so White settled for a large marijuana ring that stretched from Chicago to Mexico under the leadership of "a wealthy El Paso business man" named Arthur G. Zweier. During testimony, Zweier complained of entrapment and noted that an undercover White had "'completely and all by himself' drank a bottle of rare scotch." With a grin, the presiding judge replied, "I wondered why he looked so well and I envied him."[11] Few at the time noticed the irony of a heavy drinker arresting a network of pot dealers.

Much of White's time in Chicago was spent investigating organized crime and the notoriously corrupt city politics. As a supervisor, White occasionally stepped into an undercover role, but his growing visibility in Chicago and on the national scene suggested a more direct approach. White made a practice of brazenly questioning police officials about corruption while trailed by newspaper reporters and began paying regular visits to the city's gambling dens, where, he suspected, drug deals were also arranged. "My solution was to visit each joint nightly and break up the furniture, scatter the money and paraphernalia and walk out," he recalled. But this strategy provoked resistance from local police, some of whom were on the take. Looking back, White wrote, "I later learned that the Cap't went to the Mayor who went to the President who went to the Sect'y of the Treasury who went to the Commissioner of Narcotics who asked me, 'What's going on?'"[12]

Anslinger usually gave significant latitude to his trusted lieutenants and was apparently satisfied that White was working new angles into the narcotics traffic. But when the quixotic agent took on the city's well-oiled political machine, not even the Old Man's considerable influence could protect him. White's target was Senator Scott W. Lucas, then serving as majority whip. White suspected that Lucas was backed by financiers tied to the Chicago mob and began to dig around. The agent was repeatedly told to back off, but, he wrote to one friend, "I was having FUN." He was also making enemies, so Anslinger sent him to Detroit to keep him out of trouble. Lucas, meanwhile, ascended to the post of Senate majority leader in 1948 but was unable to bridge the growing Democratic schism over segregation and looked vulnerable going into the 1950 midterm elections. With Lucas already under fire, White surfaced some of the dirt he found during Senate hearings on organized crime and took delighted credit for Lucas's subsequent defeat.[13]

White relished such confrontations; as he told one friend after dropping the match on yet another political firestorm, "I'm also in the crusading department."[14] White's focus on corruption was mostly a product of the FBN's effort to expose the Mafia. In the late 1940s, many Americans, including FBI director J. Edgar Hoover, scoffed at the idea that organized crime could exist on a national scale. But as White noted in one 1946 memo, investigations conducted over the past several years had "indicated without a doubt the Mafia is a living organization and 'big business' today. Many of its members are no longer regarded as racketeers or criminals, but in some instances are pillars of society in the community in which they live."[15]

For a variety of reasons, White's tenure in Detroit was equally brief. Back in Washington, Commissioner Anslinger had long argued that the only effective way to fight the dope menace was to reduce global supply by sending agents abroad to disrupt trafficking networks and prevent the drugs from escaping their place of origin. In *The Protectors,* he later wrote, "It was my opinion that a few good agents overseas might help dry up the traffic at the source." By 1948 Anslinger judged the international situation ripe for such an attempt. It was also a chance to put White back into an undercover role, and, after his Chicago escapades, Anslinger reasoned that the crusading agent was "due for a 'vacation.'"[16]

Preparing a Drug War

The year 1948 marked the start of a new chapter for the Bureau and for American drug control. Agents like Garland Williams and Charles Dyar had previously gone abroad to develop investigations in the prewar era but confined most of their activities to liaising with foreign police. With orders to unilaterally initiate undercover investigations on foreign soil, Agent White's assignment was something altogether new and raised pressing political and legal issues—not least of which was the fact that the FBN had absolutely no jurisdiction in Europe or the Middle East. White later recalled, "I was the first officer to have this type of assignment and all concerned were understandably vague as to how I should go about it."[17] This uncertainty was a major reason Anslinger chose him for the task—the Old Man trusted White's ability to blaze a new trail.

White's 1948 tour included stops in Iran, Iraq, Lebanon, Turkey, France, and Italy and returned the agent to many of his wartime haunts. His task was threefold: survey the drug scene in each area, extend the FBN's intelligence network, and launch investigations against the traffickers supplying the Atlantic heroin trade. The broader goal was to begin applying FBN tactics to the larger strategy of source control; that meant focusing on Iran and Turkey, the largest poppy producers in the region.

White's first stop in Iran provides a good picture of how the agent approached his mission. He arrived in early May to find the "city reeking with fumes of opium." Opium use was widespread and lacked any outward stigma or social stratification, and White noted that many Iranian officials were "habitual opium smokers and not considered immoral." As a result, much of Iran's opium crop was consumed internally, but it was a wide-open trafficking scene, and White discovered several foreign interests competing with local brokers. The French, he reported, were purchasing enormous quantities of opium and shipping them out on flagged naval vessels to destinations unknown (most likely colonial holdings in Southeast Asia). The Soviet Union reportedly wanted to buy Iran's entire official stock, but the deal fell through when the Soviets insisted on making the purchase with riyals obtained from the sale of black-market sugar in the northern part of the country. Further testimony to the ambiguity of local controls, it's unclear from White's report if these transactions were licit or illicit. Ultimately, he concluded, "Opium situation here extremely bad and chaotic. . . . Many agents here competing for opium business and permit system apparently very lax."[18]

The good news was that White had former OSS contacts and other associates scattered throughout the region, allowing him to quickly assemble an intelligence network to monitor local conditions and prepare future cases. In Istanbul White found a large pool of acquaintances to draw upon, including friends who were former OSS and "now CIA, Robert College teachers, newspapermen, etc." The biggest challenge was to find someone capable of managing the network and running informants in the absence of a credentialed FBN agent. White suggested putting a Turkish journalist named Rizi Chandir on the payroll. In many respects, Chandir was the perfect candidate: he spoke Turkish, French, English, German, and Greek and had connections with the "Turkish Secret Political Police," but Anslinger balked at putting a foreign national in a position of such importance. White also identified a number of U.S. Air Force officials who could prove useful and thought General Hoyt Vandenberg—recently appointed Air Force chief of staff after a stint as director of central intelligence—would readily provide cover for any assets recruited from Air Force ranks.[19]

Despite White's frenetic level of activity, the network withered without a full-time FBN presence to keep it primed. Agent Siragusa was able to meet with Chandir and several of White's other contacts a few years later, but the Bureau quickly realized the difficulty of managing an intelligence network from afar.[20] White's early efforts do, however, demonstrate the Bureau's postwar effort to expand its international intelligence capacity and the generally cooperative reception it received from U.S. military forces abroad—all trends that continued in the years to come.

After spending roughly a month laying the foundation of a Middle Eastern intelligence network, White turned his attention to the actual heroin traffic. With much of Iran's opium crop consumed internally or sold legally, White judged the Turkish port of Istanbul to be the real "hot spot of the world," and the city subsequently became the backdrop for one of the most celebrated cases in FBN history. Although White was now well known to many American hoodlums, he thought his portly image would provide good camouflage overseas. "It was impossible for me to be a policeman," he reasoned. "I was too fat, too rich and obviously a stupid American who couldn't even speak the language." In late May, White began loitering around the Istanbul waterfront, posing as a gangster and attempting what agents termed a "cold turkey" approach—basically initiating an investigation without the benefit of an informant's introduction. Hanging out in seedy bars and flashing his money, however, failed to produce a lead, so White picked up an interpreter from the consulate and dropped in on the Istanbul police.[21]

As it turned out, the Turks were already monitoring several organizations. One was led by a Greek named Anastasas, operator of the Beniz Casino. Although White was able to approach him, the cautious Greek adamantly refused to talk narcotics in the absence of a trusted introduction. So White pivoted to a second figure under investigation by the Istanbul police, a local pimp named Vasil Arcan—already identified in FBN files as proprietor of the (recently closed) Piccadilly Bar, an establishment where merchant seamen were known to purchase small allotments of narcotics. White later credited a tip from an American informant, but his official report indicates that he was brought into the case by senior Istanbul detective Namik Karayel. Acting on the detective's information, White tracked Arcan through a series of squalid basement bars and nightclubs over the course of several nights. Completing the scene, when White finally caught up to Arcan, he noted, "Several girls were hustling in the place and a few drunken brawls were in progress." After cautiously quizzing White on his criminal bona fides, Arcan agreed to help purchase "a large quantity of heroin" and introduced him to suppliers Iradodos Terapyanos and Yasef Kariyo.[22]

White rendezvoused with Terapyanos and Kariyo the next morning. As a precaution, the traffickers took White on a circuitous ride around the city to shake any police surveillance prior to arriving at the stash house. The three men then got down to the business of negotiating price and quantity. White received a sample and made a show of haggling before agreeing to buy three kilos of heroin at two thousand dollars each, provided the quality was good. As the trio departed, White realized he had no idea where he was but managed to pick out the serial number on the gas meter in front of the house. (This became a key plot point later but was recorded without comment in White's report.) Reunited with Detective Karayel, the two men located the house and began planning their fateful ambush. The following morning, Karayel arranged some forty officers "disguised," White reported, "as merchant marines, soldiers, postmen, laborers, etc.," around the house in anticipation of the bust. To complete the ruse, the disguised policemen began digging up the street. "By the time the deal was finally culminated the whole street was torn up," White wryly noted. Aside from the drama of White's hurled chair, the bust went more or less as planned. As the Turkish police swept the house, they even apprehended a third suspect named Sevket Dalgakiran, who turned out to be the real supplier behind Terapyanos and Kariyo, and subsequently seized an additional fifteen kilos of heroin.[23]

The bust was front-page news in Istanbul and picked up by several major American newspapers, all of which quoted White estimating the total value of the seized heroin at one million dollars. The story quickly became part of FBN lore and was retold (with dramatic embellishment) in several outlets, including a 1950 *Reader's Digest* article titled "Our Global War on Narcotics" and a multitude of radio programs, dime-store novels, and true-crime magazines.[24]

Even before White arrived in Istanbul, American audiences got a taste of what was to come with the February 1948 release of the film *To the Ends of the Earth*. Featuring the FBN's unique brand of roving undercover investigations and story lines drawn from old case files, the movie included a cameo from Anslinger and starred Dick Powell as a protagonist modeled on Agent White. Critics praised the film's "semi-documentary" feel and message that drugs posed a common threat to all mankind, requiring a sort of extrajudicial police force to fight it. In one promotional interview, Anslinger declared, "There are no national boundaries in our work. You can't afford national sovereignty when you're trying to break up the narcotics racket."[25] Only a few months later, White seemed to vindicate Anslinger's bold claim as he flashed his American badge at the Turkish suspects.

While White's bust and globe-trotting escapades were celebrated in the American media, Turkish reporters portrayed the case in a rather different light. They noted that Arcan was already under investigation and that two clandestine heroin labs were busted prior to the agent's arrival. The *Son Telegraph* credited the Turkish police and put White in a support role. The *Yeni Sabah* was indignant that Western accounts "made a hero of the American detective," which the *Son Posta* chalked up to the chauvinism of the Associated Press.[26]

In retrospect, it also seems likely that Arcan was a police informant. He was arrested prior to the bust after unexpectedly turning up at the U.S. consulate where White and Turkish detectives were planning the raid. After testifying against his codefendants, Arcan was released and went right back into business. Agents who checked on him in subsequent years found that he was still running a busy brothel and "the biggest retail heroin business in town."[27] At best, White was a catalyst for the bust but contributed little to the actual investigation. At worst, the operation was a ploy to throw the Americans a bone and speed the agent's departure.[28]

The bust had zero impact on the regional traffic but reverberated within the American and Turkish governments for years. Treasury officials took the case as proof of the FBN's abilities and the need for a U.S. presence in source countries like Turkey. When embassy officials sought permission to return an agent to the country, however, they were informed that all of the media attention had created "a considerable amount of ill will" among Turkish leaders, who strongly preferred the FBN simply forward the names and addresses of suspected traffickers.[29]

White, meanwhile, quickly moved on to the next city and the next case. Using the same combination of rather clumsy undercover approaches and tenuous local police cooperation, White made additional busts in Marseille and Rome, but neither amounted to much or had any material impact on the Atlantic heroin trade.[30] In the end, the Bureau achieved one notable bust that produced useful domestic publicity but actually threatened its own foreign policy objectives. In a sense, that makes White's million-dollar bust on the Bosporus an even more perfect prologue to America's global drug war.

Anslinger, however, was thrilled and cabled to White that he was "much pleased with the substantial results of your investigations in Turkey" and optimistic the case would "have an excellent long-range effect."

Indeed, the bust became a central part of FBN lore and justification to extend the FBN's reach overseas. Working abroad was challenging, White noted, but his experience reinforced the belief that the FBN must take a direct hand in places like Istanbul and Tehran. "Opium is going to be produced there in large amounts from now on," he reported. "American representation will slow down the chicanery and should also result in the apprehension of smugglers in the U.S."[31]

Looking back, the warning signs are apparent. Each of White's investigations foreshadowed the kind of tensions that would emerge between the FBN and host nations and hinted at the murky political economy of the drug trade, in which local police were not infrequently implicated in the regional traffic. White's cases also raised troubling questions about the conflict between sovereign rights and the U.S. effort to extend an extraterritorial police presence under the auspices of a drug war. And, as ever in the history of America's drug wars, the narrative proved far more important than the actual results.

Between 1948 and 1951, White was followed by several other agents who toured Europe and the Middle East and further tested the FBN's approach to foreign enforcement. Those tours culminated in the creation of District 17, the Bureau's first foreign office, led by White's former protégé Agent Charles Siragusa. Over the subsequent decade, FBN agents became directly involved in law enforcement operations throughout the Mediterranean. Their impact on the regional traffic is debatable, but the stories they told about their triumphs and challenges irrevocably extended the frontier of America's global drug war—a story that began on a busy street in Istanbul.

The Wilderness

As the agents of District 17 would discover, one of the major challenges in foreign enforcement was that the local traffic was often sheltered by political corruption. Despite the consistently exceptionalist tone of drug war literature, this was no less true in the United States. And, Agent White learned, there were consequences for challenging the American system.

Despite the apparent success of his foreign tour, the years following White's return from Europe were marked by uncertainty. Aging out of undercover work, White hoped to move back into a supervisory role, but his rogue personality made him a liability in a position that required a light touch. He thought he would succeed Garland Williams as district supervisor in New York and was disappointed when the job went to James C. Ryan, a veteran from the New Orleans office. White was briefly assigned as the supervisor in San Francisco but fouled up an important case when his negligence resulted in the murder of an informant named Abraham Davidian.

The short version of the story is that Davidian was a twenty-eight-year-old neophyte drug dealer arrested just outside of Bakersfield in July 1949 with over two and a half pounds of heroin and eight thousand dollars in cash. Facing serious jail time, he offered to testify against a pair of notorious L.A.-based Mafia traffickers named Joseph and Alfred Sica. White took the case federal and stashed his star witness somewhere in San Francisco. But the isolation wore on Davidian, and, in late February 1950, he snuck off to visit family in San Jose. They reported leaving him napping on the couch as they ran errands one afternoon and returned to find his bullet-ridden corpse. The death of the FBN's main witness touched off yet another political snafu, and when White and California authorities began trading accusations, Anslinger again had to pull White's bacon off the fire.[32]

Sent to the other side of the country, White spent the next few unhappy years as the supervisor in Boston, which he described as "a sort of Siberia in the business." Rather than waste his time "chasing colored addicts down a Boston alley," as he told one friend, the restless agent entertained himself with an elaborately over-the-top report, dubbed "The Saga of Mike the Mouse," about the investigation of a former mental patient who mailed a mouse (dead from an apparent overdose) to FBN headquarters. The story later showed up in the July 1953 issue of *Real* magazine. White got a lot of laughs out of his Mike the Mouse story, but he had no fond memories of Boston.[33]

Most of White's time, however, was spent working as a special investigator for the Senate's Kefauver Committee and a little-remembered federal corruption probe led by Special Assistant Attorney General Newbold Morris. Both were enticing opportunities, and when White was tapped to work for Morris, the "political garbageman," he gleefully told one friend of his intention "to take on some of the Brass who've been kicking me around the past 18 months." For the most part, that meant settling old scores in Chicago and New York—including the strange circumstances around New York governor Tom Dewey's pardon and deportation of mob boss Lucky Luciano and the Mafia's ties to the political world. The Kefauver hearings gave White another piece of the national spotlight, but his subsequent experience with Morris was a politically bruising one and the whole thing blew up in April 1952, only a few months after it began, when half of President Truman's cabinet threatened to mutiny. Both Morris and his superior, Attorney General J. Howard McGrath, were forced to resign, and when the dust settled Morris ruefully told reporters, "It's like the end of a Shakespearean tragedy. We're all lying around on the stage."[34] That included George White, who found himself once more exposed and more unpopular than ever with the New York establishment.

Never one to shy from the limelight, White unilaterally continued (as "a personal hobby," he told a friend) investigating the political connections of mobster Gaetano "Tommy Three-Fingers" Lucchese. With Luciano in exile and Frank Costello discredited after his testimony during the Kefauver hearings, Lucchese became one of the most powerful gangsters in Manhattan, largely due to his political alliances. In November 1952, a grand-jury investigation heard testimony from White and a fellow agent about Lucchese's role in the drug trade and his ties to the mayor, the local U.S. attorney, and several federal judges.[35] The following month, however, White was briefly jailed in contempt of court after refusing to name a source in the presence of the U.S. attorney— who ran the grand jury but was among the very officials implicated by the investigation! Having lost several informants in recent years, including Davidian and Willie Moretti, an old-school mobster executed after talking to the Kefauver Committee, White was reluctant to subject his source to mob reprisal. White's imprisonment was brief (about ninety minutes), and he took a perverse pride in the affair. There are conflicting stories about the circumstances of his release, but it seems a deal was cut wherein the grand jury agreed not to ask for the informant's name after White walked back his allegations against the U.S. attorney.[36]

Once again, White's muckraking made him a target. The supervisor position in Manhattan was now totally out of the question. With narrowing opportunities for advancement, the usually irrepressible White fell into a brief depression. Determined not to return to Boston, he took an extended sick leave and hunkered down in New York. Making matters worse, a proposed second foreign assignment—this one "a grand tour of the Orient" and a stop in District 17—fell through. White seriously contemplated taking early retirement and told one friend that he intended to simply "find a spot smack on a California beach where I can lay in the sun and drink cheap gin the remaining days of my life."[37] Little did he know that the most bizarre chapter of his career lay just around the corner.

Operation Midnight Climax

White was moping in his New York apartment and considering a life outside of the Bureau when he received a lifeline from an unexpected source: the CIA. Intelligence was a career path White assumed was closed. He relished his time in the OSS, but his bull-in-a-china-shop antics were not overly welcome in the new Central Intelligence Agency. White privately complained to Garland Williams that "a couple of crew-cut, pipe-smoking punks had either known me—or heard of me—during OSS days and had decided that I was 'too rough' for their league and promptly blackballed me. . . . After all, fellas, I didn't go to Princeton."[38]

In June 1952, however, White was contacted by Sidney Gottlieb, a scientist in charge of the Chemical Division in the CIA's Technical Services Section. On the recommendation of Stanley Lovell, who had served as director of research for the OSS, Gottlieb chose White as the perfect candidate to explore the operational potential of consciousness-altering drugs like LSD. Anslinger readily gave his approval and designated White as a "supervisor at large" to provide him with sufficient freedom and rank. Only one year removed from contemplating a life of sunburns and cheap gin, White wrote again to his friend Warren Olney III (recently appointed as an assistant attorney general), "My status is still 'quo.' I'm feeling little pain and as 'Supervisor at Large' am able to play around with various interesting projects."[39]

One of those projects was another trip abroad, this time a six-week assignment in early 1953 to investigate rumors of a burgeoning poppy industry in Ecuador. As with his previous tour of Europe and the Middle East, White was again one of the first U.S. law enforcement officers to work in the country, and his subsequent escapades almost immediately became fodder for additional police adventure stories.[40] But in the mid-1950s, South America was still a minor theater of conflict, and Anslinger had bigger problems on the U.S. side of the border.

In the summer of 1954, while White waited for his CIA clearance to go through, Anslinger sent him to Houston to check out a Texas drug ring rumored to include local police officers. The investigation was a mess from start to finish and further complicated by White's renewed swagger. Several members of the Houston Police Department were discovered to be addicts, stealing drugs, and colluding with local traffickers. One detective apparently commit suicide by shooting himself in the chest—twice—shortly after being interrogated by White. The inquiry also brought the FBN into open conflict with local Customs supervisor Al Scharff, who was interested in any cross-border activity. Enraged by White's cavalier style and death of the main suspect, Scharff reportedly confronted White in a hotel lobby and challenged him to a gunfight—as if they were back in the Old West—before fellow FBN agent Henry Giordano hastily intervened. Anslinger later reprimanded White for his behavior and for reportedly being drunk for most of the investigation. White shrugged the allegations off as slander and countered that both Customs and Houston authorities were retaliating for the scandal he unearthed.[41]

With new benefactors, the episode did little to hurt White's career. By the start of 1955, White was officially a part-time employee of the Central Intelligence Agency. White's work as an adjunct to the CIA's MK-ULTRA experiments is without a doubt his greatest claim to notoriety among contemporary audiences, and much has been written about the CIA's investigation into mind control, behavioral science, and psychoactive drugs. One of the first and best accounts is John Marks's *The Search for the "Manchurian Candidate": The CIA and Mind Control, the Secret History of the Behavioral Sciences* (1979), which contextualizes this sinister and real-life conspiracy within the broader development of the behavioral sciences. White's peripheral but important role within this story, meanwhile, further illustrates the overlap between the drug war, the national security state, and the science of the mind.[42]

White's research into the operational use of psychedelic drugs actually began during World War II, with the OSS attempt to develop a "truth drug." The job was initially given to Stanley Lovell—nicknamed "Professor Moriarty" after Sherlock Holmes's mad-scientist nemesis for the devious weapons and gadgets he devised. Some, like a portable train derailer, flashless pistols, and numerous explosive compounds, were useful. Others, like the stink bomb Lovell called "Who, Me?" or the female sex hormones he hoped to spray into Hitler's vegetable garden ("so that his moustache would fall off and his voice become soprano"), were less so. A genuine truth drug, or "T.D.," was something altogether different. "Everyone wanted it," Lovell recalled, "and quite properly so." Lovell thought mescaline or cannabis might work and went to Anslinger for help. Anslinger sent him Agent White.[43]

White's team experimented with a number of different compounds— and on a number of different people, including some informants— before settling on cigarettes adulterated with an extract of tetrahy- drocannabinol acetate (THC), the primary psychoactive ingredient in marijuana. No real surprise, the spiked cigarettes produced wide varia- tion in results (read: intoxication), and White ultimately concluded the THC extract was "not a perfect 'truth drug' in the sense that its admin- istration is followed immediately and automatically by the revelation of all the secrets which the subject wishes to keep to himself. . . . [S]uch a goal is beyond reasonable expectation from any drug." The OSS's truth drug might be useful in certain circumstances, he speculated, but it was "not adaptable for mass interrogation."[44] In a strange twist, White's field testing extended to the Manhattan Project, where he partnered with future Supreme Court justice and UN ambassador Arthur Gold- berg to interrogate soldiers suspected of communist sympathies. The duo uncovered no spies, but, Goldberg contended, "The stuff actually worked" and made the soldiers quite talkative. Later he quipped, "The fellows from my office wouldn't take a cigarette from me for the rest of the war."[45]

White's OSS experiments were, to some extent, a prologue to the MK-ULTRA program, but it's important to note that while the CIA's interest in behavioral science and mind control was cloaked in secrecy until the mid-1970s, the OSS effort to develop a truth drug was openly acknowledged by the early 1960s. It was just one of the many unortho- dox stratagems pursued by the OSS. Lovell explained, "It was my policy to consider any method whatever that might aid the war, however unorthodox or untried."[46]

This no-stone-left-unturned approach extended into the Cold War, particularly once it was clear the contest would be fought via proxy war and covert action. In the minds of cold warriors like CIA director Allen Dulles, the conflict was about more than geopolitics or ideological competition—it was a literal "battle for men's minds," a struggle to control thought itself. In an April 1953 speech delivered at Princeton University (just as MK-ULTRA was secretly getting under way), Dulles warned that the communists would not hesitate to employ harsh psychological conditioning so that victims "are deprived of the ability to state their own thoughts. Parrot-like, the individuals so conditioned can merely repeat the thoughts which have been implanted in their minds by suggestion from outside. In effect the brain . . . becomes a phonograph playing a disc on its spindle by an outside genius over which it has no control."[47]

The CIA's research into behavioral science emerged directly from these fears. In the battle for men's minds, knowing what made a person tick could win the war. Using front companies like the Human Ecology Fund and the Geschickter Fund, the CIA secretly bankrolled a number of university and institutional research projects, often (but not always) without the scientists' knowledge. MK-ULTRA became the code name under which this program was conducted. (At various times, it was referred to as "Artichoke" and "Bluebird," MK-Search, and MKCHKWIT.) Operating on the periphery and unaware of these evolving code names, White referred to the whole thing as "Operation Midnight Climax," for reasons that will soon be clear. The CIA's covert influence was profound and helped drive the development of the entire field. While academics focused on the basic science of psychology and human behavior, CIA and military scientists worked on the potential applications of powerful hallucinogens like LSD, which might be used during interrogations or to disorient unsuspecting foreign leaders. As in nearly all facets of the Cold War, an arms-race mentality prevailed. Assuming the communists were pursuing similar science—and pairing it with torture and other forms of mental conditioning to program unwitting sleeper agents—CIA officials enlarged the program to encompass hypnosis, chemical and biological warfare, and covert assassination techniques.

The CIA's specific interest in operational drugs was tied to two major events: the discovery of LSD and the Korean War. The fate of American prisoners of war was a major issue in the late stages of the war and, in the eyes of the American public, reconfirmed the basic Cold War narrative as a conflict between freedom and slavery. When a pair of captured marine pilots were broadcast claiming that U.S. forces had used biological warfare agents and a small group of American POWs refused repatriation, the American people were aghast and grasped at some form of brainwashing as the only explanation. They didn't have to look far for such a seemingly outlandish answer: only a few years earlier, the entire Western world was riveted by the show trial of Cardinal József Mindszenty, a Hungarian cleric who organized antifascist and anticommunist resistance during World War II and resurfaced in 1949 to confess a bizarre array of crimes after being held by Soviet occupation forces.[48]

Right around the time of Mindszenty's shocking confessions, a new drug called Delysid arrived on the market and seemed to offer precisely such possibilities. Better known by its chemical name, lysergic acid diethylamide, or its street name, "acid," LSD was first discovered in 1938 by Swiss chemists Albert Hoffman and Arthur Stoll. The two men were using derivatives of ergot—a hallucinogenic fungus that grows on damp rye—to develop a circulatory stimulus, but the initial trials went nowhere, so the effort was shelved for five years. One day in April 1943, Hoffman was preparing a fresh batch and inadvertently absorbed a small amount through his fingertip. Almost immediately, he noticed a "remarkable but not unpleasant state of intoxication" that sent his imagination and sensory awareness into overdrive. Believing the drug required further exploration, a few days later Hoffman took what proved to be a massive dose of 250 micrograms (full efficacy is generally achieved with just 20 micrograms). Realizing the drug's incredible potential when he finally sobered up, Hoffman filed for a U.S. patent almost exactly one year later.[49]

The drug's remarkable ability to induce states of dramatically altered consciousness garnered immediate attention. Psychiatrists thought LSD could help treat alcoholism and disorders like schizophrenia, while neurologists used the drug to alleviate chronic migraines and cluster headaches. When LSD escaped the confines of the laboratory, however, it became the notorious recreational drug it is today. Although typically associated with far-out hippies and left-wing gurus like Timothy Leary, it was also very popular with elites. Mary Pinchot, wife of famed CIA agent Cord Meyer, reportedly told Leary that "top people in Washington are turning on." Years later, in an appearance on *The Dick Cavett Show,* Clare Booth Luce—wife of publisher Henry Luce and ambassador to Italy from 1953 to 1956 (where she worked directly with Agent Siragusa)—casually admitted, "Oh, sure, we all took acid. It was a creative group." LSD, however, tended to disorient and confuse as often at it enlightened, stoking the ire of intelligence officials who feared America's enemies might utilize the drug to interrogate—or, worse, reprogram—captured American soldiers. This anxiety was captured perfectly in the 1959 novel *The Manchurian Candidate* by Richard Condon, which portrayed a war hero "reprogrammed" as a communist sleeper agent and has spawned multiple film adaptations.[50]

The point is, while today they seem far-fetched, Cold War–era fears that people could be brainwashed and "reprogrammed" through a regime of torture and drugs were very real and reached the highest levels of government. And somehow it fell to George White to debunk the hoopla. White's essential involvement in the MK-ULTRA program is unquestioned. References to CIA officials involved in MK-ULTRA are scattered throughout his personal papers, as are references to "81 Bedford" and the name Morgan Hall. Senate investigations conducted in the 1970s revealed that Morgan Hall was a pseudonym used by White to operate a series of CIA safe houses, the first of which was located at 81 Bedford Street in Manhattan's Greenwich Village. Rigged with extensive surveillance equipment, the safe house was used for both undercover FBN investigations and White's experiments. The agents were responsible for keeping it stocked with food and liquor and maintaining a general "lived in" appearance. The CIA paid the rent and occasionally commandeered the apartment for its own purposes—including the sexual blackmail of foreign diplomats and spies.[51]

White confirmed his involvement in a 1970 letter to Dr. Harvey Powelson, chair of the Psychiatry Department at UC-Berkeley. "Not too many years past," he wrote, "I became a sort of liaison officer between

Federal law-enforcement and another rather obscure Dep't of the Gov't (that would like to remain obscure), which was interested in obtaining some factual information and data on the use and effect of various hallucinogens, including marijuana, tetrahydra-cannibinol and the then brand-new LSD." White described experiments conducted "under both clinical and non-clinical conditions on both witting and unwitting subjects" and to personally trying many of the drugs. "So far as I was concerned 'clear thinking' was non existent while under the influence of any of these drugs," he wrote.[52] This is a noteworthy admission, revealing not only White's participation, but also his clear skepticism about the whole project—all while flouting his ostensible duty as a federal narcotics agent.

With much of the historical record still cloaked in secrecy, MK-ULTRA has become major fodder for conspiracy theories. When the existence of the program was revealed in the 1970s, for example, Timothy Leary claimed, "The LSD movement was started by the CIA. I wouldn't be here now without the foresight of the CIA scientists." The related and mysterious circumstances around the apparent suicide of Fort Detrick bacteriologist Frank Olson—who flung himself through a closed Manhattan hotel window in 1953 after a covert dose of LSD led to a psychological break—is a particularly rich source of speculation.[53] Conspiracies do exist and MK-ULTRA qualifies, but there are simpler explanations for the rise of LSD. It was not a government conspiracy that unleashed this potent hallucinogen, but the drug's profound psychoactive properties that attracted scientists and spies, spiritual seekers and recreational users alike.

The program's effects on the career of George White, however, are clear enough and have secured him a permanent place in the history of the U.S. national security state. After the suicide of Frank Olson and White's impolitic jousting with the New York political establishment, Anslinger decided to move White back to San Francisco in early 1955, where he served as the Bureau's top official on the West Coast and continued his sideline in CIA mind control for another decade.

It was there that White's corner of the project took an even sharper turn toward the tawdry and earned the title "Operation Midnight Climax." Back in San Francisco, White set up a new CIA safe house in a luridly furnished Telegraph Hill apartment. Like the pad in New York, the apartment was rigged with extensive surveillance equipment and a two-way mirror from which to observe the action. (One agent joked that the place was "so wired that if you spilled a glass of water you'd probably electrocute yourself.") Joined by fellow FBN agent Ike Feldman and numerous CIA officials, White narrowed his focus to prostitutes and unwitting johns as subjects. In counternarcotics work, White always thought prostitutes a valuable asset: "Acquire a prostitute-informant and you've got a pipeline to the traffic," he once wrote. Now they were bait for unsuspecting test subjects. White's team was specifically responsible for testing the various prototypes produced by Gottlieb. One CIA member recalled, "If we were scared enough of a drug not to try it on ourselves, we sent it to San Francisco."[54]

Many of the documents related to MK-ULTRA were destroyed by the CIA in 1973, so there will never be a full accounting of its scope or victims, which included convicts, hospital and mental patients, enlisted men and college students, and the individuals targeted by White. The nature of the program continues to raise troubling issues. Experimenting on unwitting citizens was both a violation of the Nuremberg Code written after World War II and a profound abuse of power. Compounding the tragedy of this moral compromise was the fact that the program delivered little of genuine value. Ike Feldman, one of the agents supervised by White, later scoffed, "LSD will no sooner work as a truth drug than an aspirin." In *The Search for the "Manchurian Candidate,"* Marks summarizes, "After 10 years of unwitting testing, the men from MKULTRA apparently scored no major breakthroughs with LSD or other drugs. They found no effective truth drug, recruitment pill, or aphrodisiac. LSD had not opened up the mind to CIA control."[55] Though pressing at the time, the entire affair now seems little more than a tragic boondoggle. But the story offers valuable insights into the seeming imperatives and false trails that plague the quest for absolute security.

In terms of national defense, the MK-ULTRA experiments reflected the genuine fears of the intelligence community, as lead scientist Sidney Gottlieb testified to Congress in 1977. "I would like this Committee to know," he said, "that I considered all this work—at the time it was done and in the context of circumstances that were extant in that period—to be extremely unpleasant, extremely difficult, extremely sensitive, but above all, to be extremely urgent and important. I realize that it is difficult to reconstruct those times and that atmosphere today. . . . [S]hould the course of recent history have been slightly different from what it was," he continued, "I can easily imagine a congressional committee being extremely critical of the Agency for not having done investigations of this nature."[56]

This is a style of thought that endures, the inevitable result of even a justifiable obsession with national defense. In the midst of the 2000-era Global War on Terror, Vice President Dick Cheney famously proclaimed the "1 percent doctrine," that in the realm of national security even slim possibilities must be treated as certainties. Five days after September 11, he warned the American people that the government would have to work through "the dark side" to protect them.[57] Cheney's comments and Gottlieb's defense of MK-ULTRA both address one of the fundamental dilemmas of national security: Exactly how far does a democratic society go in pursuit of absolute security? What odd corners and eventualities is it obligated to consider?

In the 1950s, working on the "dark side" required people like George White. In *The Search for the "Manchurian Candidate,"* Marks speculates that White may have actually been the real patsy. Gottlieb and his CIA colleagues kept minimal records and in subsequent inquiries, Marks notes, "put all the blame for actual testing on George White, who is not alive to defend himself." Perhaps. But White also filled a need, and the CIA required his unique expertise. One project member recalled, "We were Ivy League, white, middle class. We were naïve, totally naïve about this, and he felt pretty expert. He knew the whores, the pimps, the people who brought in the drugs. . . . He was a pretty wild man." White was also someone who spent a career weighing the needs of security against the niceties of democratic society. "I freely admit I had a reputation for being a 'heavy-handed' cop," he remarked later in life, but he thought "it was more humane to slap a prisoner at the first sign of resistance than to shoot him if such resistance developed to the point where extreme force became necessary."[58]

White's ready embrace of that compromise make his thoughts on the MK-ULTRA project all the more pertinent. In a letter sent soon after his arrival in San Francisco, White wrote about the nuances of interrogation in a letter to Dr. Harold Wolff, a famous neurologist at Cornell who did classified research for the CIA. The experience of American

POWs "subjected to BW [brainwashing] methods" in China and Korea, he argued, was not much different from the experience of criminals interrogated by police. "How much trouble they take is dependent on how much they want the information available." Sometimes that meant the "3rd degree with rubber hose," and sometimes it meant seducing would-be informants with friendship and other appeals. (In an example of life imitating art imitating life, White recommended Eleazar Lipsky's 1947 novel, *The Kiss of Death*, as a "classic example" of how to flip a reluctant informant.) America's inability to duplicate Soviet and Chinese success with "BW techniques," he continued, "is no doubt due to our unwillingness to go to the depths of brutality and ruthlessness . . . and that is the way we like it in the long run." Yet there were circumstances, he argued, when cruelty and ruthlessness could serve the greater good. "If someone very near and dear to me—a young daughter," he speculated, "were kidnapped and threatened with death or mayhem . . . I might be willing to go to any depths of brutality. . . . For our side— this aint [sic] cricket. For the enemy, it's all in a day's work."[59] In other words, the guardians of American security were sometimes confronted with situations where nothing was out-of-bounds. The challenge lay in finding that elusive line between what was justified and what was right.

That ultimately proved a boundary White was all too ready to cross. His eager embrace of moral ambiguity was partly what led the CIA to include him in the MK-ULTRA program in the first place, but it also created an environment that was ripe for abuse. For White, it was all part of the game, and it was fittingly to Gottlieb that he wrote, near the end of his life, "Of course I was a minor missionary, actually a heretic, but I toiled wholeheartedly in the vineyards because it was fun, fun, fun. Where else could a red blooded American boy lie, kill and cheat, steal, deceive, rape and pillage with the sanction and blessing of the All-Highest?"[60]

True-Crime Action Hero

White's role in MK-ULTRA was revealed in 1977, during Senate investigations led by Ted Kennedy's Subcommittee on Health and Scientific Research. After Watergate the mid-1970s were a period of general political bloodletting; Kennedy's hearings came on the heels of the Church

and Pike Committees (in the Senate and House, respectively) that revealed considerable abuses by American officialdom. Even today, distrust
continues to linger over entire swaths of America's intelligence and police
professions. We can only speculate how White would have reacted to the
attention, but it was not the agent's first brush with celebrity.

White's return to San Francisco was a homecoming. "San Francisco,
in my book, is the greatest city in the world and I hope to stay here the
rest of my life," he wrote to one friend. But it came after several years in
the wilderness, during which it appeared his career had reached a dead
end. On the eve of his appointment to Newbold Morris's federal corruption probe a few years earlier, he confided to another colleague that
while lately he'd "been taking blows . . . I hope the day will come when I
can take bows."[61] George White craved recognition, and between March
1955 and April 1965, the most stable period of his career, he finally began
to take some of those bows. Being called on to assist the CIA likely
assuaged White's bitterness at having been excluded from the early
intelligence community. And even as "Operation Midnight Climax"
drew him further into the dark side of national security, he was also
becoming a recognizable celebrity in the true-crime literature of the
drug war.

Close analysis of these police adventure stories reveals a number of
complexities in the cultural script produced by the Bureau and indicates that figures like George White—a frequent protagonist—shaped
the way the American people thought about the nature of the threats
facing the country and the role of government in a dangerous world.
A number of archetypes illustrate the stakes: heroic agents, servile
informants, desperate dope fiends, treacherous foreigners, inscrutable
Orientals, and swaggering mafiosi; each helped convey the existential
threat posed by the dope menace. And only the brave agents of the FBN
held the danger at bay.

Exerting tight control over public perception necessitated close collaboration with journalists, so Anslinger and his agents carefully cultivated relationships with crime writers like Ed Reid, Michael Stern,
Herbert Brean, James Phelan, and other reporters sympathetic to
FBN prerogatives. Courtney Ryley Cooper, for example, wrote several books on crime, contributed to prominent newspapers, and coau-
thored Anslinger's infamous antimarijuana tract "Marihuana, Assassin

of Youth." J. Edgar Hoover considered him to be "the best informed man on crime in the U.S." (until, that is, Hoover dismissed his warnings about Nazi fifth columnists and Cooper hanged himself).[62] Both Anslinger and White were on good terms with Hearst reporters Jack Lait and Lee Mortimer, whose gossipy "Confidential" series reliably upheld the FBN worldview. *San Francisco Daily News* reporter John Spaulding Arrington was one of White's closest friends in California, and they fed each other occasional tips between 1938 and 1953.[63]

The best-documented example of such relationships is *Reader's Digest* roving editor Frederic Sondern Jr., who served as the magazine's resident expert on law enforcement, European security issues, and America's early drug war. Partnering with *Reader's Digest* was no coincidence. One of the best-selling publications in U.S. history, the *Digest* exerted a clear influence on twentieth-century American culture and had a large international audience. It also maintained a reliably conservative and anticommunist tone; advocating aggressive drug control fit perfectly with the magazine's political agenda. Anslinger wrote occasional articles, but Sondern was the glue binding the *Digest* and the FBN. "He is our favorite crime reporter," the Old Man told Sondern's editor.[64]

Sondern, in turn, received unparalleled access to FBN files and personnel, particularly in the Rome office. Armed with letters of introduction from Anslinger, Sondern had unique access to foreign police officials throughout Europe. His first piece on the FBN, "Our Global War on Narcotics" (1950), was mostly an account of White's 1948 Istanbul bust. This partnership paid immediate dividends when the article was read into the *Congressional Record* to commend FBN efforts abroad. Sondern again invoked the narrative of a global drug war in a 1956 article titled "The World War against Narcotics" that featured the work of District 17. Over time the two parties became so close that one FBN official privately remarked, "In the public mind, he is practically the voice of the Bureau."[65]

This decadelong partnership culminated in Sondern's 1959 book, *Brotherhood of Evil: The Mafia,* which included a foreword by Anslinger. "The book is highly laudatory of Treasury Department agents, particularly those in the Bureau of Narcotics," the Commissioner assured Treasury officials, and would provide "good publicity." The book spent fifteen weeks on the *New York Times* best-seller list, was widely read in policymaking and law enforcement circles, and was cited in Congress as proof of the need for tougher drug control and legislation targeting the Mafia. The book was assigned reading in FBN training courses, and Bureau officials even sent autographed copies (signed by Anslinger, rather than Sondern!) to European police agencies.[66]

In short, journalists who promoted the Bureau line were assured cooperation. In March 1959, George White encouraged a writer named Richard Hyer to contact Anslinger, confident that Hyer's project on communist Chinese drug trafficking would appeal to the Commissioner. Both Anslinger and Agent Sam Levine sat for extended interviews with J. A. Buckwalter, a high-ranking member of the Seventh-Day Adventist Church, whose book *Merchants of Misery* (1961) duplicated FBN positions on the moral peril of addiction and drug trafficking and was subsequently used as FBN training material.[67]

Despite these many cozy relationships, however, the Bureau's official stance toward the press was conflicted. For Anslinger, it was difficult to escape the conflict between the need to educate and the danger of exciting curiosity, thereby contributing to demand. FBN officials were frequently approached with projects designed to highlight their work and turned many down, adding additional weight to those that did receive their blessing. Officially, the FBN followed Treasury Department policy, which advised against participating in or expressing approval of "privately produced series." It was not a total prohibition, but Anslinger found it a useful policy that saved officials "a lot of time and grief." Even as they avoided formal relationships, FBN officials kept a close watch on radio and television programs like *Gangbusters* or *Treasury Agent* to ensure the Bureau was portrayed in a favorable light.[68]

Part of Anslinger's ambivalence stemmed from a reluctance to expose operational methods. During the 1930s, the Bureau tried to keep the names of operatives like White out of the papers. In San Francisco, White was sternly rebuked after accounts broadcast the FBN's use of drug dogs. When an informant who helped make a 1951 narcotics case against Waxey Gordon tried to take his story public, the Bureau warned him not to reveal the use of a secret wireless transmitter and then pressured the *Saturday Evening Post* to spike the story.[69]

Clearly, however, FBN officials had no problem providing access to files or exposing law enforcement techniques when it suited their purpose. The Bureau's primary concern was to remain in control of its public image and drug war narratives. One of the first accounts of the Hip Sing Tong case, for example, was less than flattering. The article's depiction of White seducing a female suspect and allegations against corrupt Customs inspectors prompted angry missives from both Anslinger and Customs officials.[70] Yet over time, the Hip Sing Tong case became a core part of FBN lore and was depicted as a daring undercover mission against long odds. Most FBN stories emphasized the heroics of individual agents, but sensationalism could also work against the Bureau. In New York, Garland Williams complained (without a trace of irony) about the media's tendency to "greatly magnify each case and each trafficker's activities and importance," leaving the impression that "we are having little effect on the growth of the menace."[71] Sensationalizing the dope menace cut both ways.

In the end, the Bureau's clear record of collaborating with sympathetic authors indicates that FBN policy was flexible and subject to opportunity. Headquarters official G. W. Cunningham artfully summarized Bureau policy in a warning sent to—who else?—George White. "One thing worse than no publicity is bad publicity," he noted. "If you can't call the tune, you had better hang up your fiddle and stay out of the orchestra."[72] This was advice White took to heart, as his celebrated cases were retold and embellished, but always for the greater glory of the FBN.

Indeed, by 1960 a slew of true-crime adventures featured George White as the protagonist. Many of the stories in this new crop of literature had been told before, but as White moved up the ranks and away from street-level enforcement, he took an increasingly visible role in the literature. The best examples come from the retellings of the Hip Sing Tong investigation and his 1948 bust in Istanbul.

White's role in the Hip Sing Tong case was initially a closely guarded secret, and Williams told reporters that the agents involved "may never be revealed to the public." That was premature; White's role was confirmed when he testified in open court against Tong defendants. An unauthorized account appearing in the October 1938 issue of *Daring Detective* also named White. Yet a nearly identical account published the following year by a sympathetic journalist in *True Detective* used a pseudonym. The first fully authorized account to identify White appears to be the 1952 book *Narcotics: America's Peril,* by Will Oursler (Anslinger's coauthor on *The Murderers*) and Laurence Dwight Smith. In the mid- to late 1950s, reporter James Phelan ran a whole series of articles on White's exploits in *True: The Men's Magazine,* including the Hip Sing Tong and Istanbul cases, as well as the escapades of White's sidekick, the mysterious con man–informant Pierre LaFitte. By 1960 White's adventures were routinely cited as part of the Bureau's self-generated mythology, and the Old Man included them in *The Murderers* (1961) and *The Protectors* (1964).[73]

Marking the prologue to the FBN's foreign enforcement program, White's 1948 Istanbul case was even more widely celebrated and put to immediate use as bureaucratic leverage and propaganda. In addition to Sondern's article, the bust was adapted into a radio program called *The Silent Man* and narrated by Douglas Fairbanks Jr., famous for his portrayals of adventurers like Robin Hood and Zorro. The telescoping of one specific moment in the case, as it was retold over the years with different emphasis, is particularly revealing. After making contact with the suppliers and going to the stash house to discuss terms, White lost his Turkish surveillance team and was unable to pinpoint his location. Realizing the need to return and prepare the bust, White noted the serial number on the house's gas meter as he departed. In his official report, White described this detail without comment. In *The Silent Man,* however, this is a moment of high drama as suspect Iradodos Terapyanos's American affectations become the group's undoing. Known to his friends as "Little Bob," Terapyanos reportedly dressed in a Western style and peppered his speech with American slang. As "Ferid" in *The Silent Man,* his affected mannerisms are played up, as are the foreign accents and exotic locale. A few lines of dialogue describe his fancy American lighter, which he repeatedly insists on using to light everyone's cigarettes. As White leaves the meeting and realizes he must confirm his location, he stops Ferid and asks for another light and then reads the number on the gas meter in the glow, which becomes the key piece of information allowing White and the Turkish police to set their ambush.[74]

As the story was told and retold, the Turks (both traffickers and police) gradually fade into mere background players and White is literally moved to the foreground. In Phelan's account, the moment when White reads the gas meter in the glow of a lit cigarette is similarly dramatic—one of only two illustrations. This time, White lights his own smoke, a heroic figure illuminated against the gloom where the traffickers lurk. Phelan painted a stark dichotomy between White and the Istanbul traffickers, right down to their physical descriptions. White was the "powerful" human "beer keg," while the Turkish traffickers were characterized by a "weak chin" and "ferret" face, speaking in "a flat metallic voice," or aping the style of a "young American hustler." Accounts in Derek Agnew's *Undercover Agent—Narcotics* and Sondern's *Brotherhood of Evil*, both published in 1959, focused even more exclusively on White's heroic attributes. These retellings all depict a battle of wits, pitting the valiant agent against the villainous drug traffickers. *The Silent Man* deliberately turned Bob's own pretenses at an American lifestyle against him as an actual "red blooded American boy" (as White described himself) went abroad to fight the criminals threatening the United States.[75]

True-crime literature was an important outlet for the Bureau's message, and the FBN furnished crime writers with a wealth of reliably lurid and easily interpreted story lines. Although it is tempting to dismiss the influence of such "middlebrow" literature on the wider populace, stories about drug investigations clearly had—and continue to have—a perverse appeal, often adhering to familiar plots and archetypes that reinforced a basic American identity as a force of moral good in a troubled world. Ambiguities abound in the real world of drug control: Is addiction a disease or a vice? Should counternarcotics strategy focus on supply or demand? Are traffickers resourceful antiheroes, operating at the margins of a closed economic system, or are they predatory criminals, exploiting the weakness of their fellow man? The great virtue of the true-crime genre, as far as the FBN was concerned, was that it cut through such intractable questions and rendered real-life cases into a readily grasped narrative of good versus evil.

And the villains in these tales were unmistakably evil. In the *Elk Magazine*, a regular FBN outlet, smugglers appear as "a moldy, unsightly part of the fabric of America." In the pages of *Reader's Digest*, *Special Detective Cases*, and *True: The Man's Magazine*, addicts were rendered in the familiar addiction-as-slavery meme as "people without souls" and "creatures of a dominating force." Dealers were invariably described by their most unflattering features, like "a slick black mustache and beady

black eyes" or as "a slick-haired, shifty-eyed gigolo." One Chinese dealer
was described eccentrically as "a grotesque figure . . . unusually husky
and tall for a Chinese and his height was topped by a high, white chef's
cap that almost brushed the ceiling."[76]

In an effort to further marginalize drug trafficking, agents and journalists repeatedly claimed that traffickers and peddlers were a class apart
even in the underworld. In Kansas City, district supervisor T. J. Walker
told radio listeners, "Certainly there is no lower criminal than one who
destroys human beings in order to make profit." In *Treasury Agent: The
Inside Story* (1958), journalist Andrew Tully similarly asserted that drug
dealers "are regarded even in the underworld with loathing and contempt." But this led to an odd disconnect when discussing the high-
ranking figures who organized the traffic and were tagged with titles
like lord, czar, tycoon, baron, king, and prime minister. Drug traffickers
were beyond the limits of respectability even for the criminal milieu,
but they were also given an unsavory aristocratic air.[77]

True-crime stories ultimately functioned to resolve popular antip-
athy toward the undercover tactics required of drug enforcement, and
highlighting the dangerous nature of the job was a reliable way to cultivate sympathy. Agents John Van Treel and Anker Bangs both lost their
lives in the line of duty, becoming two of the first martyrs of drug control, in much the same way that DEA agent Enrique "Kiki" Camarena's
kidnapping and murder at the hands of the Guadalajara cartel galvanized support for Reagan's drug war in the 1980s.[78] Anslinger frequently
invoked their deaths to illustrate the risks faced by FBN agents serving
their country. Bangs was killed when a routine search went bad, while
Van Treel literally worked himself to death in a grueling investigation
that was spun into a tragic saga, retold in *Official Detective Magazine*
and under Anslinger's byline in *The Murderers* and a 1952 issue of
SAGA: True Adventures for Men. Van Treel "served and died for neither
gold nor glory," the Commissioner wrote, "but for humanity."[79]

Practiced by honorable heroes against obvious villains, the extraordinary and duplicitous tactics characteristic of bold undercover work
seemed justified. If the threat was great and the agent righteous, the
ends justified the means—allowing men like George White or John Van
Treel to step outside of the very belief systems they worked to uphold.
The use of underhanded tactics—or, as White cataloged them, the need

to "lie, kill and cheat, steal, deceive, rape and pillage"—was defensible when deployed against a mortal threat to American values. In this context, the "vineyards," these traits became heroic. As the agents were often required to physically merge themselves with the criminal underworld, it became all the more important for the public consuming these tales to maintain a sharp distinction between hero and villain—even as the reality of undercover work undermined this critical dividing line.

One of the greatest ironies of White's career was that despite his action-hero status, his frequent attempts to tell his own story were repeatedly stymied. While still only a rookie in 1935, White sought permission to publish an article describing the work and philosophy of Treasury agents, but Anslinger shot him down with the explanation that it was "against the policy of the Treasury Department" for agents to write about their work. Even before returning from Europe in 1948, White was already talking to *Time* and *Life* about a story. Once again, the Old Man put his foot down. "Such publicity usually backfires and headquarters gets burned," Anslinger wrote. White eventually learned his lesson. In 1958 he was invited to comment on a lengthy history of the FBI appearing in the *Nation*. Expounding on the shortcomings of Hoover's Bureau was one of White's favorite pastimes, but he wisely demurred, knowing that his comments would "promote bad relations between two Government Agencies which have always had divergent opinions as the respective merits of the other."[80]

In 1961 Dean Jennings of the *Saturday Evening Post* offered White ten thousand dollars to coauthor a three-part series on his life and career and assured him the story "would really show how the Bureau fights the narcotic traffic against all sorts of odds. . . . Surely Anslinger could not protest that kind of presentation." This time White included a personal plea in his request to the Old Man. For the past several years, the notoriously hard-drinking agent had battled cirrhosis of the liver, and, he explained, "For whatever its worth, I badly need the money, having been stuck for about $5,000 in medical bills in the past nine months." Moved by his old friend's financial straits, Anslinger sought a ruling from Treasury officials and the White House. President Kennedy's press secretary signed off on the series, but Treasury balked on the grounds that officers should not write about their experiences while on active duty.[81] Anslinger, of course, was a prominent exception and often wrote about his work at the FBN and United Nations. Both *The Traffic in Narcotics* (1953) and *The Murderers* (1961) were published while the Commissioner was still on the clock. The rules were different for the Commissioner, and, for the time being, White's story had to wait.

In 1965 George H. White—OSS colonel, San Francisco district supervisor, CIA adjunct, and true-crime action hero—finally hung up the badge. A few years into his own semiretirement, Anslinger sent his congratulations, enthusing, "At last, you are going to write a book." He warned him, however, that his own latest endeavor, *The Protectors* (1964), "got nowhere, in fact, I am out pocket."[82] White was undeterred. After moving to Stinson Beach, a small coastal community north of San Francisco, he immediately set to work on an autobiography titled "A Diet of Danger"—only to find that his moment had passed. As White and a series of ghostwriters tried to attract a publisher, they found the market for detective stories and the fight against the dope menace had apparently played out. Anslinger tried to build support at Farrar and Straus (publisher of *The Murderers* and *The Protectors*) but received evasive replies. One prospective ghostwriter reported the reaction of his editors: "The whole narcotics subject is just too negative. I'm afraid that the festering nature of the subject will turn people off. Why pay six or seven dollars to be reminded of a horrible social problem?"[83]

That must have been a bitter pill to swallow, as the years between 1960 and 1975 saw a proliferation of agent-memoirs, including Anslinger's *The Murderers* and *The Protectors*. Books by other former agents followed, including White's old protégé Charles Siragusa (*The Trail of the Poppy: Behind the Mask of the Mafia* [1966]); a second edition of Malachi Harney's *The Informer in Law Enforcement* (1968); James Mulgannon, an agent who served under White in the San Francisco office (*Uncertain Glory* [1972]); Sal Vizzini (*Vizzini: The Secret Lives of America's Most Successful Undercover Agent* [1972]); and Jack Kelly (*On the Street* [1974]). White was treated well in all of these accounts, but his resentment at being excluded one last time didn't fester long.

On October 25, 1975, George Hunter White succumbed to liver failure and passed away in a San Francisco hospital at the age of sixty-seven.[84] His unfinished memoir and personal papers were donated by his widow to the Foothills College Museum in Los Altos and now reside at Stanford University. White died before news of the CIA's MK-ULTRA program broke, but he probably would have reveled in the attention. In the Federal Bureau of Narcotics, White was a unique figure, and the energetic and authentic voice displayed in his many reports, correspondences, and writings suggests "A Diet of Danger" would have been an entertaining and insightful read.

A Red-Blooded American Boy

George White was more interesting than his "rock 'em, sock 'em" cop or maniacal CIA conspirator image. As an influential figure within the FBN, White was a clear product of his time and place and served as an exemplar of the Bureau's undercover ethos. Above all, White embodied the trade-offs endemic to the worlds of drug control, counterintelligence, and national security. His career perfectly demonstrates the need to create a context in which the ambiguities of the drug war and security state can be resolved and understood.

The extensive use of undercover practices and covert operations—both at home and abroad—risked aggravating conflicted American attitudes toward spies, detectives, and national police forces. In the early part of the twentieth century, such practices smacked of authoritarianism and seemed distinctly un-American. As the twentieth century progressed, however, attitudes shifted, and the fear of a tyrannical state was transferred to a fear of crime and external enemies. Yet ambivalent attitudes toward duplicitous law enforcement methods lingered, particularly when police adapted tactics more common to espionage than law enforcement. Split between his work at the FBN and CIA, White suppressed drugs by day and experimented with them by night. Exerting control over public accounts of counternarcotics work was critical to managing expectations and resolving such contradictions.

The central role of undercover work also had a profound effect on the Bureau itself. Some agents came to recognize there was a cost to such a life—personally, professionally, and within the bureaucracy. Veteran FBN agent Martin Pera, who served abroad and hunted mafiosi in New York, later remarked that most agents "thought they could check their morality at the door—go out and lie, cheat, and steal—then come back and retrieve it. But you can't." Over time, and led by agents like White, the ends-justifies-the-means mind-set penetrated deeply into the

agency. "If you're successful because you lie, cheat, and steal," Pera continued, "those things become tools you use in the bureaucracy. You're
talking about guys whose lives depended on their ability to be devious
and who become very good at it. So these people become the bosses, and
undercover work became the credo."[85] Even Anslinger, who tried so hard
to project a world in images of black and white, would occasionally admit
that drug enforcement fell into a spectrum of gray, writing, "The truth
is that we are all characters, with a certain measure of duplicity in us,
whichever side of the governmental fence we may be on."[86]

White's career demonstrates that there was a price for privileging that
kind of compromise. Back in the late nineteenth century, in *Beyond
Good and Evil* (1886), Friedrich Nietzsche warned that whoever fights
monsters risks becoming a monster himself.[87] George White spent
much of his career staring into that abyss, and the abyss, inevitably, also
looked back into him. The same is true for any nation obsessed with
absolute security, and one of the manifestations of that abyss within the
United States was the drug war.

CHAPTER 5

CONSTRUCTING A KINGPIN

That son of a bitch Asslinger, you cannot tell where any of his men
are going to pop up. When Russia lands a man on the moon one of
Asslinger's narcotic boys will be there to search him.
—CHARLES "LUCKY" LUCIANO (1959)

Along with Communism, these traffickers in evil are a threat to the
welfare of our beloved country.
—HARRY J. ANSLINGER (1962)

It was a cold and overcast Sunday in February 1946 when New York's
most famous gangster went into exile. A run-down old Liberty ship
called the S.S. *Laura Keene* waited at the Brooklyn dock. Once it delivered Lend-Lease supplies to war-torn Europe; now it prepared to return
mob boss Charles "Lucky" Luciano to his native Italy. There were conflicting accounts of the spectacle. Frederic Sondern, unofficial voice of
the Bureau, described a "phalanx" of immigration agents and "burly
longshoremen" who held off the press as Luciano went aboard. Sid
Feder and Joachim Joesten, dedicated muckrakers both, complained
that U.S. sovereignty and First Amendment rights were trampled by
the army of stevedores who cordoned off the dock. All three bemoaned
the lavish "champagne-and-lobster" party held on board with Manhattan's finest mobsters in attendance. But all of that was written after the
fact. The *New York Times* actually had a reporter there, who described
a more sedate affair. There was a "farewell spaghetti dinner" the night
before, but Albert Anastasia was the only confirmed guest. "Except for
dock hands and a few newspaper men the pier was deserted as the

Liberty ship sailed," the *Times* reported. "Neither [Frank] Costello nor any of Luciano's ex-henchmen were at the dock to bid him farewell."[1]

In fairness, it *was* a peculiar situation. The image of a forlorn Luciano—in tailored silks once more but with only a cargo of flour for company—is a vivid one. More curious were the legal circumstances of his departure. One month earlier, Governor Tom Dewey announced that after serving ten of a thirty- to fifty-year sentence on sex-trafficking charges, Luciano would be released and deported to Italy. And it was Dewey who had famously put Lucky behind bars in the first place. But, he explained, upon U.S. entry into World War II, "Luciano's aid was sought by the armed services in inducing others to provide information concerning possible enemy attack. It appears that he cooperated in such effort though the actual value of the information procured is not clear."[2]

Luciano's pardon—and the startling questions it raised—was a nightmare for the FBN, where Anslinger and company had pegged the Mafia chieftain as kingpin of the New York City vice trade and therefore a central figure in the global heroin traffic. With the war over and international commerce restored, FBN officials feared the Atlantic heroin trade would revive even sooner with Luciano on the loose. The terms of his pardon also presented a major challenge to the FBN narrative. Luciano and his fellow mafiosi were frequent antagonists in the discourse of the dope menace. Now Lucky was not only a free man—he might even be war hero. This would not do.

The Bureau's focus on the Mafia was a major influence on the future of the agency and popular perceptions of crime in America. Anslinger, as with most of his public positions, was unequivocal: the Mafia was a threat to the nation. "I believe that the organized syndicate in America, with its strong Mafia influence, presents an immediate and present danger to our society," he wrote in *The Murderers* (1961). Convinced that organized crime was at the center of the drug trade, the Bureau spent considerable time and energy investigating the Mafia at a time when it was ignored by other law enforcement agencies.[3] Yet as FBN officials invested the Mafia with a starring role in the discourse of the dope menace, they also helped build the myth of the Mafia as an all-powerful international agency of crime.

At the center of that mythos was Charles "Lucky" Luciano, who became a critical foil for Anslinger and his early drug warriors. The irony was that by the time the FBN began portraying Luciano as an international kingpin, his reign was essentially over—a story that reveals how building support for the early drug war led to the construction of a kingpin.

The Dope-Running Murder Machine Called Mafia

The Bureau began to focus on what it would eventually recognize as the Mafia in the late 1930s. By 1950 it was a full-time obsession, rivaled only by Commissioner Anslinger's antic determination to implicate communist China in the heroin trade. During the early 1930s, the FBN's investigative efforts were often split among the Chinese, Jewish, Italian, and occasionally black gangs that populated the urban underworld. By the end of the decade, more and more cases seemed to reveal an increasing level of organization that revolved around ethnic Italian gangs. The demands of World War II momentarily allayed the Bureau's growing alarm over organized crime, but at war's end Anslinger and his agents set about picking up the thread.

For quite some time, approximately ten years, the FBN was one of the only law enforcement organizations to openly discuss the Mafia. Until a dramatic raid by local police on a 1957 mob summit in upstate New York drew national attention—held to confirm Vito Genovese's ascension to the head of the Luciano crime family and divide the spoils of the dope traffic—FBI director J. Edgar Hoover famously dismissed the notion of a national crime syndicate as "baloney." "No single individual or coalition of racketeers dominates organized crime across the country," he scoffed, reluctant to admit a failure of federal law enforcement. The FBN, however, had no such qualms and readily seized the chance to steal a march on their bureaucratic rivals. "The hard truth is that such an organization does exist," Agent White wrote to a friend preparing to join Eisenhower's Justice Department in 1952. "It doesn't matter if we call it Mafia, Unione Siciliano, Camorra, Black Hand, the Syndicate, The Organization, The Mob. . . . Personally, I like the name 'Mafia,'" he explained, because it was "sufficiently descriptive and dramatic so that an advantage is gained thru such characterization." In 1963 Joseph Valachi, a low-level soldier turned snitch, confirmed to the FBI what the FBN had always suspected: the Mafia was real. They called themselves Cosa Nostra, Our Thing.[4]

Between 1946—the year of Lucky's deportation—and the early 1960s, the FBN developed a unique expertise on organized crime and desperately tried to alert the American public to the danger posed by the mob. As the agents built their files, the Bureau compiled an extensive catalog of dossiers it called "the Mafia Book." It was actually two books—one bound in green, the other in black—and their use was a carefully guarded privilege. The green book was to share with other agencies, but the black one was classified and its circulation restricted. In time, the Mafia Book became the federal government's most detailed ledger on organized crime, and the FBN leveraged access to material and agents for influence with journalists, congressmen, judges, and other public officials. Today a reprinted version, circa 1960, is available from Skyhorse Publishing as *Mafia: The Government's Secret File on Organized Crime* (2009).[5]

FBN officials were sincere in their beliefs and there was very little daylight between the Bureau's public portrayals and internal views about the Mafia, but those concepts had only a loose association with historical reality—such as it is known. Most historians of crime in America fall somewhere between Hoover and Anslinger: the Mafia was real and its influence considerable, but it was never quite the empire of crime depicted by the FBN.[6] Again, the challenge is one of documentation. It's tricky to parse the truth from an incredibly rich mythology with a relatively sparse documentary record. Those records that do exist typically come from law enforcement and carry certain ideological and political assumptions. That makes it harder to recover an objective truth, but it does provide access to the fears and anxieties that animated the lawmen charged with protecting the American people. When Anslinger and his early drug warriors looked at the Mafia, they saw a foreign conspiracy poised to strike at the heart of the country.

Laden with such drama, stories about Mafia violence and drug trafficking were catnip to the ink-stained wretches. Sympathetic journalists and crime writers were critical partners in illustrating the threat of organized crime in the postwar era. Mario Puzo, whose 1969 book, *The Godfather,* made an indelible imprint on public perceptions of the mob, began his career writing for many of the same true-crime outlets that were regular FBN forums.[7] In establishing the threat of a drug-dealing Mafia, the Bureau helped create a mythic history of the mob that resonates still today.

When dealing with the public, the Bureau tended to project a strongly cohesive enemy. Mirroring the opportunistic way they utilized the medical vocabulary of addiction, FBN officials used the term *Mafia* inclusively and with little differentiation. What agents and officials usually meant was the *American* Mafia. Historians of the mob and true-crime writers generally agree that the American Mafia was organized around a collection of Italian American crime "families" led by a few powerful leaders who settled disputes and made governing decisions. But there's little agreement on the level of cohesion within and among the families. Partly as a consequence of its focus on international drug trafficking, the Bureau also used the term *Mafia* to refer to the *Italian* or uniquely *Sicilian* Mafia, which had only a tenuous connection to its American counterpart. The effect was to impart the American Mafia with a distinctly foreign character (despite the uniquely American circumstances of its development) and portray it as an international monolith—a characterization that echoed popular ideas about international communism and was neatly conveyed in another of the Bureau's favorite appellations: "the Syndicate."

The Bureau and its pet journalists came up with a variety of malevolent images to convey this unique enemy. Anslinger called the Mafia a "monstrous organization." Agent Siragusa described it as a "black-hearted brotherhood" and "a creature of more than 200 years." To Frederic Sondern, the Mafia was the eponymous "Brotherhood of Evil," and Luciano was that evil's literal "personification." Pulitzer Prize–winning journalist Ed Reid of the *Brooklyn Eagle* was even more demonstrative and variously described the Mafia as a vampire, a parasite, and "the brain of a system of tentacles stretching around the world." To Herbert Brean, a regular at *Life, Reader's Digest,* and numerous pulp magazines, the Mafia was "the most extensive, most effective criminal agency in the Western world."[8]

When they bothered to reach beyond such easy metaphors, FBN agents and crime writers alike struggled to define the Mafia's essential nature, variously describing it as a way of life, a criminal philosophy, or even a religion. Most accounts stressed the Mafia's relentlessly subversive worldview, and Anslinger portrayed its "peculiar Sicilian mentalities, characters, personal habits and lives" as determinative. In *Brotherhood of Evil,* Sondern described it as a philosophy, secret society, and criminal caste all rolled into one. Reid called it "the religion of the criminal classes" and cast Luciano as its "god" or "High Priest." In the tawdry *Confidential* series, Hearst reporters Jack Lait and Lee Mortimer described the Mafia as a "terroristic secret society" and "giant conspiracy." The line running through each variation was that the Mafia possessed a closed-off, alien, and deviant worldview inimical to American society. The Mafia was the perfect enemy within, provoking classic nativist responses, and came to fill a niche in the American psyche previously occupied by Freemasons, Mormons, Catholics, foreign-born radicals, and a host of other Others.[9]

To further tighten the image, Anslinger and company often reduced the complexities of the criminal realm to a single antagonist for the Commissioner to claim as nemesis. Before Luciano was Elias Eliopoulos, the purported "Drug Baron of Europe." Eliopoulos was an major figure in the nascent drug trade and reportedly organized the first global trafficking routes in response to the establishment of international controls early in the century. With excellent political connections, Eliopoulos was an elusive target during the 1930s and was finally driven into the FBN's reach by the Nazi occupation of Europe. When Agents White and Dyar (on a brief hiatus from their OSS duties) collared Eliopoulos in 1943, Anslinger issued a triumphant press release declaring the FBN had shut down "the No. 1 narcotics smuggling combination of all time." In later accounts, the Old Man painted a vivid image of Eliopoulos as "the handsome, swaggering, well-dressed baron of the business . . . always carrying his gold-topped cane which was a kind of trademark, splashing his money around for champagne parties, race tracks, opera and dinners, and an assortment of women." Anslinger then emphasized his own single-minded pursuit of this Old World archvillain by describing Eliopoulos as "the gold-tipped white whale I had to reach." Evoking Moby Dick was not just another passing literary allusion; whether in pursuit of Eliopoulos or Luciano, Anslinger proudly portrayed himself as every bit the Captain Ahab—overlooking, of course, the fact that Ahab's obsession doomed the crew of the *Pequod*.[10]

According to the FBN, Eliopoulos was the forerunner to future kingpins like Luciano. Anslinger explicitly identified him as "a historic link between the individual network and personalized violence of the 1920's and the deadly and dedicated dominance, in the late 1930's and thereafter, of the dope-running murder-machine called Mafia."[11]

Other Bureau agents and writers similarly looked to the Mafia's origins for insight and to play up its ancient and barbaric past. Many accounts began in the feudal era with Sicilian opposition to foreign occupation. During French Bourbon rule over Sicily, "Morte alla Francia Italia anela!" (Death to the French is Italy's cry!) reportedly became a common battle cry. The word *Mafia* was supposed to be an acronym for this slogan, but that is almost certainly apocryphal, as Sicilians of that era did not consider themselves Italians or even speak in the reported dialect. According to this folk history, the mafiosi, hardened by their insurgency against foreign rule, turned to crime and, by the dawn of the twentieth century, were preying on their neighbors throughout the Sicilian countryside.[12]

Between 1880 and 1920, the mafiosi followed their four million countrymen to the United States, where they continued to harass their fellows as the "Black Hand." Lait and Mortimer of the *Confidential* series described this as a period in which Italian criminals "colonized" America and began evolving into the Mafia. Most narratives paused at the site of a particularly gruesome murder or the death of innocents. It was this larvae stage of the Mafia that Anslinger encountered while working for the Pennsylvania Railroad, when Italian members of his crew were shaken down for tribute. All over the country, Ed Reid wrote in his 1954 book, *Mafia,* the mafiosi "unfurled their black flag over one city after another."[13]

It was an ominous series of images and drew an unbroken line from the decentralized terrorism of the Black Hand to the organized crime of the Mafia. Writing primarily from the 1950s and '60s, true-crime writers and FBN agents alike were distracted by their preconceived notions and desire to see the Mafia as a menacing foreign transplant rather than a problem that grew from American soil, and they overlooked a past that was far more fractious, contingent, and uncertain than they realized.

However much America's early drug warriors were projecting their presentist fears into the mythic history of the Mafia, they seem to have gotten it right when it came to Prohibition putting the *organized* into *crime.* A popular view, endorsed by the FBN and many others, was that the suddenly illicit demands of the American public created widespread criminality, as consumers turned from saloon keepers to bootleggers to slake their thirst. Most of the gangs that formed around the illicit liquor trade were naturally organized by family and neighborhood. As profits grew, so did competition. Out of this tumult, the Mafia emerged triumphant as the nation's most powerful criminal organization. "As the smaller mobs destroyed each other," Anslinger wrote, "the shadow of one grew larger with each new 'execution.' This was the Grand Council of the Mafia, with its plan of an international cartel controlling every phase of criminal activity."[14] At the head of this Grand Council was one man who purportedly rose to govern crime in America: Charles "Lucky" Luciano.

The Rise of a Kingpin

By all accounts, Luciano's ascent to power was fast. Born on the island of Sicily in November 1897, young Salvatore Lucania, as he was then known, emigrated to the United States with his family in 1907 and settled into the large immigrant community in Manhattan. Lucania disdained honest work and proclaimed throughout his life, "I never was a crumb, and if I have to be a crumb I'd rather be dead." Perpetrating minor capers with petty street gangs, an adolescent Lucania displayed a knack for criminality that earned him apprenticeships with two very important and very different organized crime figures: Arnold Rothstein, the famous Jewish gangster and gambler, and Joe "the Boss" Masseria, a tenacious survivor with a spooky reputation for dodging bullets and the leader of Manhattan's largest Italian gang. From Rothstein, Luciano learned the power of financing crime from afar; from Masseria, he learned the power of ethnic cohesion and the adept use of violence. In the course of his apprenticeship, Luciano also developed a lifelong friendship with Meyer Lansky, a Jewish gangster who remained one of Lucky's closest associates.

Around this time, Salvatore Lucania took to calling himself Charlie Luciano—he apparently felt his nickname "Sally" was too effeminate and liked the ring of his modified last name. Though he always said it was because of his luck with the dice, Luciano earned the moniker "Lucky" following an incident in October 1929 when he was kidnapped off the streets of Manhattan and found beaten half to death on Staten Island. Some writers speculated that he was worked over by an aggrieved police detective; some thought the cops were looking for Luciano's associate, the hijacker Jack "Legs" Diamond. Others insisted it was a warning from rival drug dealers. In any case, the stories agree, he was beaten within an inch of his life and "lucky" to survive—so it was a nickname his associates used with great care.[15]

Luciano was still clawing his way up the hierarchy when he first came to the attention of federal agents. In 1923 he was arrested for selling morphine to undercover agents of the Prohibition Unit. This was Luciano's second narcotics violation, so he agreed to turn over a large cache of heroin to avoid prosecution. Whether the drugs were actually his or belonged to a rival is unclear. Luciano always maintained he was no "stool pigeon," but Anslinger claimed that Prohibition agents used him as an informant for several years. Testimony to the Faustian nature of the bargain struck with criminal informants, Anslinger narrated, "One by one his competitors were sent away and Lucky improved his own position. Thus unwittingly the American government helped Lucky rise to power."[16]

Luciano's cohort had grand aspirations and realized the internecine violence associated with Prohibition hurt everyone's bottom line. The subsequent establishment of "the Commission" and purge of the older European-born leadership were usually depicted as a kind of Americanization or modernization of the Mafia. The precipitating event was the Castellammarese War (1929–31), which began as a conflict between rival gangs led by Masseria and Salvatore Marazano (formerly of Castellammare del Golfo, Sicily, hence the name). According to underworld legend, Luciano's clique of Americanized gangsters orchestrated the deaths of upper-echelon leaders in both gangs, clearing a path to the more cooperative management style of the "Commission" or "Grand Council," where disputes could be settled with less bloodshed. Journalist Joachim Joesten compared it to the Nazis' "Night of the Long Knives." It was a poor metaphor but effectively lumped Luciano with Hitler. To Anslinger, it was just another step in "Lucky's bespattered path to power."[17]

As the new head of Manhattan's largest gang and creator of the Commission, Luciano became the most powerful gangster in the city—the *capo di tutti capi*, or boss of bosses—and thereupon laid claim to a veritable kingdom of crime, presided over from his suite at the Waldorf Astoria. "No single racket was conducted without his approval," Anslinger wrote. "Name it; Lucky controlled it." In these accounts, Luciano emerges as a modernizer in the style of a chief executive officer, bringing new cohesion to the city's vice rackets. This seemed to be how Luciano, too, liked to think of himself. "We're big business, is all," he reportedly told undercover FBN agent Sal Vizzini later in life. Although his 1936 conviction tumbled him from this lofty height, Luciano supposedly duplicated this feat upon reaching his Italian exile, where, the authors of *Narcotics: America's Peril* (1952) wrote, he "reorganized Mafia gangsters into the most powerful and far-reaching international drug syndicate in the history of this traffic." Sondern likewise insisted that Luciano was a "modern mafioso" who even updated the gangster look by ditching "wide-brimmed fedoras and odd overcoats" for "quietly elegant" suits.[18]

The picture of organized crime that emerges from these accounts was surely an exaggerated one, but the combination of Prohibition and the Commission did genuinely mark the start of a new era in the history of American crime—a change not lost on contemporary observers. Around the time that Luciano was organizing the Commission, Walter Lippmann, perhaps the most influential voice in the country, wrote a pair of essays on the growth of the underworld, which he described as a sort of limbo between upright society and outright criminality. The underworld has, to some degree, existed as long as there have been cities. But the problem, Lippmann noted, had sharpened with Prohibition's galvanizing influence and the growth of the metropolis as both a material reality and a clash of cultures. Big cities like Manhattan and Chicago, Lippmann observed, represent "the place where the older American polity, its premises, its purposes, and its methods is confronted with the newer American civilization." The underworld was a manifestation of that "newer" civilization, epitomizing a kind of perverse capitalism that sprang from the paradox of a people who loved both liberty and policing the morality of their fellow man. "It is the creature of our laws and conventions," Lippmann wrote, "and it is entangled with our strongest appetites and our most cherished ideals."[19]

Unlike murderers or rapists, the denizens of the underworld served important social, economic, and even political functions. Labor racketeers brought a rough degree of order to overly competitive markets and broke strikes as readily as they consolidated labor unions; armed gangs turned out voters on Election Day, and—most important—the underworld provided the workings of a vice economy in which just about everyone was complicit. The underworld, Lippmann wrote, "lives by performing the services which convention may condemn and the law prohibit, but which, nevertheless, human appetites crave."[20]

Though small in comparison to the market for booze, sex, and gambling, one of those appetites was for narcotics, and it was around this time that an ascendant Mafia extended its influence to the drug traffic. "Dope had always been part of their operation," Anslinger explained in *The Murderers*. "Now it took on a bigger role." The timing, from a historical standpoint, was fortuitous for the underworld. The articulation of international controls led to the growth of the black market at the same time that Prohibition was creating an elaborate web of clandestine economic relationships. There were also additional patterns of ethnic succession at play, with earlier generations of Irish and Jewish immigrants moving into the middle class and leaving a void filled by incoming Italians. The Bureau, meanwhile, inadvertently did its own part by taking out the Jewish, Chinese, and multiethnic gangs that had previously dominated the drug trade.[21]

The Mafia's influence was felt all up and down the spectrum of the drug world. On the street, many addicts and low-level dealers recalled the shift unfavorably. "It was a beautiful thing when the Chinese and the Jews had it," one black dealer reminisced. "But when the Italians had it—bah!—they messed it all up. . . . I mean it was nothing but pure trash—you had more chemical in there and less narcotic."[22] At the level of public discourse and within the halls of the Bureau, meanwhile, the Italian gangs were demonstrating a worrisome ability to buy political protection. At the height of his influence, Luciano's reach reportedly extended "to Tammany Hall, City Hall, the state government at Albany and into the nation's capital itself." By the 1950s, Anslinger warned that the Mafia, backed by the profits of the dope trade, exerted control over "whole communities and cities, police departments and mayors, judges and district attorneys and juries." In *Washington Confidential,* Lait and Mortimer claimed the Mafia had "succeeded in doing that which the Communists failed to do; they infiltrated and took over the government."[23]

In other words, it was not just ethnic unity or violence but the venality of the political system that allowed the Mafia to dominate the underworld and organize the narcotics traffic. Yet aside from rogue agents
like George White, few FBN officials were prepared to assail the political establishment, reinforcing the tendency to seek external solutions
like source control and foreign enforcement to fight the drug war.

In fact, most historians agree that gambling was far more lucrative
than narcotics, which some families viewed as a liability given the cultural norms of the day. But even at the time of Lippmann's writing in
1931, it was clear that a strange phenomenon was at work. Underworld
groups like the Mafia were not only providing desired—and sometimes
necessary—services to the American people, in a sense, they had taken
on certain state functions ceded in the course of Prohibition. "Being outlawed, the liquor business cannot be regulated by law," Lippmann noted,
so it had to "improvise its own substitutes for law and order." Political corruption was a kind of informal tax and rough system of regulation—in
which revenue accrued to crooks rather than government coffers.[24]

Over time, the underworld's subversive functionality became one
of its most dangerous qualities. In 1950, twenty years after Lippmann's
writing, Illinois governor Adlai Stevenson warned Americans, "The
greatest menace is that the public will come to accept organized crime
as something inevitable, as a necessary part of our social system."[25]

That was music to FBN ears. Acknowledging any symbiosis between
the government, the mob, and the American people was heresy. So the
Bureau's early drug warriors focused their attention on lawlessness and
let their gaze drift outward to the international trafficking networks
they took as the real cause of the dope menace. In attributing the persistence of the drug problem and rise of the underworld to criminality
rather than to America's own internal contradictions, they articulated
a compelling rationale for the expansion of government authority. This
is a crucial point: just as the threat of world war and communist expansion gave rise to the national security state, the growth of organized
crime and fears of unchecked addiction enlarged the power of government and prompted officials to claim new police powers to deal with
new threats to U.S. security and American cultural values.

As with the contradictions found in drug war narratives, the numerous paradoxes and inconsistencies in popular accounts of the Mafia

suggest an active mythology in the making. That subsequent accounts lack the firm documentation necessary to resolve basic questions about the nature and reality of the Mafia makes it difficult to sort fact from fiction. But again, in construing the Mafia as a threat to national security, that is partly the point. To the Bureau, the ancient or modern character of the Mafia was a secondary concern—colorful and illustrative window dressing. Its violence and influence were dangerous, but it was the takeover of the drug trade that made the Mafia truly threatening.

Once more, fates aligned. In the same month that Luciano was deported to Italy—February 1946—Anslinger laid out his vision for drug control in the postwar era to the readers of *True Detective,* comparing poppies to the atomic bomb and proclaiming the need for U.S. leadership.[26] But with American addiction at an all-time low and the drug traffic itself all but dead, Anslinger needed a new antagonist to make the danger real to the American public. And that's where Lucky came in.

Chasing Lucky

The FBN and its allies said a lot about Luciano over the years, and little of it was complimentary. To Justin Gilbert of *True Police Cases,* Luciano was the "king cobra of crime." Joachim Joesten called him "Mr. Big Dope." Briefed extensively by Bureau agents, journalist Michael Stern remarked that "legends have flourished about him like weeds around a cesspool." Agent Siragusa described Luciano as a "Sicilian pimp and trafficker." Anslinger called him "the greatest white slaver of all times." Nearly all confided, with a knowing wink, that Lucky had syphilis, a frequently deployed trope that took the glamour out of his kingpin image and reinforced the notion that he was a marginal character—impure and rotting from the inside out. Al Capone, many noted, was driven mad and died from syphilis, and Anslinger alleged that Elias Eliopoulos, too, carried the disease.[27]

Lucky returned the Bureau's animosity in spades. While working undercover in the late 1950s, Agent Sal Vizzini noticed a stack of FBN literature in Luciano's Naples apartment, including Anslinger's *The Traffic in Narcotics,* Sondern's *Brotherhood of Evil,* Andrew Tully's *Treasury Agent,* and Joesten and Feder's *The Luciano Story.* Vizzini insisted that Luciano was barely literate, but the mob boss was paying attention.

Luciano, he reported, thought Anslinger was "worse than Hitler," usually called him "Asslinger," and spoke wistfully of pissing on the Commissioner's grave. All of which delighted the Old Man. Lucky also had cross words for Siragusa and once told reporters that for Christmas he wanted "Siragusa in a ton of cement!" Both men wore Luciano's animosity like a badge of honor.[28]

The Bureau's attack, however, came roughly a decade after Luciano's fall. Lucky's ascension in the mid-1930s was relatively quiet but put him in the crosshairs of an ambitious young prosecutor named Tom Dewey. Today Dewey is mostly remembered as a failed presidential candidate, but, for a time, he was the toast of New York and putting Luciano behind bars was among his greatest feats. In 1935 Dewey was appointed a special prosecutor to clean up the crime rackets proliferating in the wake of Prohibition. His first targets were the "beer barons" Irving "Waxey" Gordon and Arthur Flegenheimer, a.k.a. "Dutch Schultz." When Schultz found out, he allegedly demanded Dewey's assassination, but Luciano famously ordered a hit on the unpredictable Schultz instead. But Dewey then pivoted to Luciano and began seeking a case on which to prosecute the well-insulated boss. Dewey was after Luciano for his purported control over gambling and narcotics but found the city's prostitution racket a softer target. In February NYPD officers from Dewey's task force raided brothels across the city to round up suspects and potential witnesses. Luciano fled the state, and a dramatic legal battle ensued as Dewey extradited him from Hot Springs, Arkansas, and then successfully prosecuted the gangster on sixty-two counts of compulsory prostitution. The most damaging testimony came from three madams and a loan shark who all agreed to testify in exchange for reduced sentences. None were ideal witnesses, but their testimony got Dewey his conviction.[29]

Luciano's prosecution was the first time a major crime boss was convicted on charges other than tax evasion. And the fact that it was for sex trafficking, known in those days as "white slavery," perfectly complemented FBN messaging. According to Anslinger and others, Luciano—in addition to being the top pimp in the city—made a habit of dating young professional and working-class girls "eager for a way out of the enslavery of drab routine," but would get them hooked on heroin and turn them over to his brothels once he got bored. Thus, the Bureau linked Luciano to recurring anxieties about American women drawn into addiction, miscegenation, and sexual depravity.[30]

Luciano spent the next decade at Dannemora Prison in upstate New York, where, by most accounts, he was a model prisoner. His reprieve came with U.S. entry into the Second World War. The story of Operation Underworld, as Luciano's wartime assistance was called, is a complicated one, but the essentials are as follows. Early in the war, the Office of Naval Intelligence (ONI) was concerned about the number of American ships sunk by Nazi subs, particularly in the vicinity of New York City. Fearing the subs were resupplied nearby or receiving intelligence from the Manhattan waterfront, an ONI group led by Lieutenant Commander Charles Haffenden approached Joseph "Socks" Lanza for help. Lanza was a member of the Luciano family and ran the Fulton Fish Market on the southern tip of Manhattan. Concern for American security, as it often does, trumped all other considerations. Haffenden explained, "I'll talk to anybody, a priest, a bank manager, a gangster, the devil himself. This is a war. American lives are at stake." With Lanza's assistance, naval intelligence officers went out among the New York fishing fleet and monitored the waterfront for signs of Nazi agents. When Haffenden sought to expand the operation, Lanza ran into resistance from other bosses, who feared he was informing to the district attorney. So Lanza sought approval from Luciano, who still had the stature to green-light the whole thing. To facilitate communication, Haffenden had Luciano transferred from Dannemora to Great Meadow Prison (outside Albany) and afforded lenient visitation rights from Lanza, Meyer Lansky, various naval officers, and a handful of others. After helping secure the New York waterfront, the story goes, the Mafia then supplied intelligence for the invasion of Sicily. The value of Luciano's contribution has been debated ever since. The results of the Mafia's assistance were ambiguous at best, but the fact that Dewey cited Luciano's wartime cooperation when commuting his sentence made the episode controversial for everyone involved.[31]

The release of the world's most famous gangster, meanwhile, contributed to what the FBN saw as a gathering storm. Bureau officials already believed the Mafia was a major player in the drug traffic, Luciano had admitted to selling drugs in the past, and the resumption of global commerce would soon reopen transatlantic smuggling routes. So Anslinger and his early drug warriors girded themselves for the return of the dope menace by turning their full attention on the Mafia.

The first order of business was to chase down old leads. In November 1946, George White circulated copies of an address book confiscated from Mafia trafficker Nicola Gentile back in 1937 and requested that all offices immediately update their files on the individuals listed therein. "On the theory that members of the Mafia throughout the United States are generally engaged in the narcotic traffic," he explained, "the Bureau has instituted a long-range project, with the object of identifying and obtaining all available information concerning members of this criminal organization."[32]

A few months later, FBN fears were realized when news broke about a December 1946 Mafia summit in Havana, Cuba. Somehow Luciano had acquired an Italian passport and Cuban visa in order to attend. Luciano and Lansky had apparently called the meeting to discuss the future of the drug traffic and the establishment of a lucrative Cuban casino industry. Although subsequent FBN accounts claimed that agents were tracking Luciano's movements the whole time, his discovery on the island reached the public in February 1947, when columnist Walter Winchell broke the news that Luciano was in nearby Havana and allegedly up for the Congressional Medal of Honor.[33]

The Commissioner immediately swung into action and ordered an immediate embargo of all U.S. medical supplies to Cuba until Luciano was expelled from the country, a tactic that had previously forced Mexican authorities to abandon their experiments with ambulatory treatment in 1940. FBN stalwarts Garland Williams and George White backed the Old Man's play in the press. In New York, Williams briefed reporters: "We are very much concerned that Luciano has been permitted to establish a residence so close to our shores . . . where he can exercise his dangerous influence over the American underworld." In Chicago White spun a similar tale and warned that Al Capone was a "small fry" compared to Lucky. "This criminal rat Luciano," he told reporters, "has gigantic money-making plans dealing in gambling vice and narcotics." But the FBN, he assured them, was on the case. Government officials like former OSS chief "Wild Bill" Donovan also chimed in to dismiss Luciano's wartime assistance as "nothing but cheap talk from irresponsible persons and completely without foundation."[34]

The pressure worked. Cuban police took Luciano into custody on February 22, and Anslinger lifted the embargo three days later (after only five days). On March 19, Luciano was deported to Italy for the second and final time. Privately, Williams fired off a missive to Anslinger calling the embargo "one of the finest pieces of law enforcement work I have ever known."[35]

The Aircraft Carrier of the Narcotics Traffic

With Luciano back in Italy, the Bureau escalated its crusade against the Mafia, and the agents aggressively sought hard evidence of Luciano's drug dealing through a series of foreign tours between 1948 and 1951. The christening of the Rome office and creation of District 17 were physical signs of the Bureau's growing clout at home and abroad, but the office's specific location in Rome and initial focus on Italy were due mostly to Luciano.

Following stops in Istanbul and Marseille in the summer of 1948, George White finished the first of those tours in Italy, where he tried and failed to make a case on Luciano or his close associates. As in Istanbul, there were troubling signs of police collusion, and White was confronted by one target who claimed to have been tipped off by local police. Exposed, White settled for a consolation bust on three low-level players trafficking heroin and cocaine between Austria, Trieste, and Italy—an organization subsequently embellished as the Enzi Syndicate. The crucial participation of an Italian police informant, who introduced White to the suspects on behalf of the very same department that may have tipped Luciano's men, suggests that Enzi was another sacrificial lamb.[36] Even so, White had demonstrated that foreign enforcement was theoretically possible. A concrete Mafia tie-in, however, remained elusive.

In 1949 Garland Williams applied additional pressure as a UN envoy. In April he called on Italian police to discuss their control efforts but found a distinct lack of concern. In a lengthy report to Anslinger, Williams concluded, "Narcotic law enforcement in Italy is actually nonexistent."[37] Though he didn't acknowledge it, this was something of a mixed blessing: the lack of control in Italy might increase the availability of drugs in the States, but it also justified FBN intervention.

The message was driven home in June when police removed a New York man named Vincent Trupia from a passenger flight in Rome while carrying three kilos of heroin and another nine of cocaine. Bowing to FBN demands, the Italian police brought Luciano and other suspected Mafia traffickers in for questioning. Subsequent investigation by Italian law enforcement revealed that Trupia was in contact with Luciano, but the evidence was mostly circumstantial. Nevertheless, the news made the papers in the United States and jarred Italian authorities, who promptly banned Luciano from Rome.[38]

A year later, in the spring of 1950, the FBN sent Agents Benny Pocoroba and Charles Siragusa to renew the investigation. An experienced undercover, Pocoroba chased leads in Trieste and Italy, while Siragusa tried to crack a few cases further up the supply chain in the Middle East. Both agents struggled to gain traction. Though he kept his cover intact, Pocoroba suffered through the collapse of one deal after another in the quickly shifting terrain. "In my thirty-three years of undercover work," he complained, "I have never been confronted with such a kaleidoscopic investigation as this." And all of the Bureau's tough talk, he added, wasn't helping. Everyone was on high alert, Anslinger's fulminations were making Luciano "a hero in the eyes of the underworld," and the Italian police, he reported, were "still laughing at Mr. White who came here all the way from the U.S.A. to buy a few grams of dope." Pocoroba managed to cozy up to several suspects and gather some decent intelligence, but he found nothing concrete and suspected that most of Italy's narcotics were smuggled in from West Germany.[39]

Meanwhile, back in the United States, the navy belatedly joined the chorus of government agencies disavowing Luciano's war service. In April naval spokesmen issued a carefully worded statement: "There is absolutely nothing in the record to show that Luciano ever gave any information that contributed to the war effort in any way so far as the United States Navy is concerned." It was hardly a categorical denial, and Dewey's office released a similar statement, adding that there was ample precedent for deporting criminal aliens and that Luciano's pardon had relieved a burden on the New York taxpayers. Garland Williams, however, countered that now the feds had to pick up the tab by sending agents abroad to check the mobster's influence. "I regard Luciano as one of the most dangerous criminals in the world today," Williams said. "His influence in racketeering circles in the United States is almost as powerful as when he was on the scene."[40] Yet the pressure was building for the FBN to substantiate these accusations.

In August 1950, Anslinger pulled Siragusa out of the Middle East and ordered him to rendezvous with Pocoroba in Trieste, a bustling seaport and city-state perched on Italy's northeastern shoulder, then jointly governed in an awkward power-sharing arrangement between the Allies and Yugoslavia. At the time, Turkey's rich poppy fields were the largest source of supply in the region, and Siragusa had spent the previous months trying to develop cases in Istanbul, the Anatolian interior, and Beirut—fruitlessly, it turned out, as each investigation was thwarted by powerful local interests. The Commissioner knew this but wanted to show some progress in Italy, explaining, "Our pressing concern at the moment, after Turkey, seems to be Italy."[41]

Siragusa was a logical choice for European operations. The thirty-seven-year-old agent was a second-generation Sicilian immigrant, spoke fluent Italian, earned a Bronze Star for his OSS service in Italy, and explicitly saw his work as a way to counter negative perceptions of Italian Americans. "There are so many other Sicilians who have worked hard and raised decent families," he explained to Frederic Sondern. "Then there is this small group of mafiosi who make us all look like jerks." Agent Vizzini similarly complained, "The world is quick to paint all Sicilians with the same dirty brush." Fighting the Mafia was a way of striking back. In his own memoir, Siragusa wrote that his hatred of the mob gave him "the courage to fight and defeat evil."[42]

Siragusa's investigations in Italy and Trieste quickly led to a startling discovery: most of Italy's black-market heroin came from neither Germany nor underground labs supplied by Turkish opium but from legitimate wholesalers and pharmaceutical companies. In mid-September, the Bureau received information from a confidential source that two residents of Trieste, Matteo Carpinetti and Giorgio Negrin, were looking to expand a middling trafficking operation. Siragusa and Pocoroba immediately approached Carpinetti and asked for help in buying a load of heroin. The FBN agents were joined by Hank Manfredi, a U.S. Army Criminal Investigation Command officer with the Trieste occupation forces who later joined both the FBN and the CIA. Frustrated with Pocoroba's initial failures, Bureau officials in Washington hesitated with the advance funds necessary for an undercover buy, but Manfredi's supe-riors volunteered three thousand dollars in cash for a "flash roll" upon learning that Yugoslav communists might be implicated in the operation. Using Manfredi's wide-ranging authority to tap the targets' phones, the FBN team learned that Carpinetti and Negrin planned to use the pro-ceeds of the deal to open a heroin lab supplied with morphine base from Austria and Yugoslavia. In the short term, the agents discovered, they had been buying small allotments from a series of licit sources.[43]

Carpinetti was quarreling with his regular supplier, a prominent "physician-pharmacist" in nearby Padua, so the enterprising trafficker took the undercover agents to another source: the Trieste office of RAMSA Medicinale and Produti Chimici, where company officials Drs. Riccardo Morganti and Cesare Melli offered to sell Siragusa five kilos of pharmaceutical-grade heroin for ten thousand dollars. After scraping the rest of the buy money together from a combination of FBN and CID funds—and their own pockets—the agents were ready to spring their trap. Over the first weekend of October 1950, Siragusa and Manfredi arrested Morganti, Melli, and the Carpinetti gang and then retired to CID headquarters in Trieste for a jubilant celebration, complete with the requisite portraits behind a table laden with seized drugs. "It hap-pened just as in the movies—it is fantastic," a thunderstruck Morganti repeatedly mumbled. Carpinetti, meanwhile, readily gave up his Yugo-slav contacts, leading Siragusa and Manfredi to more arrests in Trieste and—in cooperation with Yugoslav authorities—Belgrade, where they enjoyed another brandy-fueled victory party with their fraternal col-leagues from across the Iron Curtain.[44]

The Carpinetti-RAMSA bust failed to turn up a definitive Mafia (or communist) angle, but it was a promising start to operations in Europe and revealed that licit diversion was a major problem. It was, in fact, probably more perilous for traffickers to operate clandestine labs, Siragusa concluded. With a little administrative sleight-of-hand and paperwork, they could buy directly on the open market. Having made a decent case, the FBN improved its standing with European police and uncovered new leads as the agents interrogated their prisoners. Per-haps most important, Siragusa believed the FBN had demonstrated the necessity of having agents stationed abroad. "The only solution to our problem of trying to strike at the source here," he wrote to Anslinger, "is to have a Narcotic Agent personally supervise investigations in Italy."[45] The task of implicating Luciano, however, still remained.

Both Siragusa and Pocoroba went back to the States for the winter of 1950–51, but Siragusa returned to Italy several months later, intent on connecting Luciano to the licit diversions. In his absence, Manfredi continued to work closely with Italian police, and by the spring the FBN had several new leads to pursue. The Bureau sent Agents Martin Pera and Joseph Amato to conduct separate investigations in Turkey and Germany, while Siragusa coordinated their efforts from Italy. Soon after returning to Rome in February 1951, he reported, "Our work is rapidly shaping up. . . . [T]here is definitely enough to keep several men busy all year round."[46]

Morganti and Melli of RAMSA, it turned out, were minor players. Identifying their supplier was at the top of Siragusa's agenda. During the bust, Siragusa found a heroin wrapper marked with the label of Schiapparelli, a major pharmaceutical company based in Turin, so he asked the Italian police to audit the records of the five companies licensed to manufacture narcotics, including diacetylmorphine (the pharmacological basis of street heroin), which remained legal in Italy. Despite lax regulation, four of the companies were legitimate. But Schiapparelli, the other four complained, broke informal price controls and sold below cost to a veterinarian supply company called SACI (Societa Anonima Italiana—which translates along the lines of "anonymous company of Italy," a designation similar to an LLC), run by a shady Milan businessman named Egidio Calascibetta. Italian police couldn't prove the company had knowingly diverted heroin onto the black market, so Siragusa dispatched an informant to make an undercover buy from Calascibetta, hoping to find narcotics from Schiapparelli. The scheme convinced Siragusa that Italian pharmaceuticals represented 90 percent of the heroin reaching the United States from Italy, possibly making Calascibetta "one of the biggest heroin peddlers of our time."[47]

With an FBN informant working up the supply chain toward Calascibetta, Siragusa focused on roping in Luciano. Part of FBN strategy was to keep Luciano isolated and off balance, and Siragusa reported, "I will see to it that the police continually harass him and I will probably do a great deal of this myself." This, of course, was not a subtle approach and likely made Luciano more circumspect. After chasing Lucky from

Cuba, FBN officials actively sought to restrict the mobster's international travel. Siragusa eventually succeeded in having Luciano's Italian passport revoked, while Anslinger warned Interpol and other European police officials that Lucky should be denied travel visas as a "potential international narcotic trafficker."[48] None of this would put Luciano behind bars, but the FBN was just as intent on disrupting Luciano's network as it was in convicting him in a court of law.

A major break came in April 1951, when an anonymous tip led Italian police to pull a man named Frank Callaci from a flight departing Milan for Palermo. Callaci was on the FBN's list of suspected traffickers, so Italian police invited Siragusa to interrogate him at the offices of the Guardia di Finanza, a police agency in the Ministry of Finance. Siragusa arrived expecting to find a middle-aged Mafia trafficker, known to the Bureau as another of the deportee gangsters from New York. He found Callaci's nephew of the same name. In an apparent repeat of the Trupia operation, the younger Callaci was recruited in New York and sent to Italy to fetch a shipment of heroin from his uncle. Under questioning, Callaci denied seeing his uncle, who, unbeknownst to Siragusa, was on the same flight and arrested when an alert policeman spotted him in Palermo. Inquiries made in New York produced little, but the arrest of the Callacis shook things up on the Italian side. Given the pressure to prove Mafia drug trafficking, Siragusa observed, "This case developed at an opportune time." Although he was reluctant to trust the Italian police, Siragusa found an effective partner in Captain Giuliano Oliva of the Guardia di Finanza. Working together, Siragusa and Oliva backtracked the younger Callaci's movements through the days leading to his arrest and discovered that he had placed several phone calls to a well-connected trafficker and known associate of Luciano named Joe Pici.[49]

Here at last was a hook on which to hang Luciano. Pici went into hiding after the Callacis' arrest, but discrete inquiries confirmed that he was a high-level organized crime figure in the region and an active participant in the Atlantic drug trade. Desk clerks at the Hotel Manin in Milan, where Luciano was a frequent guest, recognized his picture. Better yet, Milan police had spotted Luciano in the company of Egidio Calascibetta, the principle middleman in the pharma diversion scheme. Finally, a picture of Luciano's trafficking network came into focus. "Everything seems to indicate that LUCIANO is verily the head of this combine," Siragusa reported. "The loose ends are starting to tie in and most of our suppositions have turned out to be correct."[50]

But with Italian newspapers publicly linking the Callacis to Luciano and the relatively open style of investigation being run by Siragusa and Oliva, the Bureau's strategy backfired just when the case was coming together. By the end of April, critical leads were drying up. Siragusa mollified himself, reasoning, "Even if we cant [sic] put him in jail we are at least putting the 'heat' on him." Pici was officially in the wind— Siragusa called him "the most sought, hunted, and hounded man in all of Italy." Calascibetta also abruptly shut down operations, closing off an important angle of the case. Siragusa, however, was thrilled that the Bureau had flushed the network into the open, exclaiming to Anslinger, "THIS IS A HUGE CONSPIRACY." Luciano, he continued, was "the complete lord" of the Atlantic heroin trade and governed his domain "with an iron hand." Continued inquiries revealed a web spread across Italy, with regional lieutenants like Pici in Milan, Gaetano Chiofalo in Udine, and Nicola Gentile in Palermo, all presided over by Luciano and shuttling untold quantities of heroin into the United States.[51]

In the grand scheme of things, Siragusa was getting ahead of himself, and Luciano managed to avoid direct involvement. Pici was not so lucky and was arrested in September 1951—one of District 17's first major victories—but he was the most senior member of Luciano's organization caught up in the pharma investigation. For the moment, however, Siragusa was content. Luciano might be free, but his operation was in tatters. As FBN targets battened down the hatches, Siragusa abandoned his effort to make an actual case, explaining, "There is a virtual panic here, both in the instances of the criminal element . . . as well as among the guilty wholesale and manufacturer registrant diverters." The Bureau had shut down the Italian drug trade, at least for the time being, Siragusa believed, and advised his counterparts in New York to be on the lookout for signs of a panic in the American market.[52]

Any proclamation of victory, however, was premature, as several other organizations quickly resumed operations and Lucky remained on the loose. Eventually, the Bureau learned patience with respect to Luciano. A few years later, Anslinger warned Siragusa to omit public mention of Luciano "until we have him 'in the bag.'" In the short term, however, Lucky remained a useful figurehead. Siragusa's investigations in Italy failed to provide sufficient evidence for a conviction, but it was more than adequate for the Bureau's ongoing public attacks and push to establish foreign outposts.[53]

For the next several years, Anslinger and FBN-sanctioned journalists cited the Callaci and pharma cases as definitive proof of Luciano's control over the Atlantic drug trade. In *The Traffic in Narcotics*, Anslinger described these "notorious deportee gangsters of Italy" as having "a virtual monopoly" over the heroin trade. After meeting with Siragusa in Rome, journalist Michael Stern wrote about Luciano's drug lord status in both *True: the Man's Magazine* and his 1953 book, *No Innocence Abroad*, reminding readers that Luciano remained "as grave a menace to the American people as he was when he operated out of a tower suite in the Waldorf Astoria." These claims eventually prompted formal complaints from the Italian government, and around mid-decade the FBN began to scale back its accusations as Anslinger acquiesced to diplomatic necessity and took his own advice to wait until Luciano was in the bag. Questioned specifically about Siragusa's early work in Italy and asked to name names during a 1955 Senate Judiciary hearing, Anslinger readily identified Calascibetta and Pici but was coy about Luciano. He even began to ask journalists to omit mention of Luciano while covering FBN exploits in Europe.[54] By 1955 the Bureau was firmly entrenched in Rome, and Lucky Luciano, it seems, had served his purpose.

The pharma and Luciano investigations—the first sustained counternarcotic investigations ever carried out on foreign soil—were a formative experience for the Bureau. Anslinger walked a fine line in official settings or when tensions with the Italian government ran high, but he and various crime writers continued to cite Luciano's purported drug lord status as proof of the need for a global U.S. police presence. In portrayals that bore the unmistakable stamp of the early drug war, *Life* magazine characterized postwar Italy as "the aircraft carrier of the narcotics traffic." In *Brotherhood of Evil*, Sondern described Luciano's activities as "an internationally organized narcotics attack against the United States which dwarfed everything that had gone before."[55] Not everyone was convinced. J. Edgar Hoover, in particular, remained skeptical about the threat of the Mafia. But the Bureau did catch the eye of one congressman who saw organized crime as a chance for a national platform.

Senator Kefauver's Three-Ring Media Circus

Senator Estes Kefauver (D-TN) was an unlikely FBN ally. An outspoken liberal, he was both a populist and an intellectual, a mild eccentric who often campaigned in a coonskin cap, and he had a burning passion for corporate reform. He was elected to the Senate in 1948 after ten years in the House, and, over the following decade, Kefauver became a steadfast opponent of McCarthy, refused to sign the Southern Manifesto, and voted against a Democratic-sponsored bill to outlaw the Communist Party. He was a two-time presidential candidate and led antitrust probes of the auto, bread, steel, and—most famously—pharmaceutical industries. He was, in short, not the kind of politician who typically aligned himself with the FBN. Yet it was this very partnership that launched Kefauver into the public eye.[56]

Kefauver's journey began in early 1950. Alerted to the problem of organized crime by increasingly alarmist media coverage, Kefauver submitted legislation to launch a special investigation in January 1950. After some political horse-trading over membership, Kefauver got his committee, and the Senate Special Committee to Investigate Crime in Interstate Traffic was up and running by early spring. His investigation ran for the next eighteen months, into the fall of 1951, and traveled all over the country, with public hearings in nearly every major American city. The Kefauver hearings, as the whole thing was known, swiftly transformed into a traveling media circus and one of the signature events in the history of American crime.

In *The Greatest Menace: Organized Crime in Cold War America* (2002), historian Lee Bernstein describes how the advent of television elevated the hearings to a national spectacle. The New York sessions in March 1951 were particularly riveting and featured testimony from well-known crime figures Frank Costello and Virginia Hill (paramour to murdered Vegas tycoon Bugsy Siegel). Kefauver estimated the hearings captured an audience of thirty million Americans. Bernstein puts the figure at a more conservative seventeen million. In either case, the Kefauver hearings were the one of the most-watched television events of the decade, drawing larger audiences than the Rosenberg trial, the 1951 World Series, and the Army-McCarthy hearings. "Housewives have left the housework undone and husbands have slipped away from their jobs to watch," the *New York Times* observed. "The city has been under a hypnotic spell, absorbed, fascinated, angered and amused."[57] That spell was cast, at least in part, by the FBN, as its carefully honed image of a sinister conspiracy of crime led by the Mafia mesmerized the American public and policymakers.

The timing was fortuitous for the incipient drug war. Not since the days of Prohibition had the country confronted the specter of crime on such a grand scale. With the FBI denying the very existence of the Mafia, Kefauver leaned on FBN leadership to provide expert testimony and guide the committee, even granting the agents new investigational authority via congressional subpoena. The FBN, in turn, eagerly advanced its view of the Mafia as a unique transnational threat and its own image as a cutting-edge police force. Several agents played crucial roles in the committee's operations, and Kefauver frequently lauded the FBN as the "leading authority on the Mafia, because of the Mafia's dominance in the dope trade." Anslinger provided classified testimony in several early hearings, while Agents George White, Charles Siragusa, Claude Follmer, and Sam Levine all testified on the dangers of Mafia drug running.[58]

Prior to taking up his work with the CIA, George White was one of the first agents assigned to the Kefauver Committee, serving as the lead investigator and "advance man" during the committee's early travels. Kefauver praised him as "an authority on the Mafia" whose work was "invaluable." With new congressional backing, including a presidential order to open the previously restricted tax returns of important mob figures, White was able to reopen old cases and dig deeper into mob finances. Best of all, White got the chance to settle old scores from his Chicago days. His probe of Mafia financing and corrupt politicians led, he claimed, to more than a few "sudden retirements" and Senate Majority Leader Scott Lucas's (D-IL) defeat in the 1950 midterm election—a result that delighted White but did little to endear Kefauver to his fellow Democrats.[59]

In May 1951, White turned his lead-investigator duties over to Siragusa, freshly returned from Italy and ready to brief the committee on Luciano's transatlantic drug empire.[60] It was also a critical opportunity to put the Luciano-war-hero myth to bed once and for all.

During the New York hearings, the committee heard conflicting accounts from Agent White and Charles Haffenden, the ONI officer who ran Operation Underworld. White claimed the idea for Luciano's cooperation originated with the Mafia and that he rebuffed an approach from an old-school mobster and occasional informant named August Del Grazio, who offered Luciano's services to the OSS. By then old and infirm, Haffenden gave rather confused testimony but took pains to clarify that a letter he sent to Dewey indicating Luciano's "great" assistance to the navy was merely his opinion and not an official navy position. He also claimed the idea to collaborate with the Mafia came from the New York district attorney's office and not his own intelligence shop.[61]

A few months later, Siragusa provided his own testimony on Luciano's narcotics empire without the troublesome technicalities of a legal trial. In a dramatic deposition, in which the television cameras were ordered not to show his face, Siragusa recited the whole story: the arrest of the Callacis, the heroin diverted from legitimate Italian pharmaceutical manufacturers, and Luciano's purported direction of the entire operation. Nearly all of Siragusa's charges were repeated verbatim in the Kefauver Committee's final report, which blamed "the present influx of heroin from abroad" on the network "managed by the Mafia with Charles 'Lucky' Luciano, notorious gangster, vice king . . . as the operating head." When asked under oath if Luciano was the kingpin of the Mafia, Siragusa replied that he was at least "one of the royal family."[62]

The extent of FBN influence over the Kefauver hearings has not escaped the notice of historians. John C. McWilliams and Alan Block argue that both White and Siragusa offered perjured testimony and manufactured data. The purpose of such skullduggery, they speculate, was to bury Operation Underworld and protect ongoing intelligence operations. Whether the agents deliberately misled the committee is unclear, but it's certain that the agents were acting on incomplete information—unavoidable in most criminal investigations—and ensuring the fix was in on Lucky. The Bureau's influence, however, went deeper than any specific manipulations. On a more fundamental level, the FBN provided a deeply compelling analysis that the American people and their elected leaders were ready and eager to hear. Bernstein points out, "By the inception of the committee in 1950, the FBN had already established a way of thinking about the Mafia that attracted Kefauver's interest along with that of a public drawn to the secretive world of organized crime."[63] The return of the drug trade, the FBN suggested, had little to do with the problems of American life—it was something perpetrated against the nation by outside powers like Lucky Luciano.

In the end, the Kefauver Committee endorsed FBN views without reservation. The committee's final report, later revised as Kefauver's 1952 book, *Crime in America*, described organized crime as national in scale, present in both large cities and "Main Streets throughout America." The Mafia was depicted with the familiar monstrous imagery, complete with "tentacles [that] reach into virtually every community throughout the country." Drugs—"an evil of major proportions"—were central to the Mafia's activities and a primary source of income. Addiction was "a contagious disease which brings degradation and slow death to the victim and tragedy to his family and friends." And the cause of the nation's drug problem was attributed solely to the arrival of drugs smuggled from foreign lands.[64]

Kefauver even continued to promote the FBN line in his own subsequent writing. In a widely read *Saturday Evening Post* article, he warned, "America has come to the saturation point of criminal and political corruption which may pull us down entirely." The chief embodiment of that threat was the Mafia, which he called "the cement that binds organized crime." Many of the crimes committed in America, he continued, are "not isolated, self-contained local activities" but are coordinated by a "loosely organized, but cohesive" national crime syndicate "guided by an evil coalition." Finally, Kefauver twice repeated one of the Bureau's most loaded and conspiratorial charges, calling the Mafia an "outlaw" or "secret government-within-a-government" whose drug trafficking "saps the strength of America, cheats us of our rights and freedom."[65]

This was all great publicity at a time when Anslinger sought to enlarge his force and, even more important, expand FBN jurisdiction. The final report was highly laudatory of the Bureau itself and called for an immediate increase in personnel and resources, commending the agents for "serving long hours in . . . the most hazardous type of enforcement work." In *The Greatest Menace,* however, Bernstein concludes that the Kefauver Committee promised much but delivered little of real substance. It drew significant attention to the existence of organized crime, but few of its proposed remedies were translated into legislation. The 1951 Boggs Act, which introduced federal mandatory minimum sentences for narcotics violations, was a major achievement for the FBN but was basically the only tangible result of the Kefauver hearings. Law enforcement had to wait another twenty years for the passage of the 1970 Racketeer Influenced and Corrupt Organizations (RICO) Act before it received the tools to really dismantle organized crime. But that's not to say the Kefauver hearings were without value. "Ultimately," Bernstein concludes, "it was the glitz that became the lasting contribution of the Kefauver Committee."[66]

The "glitz" was important. Kefauver went on to run several high-profile investigations into price-gouging and other forms of corporate malfeasance, while the FBN pursued its drug war with improved stature and recognition. The convergence of television and politics, meanwhile, meshed seamlessly with the "infotainment" produced by the Bureau. A democratizing medium, television allowed the American people, regardless of geography or social standing, to see for themselves the clear distinction between the agents and their prey. One of the most famous episodes of the Kefauver hearings came when gangster Frank Costello abruptly quit the stand after two days of questioning during the widely watched New York hearings. Costello's racket was gambling, but, following Luciano's exile, he took on a prominent leadership position as the politically astute "prime minister" or "czar of America's underworld." Reluctant to make a spectacle of himself on national television, Costello demanded that his face not be shown, so the cameras famously focused on his hands instead and Costello's nervous fidgeting seemed to betray his guilt to the captivated audience. Immediately after Costello's dramatic departure, FBN agent Sam Levine took the stand and likewise had only his hands shown. Well liked, expressive, and articulate, Levine delivered a composed performance that drew a sharp contrast between the self-assured agents and the shifty mobsters they hunted.[67]

While the Kefauver hearings produced few legislative victories aside from the Boggs Act, they clearly captured the imagination of the American people, and much of that fascination was with the mysterious agents who fought the menace of organized crime. That, as far as the FBN was concerned, was priceless, and the image they presented of the Mafia as a subversive government of crime lingered for years to come.

In time, even the FBI adopted FBN positions. When the fallout from the 1957 raid on a mob summit in Apalachin, New York, finally forced Hoover to acknowledge the Mafia, he ordered the FBI to quickly draft an in-house monograph titled *Mafia,* completed in July 1958. Echoing FBN claims made over the preceding decade, the FBI study fixated on the Sicilian rather than American character of the Mafia and described it in familiar terms as "a diabolical criminal philosophy, offering its adherents domain over crime in return for their souls." The Mafia, the report continued, took control of the drug trade sometime in the 1950s and "acquired its monopoly of this racket through a long, deadly, but unpublicized [effort] launched as far back in the past as the late 19th Century." In other words, the FBI endorsed the well-established FBN view that the Mafia was an alien parasite rather than an internal development, symptomatic of American socioeconomic trends.[68]

One additional legacy of the Kefauver hearings was the continued collaboration between the FBN and subsequent congressional investigations. Bureau agents played a key role in inquiries led by Senator Price Daniel (D-TX) in 1955, which repudiated attempts to medicalize the drug problem and produced the 1956 Narcotic Control Act. Senior FBN agents partnered with Robert Kennedy to investigate labor rackets under the leadership of Senator John McClellan (D-AR) in 1958, hearings that laid the groundwork for the formulation of the RICO laws and Kennedy's best-selling book on labor racketeering, *The Enemy Within* (1960), and, when reconstituted in the early 1960s, prominently featured Mafia snitch Joseph Valachi.[69] Beyond influencing legislative goals, the links forged during all of these congressional efforts deepened the connection between the FBN and key policymakers—relationships that Anslinger exploited to protect the FBN and ensure that no one ever lost sight of the dangers posed by the dope menace.

The King Is Dead

Lucky Luciano remained a central FBN antagonist for the rest of the 1950s and a focal point around which Bureau officials shaped the dangers of the dope menace. Blaming distant communist China for supplying the Pacific drug trade was useful in geopolitical situations, but the Mafia presented a danger that was both here and abroad, and Luciano was always a top target for the agents of District 17. Ironically, the former mob boss even managed to outlast Siragusa when the agent returned from Italy to take a headquarters job in 1958.

In fact, Siragusa never again got as close to Luciano as he did in the spring of 1951. The following year, the Bureau calculated that, between 1948 and 1951, 600 kilos of heroin were diverted from legal sources in Italy and smuggled to the United States. A Schiapparelli chemist named Carlo Migliardi was suspected of diverting 423 of those 600 kilos, mostly to middlemen like Calascibetta and RAMSA. Yet even as Siragusa uncovered rival organizations, he insisted that Luciano was behind it all. A significant component of this traffic went through an organization run by Frank Coppola, described in Siragusa's memoir as "an arch competitor of Luciano." That investigation was spun into another police adventure story as the "Green Trunk Case" and used to pressure the Italian government to end the legal manufacture of heroin. But in public, the FBN continued to insist that Luciano was the principal figure behind the Mafia's "virtual monopoly" over the Atlantic heroin trade.[70]

Later agents of the Bureau complained that the focus on Luciano was a product of bureaucratic politics rather than his actual stature. Siragusa "played up to the Old Man," Howard Chappell griped to journalist Douglas Valentine many years later, and "made a career out of writing memos about Lucky." Tom Tripodi, a veteran of the FBN and CIA, similarly came to dispute many of the qualities once attributed to the Mafia. "As powerful as the international Mafia is," he wrote, "it is still not nearly as organized or as big as it has been portrayed. There is no single man sitting in Palermo wearing a black fedora and pulling strings that trigger an assassination on the south side of Chicago." Siragusa, too, later repudiated many of the same myths he helped to create. "The theory of a single Mr. Big is obsolete," he said in a 1975 interview. "There's collective leadership now. . . . No Don Corleones."[71]

Discrediting rumors of Luciano's war aid, meanwhile, remained a top priority that left Tom Dewey increasingly in the line of fire. While a steady drumbeat of officials from the navy and OSS continued to deny that Luciano contributed anything of substance, the FBN surfaced rumors that Luciano made payoffs to Haffenden, Dewey, and Republican party officials in a 1952 magazine article by Michael Stern. The target, however, was always Luciano; smearing Dewey by undermining the rationale for Luciano's pardon was simply collateral damage. Bureau agents also suggested that the compulsory prostitution charges upon which Luciano was convicted were rather thin and that Dewey wanted the gangster out of the country before, George White confided to a friend, "suborned witnesses threatened to blow the whistle"—a charge repeated in Feder and Joesten's *The Luciano Story* (1954).[72]

The exact circumstances of Luciano's pardon remain murky and controversial but ultimately have more to do with Dewey than Luciano. In many ways, Dewey was an innocent bystander. The plan to use Luciano to secure the mob's cooperation came from the partnership between Haffenden at ONI and Socks Lanza at the Manhattan waterfront. After the war, the whole thing got dumped in Dewey's lap when Luciano came up for parole with a deportation order already in his file alongside Haffenden's note citing unspecified contributions to the war. In *American Mafia* (2004), Thomas Reppetto summarizes, "Whatever the explanation, by 1946 Dewey had transformed himself from racket buster to politician, and in that capacity his interests were better served by a free Luciano 3,000 miles away than one carrying on a high-powered campaign to obtain release from a New York State prison cell."[73]

Dewey was also not without resources of his own. In 1954 he authorized New York State commissioner of investigation William B. Herlands to lead a secret inquiry into the whole mess. Herlands discovered that the results of Operation Underworld were ambiguous at best; it appears the Mafia did help secure the Manhattan waterfront and prevented one potentially damaging labor strike but contributed little to the invasion of Sicily. That should have vindicated Dewey, but all of this remained unknown to the public because the U.S. Navy demanded total secrecy in exchange for cooperation. As Dewey himself explained, "Since the Navy allowed the officers to testify only with the expressed wish that the report not be made public, I never released it." As a result, Herlands's inquiry was kept under wraps until 1977, when Dewey's estate authorized the publication of *The Luciano Project: The Secret Wartime Collaboration of the Mafia & the U.S. Navy,* by Rodney Campbell.[74]

In the meantime, the FBN still had a kingpin to chase. The closest the Bureau ever got to Luciano was an periodic deep-cover operation featuring FBN agent Sal Vizzini as the morally compromised U.S. Air Force major Mike Cerra. For the better part of three years, from 1959 to 1962, Vizzini shuttled between Istanbul, where he led FBN efforts in Turkey, and Naples, where he worked undercover to gain Luciano's confidence during the final years of the gangster's life. The Bureau spent countless hours and resources trying to uncover Luciano's authority. Vizzini claimed that Luciano's "tentacles were long and his influence powerful" but failed to turn up any hard evidence of his criminal associations or activities. The best Vizzini was able to do in the three years he spent in and out of Luciano's company was to obtain some marked U.S. currency used by agents in New York for an undercover buy, indicating that Luciano still received occasional tribute from the American Mafia. "The king might be in exile," Vizzini concluded. "But it was now absolutely clear that the king wasn't dead."[75]

Not yet anyway. The Bureau lost its archnemesis on January 26, 1962, when Luciano suffered a fatal heart attack in the Naples airport. Lucky died in the arms of a would-be movie producer named Martin Gosch, who was developing a book or film based on the mobster's life. Although American Mafia chieftains quietly opposed the endeavor, Gosch's account emerged as the error-filled *The Last Testament of Lucky Luciano* (1975). An FBI memo sent to J. Edgar Hoover a few months later indicated that narcotics agents were still working on Luciano's ties to the drug traffic, "but all indications are that the case will be closed with no startling developments."[76] Vizzini's three-year investigation, the Bureau's most successful and sustained undercover operation against Luciano, ultimately revealed little. Luciano took most—but not all—of his secrets to the grave.

Constructing a Kingpin

Comparing the image of Luciano created by the FBN to the real one is a difficult task, and there's little certainty in the history of crime. If Lucky ever did attain a status approximating that of a kingpin, it was during the five-year span between the creation of the Commission and his 1936 conviction—a time when the FBN was more interested in Chinese and Jewish gangs than the Mafia. After Luciano's pardon and exile, the Bureau insisted that he was the "lord" of the Atlantic heroin trade—but that was well after his reign was over. As his brief sojourn in Cuba demonstrated, Lucky's notoriety made him a liability to any kind of criminal endeavor. Even during Siragusa's investigations in Italy, there were hints that Luciano's drug lord status was, at best, an overstatement. He remained a respected figure in the American Mafia and received tribute during his forced retirement. But Lucky was no drug baron, possessed little real influence, and was avoided by Italian gangsters.[77] His life in Naples was comfortable but hardly affluent, and it was a big step down from his days in the Waldorf Astoria. At most, Luciano functioned as an organizer or facilitator. He remained a person who, for a cut, could make introductions and put people together in a room—an interpretation that comes through between the lines of many FBN reports, even as the agents typed platitudes about Lucky the Kingpin.

So was the Bureau acting out of ignorance or deception? There are few satisfactory answers. Some observers point to cynical motivations, arguing that Luciano was a prop used to sustain ever-higher law enforcement budgets or a clever diversion to protect an ongoing alliance between U.S. intelligence and organized crime.[78] There's not a great deal of evidence to support either conclusion, but public depictions of Luciano's trafficking activities definitely helped justify the expansion of U.S. power at home and abroad. The earnestness apparent in FBN field dispatches suggests that Anslinger and his loyal drug warriors were falling into a trap of their own design. In short, the Bureau already thought Luciano was a drug lord; it just needed proof—proof that was always tantalizingly out of reach.

Luciano, of course, was not the first or the last of his kind. Throughout the long history of American drug wars—a framework that can reasonably be pushed into Prohibition—a succession of drug lords and kingpins, from Arnold Rothstein, Al Capone, Eli Eliopoulos, Lepke Buchalter, and Lucky Luciano all the way through to Khun Sa, Pablo Escobar, and Joaquín "El Chapo" Guzmán, have been identified by U.S. law enforcement and neutralized. Yet the fall of the "beer barons" did nothing to stop the flow of alcohol during Prohibition, and the capture, death, or isolation of various drug lords has done little to impede the flow of drugs. Kingpin imagery actually risks making law enforcement look worse: if it's as simple as taking out one guy (inevitably, it is a he), why is he still walking the earth? Since this tendency toward constructing kingpins appears ineffective yet supersedes any one person, agency, or era, it's worth asking: why does it persist?

Kingpins do, of course, exist, rooted in both historical fact and the material realities of the criminal underworld. But the pronounced tendency to overstate their power and influence is revealing. Ultimately, kingpin imagery is the product of hidden assumptions and the need for simplicity. A drug lord renders all the complexities of the drug trade into an easily rendered picture that reinforces the basic notion that drugs are a problem of supply and not the more complicated and elusive problem of demand. This imagery is cyclical, reinforcing the same assumptions that create it. Kingpins demand little self-reflection, only an enemy to destroy. In the context of Luciano, the American public had little inclination to acknowledge the complexities of licit diversion, the shifting terrain of the drug traffic, or their own thirst for narcotics at a time when the country was supposed to be the leader of the free world. But a drug-dealing monopoly run by a notorious gangster complemented public expectations and reinforced ethnic and class prejudice. Kingpin imagery is also incredibly malleable, simultaneously rendering the mysteries of the criminal underworld tangible (by singling out one mortal individual) and intangible (by evoking complex conspiracies). This tension between specificity and ambiguity is useful—and, more important, persuasive—in a bureaucratic context.

Above all, kingpins serve to identify enemies and reinforce a certain way of thinking about the world. For the FBN, Luciano put an instantly recognizable face on the nascent drug war; he helped the Bureau draw the lines. Though the FBN never caught him (in some ways, he was more useful as a free man), Anslinger and company were quite pleased with the effect of their portrayal. When *Brotherhood of Evil* was published in 1959, glorifying a decade of foreign drug enforcement and the FBN's war on the Mafia, Sondern practically crowed, "The Boys aren't going to like this a bit. It will, I think, be the biggest publicity blast that ever hit them." Comparisons between the Mafia, the drug traffic, and the threat of international communism were often explicit and drew the FBN into the growing realm of national security. One of the most frequent claims about the Mafia was that it represented a "government within a government," a framework adopted by the Kefauver Committee and many others. Popular writers like Lait and Mortimer echoed the Bureau in describing the Mafia as both a "well-organized and semi-sovereign state" and "an international conspiracy, as potent as that other international conspiracy, Communism." And finally, there was Anslinger's warning that drugs could serve as a "political weapon" and allow the communists and Mafia to "make narcotics a new 'sixth' column to weaken and destroy selected targets in the drive for world domination."[79] Such a threat demanded the existence of a police agency capable of following organized crime into the underworld and around the globe.

Many of these claims are a product of their time and place, but the Bureau's pursuit of Luciano—the manner in which it constructed a kingpin—had a determinative influence on the agency itself and, ultimately, on the future of American drug wars. The focus on kingpins remains an obvious component of modern drug control and is symptomatic of the stubborn adherence to supply-side solutions: government attention remains fixed on traffickers and producers, while the conditions leading to drug abuse are mostly ignored. In its day, the Bureau spent considerable time and energy managing public perceptions of Luciano specifically and the drug war more broadly, and that, in turn, shaped actual counternarcotic operations. The problem of licit diversion in Italy was significant in the early 1950s, but it paled in comparison to the volume of drugs moving through the Turkey-Marseilles–New York pipeline later dubbed the "French Connection," and as early as 1948 the agents knew that Turkey was the real source of supply in the region. Kingpin politics, in other words, played a greater role in determining where the Bureau focused its initial efforts abroad than did actual counternarcotics strategy. This, too, remains an important legacy of the early drug war, as domestic politics and a certain cultural stubbornness continue to impede effective treatment of America's drug problem.

CHAPTER 6

THE DRUG WAR GOES ABROAD

It is necessary for one of us to direct operations, give orders,
see that things get done.
—CHARLES SIRAGUSA (1950)

One might well state that the Lebanese Government is
in the narcotic business.
—PAUL KNIGHT (1954)

There were times when Charles Siragusa rued the life of an undercover agent, like in September 1950, when he got stuck working a dead-end case in Athens. A rising star at the FBN, Siragusa was in Europe with the understanding that if he could make a few cases abroad—ideally one involving Lucky Luciano—he would get his own office in the region. But for now the agent was going nowhere fast. Posing as "Cal Salerno," a New York gangster in need of a European heroin connection, Siragusa spent the last days of summer on a bender with Anastasio Voutsinas, an Athens jeweler reputed to be one of the biggest traffickers in the city. For five days in a row, the two met for idle chitchat over endless glasses of whiskey and brandy. "I think he plied me with liquor in an effort to assure himself that I was o.k.," the agent surmised. Voutsinas, he noted, was the "very personification of geniality" but got evasive whenever drugs came up. "We have drank countless cognacs together and swapped numerous obscene stories. He appears to completely trust me, but he will not sell me heroin," Siragusa complained in a report to Anslinger, likely through the fog of a hangover. Finally cutting his losses, Siragusa decamped for Beirut, promising to keep in touch with Voutsinas and send some penicillin and "obscene photographs."[1]

Siragusa's stop in Greece was part of a series of tours through what would soon be known within the Bureau as District 17: a region encompassing Europe, the Middle East, and North Africa. The establishment of District 17 was a critical—though largely unacknowledged—milestone, not just for the Bureau but also in the wider history of American drug wars. The United States had long supported a counternarcotics policy of source control, but District 17 represented the dawn of a new era in which the FBN tried to directly implement U.S. policy solutions abroad instead of relying on diplomacy or moral suasion. This was the first time that American police agents were stationed on foreign soil in an operational capacity. From that moment on, September 1951, an American drug enforcement presence has continued to expand throughout the world in an effort to fight the drug problem "at the source." As of this writing, the Drug Enforcement Administration maintains ninety foreign offices in sixty-nine countries.[2] The history of those outposts—and of America's global drug war—starts with Charles Siragusa and District 17.

Due partly to neglect and partly to the only recent declassification of many FBN records, the story of District 17 remains largely untold until now.[3] But it's an important chapter in the larger history of U.S. foreign relations and offers fresh insights into the evolution of America's role in the world. Law enforcement is an inherently sovereign priority, and the arrival of U.S. agents was a serious political challenge to host nations, requiring diplomatic finesse and a light touch. The agents, Siragusa noted, functioned like the "roving ambassadors of the Federal Bureau of Narcotics."[4] They were not always effective, but their successes and failures offer a close look at the point where the rubber of American expectations met the road of global realities.

Source control and foreign enforcement became a major component of the larger effort to project American influence and bring foreign nations—particularly troublesome "producer" or "transit" nations—into line behind U.S. policy goals. With their frequent invocation of ostensibly universal values like freedom, liberty, and security, American policymakers assumed their goals, including defeat of the dope menace, represented the collective aspirations of the whole world. The gradual iteration of America's global drug war reflected widespread belief in the necessity of a Pax Americana and the importance of global leadership. As the Commissioner himself argued in 1946, "The United States will always have to lead—if for no other reason than self-protection."[5]

The history of District 17, however, offers a record of mixed success. Within the United States, the FBN consolidated support for a punitive, quasi-paramilitary, and transnational approach to the drug problem. Abroad, the Bureau facilitated greater cooperation between police agencies and developed a better (though still fuzzy) picture of the global drug trade. The presence of narcotic agents was challenged by local authorities more often than not, but—despite frequent political conflicts and international turf battles—the Bureau steadily extended the reach of its operations, opening satellite offices throughout District 17 and then establishing new FBN districts in Latin America (District 18) and the Far East (District 16). The actual impact of these offices on the drug trade is debatable, but the fact that they remain—many of them to this day—reveals the undeniable impact the Bureau had on U.S. foreign policy. The Bureau achieved its goal of making source control an international norm, even if it failed to stop the traffic at its source.

The Road Ahead: Beirut, 1950

On the afternoon of September 8, 1950, Agent Siragusa rushed to keep an appointment at the American Embassy in Beirut—a city that perfectly illustrated the legion of challenges facing the early drug war. It had been a frustrating summer and things were finally starting to look up for the itinerant agent, but as Siragusa left the dim confines of the Victory Bar, a waterfront dive frequented by sailors and roustabouts from a nearby pipeline, all he could think about was his tender stomach.

His plan had been a simple one: acting on intel in FBN files, Siragusa was to approach proprietor Artin Guedikian, get a quote on six kilos of opium, and then turn him over to local authorities upon delivery. Guedikian was a Fagin-like character who lorded over a small band of knife-fighting street urchins, adolescent pimps, and teenage pickpockets, and his garrulous boasting seemed to confirm his connections in the Beirut underworld. He knew which Customs and police officials to grease with a little bribe money (*baksheesh* in the local idiom), and, for the right price, he could acquire all kinds of drugs: hashish, opium, heroin—pick your poison.

When approached the previous night, Guedikian was eager to do business and asked Siragusa to return the following afternoon. Intent on wooing his prospective buyer, Guedikian insisted on making a big lunch of steak, potatoes, and eggs. Siragusa arrived to the horrific scene of Guedikian busily preparing this feast on a small gasoline stove located in a sink right next to a "wall urinal which was in constant use" by his adolescent minions. Guedikian exhibited "great pride" in the meal, so Siragusa choked back his bile and sat at an "equally filthy table to dine," where they were joined by a (presumably crooked) police captain in civilian clothes. The agent dutifully picked at his food and managed to get his quote: seventy U.S. dollars per kilo of raw opium or fifteen hundred for heroin. But when Siragusa finally typed up the details of his meeting, he was morose. "I am merely describing these irrelevant details," he wrote, "to illustrate the hardships I am suffering for the sake of duty. Between the extremely unsanitary food I am eating and the bad liquor I am consuming, I will undoubtedly contract our occupational disease—ulcers."[6]

Tummy ache aside, this was progress and not a moment too soon. The Bureau's ambition to build an aggressive foreign enforcement program was at a delicate stage. Before making a bid for a permanent office, the Bureau had to demonstrate that source control—and FBN agents operating on foreign soil—could actually work. So far they had little to show. George White's 1948 busts in Istanbul, Marseille, and Rome had a negligible impact on the international traffic. Garland Williams spent much of his brief 1949 diplomatic tour bullying police officials throughout the region—which may or may not have helped the FBN cause. Agent Benny Pocoroba, a veteran undercover, had been in theater for six months, but his investigations of Mafia trafficking in Trieste and Italy were excruciatingly fruitless.

Siragusa, too, was off to an inauspicious start, despite finding drugs and drug traffickers everywhere he looked. Arriving in target-rich Istanbul in late July, Siragusa received a decidedly tepid reception from Turkish officials, who were sharply resistant to the idea of another FBN agent running amok in their city. Under pressure from the State Department, the Turks reluctantly agreed to clear Siragusa, provided he adhere to strict guidelines—the most important being that he keep his presence "completely secret" and do nothing without the supervision of Turkish police. Kemal Aygun, the chief of police in Istanbul, kept a close eye on Siragusa and feigned cooperation while quietly thwarting all of the agent's endeavors.[7] The next stop was Athens, where Siragusa was stymied by the hard-drinking but wily Anastasio Voutsinas. Determined to snap his streak of bad luck, Siragusa set his sights on Beirut and Artin Guedikian.

But he was in for another rude awakening at the embassy. Shortly after Siragusa's lunch meeting at the Victory Bar, U.S. diplomats Robert Stanger and Paul Tenney sat the queasy agent down for a crash course on Lebanese politics. *Under no circumstances,* they stressed, was he to arrest a Lebanese national—including Guedikian. The Lebanese government, they explained, had no love for Uncle Sam. U.S. recognition of Israel, cavalier treatment of other Arab states, and refusal to lend aid under the Marshall Plan had all created serious resentment, and the Lebanese would look with "extreme disfavor upon any act covert or overt" by the FBN. Any attempt to develop a case, the diplomats warned, was more likely to end with a dead agent and Lebanon in the Soviet orbit. Tenney warned Siragusa to keep his cover intact at all costs—or he might "conveniently disappear."[8] Though the diplomats didn't frame it in quite these terms, it was clear that Lebanon, an independent nation for going on seven years, would insist on its sovereign rights and actively resist any U.S. claim on extraterritorial powers.

Making matters worse, the diplomats continued, Beirut's thriving drug trade was under the protection of top government officials. A prominent legislator named Sabri Bey Hamede, for example, was head of Lebanon's unicameral parliament and "the richest and biggest landowner in the Bekaa district," a major center of hashish production. Hamede occasionally ordered showy suppression campaigns but usually only destroyed the crops of his rivals. Heroin was a minor problem, the diplomats noted, but hashish, a highly concentrated form of marijuana resin, was woven into the very fabric of the Lebanese economy. Stanger and Tenney estimated the government drew at least 15 percent of its total revenue from the hash trade. In *The Lebanese Connection: Corruption, Civil War, and the International Drug Traffic* (2012), Jonathan Marshall describes hashish as the "petroleum of Lebanon" and one of the country's most lucrative exports, rivaling silk, olive oil, and tobacco. In sum, there were deep structural components to the regional traffic, which shaped long-standing political, economic, and social relationships in Lebanon.[9]

The historical conditions leading to drug use and an active black market were not totally lost on the agents. In Beirut Siragusa reported on a permissive drug culture and observed that a sharp class divide created both a "fertile ground for breeding Communism" and an incentive to participate in the lucrative drug traffic. Rather than a reflection of differing cultural perspectives and economic realities, however, the agents usually interpreted tolerance for drugs or the involvement of local power brokers like Hamede as a sign of the venality of foreigners.[10] This cultural bias led the agents to overlook signs of political corruption within the American system and bred an attitude dismissive of long-term social and political trends.

Despite the admonition to make no arrests, Siragusa stuck around to see what else he could learn and rejoined Artin Guedikian for a night on the town. The gregarious barkeep took the agent to a restaurant owned by a friend on the outskirts of Beirut, where the three men retired to a scenic balcony to discuss the nightlife and Guedikian proceeded to roll two large hash cigarettes. Heeding Tenney's warning to maintain his cover, Siragusa reported, "I was compelled to take a few 'drags' but put on a good show." Siragusa pocketed the remainder of his reefer and told Guedikian he would keep it as a sample—which was true, but Guedikian probably never imagined it was destined for FBN labs. Though he chafed at the inability to make arrests, Siragusa readily agreed to accompany the amiable Guedikian on a road trip into the Bekaa Valley, where they saw the marijuana fields up close and visited another friend who was sitting on a massive stash of opium and hashish. Along the way, they encountered a marijuana farmer who posed for photographs with the duo while Guedikian and Siragusa took turns brandishing a pistol.[11]

The agent's time in Beirut revealed a drug scene that was "wide open." As was often the case, Siragusa railed against the diplomatic and political constraints that prevented him from making cases. "I am powerless," he complained, for neither the first nor the last time. "The unbelievable situation here enables me to understand what tremendous quantities of narcotic drugs and hasheesh reach our shores, and there is very little we can do to stop it!"[12] Most of the hash went to Egypt and not the States, but he was right about the absence of control.

Fortunately for the FBN, Siragusa's luck improved in Italy and Trieste, where the discovery of massive pharma diversions provided a much-needed opening for the Bureau. His initial foray into Beirut, however, indicated that an array of diplomatic, political, social, cultural, and economic obstacles stood before the nascent American drug war.

Headquarters: Rome

The years immediately following World War II were a time of general belt-tightening, so the Bureau initially faced an uphill battle in returning to its prewar budget and lacked the resources to take on the role of global drug cop. Anslinger, however, scored an important strategic victory when his old friend Charles Dyar was tapped to set up a drug control regime in occupied Germany, America's former rival in the commercial drug industry. In March 1947, just as Luciano was departing Cuba, the two men discussed the need for an FBN presence in Europe but worried about congressional foot-dragging. Watching the House slash the Treasury budget, Anslinger feared the worst. "Our funds are so low that we couldn't even send an agent across the border from El Paso unless he walks," he wrote Dyar. "To send someone to Paris . . . would just about take our whole appropriation." Fortunately, Anslinger had influential allies and credited advocates like Helen Moorhead, a drug control expert at the Foreign Policy Association, and Representative Gordon Canfield (R-NY) with helping to secure the necessary funds.[13]

Siragusa's travels throughout the Middle East and Mediterranean—together with those of George White and Garland Williams before him—represented the FBN's first sense at what it meant to fight the drug war "at the source." Wherever they traveled, the agents found an assortment of drugs ready for consumption and smuggling. Gradually, they developed a picture of the Atlantic heroin trade: poppy crops raised in the hinterlands of Turkey and Iran were processed into raw opium by local brokers; then sold to larger traffickers for refinement in clandestine labs located around trade centers like Istanbul, Milan, and Marseille; and were finally shipped as crude heroin to North America via any number of smuggling routes believed to be under complete Mafia control. By the late 1960s, this supply line was known as the "French Connection," but it was only loosely organized in the 1950s. The agents consistently exaggerated Luciano's role in the system, but Anslinger felt the well-publicized busts in Italy had demonstrated the value of a preventive and outreaching enforcement posture.[14] In order to get District 17 up and running, however, the Bureau needed to put down roots and establish a regional headquarters—a process that revealed a great deal about the complicated politics of international drug control.

Nearly every city the agents visited seemed ripe for an FBN office. Given the importance of Persian and Turkish poppy, White and Williams favored a Middle Eastern focus. In Tehran White found that opium dens were "about as difficult to locate as New York speakeasies during prohibition" and reported to Anslinger, "Situation here requires full time Bureau representative for proper treatment." Either Tehran or Istanbul, he wrote, would make an ideal headquarters.[15] During his brief visit in 1949, Williams, too, was struck by the scene in the Iranian capital. He estimated the city was home to around 160,000 of Iran's estimated 1 million addicts and serviced by 250 to 500 opium dens. Addiction lacked any stigma or social stratification, and he quipped to White that proof of drug use in Tehran was "like getting evidence that they are selling rubbers in New York." As in the United States, Williams associated drug use with deviance and claimed the dens were patronized by homosexuals, "child prostitutes," and even infants who became addicted "at their mother's breasts." Reports of smuggling to and from Iraq, Syria, Afghanistan, and Turkey indicated that Iranian opium contributed to the regional traffic, and Williams thought the "weakness" of the shah and the central government was a contributing factor. Moreover, just as Siragusa would discover in Beirut, the Iranian poppy industry was protected by large landowners, including the royal Pahlavi family.[16]

In typical fashion, Williams took all of this as proof of the need for American leadership—specifically, his own. The first step, he wrote, was to appoint "an informed and energetic person" to advise the Iranian government. The 1953 CIA-engineered coup drew Iran firmly into the American orbit, and, two years later, the shah banned the recreational use and production of opium. From 1957 to 1961, Williams actually did serve as a State Department police adviser to the Iranian government and ensured its drug control system met U.S. expectations. His effectiveness as an international police adviser, however, was limited by his often imperious manner. "Williams smacked of official Washington," Anslinger observed, "and the police over there, like their governments, took a dim view of Washington venturing into places where it was not only unwelcome but not overtly tolerated either."[17]

The rise of the postwar heroin trade was due primarily to the recovery of the global economy, but the Bureau tended to scapegoat foreign governments for lax control over a deadly commodity. When he encountered a display featuring opium production at the Turkish Ministry of Commerce, Williams lectured his hosts that it was "a shameful thing" to promote "a drug that the world considered a menace" and "terrible to profit from the destruction of others"—never mind that much of Turkey's crop went to legal sources. After getting a close look at the situation in the region, Williams painted a dire picture: "Those governments are so unreliable and their motives are so contrary to ours, that they will never regulate themselves," he wrote. "Now that the Middle East is kicking over the last of Anglo-Saxon control, I expect the flood gates will be open wider than ever before."[18]

Indeed, governments throughout Europe and the Middle East were quite resistant to what they saw as an unwelcome intrusion into a purely domestic concern. White's bust in Turkey resulted in spectacular press for the Bureau but hindered relations with the Turks for years. French officials showed zero patience for American meddling, and Siragusa's experience in Beirut indicated that cooperation would not soon be forthcoming from the Lebanese either. The only places the Bureau could count on total cooperation were in occupied territories like Trieste, West Germany, and Japan. Even in Italy, where the FBN enjoyed the most tangible success during these early years, Bureau agents saw little sustained interest in drug enforcement.

Yet after defeat in World War II, Italy was also under unique pressures that the FBN was eager to exploit. While the Bureau's initial efforts in the Middle East were greeted with muted but active resistance, all of the noise about Luciano, Williams observed, had lit "a fire under the Italian police" at a time when the country was eager to "reestablish herself in the community of Nations." The discovery of pharmaceutical diversions and lax controls, meanwhile, demonstrated to Siragusa that the Bureau needed a "permanent base" in the region. "It is necessary for one of us to direct operations, give orders, see that things get done," he argued. Then winding down his service with the Kefauver Committee, Agent White, too, recognized that political developments augured a European focus. The Turks, he observed, are "fiercely nationalistic and can not be kicked around in the same manner we treat the conquered Italians."[19]

Seizing the opportunity presented by Luciano and the pharma diversions, the Bureau turned the screws on the Italian government throughout 1950 and 1951. At the United Nations, Anslinger pointed out huge disparities in the licit narcotic production estimates provided by Italy and its neighbors. In country, Siragusa hounded health and police officials, who, he reported, were shaken by the Schiapparelli scandal and eager to correct their reputations. After a few good busts and exposure to FBN methods, Siragusa thought the Italian police were becoming "increasingly narcotic conscious," and "circumstances here auger well for our type of vigorous enforcement." Siragusa's dramatic testimony before the Kefauver hearings was the final coup de grâce and convinced U.S. policymakers that Italian negligence and foreign criminals were to blame for the resurgence of the American drug problem. The committee's final report, released in August 1951, depicted Italian heroin going straight "from the back door of the factory in Italy to addicts' blood" in New York.[20]

When Siragusa returned to Italy after his victory lap with the Kefauver Committee, it was as the newly promoted supervisor of District 17.[21] There was no going back to a purely domestic drug war.

Siragusa briefly considered locating the FBN office in Milan, where much of the Italian pharmaceutical industry was based, but practical considerations favored Rome. The Italian capital was a convenient travel hub, easing logistics for investigations scattered throughout the region. The Bureau could use State Department facilities at the embassy, and the heads of the various national police services were all nearby. Italy also had one further advantage: despite lax controls, there was relatively little drug use compared to Turkey, Iran, or Lebanon. Italy was primarily a "transit" rather than a "producer" or "consumer" nation. To demonstrate progress, all the Bureau had to do was plug the leaks from the legal industry and disrupt the Mafia trafficking networks, a simple task compared to the structural changes necessary to challenge the deeply entrenched poppy agriculture and broad cultural and economic trends that produced drug use in Middle Eastern cities.[22]

Rather conspicuously missing from this account, of course, are the Italians. FBN records include substantial correspondence with various Italian officials, but the files are quiet on the terms of the FBN presence or any Italian debate on the matter, as are U.S. State Department records. Italian officials were, however, definitely consulted, and Siragusa was issued new credentials by the Italian government on his return.[23]

Giuseppe Dosi, the Italian representative to Interpol, played a key role. Every agent who encountered Dosi considered him, to put it mildly, an unpredictable eccentric and threat to the operational security of any investigation. Working around his office was a delicate dance that caused frequent complaints. Anslinger preached patience and reminded Siragusa that "it was his acquiescence which originally allowed us to place you in Italy." Dosi was part of the deal, and Anslinger warned the agents not to "antagonize" him. "Dosi may be irrational and unpredictable," the Commissioner lectured, but "if his Interpol connections can help keep from you the onus of a 'meddling Yankee' that is worth some special effort on your part." A few years later, Treasury official Malachi Harney briefed Ambassador Clare Booth Luce as she prepared to take up her duties in Italy. He explained that stationing American police on foreign soil was "a delicate matter," but the FBN had utilized "UN connections and prestige, treaty background," and "some protective coloration" from Interpol to open the Rome office.[24]

Although the Italian government outwardly welcomed the Bureau, there was serious resentment about Italy's portrayal as a platform for drug smuggling. The frequent accusations regarding Luciano were particularly irritating and eventually compelled the Italian Embassy in Washington to politely ask the FBN to put or up shut up. Officials from the Italian Public Health Commission, responsible for regulating the legal trade, were often combative with the agents; one even publicly suggested the Italian drug trade was run by American communists rather than the Mafia. Police officials, meanwhile, bristled at the FBN claim that "deportee gangsters" controlled the drug trade and complained that Italy was being treated like an American "penal colony."[25]

Part of FBN strategy revolved around shaming other countries into accepting an office or increasing their own control efforts. Italy was more vulnerable to this kind of pressure than most, but there was a danger in going too far. The style of language used to discuss drugs was so laden with moral argument that is was difficult to avoid giving offense. In time, Siragusa became more attuned to the requisite balancing act and, shortly after taking up his official duties in District 17, reported to Anslinger, "I have been very careful not to infer that all of my activities are restricted to Italy—that I am sort of a watch-dog. . . . I do not wish to offend the Italians."[26] Privately, the agents continued to grumble about the failures of Italy and other foreign governments, but, in a pattern repeated in each country into which it expanded, the Bureau abruptly switched from condemnation to praise once it established a formal presence.

"Don't Wear Spats"

District 17 swiftly became a central focus of FBN operations, but it had humble origins. For the first few years, Siragusa was something of a bureaucratic nomad. Shuffled between different embassy properties, he later recalled the period as one when the office was "headquartered mostly in my briefcase." *Brotherhood of Evil*—a book that was half paean to District 17—romanticized a shoestring operation: Siragusa "wrote his meticulous reports on a battered old portable, kept his individual records in shoeboxes, and caused one important arrest after another with the seizure of enormous quantities of narcotics before they reached the American market."[27]

The details of those cases are lost unless they were set aside as material for true-crime stories, but it's clear from extant FBN records that Siragusa was a busy man. In October 1951, he was joined by Hank Manfredi, the army CID agent who worked on the Luciano investigations. After transferring to the FBN, Manfredi split his time between Rome and Trieste and became one of the most valued agents of District 17—so much so that his services were occasionally commandeered by the CIA and Secret Service. The FBN's modest budget meant there were usually only three or four agents stationed in District 17, plus a few clerks, and Siragusa frequently complained, "We have an enormous amount of work." The Bureau rotated up-and-coming agents through the district for seasoning—Agents Jack Cusack and Mike Picini both served early tours and later returned as supervisors—but the office was chronically understaffed and often swamped by the demands of undercover work, administrative hurdles, and a general lack of hard intelligence about the regional traffic.[28]

Much of the district's early success was due to Siragusa, who served as supervisor from September 1951 to July 1958. The job was a tough one, and most of its challenges revolved around the unique nature of the assignment. Siragusa characterized the agents of District 17 as "roving ambassadors," but they weren't quite diplomats, and Anslinger explicitly warned him, "Don't try to wear spats." They were American cops a long way from home with a vaguely defined authority, a deeply ambiguous position, and a wildly ambitious agenda. "My present 'neither fish nor fowl' status has had its disadvantages," Siragusa remarked after a few years. Countless political and bureaucratic sensitivities compounded the challenges of developing and running criminal investigations in foreign lands, turning the job into a constant high-wire act. Anslinger, however, had great expectations and rare affection for Siragusa and hoped to groom him as a successor. "You are on this job because you have been able to balance intelligence and aggressiveness with discretion," he wrote. The balance between cop and diplomat was a tricky one, but Siragusa promised to avoid "the social whirl."[29]

One of the biggest challenges for the agents was tempering their jingoistic attitudes and frustration with local police. Siragusa was prone to impolitic statements like "It is necessary for one of us to direct operations, give orders, see that things get done." In Turkey Siragusa found the quality of local authorities decidedly lacking and commented, "I simply can't appreciate or sympathize with their evasive and ambiguous language, their double talking, double dealing, etc." Such language reflected a pervasive mind-set that did little to ease tensions over an already sensitive issue, even when confined to internal reports. "In deference to the fact that we are guests in a foreign country," one Bureau official dryly remarked, "statements indicating that you are taking charge of foreign police should be avoided." Siragusa's élan was one of his virtues as a narcotic agent, but his headstrong attitude caused periodic trouble in a delicate position. Malachi Harney, then supervising all Treasury law enforcement, warned, "Just one incident might upset an applecart."[30]

The ambiguity of the FBN's status also complicated life for U.S. Embassy officials, and the agents ran a constant risk of wearing out their welcome. Upon his return to Rome in September 1951, Siragusa was fortunate to share the voyage with the new resident minister of the Rome embassy, who agreed to provide him with office space. The agents also received valuable cooperation from U.S. military officers and diplomatic security officers in Rome and elsewhere, who invariably stressed discretion. One security officer warned Siragusa not to let FBN brass circulate documents sent via cable, or the State Department "will raise hell for possible compromise of secret codes." Anslinger and other HQ officials took the issue to heart and were diligent with adulatory thank-you letters and other gestures of gratitude.[31] As long as it was informal and off the books, most U.S. government personnel were willing to assist the Bureau in its mission of preventing dangerous drugs from reaching American shores.

In the summer of 1955, Siragusa tried to resolve some of the ambiguity by requesting formal diplomatic status. He had been careful to heed Anslinger's advice: "I have yet to wear 'spats' nor do I think I ever will," he explained, but diplomatic status would add leverage to his dealings with the Rome embassy, other diplomatic outposts, and foreign police. The State Department flatly refused the idea, no doubt fearful of what consequences might follow a U.S. diplomat running around apprehending foreign nationals. Anslinger agreed, writing, "You are extremely fortunate to be in Rome in your present status which we feel is very generous of the Italian Government. . . . [A] similar assignment could not be accomplished in most other countries."[32]

By necessity the agents of District 17 were to be in but not of the world of European diplomacy. When Siragusa began to circulate business cards advertising the FBN office in "Roma" a few years later, Anslinger insisted he switch to an English spelling to distinguish the American agents from their European counterparts.[33] Like it or not, however, diplomacy remained a critical component of District 17's work and an inevitable counterweight to operational concerns.

Ironically, the agents' biggest competitors were not a foreign police force but their own Treasury Department brethren: U.S. Customs. One FBN agent characterized their long-simmering rivalry as "like one of those mountain family feuds which can't be traced to any specific incident."[34] Both agencies had a strong claim on foreign enforcement. The

FBN was tasked with breaking up major drug trafficking rings, but Customs had a mandate to police smuggling in general and already had personnel overseas. Prior to World War II, Customs often took the lead on foreign investigations for just this reason. The problem, as far as FBN officials were concerned, was that Customs agents didn't do much investigating; their primary function was to exchange information and liaise with foreign police. Most Customs officers, Harney later recalled, considered themselves "some sort of a sub-diplomat who could not dirty his hands with the actuality of narcotic investigations."[35] There were also major differences in strategy. Customs felt that intelligence should be exploited to make seizures at the borders and ports, while FBN agents were more interested in disrupting the actual trafficking networks. You might say that Customs focused on the product while the Bureau concentrated on the perps.

The establishment of District 17 therefore represented not just a challenge to the sovereignty of other nations but also an implicit rebuke of U.S. Customs and a fundamental shift in American law enforcement posture. Customs, of course, was vocal in protest. Soon after the creation of the Rome office, Treasury officials huddled in Washington to quash the beef and iron out a new working relationship. Behind the scenes, FBN officials were harshly critical and claimed that Customs was "completely falling down on the job." "While there is little effective activity from Customs," Harney complained, "heroin is available practically every place in the country . . . and narcotic agents are worked to the limit of physical endurance." Assistant Treasury Secretary John Graham evidently agreed and, with the wisdom of Solomon, split jurisdiction between the two agencies. Customs retained authority over Latin America and the Far East, but the FBN got the lead in Europe and the Middle East, where it would continue to apply its aggressive undercover approach. Thus began the FBN's slow but almost total eclipse of Customs in the realm of foreign drug enforcement. Outwardly gracious in victory, Anslinger encouraged Siragusa to exhibit team spirit by forwarding any information on gold or diamond smuggling to local Customs attachés. When Graham visited Rome soon after, Siragusa extolled the virtues of undercover work and explained that it was a style of investigation generally eschewed by Customs and European police but was absolutely key to the Bureau's success.[36]

Stateside, meanwhile, the most pressing need was simply for better intel. In June 1952, James Ryan, the district supervisor in Manhattan, bemoaned the FBN's inability to keep up with new smuggling routes. "In spite of the excellent work being done by you and your aides in Europe," he wrote to Siragusa, "heroin is still reaching this country in ample quantity, and we would like very much to know how this is being accomplished." What little the Bureau did know, he groused, was based entirely "on hearsay from informants." Much to the FBN's chagrin, informants played an even more central role in foreign operations, where agents were denied the authority to make the kind of routine street arrests that generated leads at home. District 17 was so pressed for good intelligence during the early years that the agents occasionally stooped to poaching informants from other agencies.[37]

There were also important changes afoot within the Atlantic drug trade. In the summer of 1952, Siragusa and Ryan believed that "most of the heroin reaching this country is carried ashore at New York concealed beneath the clothing of passengers." Publicly, the Bureau was consistent in depicting the drug traffic as highly organized and hierarchical, but early analysis indicated a decentralized, low-scale, and piecemeal traffic carried out by small-time entrepreneurs. As the agents gathered better intelligence, however, they saw an increase in both volume and complexity. It wasn't quite the "internationally organized narcotics attack" portrayed by FBN allies, but cases made in New York and Italy signaled a growing level of sophistication and steady increase in large-scale shipments concealed in cleverly designed trunks and shipping containers.[38]

Due to the fact that the drug trade operated in the shadow of legal commerce, American private companies, particularly in the airline and shipping industries, were important partners. While monitoring their own workforce for smuggling, executives readily furnished the FBN with cover and informants. Among Siragusa's official disguises was "Constantino Salerno," a pilot for Trans World Airlines. The agents promised (improbably, since they often posed as bagmen) not to use their cover identities in a way that would "reflect unfavorably" upon the companies and returned the favor with specialized training for private security personnel.[39]

Over the years, the ambiguous nature of the foreign office caused some confusion with agents who ranked liaison and diplomacy ahead of actual policing. The Bureau wanted aggressive and resourceful agents who made cases regardless of the challenges. Collecting and exchanging intelligence was important but only in service to tangible results: seizures, arrests, and headlines. In short, the Bureau valued operators over analysts. Agents with a more contemplative and patient style often faced criticism for relying on informants instead of going directly after suspects.

The undercover ethos celebrated in FBN literature was even more of a defining feature in District 17 and made a sharp contrast with European services that were leery of undercover tactics due to their historic association with political policing.[40] Several agents were recruited specifically on the strength of their previously established relationships with European police agencies, adding to the confusion of being caught between the culture of the FBN and the reality that agents serving abroad were required to work through local police. But as one of Anslinger's assistants sternly clarified, "The only purpose of liaison is to make cases. . . . [T]here is absolutely no place in our organization for social fraternizing under the disguise of official liaison."[41] The lines between fraternizing and liaison, however, were always blurry, and the cop-to-cop diplomacy that paid repeated dividends for agents like Siragusa and Manfredi often took place during social hours and over (many) drinks.

None of these challenges proved insurmountable, and District 17 quickly became the centerpiece of FBN global counternarcotics strategy. With each passing year, Anslinger claimed that an ever-greater percentage of illicit drugs was stopped before it reached American shores.[42] In October 1953, Siragusa was rewarded with a permanent home in an annex across the street from the Rome embassy. Sondern described the scene in *Brotherhood of Evil:* "Siragusa was given the secretaries and the office space he needed, along with an electronically controlled wire mesh door, combination lock files and the rest of the trappings of a highly secret government operation."[43]

By mid-decade the future of District 17 looked promising. The Bureau had strengthened its hold on Rome and slowly brought the Italians around to supporting American control efforts. From their headquarters in Rome, FBN agents circulated throughout the region—even in places where they were not especially welcome—and gradually began to consolidate and normalize the foreign enforcement program. Internally, the Rome and New York offices, bookending much of the Atlantic heroin trade, developed a close working relationship, and over the years a dedicated "Mafia Squad" in New York evolved into an "International Group" and later a "District 17 Liaison Group" to pursue leads generated overseas. In November 1955, Siragusa proudly declared to one Bureau official, "This office, jointly with District 2 and other districts, has made several big international cases involving professional large-scale smugglers. I would think that we are achieving our mission."[44]

Anslinger agreed. The dope menace was a persistent foe, and District 17 was now the front line. During Senate testimony in June 1955, the Commissioner made the case for a new, more global drug enforcement strategy. Trying to intercept drugs at the border was hopeless, he claimed: "If you had the Army, the Navy, the Coast Guard, the F.B.I., the Customs Service and our service, *you could not stop heroin coming through the port of New York.*" The only solution was to go abroad and fight drugs at the source, where, he argued, the agents of District 17 were "worth 100 men here."[45]

The implications of this shift in U.S. counternarcotic posture go well beyond drug enforcement. While most of the world's attention was fixed on the Cold War and the specter of nuclear war, more prosaic—but no less fundamental—transformations were taking place in the global security environment, and policymakers like Anslinger faced the cutting edge of those dilemmas. The processes of globalization begun earlier in the century, temporarily stymied by global depression and war, returned with a vengeance as Western leaders sought to forge an open and interconnected economic system capable of resisting communism and supporting Western democracy. Buried within that system, like a symbiotic parasite, was the drug trade, and the Commissioner grappled with a problem that, to his mind, threatened to undermine the very same political economy that enabled it. Globalization rendered America's traditional reliance on borders and distance obsolete; the only solution was to make the entire world safer for American society. The counternarcotic strategy that this worldview engendered—source control—reflected a genuine reading of the changing threat environment. But it didn't hurt that source control and aggressive transnational police operations also gave the FBN a leg up on its bureaucratic rivals.

Anslinger's claims about the efficacy of this outward-reaching strategy are difficult to corroborate. Seizure numbers, after all, signify merely an unknown percentage of the overall traffic. Prominent busts and confiscated drugs represented hard-won bureaucratic victories and strengthened the FBN's argument that American security required global leadership, but progress in the drug war is difficult to measure and the illicit traffic continued to grow even as the FBN improved its footing at home and abroad. Increasingly sure of themselves, Siragusa and the agents of District 17 turned their attention to structural reforms and meaningful investigations they hoped would reduce the global supply of narcotics.

"A War of Attrition and Memoranda in Quadruplicate"

One of District 17's first tasks was to eliminate legal heroin production in Italy. Compared to fixing elections or staging coups, this was relatively minor stuff in the broader scope of U.S. intervention.[46] But the FBN's quest to outlaw global heroin production illustrates the way U.S. drug policy led the country to interfere in the affairs of foreign nations and push domestic reforms aligned with American expectations. Around 1953 Siragusa and Anslinger dropped their focus on Lucky Luciano and started pressing the Italian government to adopt a total ban on the use and production of diacetylmorphine—the pharmaceutical analogue of street heroin.

Following the international furor provoked by the Carpinetti and RAMSA busts in Trieste, the Italian Public Health Commission announced an indefinite suspension of diacetylmorphine production, effective July 1, 1951.[47] The Bureau wanted to make that permanent and wean the Italian medical community off the powerful narcotic. But much of the damage was already done; follow-up conducted by Siragusa and the Guardia di Finanza indicated that approximately six hundred kilos had escaped to the black market between 1948 and 1951. The main culprit was Carlo Migliardi, a chemist and executive at Schiapparelli, whose product was discovered in the RAMSA busts, in the possession of the Callacis, and in the hands of Luciano-rival Frank Coppola. Using Egidio Calascibetta (of the SACI company) as a middleman, Migliardi was suspected of single-handedly diverting nearly a half ton of legally manufactured narcotics into illicit channels. Though denounced by judicial officials, he wasn't actually arrested until 1953, when prosecutors finally assembled a legal case. Schiapparelli, meanwhile, remained open, and the company's license was even renewed, Siragusa suspected, after the owners "contributed heavily towards the Democrat Christian campaign funds."[48]

Italy did eventually outlaw diacetylmorphine, but it was a slow process and many Italian physicians insisted on their right to use the powerful analgesic. First the agents had to figure out where to apply pressure. Short of a legislative decree, they learned, the decision rested with the commissioner of public health (part of the Ministry of the Interior), who was advised by a Superior Health Council composed of distinguished scientists, physicians, and industry leaders, plus a Narcotic Section that oversaw the pharmaceutical industry. Commissioner Giovanni Migliori—the same official who blamed American communists for the Italian drug trade—was quick to issue a temporary hold on heroin manufacture in the wake of the Schiapparelli scandal, but it was more than two years before Italian health officials revisited the subject.

In the spring of 1953, Siragusa was hopeful that an upcoming meeting of the UN's Commission on Narcotic Drugs would coax the Italians into action. Anslinger broadcast his intention to raise the issue, and several members of the Health Council privately expressed their wish to counteract "the unfavorable publicity" created by Schiapparelli. But the Italian public health office failed to act and faced sharp criticism from Anslinger and other UN representatives. Back in Rome, Siragusa noted an abrupt change. The chief of the Narcotic Section, he reported, had "previously been indifferent, unfriendly and even antagonistic" but was suddenly "most convincing and very friendly." He promised the temporary ban would remain in force and "went on at great length" about the "political embarrassment" caused by the UN discussion.[49]

Siragusa set to work pulling every available string in advance of the next meeting of the Public Health Commission that summer, promising Anslinger that he would "push this thing along" and "influence the votes of some of the council members." After convincing several of the physician-advisers on the Superior Health Council to remove diacetylmorphine from the official Italian *Pharmacopeia,* Siragusa was optimistic: "The outlook has never been better for this heroin ban." At the meeting, however, most of the physicians continued to insist on the right to administer the drug, even as they accepted the wisdom of an overall production cap. This reduced the amount of pharmaceutical-grade heroin available for diversion, but it was not quite a total ban and Siragusa sheepishly informed embassy officials, "The victory to us was not total."[50]

Progress on the heroin ban was further slowed by turnover among health officials. Elections in the summer of 1953 produced a new government, and the heroin debate was put aside as the entire Public Health Commission prepared to find new jobs. Giovanni Migliori, the current commissioner of public health, was the first to go. Carlo Angius, supervisor of the Narcotic Section, convinced the incoming commissioner to delay comment in the hope that a new council would accept total prohibition. Under the production ban, the Italian government intended to use confiscated heroin instead of importing a new supply, but Anslinger worked behind the scenes to ensure that the UN's Permanent Central Opium Board would deny this request and "force Italy's hand" toward "total prohibition."[51] The Americans, however, were dealt another setback when Tisiano Tessitori, the new public health commissioner, made it clear that he resented the depiction of a vibrant Italian trafficking scene. Siragusa calmed Tessitori with platitudes about support for Italian policing and assured him that FBN officials viewed Red China, and not Italy, as the largest source of illicit supply, but relations with Italian health authorities remained tense in the face of FBN accusations of Mafia trafficking.[52]

The Bureau kept the pressure on throughout 1954 and 1955. Using a carrot-and-stick approach, the FBN praised the Italian government for improved control over the legal trade and the promulgation of punitive prison sentences, but officials also continued to feed the Mafia-controlled heroin traffic story to the media as proof of the need for robust policing and a global heroin ban. An FBN-sanctioned article appearing in the June 1955 issue of *Bluebook* magazine further escalated tensions. The article's sensationalist rhetoric and title—"How Italy's Government Lets Heroin Flood the U.S."—provoked ardent protest from Italian authorities, discussion within the White House, and disavowals from the State Department.[53] But there were few consequences for the Bureau, which had mastered the art of escalating and de-escalating its rhetoric to suit its short-term agenda.

That same month, Anslinger again raised the issue during Senate testimony—the same in which he spoke of the need for a global enforcement posture. Contending that heroin should be outlawed "in every country," the Commissioner described international efforts to effect a global ban and told senators, "We really only have six more countries to convince. One of those countries is Italy, which should have made the decision a long time ago." When asked about the controversial *Bluebook* article, Anslinger confirmed the facts were "absolutely true" and blamed the "last wave of drug addiction" on the Schiapparelli scandal. Ultimately, Anslinger contended, Italy must enact a permanent ban on both the production and the use of diacetylmorphine (even under medical supervision) and ratify the 1953 Opium Protocol, a UN treaty that limited global opium production. While Anslinger rallied the Senate, Siragusa enlisted the direct aid of the diplomatic mission in Rome, including Ambassador Luce and chargé d'affaires Elbridge Durbrow, both of whom wielded formidable influence and "promised to apply diplomatic pressure."[54]

In the spring of 1956, the Italian government finally bowed to American demands but only after a final bit of chicanery from Siragusa. In early March, Siragusa encouraged an informant named "Carpi," a lawyer representing pharmaceutical concerns, to issue a letter declaring support for the heroin ban. After Carpi's letter circulated among members of the Italian public health office and "about 700" other physicians, Commissioner Tessitori finally signed an official decree permanently prohibiting the import and manufacture of heroin. Although the use of heroin under medical supervision wasn't addressed, the restriction on imports effectively ended the medical use of diacetylmorphine once current stocks were exhausted. Siragusa declared victory and fired off a cable to Anslinger: "Happy we won our five year battle." He reported some trepidation that Italy would face criticism at another upcoming UN meeting but ultimately thought his self-described "scheme" with Carpi was "instrumental" in achieving the ban. Not long thereafter, Italy formally ratified the 1953 Opium Protocol, coming fully into line with American expectations.[55]

Lobbying for the heroin ban revealed new aspects of the challenges faced in exporting U.S. drug control policies. The Italian medical community resisted abandoning a powerful and fast-acting opioid, and

Siragusa was immediately drawn into Italian politics and conflicts between the pharmaceutical industry and public health bureaucracy. The Bureau's hard-line stance created conflict between the Public Health Commission, which tried to accede to international pressure, and the Superior Health Council, which represented manufacturers and doctors who resisted political intrusion into a medical debate. The various pharmaceutical houses were always competing for commercial advantage, and Siragusa's industry contacts tried to pull him into their legal and political maneuvering. Carpi, for example, acted out of clear self-interest and spent years trying to undercut rivals, including Schiapparelli and other companies accused of licit diversions. Providing support for the "balloon theory" that suppression in one area simply shifts production and trafficking routes to new areas, the Italian heroin ban seems to have encouraged new diversions from the French pharmaceutical industry and the growth of clandestine manufacture throughout the region.[56]

On the whole, however, the Bureau was extremely pleased with the results of the Italian heroin-ban campaign. It was a drawn-out affair, but in FBN literature these events were compressed and held up as an important victory for global drug control. Anslinger summarized, "It was a long and difficult war of attrition and memoranda in quadruplicate, but . . . heroin was no longer legally manufactured in Italy."[57] The episode serves as a good example of the way the Bureau pursued additional control-related policies in each country in which it gained a presence, including criminalizing drug use, instituting punitive prison sentences for drug offenders, and creating specialized police agencies.

Beirut Redux

Both George White and Garland Williams had originally pushed for an outpost in Istanbul or Tehran, each of which was close to the poppy farms that ultimately supplied the illicit trade and where U.S. authorities enjoyed relatively warm relations with the national governments. Yet it was in Beirut, where Siragusa experienced such morale-sapping powerlessness, that the FBN gained its first foothold in the Middle East in November 1955.

After his visit in 1950, Siragusa was aware of the complicated Lebanese drug scene. Although the Bureau was more concerned with heroin than hashish, the hash trade forged clandestine relationships among producers, traffickers, and the politicians who protected them. Given Lebanon's proximity to Turkish and Persian poppy fields, both Siragusa and the American diplomats knew it was only a matter of time before opiates began to circulate through Beirut's already primed black market.

The first signs of a Beirut opiate trade reached Rome in fall 1952, when Siragusa heard rumors that vast quantities of Turkish opium and morphine base (a semirefined precursor to heroin) were arriving by way of Lebanese couriers, many of whom used diplomatic status as cover. In hindsight, Italian traffickers were probably looking east to compensate for the loss of product diverted from pharma. In October the Italian police came to Siragusa with a promising lead. Adopting FBN tactics, an Italian undercover officer targeted a Rome merchant who claimed his Lebanese partners "could supply any amount of morphine base and opium" in exchange for cocaine. Using this as a teaching opportunity, Siragusa briefed the officer and set him up in a hotel but refrained from direct involvement to avoid "the complaint of provocation and Yankee meddling."[58]

The case never developed, but Siragusa and the Italian undercover were able to identify the courier as Habib Khoury, a Lebanese diplomat assigned to the Vatican. Back in Washington, Anslinger and State Department official George Morlock contacted Charles Malik, the Lebanese ambassador to both the United Nations and the United States. Malik was an influential figure at the UN, close to Lebanese president Camille Chamoun, and generally supportive of the FBN, so the Old Man was optimistic that a discrete approach would yield goodwill. Malik duly notified Beirut and several diplomats (including Khoury) were fired, but the Lebanese government slammed the door on official cooperation, arguing that an FBN presence was "unwarranted" since the diplomats had been removed. Momentarily stalled, the Bureau opted for gentle prodding as Siragusa and Anslinger kept tabs on suspected Lebanese traffickers.[59]

In the fall of 1954, Siragusa began developing cases in Rome with the intention of working back toward Lebanese middlemen and using proof of their participation to pry Beirut open to the Bureau. In Rome he sent an informant to socialize with Lebanese diplomats in the hopes one would sell a few kilos of heroin. In the meantime, Siragusa sent

FBN agent Paul Knight to build a covert intelligence network in Beirut. A handsome man who bore a striking resemblance to actor Paul Newman, Knight started with District 17 in July 1952 and, with a knack for intrigue and foreign language, became one of Siragusa's most effective lieutenants.[60] Posing as a travel agent named Robert Martel, Knight entered Beirut under cover and quickly established a network managed by two local gatekeepers, who, in turn, recruited a variety of lookouts to send word of possible drug shipments in exchange for cash rewards.[61]

Knight concentrated his network on the shipping industry and the notoriously corrupt Lebanese Customs service, but it was a delicate operation and the FBN remained officially unwelcome in the country. Siragusa cautioned him to protect his cover but also to collect any evidence that could "serve as added ammunition" to use on the Lebanese government. By December 1953, Knight had a stream of tips flowing back to Rome and Washington. Many leads went unexploited while the FBN presence remained covert, but Knight thought the intelligence could still be used to "embarrass the local constabulary."[62]

In a lengthy report sent that spring, Knight described a situation essentially unchanged since Siragusa's visit in 1950. Like Istanbul, Beirut's geography and thriving port made the city a critical transshipment point. Economic woes also played a role, as "large numbers" of Palestinian refugees—including many "old-time narcotic smugglers"—depressed an already poor standard of living, sharpened a glaring class divide, and provided ready recruits to local gangs. Drug use was common and lacked any apparent stigma. Lebanese diplomats continued to function as bagmen, and corruption posed a serious impediment to law enforcement. So many government officials were apparently implicated that Knight remarked, "one might well state that the Lebanese Government is in the narcotic business." Cases made in Rome were forcing the government to acknowledge the problem but produced few lasting results. And layered atop all of this were Lebanon's deep-rooted religious divisions and chronic political instability.[63] In short, the enforcement situation was bleak, but Beirut's pivotal role in the regional drug trade demanded FBN attention.

Throughout the summer of 1954, the Bureau applied pressure from multiple fronts. Knight remained undercover and continued to expand his network of eyes and ears, which grew to include foreign nationals,

Lebanese officials, and a handful of highly placed criminal informants—
including known traffickers. In Europe Siragusa enlisted the aid of Interpol and French police to cultivate Farid Chehab, director of the Sûreté
Générale (Lebanon's security and intelligence service). In Washington
Anslinger brought fresh intelligence to Ambassador Malik and again
requested permission to work cases in Beirut. This time the potentially
damaging reports did the trick, and Lebanon was spared the degree of
public shaming the FBN inflicted on Italy. In August President Chamoun
personally authorized an agent to visit Beirut, and Chehab agreed to
exchange information with the FBN after Siragusa furnished him with
evidence against two wanted fugitives.[64]

Operating in the Middle East posed new problems. Knight spoke
some Arabic, but the agents struggled with the language and spelling
of Arabic names. (Siragusa discovered that many suspects were indexed
in FBN files under separate phonetic spellings of the same name.) For
this first official venture, Bureau officials needed someone capable of
going undercover in an Arab region and chose Agent George Abraham.
Though new to the Bureau, Abraham was of Syrian descent, spoke fluent
Arabic, and, in Siragusa's opinion, was "an excellent undercover man."[65]

Arriving on September 17, 1954, Abraham immediately set to work
with a broad "sweep" strategy designed to implicate as many suspects
as possible, including Siragusa's old chum Artin Guedikian, the Fagin-
like tavern keeper. Most of Abraham's targets were small-time players
operating at the retail level, but his tour was an explicit trial balloon,
so the idea was to hit as many targets as possible to impress the city's
traffickers and Lebanese authorities.[66]

Abraham successfully brought in nine separate defendants over
a two-month period but faced several obstacles. Farid Chehab was
a reluctant collaborator, and there was an added legal technicality to
overcome in that an undercover drug buy was insufficient grounds for
arrest in Lebanon, requiring the guilt of each party to be independently
corroborated. Undercover tactics were very unpopular, and Abraham
faced a decidedly hostile reception from the Lebanese judiciary when
the cases went to trial.[67]

But the real problem was the dubious loyalty of the Bureau's own
informants. One of the key figures in Knight's network was a man
named Darwish Beydoun, described by Siragusa as a treacherous but

"powerful political and underworld figure in Lebanon." Beydoun put his own network of minions at Knight's and Abraham's apparent disposal but was viewed with trepidation by other informants. American largesse often smoothed foreign cooperation—usually in the form of reward money or modern equipment—and relations with foreign informants were no different. At their first meeting, Abraham showed up with a squirt gun for Beydoun's kid nephew and clothes and cigarettes for Beydoun and his men. But loyalty did not come so cheaply. When Abraham and Beydoun sat down to plan their strategy, Abraham quickly realized the gangster was conning the Bureau.[68]

FBN funds remained tight, so Abraham was instructed to make small purchases from each target. Beydoun, however, was adamant that he and his men make first contact and buy expensive samples of at least one kilo to demonstrate good faith. Abraham made a few direct purchases, but Beydoun kept his own people between Abraham and the targets and made a show of sending another nephew to purchase samples from various suppliers. Those samples, however, proved suspiciously uniform, given the rudimentary nature of the different labs in which they were supposedly refined. When Abraham dutifully sent them off to Washington for analysis, the samples turned out to be morphine base refined in a single lab rather than heroin purchased from separate suppliers. Beydoun, the agents realized, was pocketing the buy money and providing his own product—which meant the FBN was buying drugs directly from its own informant. Chagrined, Siragusa and Knight instructed Abraham to proceed with whatever investigations he was able to, but with the Lebanese authorities providing little real support, the Bureau continued to rely on Beydoun for introductions and information.[69]

Nevertheless, Abraham was able to collect evidence against a number of targets, and, on November 19, he and the Lebanese police rounded up their suspects. In a report filed the next day, Knight noted that most of the targets walked because few of the arrests were accompanied by seizures—a clear indication that Abraham's cover was blown and the underworld forewarned. Still, Knight thought this first group of cases represented "a great step forward" and likely to slow the local traffic and impress the Lebanese police, who would be more accepting of formal cooperation.[70]

Abraham's cases imparted some valuable lessons about working in Beirut. The most important concerned operational security; Knight's sources confirmed that most of Abraham's targets knew of their impending arrests. It was time to switch tactics. "I do not feel that we should attempt to prepare a large number of simultaneous cases here again," Knight wrote, suggesting it would be more prudent to concentrate on one high-level target at a time.[71] Fortunately, District 17 had a perfect case already lined up, and while Abraham was rounding up suspects in Beirut, Knight and Siragusa were climaxing an investigation destined to become another of the Bureau's true-crime legends.

The Abou Sayia Case

Featuring police from five different countries, the Abou Sayia case was a model of international cooperation in the fight against the dope menace. The investigation began in Greece in the summer of 1954 with a night of drinking. As they bonded over their shared identity as policemen, Agent Siragusa and Gerasimos Liarommatis, director of the Greek National Police, hatched a plan. "Jerry," as Siragusa called him, offered to lend the Americans one of his best informants, a smuggler and con man named Carlo Dondola. Seeking revenge after getting cheated on a counterfeit-money deal, Dondola proposed setting up an associate in Beirut: Abou Sayia, the purported head of a gang of international drug dealers and a principal figure in the Mediterranean supply chain. Siragusa agreed immediately.

Over the next few months, Dondola approached Sayia on behalf of a fictional American buyer and introduced Agent Knight as the bagman. During their talks, Dondola somehow convinced Sayia to identify his source in Aleppo, Syria. Accompanied this time by Agent Abraham, also in the role of a prospective courier, Dondola met with Sayia's supplier, a large man who introduced himself as Tifankji (later identified as Haji Mehmet Deniz). The silver-tongued Dondola then convinced Tifankji to cut Sayia out of any deal and introduce his own source in Adana, Turkey. Thus, a third angle opened up, and off the agents went. This time Siragusa and Liarommatis met Dondola in Turkey to woo Mehmet Ozsayar, the wholesale supplier. Dondola then enlisted Ozsayar in a triple cross, proposing to cut out both Sayia and Tifankji.

Ozsayar, however, insisted on a large purchase of 250 kilos of raw opium with payment of twenty-five thousand dollars up front. Siragusa, interestingly, turned to Turkish official Kemal Aygun for the buy money. As the police chief in Istanbul, Aygun had torpedoed all of Siragusa's cases back in 1950. Now governor of the Ankara province after serving as head of Turkey's Directorate of Public Safety (and still exerting considerable influence), Aygun dropped his obstructionist tactics and agreed to provide the funds. That left the Bureau with three sets of targets scattered across three different countries.

In November 1954, just as Agent Abraham was wrapping things up in Beirut, Siragusa and Knight orchestrated a series of raids and busts to conclude the Abou Sayia case. Over the course of twenty-four hours, the agents and local police arrested the three principals (plus nine additional suspects) in Beirut, Aleppo, and Adana; issued warrants for another five fugitives; and seized over 700 pounds of narcotics worth an estimated forty million dollars retail. Siragusa was justifiably proud and summarized in his official report, "This case, in addition to wiping out what was probably one of the most important international organizations of narcotic traffickers, may serve as a heartening and exemplary pattern of international cooperation of police agencies combating the international traffic in illicit narcotic drugs."[72]

The case became a celebrated part of Bureau lore, and the tale was retold in several outlets. Frederic Sondern called it "one of the Bureau's classic stories." As an artifact of true-crime literature, the story was perfect for clarifying the various roles and identities in the drug war. Dondola (identified in Siragusa's account as "Dimitri"), the con man–informant who offered such an irresistible case that Siragusa was willing to "work with the devil," was humanized with "gall and imagination" and enthusiasm for the hunt. Abou Sayia was villainized as a "depraved" fat man who reveled in violence and callously inducted his own small children into a life of crime. Tifankji was parodied as "a curious mixture" of East and West, attired in tailored suits and "a flaming red fez," while Ozsayar appeared as a monosyllabic barbarian warlord. The cops, meanwhile, were valorized for their moxie and eagerness to overcome historic national enmities for the sake of a good case.[73]

Reading between the lines, however, indicates the case was never quite what the Bureau made it out to be—in either internal reports or subsequent retellings. FBN records describe the ring as "a large, well-organized, international gang of narcotics traffickers" led by Sayia, whom Siragusa identified as "a major source for the Mafia bosses." But that was pure speculation. The Bureau had no evidence to link Sayia to the Mafia or any other buyers. Siragusa's own narrative suggests that Sayia's influence was limited and he was eagerly betrayed by his confederates. The double crosses orchestrated by the FBN indicate the ring had little cohesion and likely functioned only one deal at a time—a loose association of independent entrepreneurs rather than a hierarchical gang. The picture of a tightly organized ring was a product of the Bureau's tendency to see and depict kingpins rather than a genuine reflection of the drug trade, where actual kingpins were few and far between. The Bureau characterized the group as "one of the most important international organizations of narcotic traffickers," but this, too, was something of an overstatement, as the regional traffic continued unabated.[74]

The case did feature officers from the United States, Greece, Turkey, Syria, and Lebanon all acting in an operational capacity, but this much-vaunted cooperation was also far more tenuous than depicted. In *The Trail of the Poppy,* Siragusa ended his narrative with another raucous victory party featuring drunken toasts to the fraternal bonds of policemen, but the whole operation was nearly derailed on at least three separate occasions when various officials balked at cooperating with national rivals. Siragusa cited Farid Chehab, of the Lebanese Sûreté, for special credit, but internal FBN communications reveal that Siragusa carefully kept Chehab in the dark to protect FBN informants.[75]

In a way, the tension between the image the Bureau wished to project and the material reality of the drug world makes the Abou Sayia case a more perfect illustration than Siragusa and his men imagined. Multilateral cooperation in the drug war was possible, but—much like the traffic itself—it was tenuous, transactional, and contingent on the regional political economy.

Nevertheless, the case was a critical step in the development of District 17. Abraham's series of cases and the Abou Sayia investigation make a useful comparison: a "sweep" versus a "probe." Though it was a more frugal endeavor, Abraham's scattershot investigation against a handful of unaffiliated traffickers was a classic sweep operation, the equivalent of "clearing the corners" in the American drug war. The better-financed Abou Sayia investigation, in contrast, aimed to neutralize one major target at a time—a probe or kingpin strategy. Neither made much of an impact, but the glory of the Abou Sayia case convinced the FBN that it might be possible to dismantle the regional drug traffic one piece at a time and eventually make discernible progress in the foreign drug war.

The Beirut Office

At home Anslinger used the dramatic conclusion of the Abu Sayia case to turn up the heat on Lebanon and identified Beirut during Senate testimony as "the center of an enormous traffic in heroin." (It's worth noting the agents found only morphine base, street heroin's final precursor.) Faced with international embarrassment, the Lebanese government indicated it was ready to cooperate. In Washington Anslinger encouraged Ambassador Malik to file these investigations with the UN Commission on Narcotic Drugs to show Lebanon's determination "to stamp out this illicit traffic."[76] Agent Knight, meanwhile, was left to sort out the complexities of Lebanese law enforcement.

What he discovered was a complicated quilt of overlapping jurisdictions—not unlike the American system—with the Sûreté and Customs service in frequent conflict. Officially, the Sûreté handled all criminal investigations, and the Bureau was only authorized to work with Director Farid Chehab, who remained a deeply reluctant collaborator. Lebanese Customs, on the other hand, was generally more active in drug enforcement, and the agents found a willing partner in Edmond Azzizeh, captain of a small investigative squad. There was also a religious coloration: Chehab owed his patronage to the Maronite Christians, while Customs was the domain of Muslim factions. That meant there was little cooperation between the two agencies, and the embryonic Beirut office soon found itself in the middle of a bureaucratic proxy war. "This is a bad situation from an enforcement viewpoint," Knight remarked.[77]

Once again, the drug war inextricably drew U.S. law enforcement into the internal politics of a foreign country. Chehab was cousin to Fuad Chehab, the influential commander of the Lebanese army (and president from 1958 to 1964), but French police officials cautioned Siragusa to keep his distance. They warned him that Chehab was a difficult man, rumored to be active in black-market currency counterfeiting. By January 1955, Agent Knight's concerns were also mounting, and he urged "somewhat more discretion" in the Bureau's relationship with Chehab. Knight's sources corroborated reports of Chehab's counterfeiting and close association with a Sûreté officer named Hadji Touma, widely thought to be "completely corrupt" and allied to Samil Khoury, Lebanon's most notorious drug trafficker. There were other troubling signs: FBN mail was routinely opened, and Sûreté detectives targeted Knight's informants for minor offenses. Knight suspected Chehab was actually under orders to obstruct the FBN. "In this regard," he added in a cryptic note to Siragusa, "I might note the remote possibility that another agency, even an American one, may have suggested to the Amir that he slow up in his work with us, for one reason or another." Both Chehab and Touma were rumored to be agents of British intelligence, and Siragusa was explicitly told to back off by an unnamed CIA official after Knight unknowingly tried to recruit a CIA asset in the Lebanese shipping industry.[78]

There was little the agents could do but scale back their cooperation with Chehab. "We will have to work more closely with the Customs and try to keep Chehab from knowing about it," Siragusa concluded. Above all, he emphasized, "We will do our best not to give Chehab or anyone else in Lebanon an opportunity to 'invite' us to leave that country. It took the Bureau many years to effect this collaboration and we will try to sustain it—the area is too important to us."[79]

Fortunately for District 17, the drug war produced a reliable succession of enemies, and, once again, another case developed right when needed, this time involving Samil Khoury. Working with the FBN, Captain Azzizeh made a handful of arrests and seizures targeting the leadership of Khoury's gang and even captured their "secret weapon," a Jaguar sports car modified to conceal 140 kilos of contraband. Further testimony to the unstable political environment and welter of conflicting loyalties in the Lebanese government, however, Azzizeh was unceremoniously jailed for his efforts and held for five days while Khoury evaded capture.[80]

It may have been a product of bureaucratic or religious rivalry, but Azzizeh's willingness to go after Khoury (a Christian) cemented the Bureau's decision to throw in with Customs. Thereafter, Siragusa took to calling Azzizeh "our sparkplug collaborator." Yet troubling rumors swirled around him as well, including sudden wealth and association with known traffickers. A short time later, Farid Chehab's nephew Claude went to work as an FBN informant in Istanbul and claimed that Azzizeh actually worked for Khoury. Claude said his uncle had no knowledge of his actions, but he was almost certainly a plant. The truth, as ever in the underworld, was murky. But in Lebanon, the Bureau was prepared to take what it could get. Siragusa rationalized that "no one in an enforcement job there can be assumed to be of unqualified integrity," and he described Azzizeh as the "one person upon whom we have been able to rely." Knight even began to advertise his services to the rest of the American intelligence community. "Through us," he wrote, Azzizeh "is at the disposal of any such agency which cares to ask information of us," adding that Azzizeh had already provided useful tips to naval intelligence and economic defense officials.[81]

Chehab and his cohort within the Sûreté were not passive observers and let the agents know that the FBN remained in Lebanon only on their sufferance. One day in April 1955, a newly assigned agent named James Attie was working undercover to locate a suspected heroin lab run by the Khoury organization when he was abruptly arrested by Sûreté detectives. Cuffed and brought before Sûreté officer Hajdi Touma, a close associate of Chehab and suspected ally of Khoury, Attie was interrogated and savagely beaten but refused to break cover. He was then openly paraded on the street before an alert Lebanese prosecutor secured his release. Azzizeh suggested it was because Attie was getting close to Khoury. Both Knight and Siragusa were furious, but there was little they could do. As one headquarters official cautioned, "If we made too much of an issue of this matter, we might be told to leave the country." After that, Siragusa was settled: "Our future lies with the Customs."[82]

The Attie episode capped the period of uncertainty that accompanied the Bureau's initial attempts to gain access to Beirut. Once the agents cast their lot with Customs, it was comparatively smooth sailing, and, in November 1955, Agent Knight was finally authorized to open District 17's first official branch office.[83]

Significant challenges remained. The first, Knight discovered, was that the investigative wing of the Lebanese Customs service was woefully unprepared to take on a productive partnership and lacked basic resources like index files, duplication services, modern office supplies, or photography and fingerprinting equipment. One of the benefits of partnering with the FBN, however, was a crash modernization. Modest appropriations prevented the Bureau from footing the bill, but the agents readily provided training and advice on modern investigative technologies and pulled strings to acquire specialized equipment. In Beirut Azzizeh's office was the beneficiary of this attention. Knight explained to Siragusa, "If our assistance to the Customs produces an increased speed and efficiency of operation, we too shall benefit in our work with them." After picking out equipment and designing a new filing system for his office, Knight pointedly wrote to Azzizeh, "I look forward to a really permanent association between us in Lebanon."[84]

This kind of treatment was a fixture of FBN foreign operations and ensured the agents remain on good terms with their hosts. Another way of institutionalizing American influence was to bring foreign policemen to the United States for training, a policy the FBN began in Lebanon soon after opening the Beirut office. Typically working through the State Department's International Cooperation Administration (later USAID), the FBN helped recruit foreign officers to receive training at the Treasury Department's Law Enforcement Officers Training School. Most of the policemen were drawn from the gendarmerie or municipal police forces, expanding the Bureau's influence to new branches of Lebanese law enforcement.[85] Although Azzizeh never benefited from the policy (due to his troubled reputation), he was awarded a consolation prize (at his apparent request) in the form of a unique certificate from the Treasury Department thanking him for his service. "He attaches tremendous importance to receiving it," Siragusa wearily apologized, and "it took us a long time to get to first base with the Lebanese police." American firearms and blackjacks were particularly effective gifts and universally desired by foreign officers. As Siragusa explained to FBN HQ officials a few years later, "With a gift costing about $75 we can get thousands of dollars worth of necessary investigations conducted for us, at no cost. It is a regrettable fact, but one we have to face realistically, that often it is necessary to 'purchase' foreign friendships to ensure future good will and cooperation on official matters."[86]

The FBN solidified its position in Lebanon over the years, but the Beirut office continued to face intractable problems. There was little follow-through from the Lebanese judiciary, which passed lenient sentences on drug offenders—Siragusa was particularly incensed to learn that Abou Sayia was released after only one year. Knight continued to struggle with devious informants, and the Lebanese government remained torn by factional rivalries. In a letter sent soon after opening the new office, Knight itemized the challenges in Beirut and complained that everything "is a technicolor production here." Working around Chehab remained a delicate issue. But, Knight reasoned, "if I were in his position, and felt the way I am certain he feels about our having a man in his country permanently, I would do *precisely* what he is trying to do." That is, put on a show of cooperation while doing everything possible to ensure the Bureau failed. This made for a difficult enforcement situation, and the agents constantly chafed against their constraints. Siragusa tried to smooth relations by securing Chehab various appointments with Interpol and patronizingly explained to officials at the European police agency, "Our policy has been never to become frustrated with the Lebanese authorities. Instead we try to be as patient and understanding as possible."[87]

Despite these challenges, the office endured to become a critical front in the FBN's global campaign. During his June 1955 Senate testimony, Anslinger cited the example of Lebanon to argue for a multifront drug war that paired aggressive international investigations with harsh penalties at home—an argument that led directly to the 1956 Narcotic Control Act. Operations in Lebanon led the FBN's 1957 summary of important cases, as leads developed in Beirut led to arrests downstream in Marseille and Detroit. The Beirut office facilitated Lebanon's cooperation with other law enforcement agencies in the region, and the agents began to see the country's endemic internal conflicts as a way to encourage competition for influence with the FBN.[88]

The office also managed to survive Lebanon's political crisis of 1958. Although the turmoil heightened political and religious tensions and dramatically slowed FBN operations, it also cleared the decks when a new government was formed. Farid Chehab and Edmond Azzizeh were both replaced and investigated for their ties to the drug traffic. The Bureau quickly established new and more effective liaison with their replacements, most of whom were military officers. The new government had a more Islamic and ostensibly anti-Western character, but Knight optimistically reported, "I think that we shall be able to cooperate with the new Security Forces and with any new group in the Customs, if we get off to a good start and win their confidence." A dedicated narcotic squad was even created within the Lebanese Gendarmerie, based explicitly on the model established by Garland Williams in Iran.[89]

By the end of the decade, District 17 had strengthened its institutional bonds to Lebanese police and security forces. Beirut remained a problematic area, but FBN operations continued to grow, and the agents built a noteworthy case record: the FBN estimated that roughly seventy-five joint investigations were initiated between 1952 and 1960, producing around 150 defendants. Most were let off easy by a judicial process the Bureau deemed "unrealistic, antiquated and ineffective," and law enforcement remained "badly splintered."[90] Yet from a bureaucratic standpoint, all of this sustained the rationale for an FBN presence and American intervention.

The details changed from country to country, but this, too, was a pattern common to the FBN's foreign drug war—an example of where the Sisyphean policy of source control strengthened the interventionist claims of the Bureau and echoed a broader U.S. national security strategy of bringing foreign institutions, rather than physical territory, under American influence.

Exit Charlie Cigars

By 1958 things were going well for Agent Charles Siragusa—now referred to in some quarters as "Charlie Cigars" due to his fondness for stogies and predilection for smuggling them via diplomatic pouch.[91] Under his leadership, District 17 established a regional headquarters in Rome, added the office in Beirut, and strengthened ties to police services in France, Italy, Greece, Turkey, and Lebanon. Siragusa was even knighted by the Italian government and awarded the Order of Merit. As tales of District 17's exploits spread, Siragusa joined the ranks of FBN celebrity crime fighters, much like his mentors, George White and the Old Man. "I suppose you read Toni Howard's article glamorizing Charlie Chan, alias Sherlock Holmes, alias Charlie," Anslinger teased after reading an advance copy of a profile on Siragusa.[92]

Appearing in the April 1957 issue of the *Saturday Evening Post*, the article revealed just how much Siragusa's position had improved since 1951. No longer merely tolerated by U.S. Embassy and foreign police officials, District 17 had put down roots. The agent who promised to avoid the "social whirl" and never wear spats was photographed squiring actress Marlene Dietrich at a posh Rome cocktail party, while the text romanticized the "brash, fast-talking New Yorker" as a "character straight out of murder-mystery fiction." The story glamorized District 17's exploits against the Mafia and concluded with a detailed account of the Abou Sayia case. If there were any doubts that Siragusa was Anslinger's man, this article put them to rest. At a time when other agents were denied permission to publicize their work, the Old Man personally cleared the *Saturday Evening Post* article and only gently rebuked Siragusa for allowing his photograph to be "splashed across the front page of magazines."[93]

In fact, like George White, Siragusa's undercover days were mostly behind him. Within the Bureau, he was rumored to be Anslinger's pick as the next commissioner, and his work overseas seemed to put him on the fast track. In July 1958, he was brought home and promoted to supervise all field operations—and liaise with the CIA, taking charge of the FBN-CIA safe houses established by White in Manhattan. In September 1962, Siragusa was promoted again, this time to the rank of deputy commissioner, but he was ultimately on the losing side of the infighting touched off by Anslinger's retirement. The following year, he left the FBN to run the Illinois State Crime Commission and continue his crusade against the Mafia.[94]

Not everyone was impressed with Siragusa, and many agents found his grandstanding irritating. Howard Chappell, an agent close to George White, remarked that "Charlie was a good report writer but to my knowledge never initiated anything." When former agent Arthur Giuliani stumbled upon Siragusa's memoir, *The Trail of the Poppy* (1966), while killing time at an airport, he observed to White that Charlie was "still on the horseshit circuit" and delightedly remarked, "Ick! Noted the copy I looked at was dusty, which is about right."[95]

Assessing Siragusa's importance to the history of the FBN and the success of District 17 is further complicated by unresolved questions about his relationship to the Central Intelligence Agency. In journalist

Douglas Valentine's account, District 17 was little more than a CIA cutout where Siragusa and Manfredi ran errands for counterintelligence chief James Angelton, shuttling "black-bag CIA money to Italian politicians" and providing access to the criminal underworld and foreign police files. Both Valentine and historian Alan Block contend that Siragusa may have recruited or even been a mysterious CIA assassin code-named QJ/WIN. When called before Senator Ted Kennedy's committee to answer for FBN and CIA misdeeds, Siragusa emphatically denied ever working for the CIA. He did admit to maintaining the New York safe houses, but disavowed any knowledge of human drug testing. Around that same time, however, he told a *People* magazine reporter that, although he had no personal knowledge of CIA operations, he put the odds at around "70 percent" that "the CIA was seriously talking to the Mob." It's doubtful that Siragusa was a CIA assassin or recruiter—he had too great a personal animus toward the Mafia—but it's almost certain the relationship ran deeper than he acknowledged, and there's strong evidence that Siragusa served as a "singleton" agent reporting to future CIA director Bill Colby during his time in Rome.[96] Given the dearth of evidence directly linking the Bureau to some of the Company's more questionable practices, the extent of Siragusa's involvement with the CIA will remain at least partly a mystery.

FBN records strongly indicate that drug control was always the Bureau's first priority—even if not for the rest of the American intelligence and security community. The Bureau knew it was playing second fiddle to the Cold War in terms of demands on resources, but preventing deadly drugs like heroin from reaching American shores was an urgent priority that the agents took very seriously, even if they reveled a bit in their "bad boy" status.

Siragusa played a unique and important role in the history of the Bureau, particularly in the growth of foreign drug enforcement, and his departure from District 17 ushered in a period of dangerous instability in the foreign drug war—a situation that Siragusa actually precipitated from his new perch in Washington.

CHAPTER 7

THE GLOBAL DRUG WAR

It is a regrettable fact . . . that often it is necessary to "purchase"
foreign friendships to ensure future good will and
cooperation on official matters.
—AGENT CHARLES SIRAGUSA (1957)

These efforts have been so successful that the activity of the Bureau
of Narcotics is being expanded to other parts of the world.
—PRESIDENT JOHN F. KENNEDY (1962)

Jack Cusack had a problem. Actually, he had a lot of problems, and two of them were Charles Siragusa and Wayland Speer. Newly appointed as supervisor of District 17, Cusack arrived in January 1959—right in the middle of an exasperating dry spell. Making matters worse, direction of the foreign drug war had become a pawn in the intramural competition to replace Anslinger. Speer and Siragusa both coveted the Old Man's job and seemed intent on micromanaging every aspect of District 17's affairs from their perch in Washington. Cusack had scarcely unpacked his bags before FBN headquarters began to announce abrupt shifts in policy and second-guess decisions made in the field, all while demanding more arrests and bigger seizures. The flood of memos—and Siragusa and Speer's attempts to outdo one another in feats of administrative prowess—generally ensured that Cusack spent as much time fighting Washington as he did the dope menace.

Cusack's tenure as supervisor of District 17 is best described as embattled, and the sustained conflict between Rome and Washington hastened his departure in May 1963. The odd thing was that it should have been a time of celebration. Even in the face of budget constraints and fewer cases, the district continued to grow under Cusack's leadership and won several hard-fought bureaucratic victories, including the establishment of long-anticipated branch offices in Paris, Marseille, and Istanbul and the Bureau's final triumph over Customs. By the time Treasury gave the FBN total jurisdiction over international drug enforcement in September 1962, the Bureau stood among the world's preeminent law enforcement agencies—an accomplishment that makes the conflict between headquarters and District 17 all the more perplexing.

The Bureau's expansion into France, Turkey, and Thailand put it on a trajectory to assume global responsibility for all U.S. drug enforcement. But the FBN was riven by internal rivalries as Anslinger's once firm grip on the agency slipped and the competition to replace him directly influenced operational matters. By the mid-1960s, significant changes were afoot within U.S. foreign policy, the drug war, and American culture. The tactics used in the early days, on both traffickers and foreign governments, grew less effective as the years wore on, requiring the agents to refine the manner in which they cultivated influence and attacked the dope menace. Yet there were also remarkable continuities in the way the FBN conducted itself on the world stage and approached the challenges of international enforcement—many of which last into the present.

This story has real implications. District 17 established and shaped many of the law enforcement and control strategies that remain in place today. The Bureau's victory over Customs signaled a critical total shift in U.S. counternarcotics strategy from a conflicted and passive stance focused on borders to a far more aggressive posture in which federal narcotic agents went out into the world—not just Europe and the Middle East—to disrupt the global drug trade. Subsequent decades witnessed a sharp increase in the geographic reach and number of interdiction programs run by the FBN's successor agencies, the BNDD and DEA, but the shift—the events that put the United States on this path—came out of the Bureau's experience in District 17.

Musical Chairs

By most accounts, Jack Cusack was a widely respected agent. He had a reputation as a sharp detective with a knack for handling informants.

Sal Vizzini, one of his subordinates in Europe, remembered him with a bald head, "a blacksmith's jaw and hard blue eyes." Others recalled Cusack's natty Brooks Brothers suits. He had a temper but was usually mild in manner and avoided the resentment that flamboyant agents like White and Siragusa often engendered.[1] He was, however, a true believer. Like Anslinger, Cusack dismissed public health advocates and other challengers to drug war orthodoxy as "false prophets." He also had the distinction of busting jazz legend Charlie "Bird" Parker for possession of heroin paraphernalia back in 1948. During the early days of District 17, Cusack was among the first agents to rotate through France. But he wasn't good with languages and struggled to make a case, so he concentrated on feeding Anslinger's jones for tales of drug-addled jazz musicians and filed reports claiming that figures like Bird, Thelonious Monk, and Miles Davis corrupted their European counterparts with their evil habits and should have their passports seized as carriers of addiction. Following his initial foreign tour, Cusack worked out of the New York office for a while and served one year as the district supervisor in Atlanta before replacing Siragusa in Rome in 1959.[2]

Cusack's appointment was itself partly the result of infighting in Washington. By the late 1950s, Anslinger was focused on diplomatic affairs and desperately trying to sink the UN Single Convention, a treaty that unified disparate international control agreements but, to his mind, did little to curb global poppy production. Day-to-day affairs fell mostly to the rest of the FBN brass—Henry Giordano, Wayland Speer, and Charles Siragusa—each of whom sought to keep the others from reaching the Commissioner's office. When Siragusa left Rome, most of the rank and file assumed the supervisor job would go to Knight or Manfredi, effective agents who had been with District 17 from the start, but that would have left the foreign drug war under Siragusa's influence. Giordano, newly elevated to deputy commissioner, swung the job to Cusack to consolidate his own claim on Anslinger's soon-to-be-vacant throne.[3]

Meanwhile, Wayland Speer, a more recent arrival to the Bureau, was preparing his own bid for influence. Speer first came to Anslinger's attention while serving as a narcotic control officer with occupation forces in Japan and ingratiated himself to the Old Man with his readiness to see a Red Chinese hand behind the Far Eastern dope traffic.

The fact that he provided access to East Asia, technically Customs turf under the 1951 jurisdictional agreement, made him doubly useful. Speer officially joined the Bureau in early 1953 and was swiftly promoted to field supervisor, but he spent most of his time on special assignment—first on several additional tours of the Far East, where he sought proof of communist Chinese heroin trafficking, and later as the lead investigator for the Senate's Daniel Committee, which produced the 1956 Narcotic Control Act. Speer's unusual career path (and grating personality) bred some resentment among the agents, but his congressional experience brought new allies on Capitol Hill and secured the number-three job of assistant to the commissioner in 1958.[4]

When Siragusa returned from Europe that summer, the only remaining leadership posts were a brief stint as field supervisor and the number-four job of assistant deputy commissioner. Tom Tripodi, a new agent assigned to help update the Mafia Book, described Siragusa as "clearly the least political of those enmeshed in a power struggle for control of the bureau." But it was apparent that Siragusa still felt the tug of old duties and resented getting trapped at the bottom of the headquarters hierarchy after all the acclaim and excitement of Rome. "I regret my inability to restrain my impulse to run District 17," he apologized in one memo.[5] He did, however, quickly come to appreciate that the view from Washington was very different from that of Rome and began to order sudden changes in District 17 policy and strategy.

The fundamental problem was an abrupt drop-off in cases. Drug seizures in District 17 declined after 1955 and reached an all-time low of around 34 kilos in 1959. Seizures in New York, meanwhile, climbed steadily, from roughly 36 kilos in 1957 to 64 in 1958 and 73 in 1959, and then exploded to around 172 kilos in 1960. Bureau officials believed that most of New York's heroin arrived via France, but cases there were hard to come by.[6]

The pressure to drain the illicit traffic exacerbated another long-running problem: money. In September 1957, Treasury officials ordered department-wide austerity measures, which trickled down into the field offices. District 17 was hit particularly hard, as costs associated with turnover and operational expenses continued to mount while appropriations remained flat and the rivalry to succeed Anslinger began to heat up.[7] It wasn't (entirely) personal, but Cusack's appointment signaled a dramatic shift in the resources allocated to District 17. It was as if the party of the Siragusa years was over and Cusack got the check.

One of Siragusa's major initiatives was modernizing the Lebanese and Italian police services partnered with the Bureau, but Cusack arrived to find the Rome office badly in need of its own modernization, with obsolete equipment and agents going out of pocket on routine expenses. The office's reel-to-reel recording device, he complained, was "a relic," and the agents lacked the modern photo equipment necessary to build case files. Where Siragusa had once happily covered the tab when entertaining foreign officials or undercover targets, the men were now admonished to "be careful and discriminate in the manner of expending Government money."[8]

The budget pinch worsened the case slump in District 17. Privately, Speer and Siragusa considered easing up. "Their morale is low but one good seizure should bring them out in the front again," Siragusa remarked. In their communications with Cusack, however, both men indicated they expected the district to do more with less. When Cusack countered that ramping up field operations would strain his already meager funds and begged for an increase, he was denied, and Giordano barked at him to stop "continuously taking exception to instructions" sent from Washington. Caught between the need to make cases and empty coffers, Cusack reluctantly implemented austerity measures that further hampered investigations.[9]

The battle over District 17's expenditures continued for years. Personal favors and gifts were a key feature of operations under Siragusa, and, Cusack pointed out, the agents needed to spend money for the Bureau to "remain competitive with other U.S. agencies operating abroad." It's telling that Cusack framed it in the context of American bureaucratic competition and not global counternarcotic strategy, but, he rightly pointed out (echoing arguments first made by Siragusa), "whenever you give a foreign police official a bottle of whiskey, a carton of cigarettes or a box of cigars he owes you something and will come through with that little extra favor when needed." When, less than a year later, Siragusa decreed that all such purchases would have to come out of pocket, Cusack canceled bulk cigarette purchases for the entire office in a fit of pique, prompting a wordy rebuke from Siragusa: "Your unabated and impertinent manifestations of philological prowess reflect a disconcerting retrogressive comprehension of basic standard operating procedures in the administrative area."[10]

It's unclear if Siragusa was responding to institutional pressures or trying to hamstring a rival. It was probably both. Eventually, the pressure began to get to Cusack, and he took his frustration out on underperforming agents, which Siragusa took as further proof that he was unfit to lead the district. Personal antagonisms actually crowded in to such a degree that Speer rebuked Cusack for delaying an undercover buy to remain with his pregnant wife during a difficult labor that resulted in the stillbirth of their infant son.[11]

The fight over District 17's budget injected a damaging level of animus into foreign operations, but the underlying problem was the natural dialectic between trafficking and enforcement tactics. The Beirut office generated a lot of work at mid-decade, but it went quiet during Lebanon's 1958 political crisis and exposed the lack of cases elsewhere in the district. In response, Siragusa and Speer pushed Cusack to stop relying on informants and get his agents into the field. In May 1959, Speer noted that "tremendous seizures" made in New York over the previous six months indicate "there is a fertile field and ample opportunity for District #17 agents to initiate cases leading to comparable seizures." The problem, headquarters felt, was that agents had become overly reliant on informants, few of whom could be trusted. Instead, Speer and Siragusa instructed the agents to attempt "cold turkey" approaches (without the benefit of an informant's introduction) in the "ginmills, taverns, etc.," despite the admonition to spend less money.[12]

The dubious reliability of informants in District 17 was a real and pressing issue. Aggravating the problem, however, was the fact that officials like Speer and Giordano lacked prolonged investigative experience overseas and believed—incorrectly—that "making cases in Europe is no different from making cases in the States." In point of fact, it was very different—as Siragusa, at least, knew all too well. Cusack acknowledged that there were cases to be made. But, he countered, why hadn't New York generated leads for District 17? The real impediment, he countered, was that "our means are not the equal" of the New York office, particularly when it came to police authority. With the mandatory minimums introduced by the 1951 Boggs Act and 1956 Narcotic Control Act, the Bureau could generally count on a steady supply of informants looking to avoid jail time. But in District 17, Cusack pointed out, that mechanism is "not available to us nor is the manpower nor technical equipment." Penalties for drug violations were often significantly less punitive in Europe and the Middle East, and the agents lacked the authority to intervene with prosecutors or make routine street arrests. In places like France, the FBN was explicitly prohibited from making "exploratory cases." That meant the agents had to settle for slow-developing conspiracy cases or informants motivated by cash rewards. The results were predictable, and, Siragusa observed, "Too much time has been wasted on unreliable informants who in addition rob our money."[13]

Speer and Siragusa pushed "cold turkey" approaches—a term typically associated with abrupt withdrawal from heroin—as the solution for all that ailed District 17. No more per diems or venal informants, just an undercover agent mano a mano in a battle of wits with a drug dealer. Cusack, however, was aghast and argued the technique was outdated, ineffective, and "a last resort." Few agents had much confidence in the method. "I did not believe that I could arrive in Paris or any other city and simply go out and make a case without a Special Employee," one agent replied after facing reprimand. The real cause of District 17's case slump was simply that regional traffickers had caught on to American tactics, and cold-turkey approaches only made it worse. "The traffickers have all heard of the dangers of dealing with anyone who looks American," Agent Knight reported during a 1959 stop in Istanbul. Siragusa, again, knew better and frequently observed the same during his tenure in Rome. After ten years, the traffickers had caught on. "We are wearing out the gimmick in many areas," Cusack warned. And given the pressure to cut expenses, it took a seriously canny agent to make cold undercover approaches in "ginmills and taverns" without buying drinks.[14]

While the agents in District 17 tried to do more with less, impatience grew in Washington. In early 1960, headquarters issued new guidelines requiring each agent to submit quarterly progress reports.[15] For the first time, agents were held to a quota, and those who failed to make a case every three months were unceremoniously shipped home, creating pressure to focus on results-oriented short-term busts at the expense of more valuable long-term investigations. The freewheeling days of District 17 were officially over, and the only agents afforded any latitude were those who consistently made cases. Fortunately for the Bureau, however, three new branch offices were on the horizon, offering new leads and new opportunities.

"Getting Our Foot in the Door"

Even as District 17's caseload sank to an all-time low, the institutional bonds painstakingly forged with foreign police over the previous decade facilitated a critical expansion, particularly in France, which rapidly became the focal point of U.S. counternarcotic efforts. By the summer of 1959, Cusack reported, it was "increasingly evident that almost all heroin smuggled to the United States is of clandestine manufacture in France." The name hadn't stuck yet, but the Bureau was witnessing the crystallization of the infamous "French Connection," as opium and morphine base from around the Mediterranean was increasingly destined for the Marseille region of France, where it was processed into heroin in clandestine labs and smuggled across the Atlantic. "The narcotic situation in France, so far as it concerns us, is as serious as it has ever been," Cusack concluded. For once the suits in Washington agreed, and Speer relayed word to Anslinger that the FBN "will make little progress in District 17 until the continuous flow of heroin from the Marseille underworld is blocked."[16]

Enforcement in France, however, was a daunting prospect. The Bureau quickly zeroed in on the "Corsican Mafia" as its primary antagonist, believing it had "almost complete control" over the French underworld and a monopoly on the critical heroin manufacturing process. Much like Sicily to Italy, Corsica is a Mediterranean island under French domain. Both were home to communities that tended to be separatist in outlook and marginalized on the mainland—a background that facilitated their cooperative ventures and reinforced the FBN's predisposition to see the Corsicans as a unified "Mafia" rather than a series of disparate gangs sharing a common heritage. One 1966 FBN briefing paper described the Corsican mob as "very similar to and operates by almost the same criminal code as does the Italian Mafia." Though present throughout France, Corsican influence was concentrated in Marseille, and there were troubling rumors that many Corsican criminals had ties to French intelligence (as well as the Gestapo) that dated back to the Resistance. Historian Al McCoy contends that some gangsters also received backing from the CIA as a check on Marseille's influential labor movement.[17]

Profound differences of opinion between French and U.S. law enforcement further compounded the challenge of working in France. As one agent observed, the French have "a deep feeling of independence and do not like to be advised [on] the manner in which to conduct an investigation," nor were they overly fond of undercover work or informants. The Bureau had long sought better access to the country, but the relationship was strained by Gallic ambivalence toward the United States in general and FBN methods in particular. Anslinger pressed to get an agent or, at minimum, a sympathetic consul stationed in Marseille as early as 1947 but to no avail.[18]

During his own tenure, Siragusa tried to cultivate a Sûreté official named Edmond Bailleul, who took over the country's Central Narcotics Office in 1952. Bailleul professed great affection for George White but didn't trust Siragusa and (understandably) demanded close supervision of any FBN activity in France. Siragusa thought him well intentioned but suffering "illogical illusions of grandeur," a charge leveled at any foreign official who dared insist on oversight of FBN operations. It's possible that Bailleul was dirty, and his bureaucratic rivals forced him into retirement in 1955 with the accusation that he associated with Corsican traffickers. The Bureau managed to carry out a few operations behind Bailleul's back (with poor results), but it faced a real problem in the clash of cultures between American and French law enforcement, and FBN access remained sharply limited by his replacement, Commissaire Charles Gillard, a former Vichy homicide detective.[19]

Tensions between the FBN and French police increased during the 1950s, as Bureau officials began to suspect the American heroin market was swollen with diversions from the French pharmaceutical industry. After his men captured large quantities of high-quality heroin in the fall of 1955, New York district supervisor James Ryan commented, "There is no question that a tremendous quantity of heroin is being smuggled into the United States directly from France. It is my opinion that clandestine factories could hardly be responsible for this output." Siragusa was less convinced. "The root of the evil is excessive Turkish opium production," he countered, and "there are enough clandestine laboratories in France, Turkey, Lebanon, Syria and maybe Italy too to feed heroin into the United States in large quantities and continuously." FBN inquiries and a check on French production figures at the United Nations, however, indicated that a considerable volume of narcotics (labeled as ethylmorphine or dionin) may have leaked into the illicit traffic. When the Bureau pressed, French officials stonewalled and reported "nothing abnormal." Dissatisfied with what they took as a "whitewash," FBN officials sent an agent and informant to take an unsanctioned look at the suspected factories, a sensitive operation only elliptically referenced in FBN records.[20]

Paradoxically, the Bureau enjoyed strong relations with Interpol, which was headquartered in Paris and staffed primarily by Sûreté officers. From early on, both Siragusa and Anslinger found Interpol a useful ally in monitoring suspected traffickers and gathering intelligence. Although tension between the Sûreté officers assigned to Interpol and those operating out of the Central Narcotics Office sometimes complicated liaison for the Bureau, Siragusa ensured his relations with Interpol remained "correct and never strained." In 1958 the FBN was even designated the formal U.S. representative to the international police body, making official a de facto relationship in place since J. Edgar Hoover abruptly withdrew FBI membership in 1951 (after realizing he could not dominate the organization).[21]

Siragusa pressed for a Paris office as early as 1957, but it took two years to wear down the Sûreté. In June 1959, Gillard finally acquiesced to a branch office after negotiations with FBN brass in Washington. *Agreed* is too strong a word; as one agent put it, "I received a very definite impression that they were waiting for us to open the office. . . . [A]t no time did they ever express approval." Once again the FBN's entrance was tenuous, but it was a start. For Andrew Tartaglino, the agent chosen to run the Paris office, it was good enough. "In my opinion this is getting our foot in the door," he wrote. Further testimony to the deteriorating relationship between Washington and Rome, however, Cusack was not even informed until he was suddenly ordered to dispatch Tartaglino to Paris before the French could change their mind. Cusack's objections— that all of his manpower was tied up in Turkey and French officials were about to go on summer holiday—fell on deaf ears. "It is imperative that we do not lose our foothold in France," Giordano remonstrated.[22]

When news of the Paris office arrived, Cusack's attention was fixed on the Middle East. In an effort to pull the district from its doldrums, Cusack traveled to Ankara to renew the FBN's standing request to allow joint investigations in Turkey. The Anatolian peninsula remained the largest source of opiates (both licit and illicit) in the region, but Turkish officials successfully kept the FBN at arm's length for more than a decade and had just recently thwarted Garland Williams's appointment as a State Department police adviser. To retain control over the few token investigations that were allowed, Turkish officials required the agents to work with two specially designated detectives from the Directorate of Public Safety, named Ali Eren and Galip Labernas. Cusack's personal diplomacy, however, earned the Bureau tentative permission to send agents to Istanbul for extended assignments. With several promising cases already lined up, Cusack was optimistic this temporary arrangement would soon result in a permanent office in Istanbul or Ankara.[23]

Here, finally, was cause for optimism. The Bureau's eastern flank had been mostly secure since 1955, when the shah of Iran announced a comprehensive anti-opium campaign and cracked down on both use and production. Encouraged by police advisers like Garland Williams, Iran even signed on to the 1953 Opium Protocol, the strict control treaty championed by Anslinger.[24] Now with branch offices either newly opened or soon to open on both ends of the regional supply chain, the Bureau no longer had to content itself with straddling the traffic from Rome or Beirut. By the summer of 1959—roughly six months after Cusack's arrival—District 17 could finally direct its efforts against the entirety of the Mediterranean and Atlantic heroin traffic.

Back in Washington, however, Siragusa was showing the strain of his headquarters rivalries and attempt to undermine Cusack. In the margins of Cusack's report on the prospective Istanbul office, Siragusa scribbled a note to Anslinger, complaining that with so many agents manning branch offices, no one was left for undercover work. "Looks like too much empire building and no cases in immediate sight," he wrote. When the Turks rebuffed Williams's appointment four months earlier, however, Siragusa advised Anslinger that "District #17 could set up a branch office there quietly and without any fan-fare."[25] In other words, when the Istanbul office was Siragusa's idea, it was quiet diplomacy; when it was Cusack's idea, it was empire building.

Despite the turmoil at FBN headquarters, results in Turkey exceeded all expectations. A large part of the district's success lay in the selection of talented undercover agent Sal Vizzini to head the office. With a flair for operations and a gift for language, Vizzini quickly learned Turkish and achieved such effective collaboration from local police that he almost single-handedly ended District 17's case slump. Between January and April 1960, he and fellow FBN agent Frederick Cornetta participated in the seizure of over 250 kilos (about 550 pounds) of raw opium. In Rome Cusack estimated the Istanbul office would be ready to open by midsummer. In Washington Speer and Siragusa continued their gamesmanship: Siragusa suggested partnering Vizzini with underperforming agents to squeeze out more cases, and Speer pointed out that two of Vizzini's cases had featured "cold-turkey" approaches.[26]

Plans for Istanbul were thrown into momentary disarray, however, when the administration of Prime Minister Adnan Menderes was suddenly overthrown by military coup in May 1960—an event that took both the Bureau and U.S. military observers by surprise.[27] The FBN's designated collaborators Eren and Labernas were sidelined and exposed, Cusack reported, as "counter-espionage or security agents operating as a special squad" for Kemal Aygun, an important figure in the Menderes regime frequently identified as the FBN's best patron in Turkey. It's unclear if Aygun was in cahoots with Turkish traffickers, as the new military authorities alleged, but Eren and Labernas were definitely meant to keep the Bureau on a short leash.[28]

In any case, Vizzini was a resourceful agent and earned the new regime's gratitude by capturing a wanted bank robber. The Istanbul office opened on schedule in July 1960. Soon after, Vizzini oversaw the creation and training of a new dedicated narcotic squad. By the fall of 1960, FBN-Turkish relations were stronger than ever and led to an unprecedented string of successful cases, most involving the traffic in raw opium. It's noteworthy, however, that Vizzini attributed much of his success to an informant network kept secret from the Istanbul police. "I had some of the most talented thieves in Istanbul on my payroll," he wrote, "and it gave me a better intelligence system than the Istanbul police ever had." The seizures made throughout 1960 represented a record haul, and, soon after the new year, Cusack congratulated Vizzini on joining the "One Ton Club," writing, "So far as I know, you are the first narcotic agent . . . to have directly and personally participated in the seizure of over a ton of opium in the course of one year." In short, the future looked promising in Turkey, where the authorities were staunchly pro-American and increasingly ready to implement American-style drug control.[29]

The future, however, was less bright on the other side of District 17, where the FBN struggled with the French. Agents like Knight, who took over in Paris in 1961, must have experienced some déjà vu, as developments in France echoed FBN growing pains in Lebanon. Prohibited from exploratory investigations, the agents fumed under the tight supervision of the Sûreté and had to settle for a strategy of exploiting outside leads back into the country before the French would act. Unsanctioned investigations were tempting but far too risky. Informants were scarce and were certainly not going to be provided by French authorities, so the Bureau again had to beg, borrow, or steal from other U.S. intelligence services (primarily army and air force investigative units—no mention of the CIA). And, once again, domestic rivalries complicated FBN efforts. Although approval for the Paris office came from Charles Gillard, supervisor of the Central Narcotics Office, tensions between he and his superiors in the Sûreté quickly became so apparent that the agents cut him out in favor of a direct relationship with his boss, Michel Hacq, director of the Sûreté's investigative wing.[30] The Bureau's relationship with Interpol remained steady, and Agents Tartaglino and Knight were on good terms with Michel Hugues, a midlevel official who ran the day-to-day operations of the Central Narcotics Office.[31]

Getting into Paris was an important development, and the office took on real significance over the years. In 1968 it became the European headquarters for the FBN's successor, the Bureau of Narcotics and Dangerous Drugs.[32] From an operational standpoint, however, Marseille was where the action was. In August 1960, Speer announced that he was sending Agent Martin Pera to develop cases in the area. Pera was an experienced veteran, and Speer likely intended him to supplant Cusack in District 17. No dummy, Cusack realized he was being frozen out of operations in France, particularly after Speer and Giordano designated Pera and Anthony Pohl, a French-speaking agent from the New York office, to liaise with French officials. Cusack bristled at Speer's transparent maneuvers and exasperatedly pointed out that Pera and Pohl had stumbled directly into internal Sûreté rivalries that the Rome office had scrupulously avoided.[33]

Once more, a big case intervened at just the right moment. This time the setting was New York, where, in October 1960, FBN agents arrested a Guatemalan diplomat named Mauricio Rosal and his French accomplice, Etienne Tarditi, in possession of 50 kilos (roughly equal to 110 pounds) of uncut heroin. Their interrogation led to the discovery of another 50 kilos in a Long Island stash house, making the Rosal bust one of the largest seizures of heroin in FBN history. The "Ambassador case," as it was called, began with a tip from one of Knight's criminal informants in Beirut, who reported that a rival organization was using a diplomatic courier named "Maurice." Working with U.S. Customs and the French Sûreté, the Bureau identified the prime suspect as Mauricio Rosal Bron, the Guatemalan ambassador to Belgium and Holland—and, they discovered, a pedophile blackmailed into service by Tarditi.[34] The intended buyers, Trans World Airlines purser Charles Bourbonnais and longshoreman Nick Calamaris, had ties to the Mafia. Tarditi, however, was the key figure and, under questioning, provided a detailed overview of the trafficking scene in Marseille while hinting that he was protected by French intelligence. On the surface, this looked like a great case, but the Rosal bust ultimately revealed that some 200 kilos of heroin were smuggled into the United States from France *every month*.[35]

In retrospect, the enormous volume of drugs arriving via the French Connection shows that the Bureau had a rather poor grasp on the Atlantic heroin trade. At the time, however, it was precisely what FBN officials needed to galvanize French counternarcotic efforts and kick open the door.

In Paris, Tartaglino enthused, the case "could not have happened at a more opportune time" and demonstrated the need for an FBN outpost in the French capital.[36] The case also lent new urgency to the Bureau's effort to gain regular access to Marseille. As Anslinger, Speer, and Siragusa spread out to canvass French officials, the Bureau increasingly began to identify France as a "principal source of supply of pure heroin" and compared it to communist China or Italy during the Schiapparelli scandal. Back in New York, Agent Pera took a French consul on a few ride-alongs and introduced him to addicts who cheerfully acknowledged that everyone knew the good stuff was from Marseille.[37]

Anslinger even pressed President Kennedy to raise the issue with Charles de Gaulle during a diplomatic mission to Paris. The matter was relegated to written exchanges, but Treasury and State Department officials readily accepted Anslinger's contention that France was "responsible for nearly all the illicit heroin" east of the Mississippi, leading to an estimated three hundred million dollars in economic losses to drug abuse and crime.[38]

Once again, the combination of threatening a host nation's international reputation and enlisting officials from across the diplomatic, political, and law enforcement realms was key to the Bureau's success. In May 1961, Speer warned French police that the Bureau had gone easy on them in the past, "but that another year would be different." Later that day, he reported to Anslinger, "Now the French not only agree to having our agent in Marseilles but are eager to have one there."[39]

The Bureau chose a new recruit named Anthony Pohl to run the Marseille office. Pohl grew up in France, fought with the Resistance during World War II, and had nine years of investigative experience in Europe with U.S. Army CID. Though new to drug enforcement, Pohl was recruited largely on the strength of his ties to French officials and demonstrated his mettle while interrogating Etienne Tarditi, but he found an uphill struggle waiting for him in Marseille.[40]

Taking up residence over the summer, Pohl had the new office up and running out of the American consulate by September 1961. Marseille, however, was a mess, one that was a long time in the making. Years earlier, the Bureau enjoyed some success working with Sûreté detective Robert Pasquier. But when Siragusa paid a social call on Pasquier back in 1951, he found the officer living with his pregnant wife and six-year-old son in "squalid" conditions, "reminiscent of the filthy New York City tenements." It was little wonder, the agents concluded, that police in Marseille were so easily bought. Ten years later, Pohl reported that the local narcotic squad remained "paralyzed by their fear of the Marseilles underworld." Pasquier was still on the job, and Cusack thought that he was probably "protecting some violators" but would move against low-ranking traffickers. Contributing to the "appalling" lack of enforcement in Marseille, Pohl observed, was a growing addict population swollen by the "return of the 'colons'" from Indochina and Algeria. The FBN's presence in the city also put new strain on the Sûreté command structure, as the national leadership of the Services de Police Judiciaire sent new men and resources to Marseille but removed the local squad from the supervision of Gillard's Central Narcotics Office. On the American side, FBN headquarters had to check Cusack's impulse to issue ultimatums and demand changes in French police administration.[41]

It was slow going, but within a few years the Marseille office established good liaison with local police and developed some productive leads. The famous NYPD "French Connection" case, immortalized by the book and movie of the same name, took shape between October 1961 and February 1962 and galvanized operations in Marseille. However, it also indicated that international law enforcement still had a long way to go toward effective control over the Atlantic heroin trade. In New York, the case resulted in the seizure of about fifty kilos of heroin, smuggled into the country via an automobile belonging to a minor French celebrity. But like the Rosal bust a year before it, the case confirmed that huge shipments of heroin continued to reach New York. Even worse, the main suspect, supplier Jean Jehan, escaped, and most of the contraband later disappeared from the NYPD's evidence locker, a postscript glossed over in the Hollywood version.[42]

This is what victory looked like in the early drug war. A decade into the FBN's foreign enforcement program, the Atlantic drug trade showed no sign of diminishing—if anything, it was growing. From a bureaucratic perspective, however, the expansion into France and Turkey was an achievement of the highest order. The FBN had secured the cooperation of the recalcitrant French and further institutionalized its influence with police agencies across Europe and the Middle East. By 1961 the district even began to look south, toward Africa, which had previously been an afterthought but was formally added to District 17's domain.[43] And the biggest expansion of the foreign drug war was still to come.

Bangkok and the Global Drug War

With District 17's growth into Lebanon, Turkey, and France, the FBN had demonstrated—depending on the measure—that it was the most effective tool with which to extend the reach of U.S. drug control. As Bureau officials looked to new areas, however, they risked aggravating the long-running feud with Customs. Since the original 1951 power-sharing agreement, FBN and Customs agents alternated between working cooperatively and sniping at one another. By the early 1960s, the bickering was intractable. Siragusa chalked the growing tension up to institutional jealousy, particularly over the Ambassador case. In the summer of 1962, Philip Nichols Jr., the commissioner of Customs, complained that very little intelligence reached his agency and FBN agents were actively withholding information on suspected drug shipments in order to bust the recipients in the United States.[44]

Better known as a "controlled delivery," the strategy was high risk/high reward, and its use was somewhat ambiguous in FBN policy—the agents were forbidden from posing as foreign suppliers and bringing drugs into the country themselves, but they sometimes let a shipment go through if they had a reasonable chance of recovering the cargo and wrapping up multiple wings of an organization. The danger, of course, was in losing track of a drug shipment allowed past the border. Despite the risks, the strategy was not uncommon. The Ambassador case is a perfect example, and Bureau officials had to convince the French to allow Rosal to leave Paris unmolested in order to arrest him in New York with Tarditi and the buyers. The technique, however, irritated Customs officials, who thought the "primary purpose" of foreign enforcement was "to feed information to the Customs officers at the ports," and they protested that many FBN busts were made "so soon" after the shipment arrived that it was obvious "narcotics agents knew by whom, where, and at what time the narcotics were to be smuggled, yet Customs was not informed."[45]

FBN officials responded with their own list of grievances and complained that Customs was trying to edge back into European drug enforcement, throwing several already delicate liaison relationships into confusion. The FBN, headquarters officials protested, was a model of interagency cooperation and continued to exchange information with Customs even as that agency infringed on FBN jurisdiction and disdained genuine police work. In the end, Siragusa and others pointed out, drug enforcement was "highly specialized," and Customs agents, with their myriad other duties and reluctance to go undercover, were simply not up to the task.[46]

The specific catalyst for the most recent skirmish was a set of dueling proposals from Customs and the FBN to open an office in Bangkok.[47]

Given the region's history of opium production and China's alleged role in the global drug trade, the Bureau was eager to get into Southeast Asia but constrained by resistance from Customs, the U.S. State Department, and local governments.

Following Mao Tse-tung's victory in the Chinese Civil War, it soon became apparent that the real problem in Southeast Asia was the poppy-rich area known as the Golden Triangle, a lawless region where the borders of China, Burma (now Myanmar), Laos, and Thailand all converge. The area was also home to remnants of General Chiang Kai-shek's routed Kuomintang Army (KMT), many of whom went to ground among the natives instead of retreating to Taiwan, becoming minor warlords and significant players in the local opium trade. The Bureau, however, was absolutely convinced that communist China was the ultimate source of the regional opium traffic and therefore the Pacific heroin trade. Proof of China's role would have paid handsome geopolitical dividends and remained a top FBN priority. In 1953, for example, HQ officials instructed agents in San Francisco to "be sure to include one defendant in Communist China" in an indictment being prepared against a band of merchant smugglers, as this would "be worth a great deal to the Commissioner in the United Nations."[48]

From the Golden Triangle, a significant portion of the region's opium trade moved south into Thailand, through Bangkok, and then by ship to major port cities like Singapore, Hong Kong, and Macao. As a result, Thailand assumed tremendous importance for regional control efforts, much as Rome and Beirut straddled the Mediterranean traffic in District 17. Two additional factors further complicated enforcement in Thailand. One, as of 1945, Thailand was the only remaining country in the world to sanction a legal recreational opium industry. And two, as historian Alfred McCoy details in *The Politics of Heroin: CIA Complicity in the Global Drug Trade* (2003), it's all but certain that the CIA turned a blind eye to the drug-running activities of regional partners working to contain the spread of communism from China and North Vietnam.[49]

Southeast Asia was Customs territory, so the FBN had to rely on indirect representation for most of the 1950s. One of Anslinger's favorite sources on Red China trafficking was a Japan-based American labor organizer named Richard Deverall, an eccentric red-baiter and likely CIA asset.[50] Anslinger also found a ready ally in the so-called China

Lobby, an amorphous group of politicians and activists who sought to prevent diplomatic recognition of communist China. The interest of such groups in FBN allegations of ChiCom trafficking created yet another feedback loop, amplifying FBN claims of Red China wrong-doing. Some contemporary observers have taken this relationship as yet another indication that Anslinger was a creature of special interests and corporate America, but the Commissioner was ready to use any tool that could shape the larger narrative around drugs. Such anticommunist groups and the FBN were essentially preaching to one another's choir.[51]

Fortunately, the Old Man also had credible sources in the form of U.S. diplomats stationed in Burma, Thailand, and Hong Kong—all of whom sent regular updates and described a wide-open trafficking scene in which nearly every regional player was complicit. One American consul in Rangoon dryly summarized, "The question of whether opium is coming in to Burma from Communist China has been answered with yes, no and maybe." The reality is that everyone was involved, and there was little state control over the inhabitants of the Golden Triangle on either side of the Bamboo Curtain. The Bureau even received one report from U.S. Army intelligence that depicted former KMTs, Shan, communists, Hmong, and Thais all cooperating smoothly, with communists in Yunnan directly handing shipments of opium over to the KMTs, despite their ostensible enmity.[52]

The Bureau was able to send its own people in on occasion. Toward the end of World War II, George White toured the region and reported on extensive poppy cultivation in the Shan states of Burma, pointing out that corruption was rampant and chances for prohibition slim.[53] Between 1953 and 1955, Anslinger received frequent dispatches from Wayland Speer. Intent on currying favor with the Old Man, Speer scoured the region for intel on ChiCom traffickers, who, he confidently reported, targeted American troops and used narcotics to "lower the fighting strength of colored soldiers in Japan and Korea." Speer came up empty but, in classic conspiracy thinking, took the absence of evidence implicating the communists as an "attempt to 'cloak and dagger' the investigation," and he dismissed indications of KMT trafficking as a "ruse to confuse the issue." Unsurprisingly, Speer came away from his tours convinced, he wrote, that "Red China Communists are having a field day pouring opium out of Yunnan into the Shan State for Thailand, Burma and the ends of the earth."[54]

Speer's cognitive acrobatics aside, there was quite a bit of opium in Thailand, and it had an undeniably pernicious influence on state institutions. In the summer of 1954, Speer traveled to Burma and Thailand to meet with local police and U.S. intelligence officers—including former OSS director "Wild Bill" Donovan, then serving as ambassador to Thailand. What he heard corroborated reports the FBN had received secondhand throughout the decade: involvement in the lucrative opium trade was universal. One former OSS man turned silk magnate told Speer that Thailand was "the most corrupt place on the earth. . . . [E]veryone is in the opium traffic from the top to the bottom."[55]

One of the more colorful characters Speer met was another former OSS China hand named Willis Bird, who now drove the streets of Bangkok with a machine gun in the trunk and two .38s in easy reach. Speer gathered that Bird was helping the CIA organize local anticommunist resistance and extract the remaining KMTs, but he also heard repeated allegations that Bird was directly involved in the opium trade. (Bird also later helped create the Thai stock exchange.) At one point, Speer met Bird for lunch together with a Thai police official "dressed in a perfumed silk suit, nylon mesh shoes, diamond ring, diamond tie clasp, miniature pearl-handled six shooter cuff links set with diamonds, and an automatic tucked under his alligator belt." Realizing that both men were dirty, he wrote Anslinger, "I refrained from asking embarrassing questions."[56]

The Thai military and police, Speer learned, were active participants in the opium traffic. Each were known to buy and sell bulk opium, and the two frequently competed to hijack caravans coming down from the highlands. Other observers told Speer that General Phao Sriyanond, director of Thailand's national police force and an important CIA client, had a hand in the traffic. This, obviously, complicated the enforcement situation. Speer was adamant that the conditions in Thailand were merely symptoms of the China disease, but he did occasionally stop to ponder: "How does one go about knocking off an army[?]" Ambassador Donovan assured Speer the Thai services were extricating themselves from the drug traffic, and Bureau officials did what they could to pressure the Thai government from afar.[57]

For the most part, that meant convincing the Thai government to close the state-licensed opium dens. In 1955 Anslinger publicly called on Thailand to enact a total ban on opium consumption. He was rebuked by U.S. diplomats, who warned that his "frontal attacks" at the United Nations were undermining a critical allied government and that, furthermore, prohibition would drive opium consumption underground and Thailand would "lose what control over opium smoking it has now." In keeping with drug war orthodoxy, however, the Bureau countered that treatment programs were useless and, Garland Williams informed one embassy official, "not needed for the great bulk of opium users." It would be "more productive," he continued, "if available funds are spent on eliminating the sources of supply of drugs." Perhaps in an effort to Westernize, the U.S.-backed military government agreed to criminalize opium consumption and close the dens, a process that began under Prime Minister Plaek Phibun in 1956 and was completed in June 1959 when the ban finally went into effect under Field Marshal Sarit Thanarat. As U.S. diplomats predicted, however, cracking down on consumption without addressing demand only pushed the opium economy underground and actually led to the development of a sizable heroin industry for the first time in the country's history.[58]

In retrospect, the creation of a Thai heroin market where there had previously been none is a damning development that can be laid partly at the feet of the FBN. But here again, the Sisyphean policy of drug control worked in the Bureau's favor and lent new impetus to the FBN's presence abroad. In the case of Thailand, the FBN was part of the problem and the solution.

In the fall of 1961, Cusack traveled to Southeast Asia to rally last-minute opposition to the UN Single Convention and gather proof of Customs' failure to crack the regional drug traffic or implicate communist China. Like Speer before him, Cusack met with various police authorities, diplomats, and U.S. intelligence officials—including Harold Young, an American missionary and zookeeper who, along with sons Gordon and William, helped organize local anticommunist forces for the CIA. They again confirmed that both communist and KMT forces participated in the regional drug trade, often in cooperation, but claimed the vast majority of the region's opium came from Burma and not China. None of the Youngs were avowed CIA officers, but Cusack was aware of their connection to U.S. intelligence, and the family's later involvement in the Nugan Hand banking scandal, which exposed CIA money laundering and connections to the drug trade, indicates they may have been players rather than mere observers. As usual, the situation was murky and the various clandestine relationships difficult to sort from the outside—and FBN records clearly indicate that the agents were on the outside looking in. Regardless of the complexities (or U.S. complicity, for that matter), Cusack concluded that the narcotic situation in Thailand was "extremely dangerous" and in need of immediate FBN representation.[59]

By the summer of 1962, Thailand's role as a new front line in the drug war was a foregone conclusion. The only real question was which Treasury Department agency would open an office in Bangkok, FBN or Customs. At stake, however, were much larger questions about the over-all posture of U.S. global counternarcotic strategy. As the Bureau's point man on foreign enforcement, Cusack was fully aware that the future of the drug war hung in the balance, and he knew just the man for the job: Salvatore Vizzini. Having pried open Istanbul, seized record-breaking quantities of contraband narcotics, and infiltrated the inner circle of FBN nemesis Lucky Luciano—all within the previous few years—Vizzini had a hot hand. In his memoir, Vizzini recounted that he was in the midst of a well-earned vacation when he was summoned to Washington and told that his next assignment would be, in his words, "to euchre Customs out of the Far East and add that to the Bureau's command." Before he left, Cusack pulled him aside and confided, "Pull this off, Sal, and we'll get the green light on Far East jurisdiction and take over from Customs. Then we'll really get the job done."[60]

In order to avoid tipping off Customs, the FBN arranged to have Vizzini sent to Bangkok under official U.S. military cover. He began his ninety-day assignment in August and split most of his time between lecturing U.S. military personnel and setting up busts for the Thai national police. Records are spotty here, but the cases Vizzini made with the Thai Central Narcotics Bureau were quite substantial and led to the seizure of more than one ton of raw opium and morphine base.[61]

Even before the results of Vizzini's exploratory work came in, how-ever, debate over the future of global drug enforcement was intensify-ing back in Washington—just as Henry Giordano was sworn in as the new commissioner of narcotics. Throughout August and September, top

FBN and Customs officials battled back and forth over which agency was best-suited to carry out U.S. global counternarcotic objectives. Although the link wasn't explicit in official exchanges, word of Vizzini's success in Thailand helped tip the Treasury Department toward the FBN. Interestingly, however, the Bangkok embassy received confidential word that Treasury was planning to relieve Customs of foreign drug control on August 8, only a week after Vizzini's arrival and prior to his meeting with Thai police. So it looks like Vizzini's assignment was something of a fait accompli—though Treasury could still scuttle the whole thing if Vizzini bungled the situation.[62]

Formal announcement of the FBN's new global jurisdiction was left to President Kennedy. On the opening day of the high-profile White House Conference on Narcotic and Drug Abuse in late September, Kennedy described American drug use as "a national problem" of "national concern." Although he complained of a "discouragingly high degree of relapse among addicts" and a field riven by "conflicting approaches," Kennedy found a sliver of hope in the foreign drug war. Like the FBN, Kennedy framed the drug problem as one that transcended national borders and sovereignty. "Our focus on national issues must not obscure the international aspects of our drug abuse problem," he remarked. "Criminals responsible for [this] international traffic in narcotics have no respect for national boundaries." In that regard, he continued, the FBN's efforts to "strike at the foreign sources" of the global drug trade "have been so successful that the activity of the Bureau of Narcotics is being expanded to other parts of the world."[63]

Back in Rome, Cusack immediately sent Kennedy's remarks on to the rest of District 17, adding, "It is a great honor for all of us to have the President of the United States mention our district and on the basis of our success to have the Treasury Department expand the activity of the Bureau to other parts of the world." By the start of the new year, Districts 16 and 18, covering East Asia and Latin America, were added to the Bureau's overseas holdings, and agents were dispatched to new offices in Bangkok, Mexico City, and Monterrey, followed by Lima, Hong Kong, Seoul, and Singapore.[64] Anslinger's dream of turning the FBN into a "cop at the crossroads of the world" was finally a reality.

In a cover letter transmitting the official edict, Assistant Treasury Secretary James A. Reed explained that the decision was not a reflection on Customs, but that the "dual jurisdiction" system in place since 1951 wasn't working and the FBN would now take the lead on all foreign drug investigations. The Bureau's argument about the unique challenges of counternarcotics carried the day; as Reed noted, "The principal work of the Bureau of Narcotics is concentrated in the narcotics field. Customs on the other hand has many other types of enforcement activity." The new arrangement, he reasoned, would lead to greater efficiency for both agencies.[65]

Meanwhile, back in Thailand, Vizzini was adding an explosive coda to the Bangkok affair—an episode recorded in his memoir but conspicuously absent from FBN records. Right around the time of Kennedy's remarks, Vizzini traveled north to the Thai border and secretly crossed into Laos to destroy a KMT heroin lab with the connivance of a local CIA agent who provided the explosives. If true, the incident suggests the CIA was not entirely complacent about the local heroin trade. Having apparently worsened a recurring bout with malaria during his foray across the Mekong, Vizzini received permission to cut his trip short and go home, mission accomplished. He returned in January 1963 to cut the ribbon on the Bangkok office and introduce Thai officials to Agent Bowman Taylor, the agent chosen to run the new office. After a few more years and a few more adventures, Vizzini retired from the Bureau to become chief of the South Miami Police Department. The Bangkok office continued on in his absence, though with somewhat less excitement.[66]

The Bureau had high hopes for Thailand. Agents operating out of Bangkok found a lot of opium but failed to conclusively implicate China. In late 1963, almost exactly one year after the establishment of District 16, Bureau officials ventured a "conservative estimate" that roughly one thousand tons of opium were produced in the Golden Triangle every year. Working with the Thai Central Narcotics Bureau, two FBN agents succeeded in making "some of the largest seizures ever . . . effected in this area." But, officials were forced to admit, "We do not have any true idea of the amount now being produced in China." After the explosive conclusion of Vizzini's trip, the FBN also had to overcome the heightened concerns of U.S. Embassy officials who feared the possible consequences of "operations carried out in cloak and dagger style."[67] Once the initial dust and excitement settled, it became clear that Southeast Asia was not quite the bonanza FBN officials had hoped. In January 1967, one FBN official reported that most of the opium produced in the area was consumed locally, limiting its contribution to the American market. "At the present time," he wrote, "the Far East is not considered to be the major source of illicit narcotics being smuggled into the United States. We have estimated that 80% of the heroin reaching our shores is produced in France from opium diverted from legitimate cultivation in Turkey."[68]

District 16 may have disappointed in terms of actual value to global counternarcotic objectives, but the FBN's triumph over Customs and expansion into East Asia and Latin America were nevertheless of great importance. Although the rivalry between Customs and the FBN and its successors continued for years, the terms of debate had shifted in the Bureau's favor, and the drug war was now irrevocably global in scope. The FBN's triumph at the strategic and bureaucratic level left an indelible imprint on the future of American drug enforcement and confirmed that source control, foreign intervention, and a hegemonic U.S. police presence would remain first principles.

The enlarged scope of FBN operations also helped to compensate for faltering diplomatic endeavors. In *Drug Diplomacy in the Twentieth Century*, William McAllister observes that control efforts at the United Nations "began to splinter between 1953 and 1961," precisely the years during which District 17 strengthened the FBN's grip on Europe and the Middle East. Anslinger and other source-control hard-liners put their faith in stern agricultural production limits, codified in the 1953 Opium Protocol. But its strictures were too severe to win enough signatories, and there was great pressure to simplify the welter of international treaties and regulatory bodies, which ultimately led to the 1961 UN Single Convention.[69]

The triumph of the 1961 Single Convention over the 1953 Opium Protocol was but one of the signs that Anslinger had lost his once formidable sway over the international process, a change visibly symbolized in the UN's 1955 transfer of drug control operations from New York to Geneva.[70] Starting around 1960, Anslinger was also frequently absent as his wife took ill and he moved home to Pennsylvania to care for her in her final days. By 1962 Anslinger was on his way out, and U.S. drug control policy drifted in his absence.

The expansion of the Bureau's foreign enforcement program from Europe and the Middle East to the rest of the world thus came at a critical time and ensured that, even if political and diplomatic attention had wandered, police forces all over the world remained focused on source control and supply-side enforcement strategies. The ultimate irony was that even as the FBN successfully took the drug war global, its own demise loomed. And, of course, the illicit drug traffic continued to grow and evolve, providing drugs to American addicts and tempting unwary enforcement officers with infinite opportunities for corruption. Only six years later, the Federal Bureau of Narcotics was finally swallowed by the ever-present threat of federal consolidation. But the war it began marched on.

This leaves some crucial historical questions: How did the foreign drug war continue even while the consensus supporting it began to splinter? What, ultimately, were the keys to District 17's success, and what is its legacy?

A Devil's Bargain

Making cases was the most visible—but not necessarily the most accurate—way to measure the success of the FBN. The poorly documented nature of the drug trade makes certain elements of its history unknowable. Certainly, we can say that District 17 failed to curb the Atlantic drug trade, but, beyond that, we can only speculate as to how distant the agents remained from their larger objectives. From a contemporary standpoint, it is ultimately more useful to gauge the Bureau's success in terms of its bureaucratic relationships and ideological influence—trends that, unlike the volume of the illicit drug trade, can be measured in the historical record. The Bureau's institutional success overseas depended, in nearly equal measure, on its relations with foreign governments and other U.S. agencies. Without the approval or tolerance of host nations, there would have been no foreign program to speak of. And without support from the rest of the U.S. government— particularly the grudging acquiescence of the State Department—the Bureau would have lacked the foundation necessary to go abroad.

One of the biggest questions hanging over the history of the foreign drug war concerns the relationship between the FBN and CIA. A number of authors—particularly those interested in the "deep politics" of the American national security state—claim the FBN countenanced or even protected the drug-running activities of certain assets, either by recruiting high-level traffickers as informants or by turning a blind eye to CIA-backed traffickers.[71] Given the clandestine nature of the Bureau's work and the murky criminal milieu in which the agents were submerged, it's easy to see how the worlds of drug trafficking and espionage would converge.

It's no real surprise, however, to find there is little direct evidence to support such claims in FBN records. That does not mean these charges, conspiratorial though some may be, are untrue—a number of them undoubtedly are, and bread crumbs scattered throughout FBN files offer intriguing hints. A folder randomly located amid overseas reports, for example, holds a chemical analysis of a wrapper from a package of heroin—performed by Sidney Gottlieb, a critical figure in the MK-ULTRA program.[72] There are also several of the kind of examples expected of two agencies that presumably should exchange information on a regular basis. Reading between the lines of FBN records reveals countless elliptical references to the CIA, suggesting that at some point it became official policy to avoid explicitly naming the Central Intelligence Agency.[73]

A number FBN agents pulled double duty for the Bureau and CIA. According to the memoirs of CIA director William Colby, Siragusa was almost certainly one of his sources in Rome. The FBN's emphasis on undercover work meant that the agents' field craft was second to none, and those who were able to thrive in the challenging overseas environment were particularly effective operators. Some agents, like Sal Vizzini, performed missions for the CIA while remaining with the Bureau. Other agents, like Tom Tripodi, who worked in counterintelligence, formally transferred back and forth. Paul Knight was definitely approached and may have been recruited by the CIA during his time in Beirut and France.[74]

The best-documented example is Hank Manfredi. A series of memos between Siragusa and Anslinger in the spring of 1957 indicate that Manfredi worked on several highly classified CIA projects while attached to the Rome office. During one of his semifrequent absences, Siragusa sheepishly wrote, "My ignorance of Manfredi's future plans is rather embarrassing to me, more so since I am ostensibly his Supervisor."

Journalist Douglas Valentine claims that Manfredi was, in fact, Lucky Luciano's CIA case officer.[75]

A number of authors have argued, as Bruce Bullington and Alan Block do, that cooperation between the Bureau and the CIA—or the CIA's infiltration of the FBN—indicates the drug war serves primarily "to mask the U.S. counter-intelligence and paramilitary presence abroad."[76] This is true to a degree, particularly once the drug war migrated to Central America in the 1980s and '90s, but the global drug war is no charade and not merely an elaborate front for U.S. intelligence.

The records and history of District 17 reveal a complicated story. Because most of the Bureau's case files were destroyed, it's hard to say with any certainty whether the CIA influenced any given investigation. Nevertheless, two conclusions are inescapable: first, the FBN was absolutely sincere in its efforts to disrupt the global heroin trade, which it perceived as a genuine threat to American security, and, second, the agents spent far more time on drug control than they did on extracurricular intelligence operations.

Returning to the idea of drug control as a "devil's bargain" explains many of the apparent tensions and contradictions of the American foreign drug war. Because drug use (like many vices) is a consensual crime, it requires a proactive style of enforcement and a burdensome dependence on informants. Working on foreign soil, FBN agents were denied the kind of low-level roundups that produce informants in domestic law enforcement. As a result, the agents turned to financial incentives to encourage their special employees or to even more specious motivations like revenge. The Bureau also had to rely on the cooperation and assistance of local police officials who were often similarly compromised by the local drug trade. This was not necessarily an indication of treachery; it was a political reality in places where the drug traffic had influential patrons, including the United States. And just as the Bureau had to tolerate informants or collaborators who might participate in the very traffic they sought to police, these same foreign police services were asked to tolerate the presence of American cops who represented foreign intervention and a compromise of their own sovereignty.

Needless to say, this required a delicate balancing act. Some agents, at least, were sensitive to the dilemma in which they placed their foreign collaborators. "If, for example, Scotland Yard had sent men over to District #2 [New York]," Agent Knight once mused, "and these men had had successes which outshone the work of the District, I feel that perhaps our own attitude would be unfairly but understandably cool." On encountering resistance from Lebanese officials, Knight reasoned that he would behave in precisely the same manner if the roles were reversed. "I should be friendly to the boss, and show that I am most cooperative and socially am a good fellow," Knight remarked. "I should give the boss and his service a few examples demonstrating that I am willing to cooperate. . . . BUT I would see to it that the man here got no real help, and accomplished as little as possible. . . . Then I could say, in effect: you see, they sent one of their hot-shots to do a job (thereby implying that my outfit could not do it), and look what the hot-shot accomplished—nothing."[77]

It's worth pointing out, of course, that U.S. officials would never permit such a role reversal. Yet another of the ironies of drug control was that the extension of U.S. law enforcement beyond territorial borders and claims on a kind of supranational jurisdiction for drug control were accompanied by vociferous opposition to the introduction of international law into American jurisprudence.[78] In U.S. hands, the authority vested in drug control flowed in one direction only. Officials like Turkish security chief Kemal Aygun paid lip service to the idea that the Turks were somehow culpable for American addiction and told one diplomat that he "felt responsible when he read of the addiction of New York school children."[79] But it's unlikely that anyone in the U.S. government would have accepted responsibility for something like Turkish teens puffing Lucky Strikes.

The confluence of international law enforcement, politics, and corruption meant the agents in District 17 had to live by a bastardized version of the "Serenity Prayer" immortalized by Alcoholics Anonymous, finding the serenity to accept the things they could not change—like local drug use or police complicity—and the wisdom to engage in compromises that might allow them to make a meaningful impact on the international traffic. No wonder Siragusa complained so frequently of ulcers. If the Bureau wanted to make cases, it had to roll with the punches—sometimes literally, as in the case of Agent Attie's beating at the hands of Sûreté officials in Lebanon. Samil Khoury, the trafficker whom Sûreté detectives were ostensibly protecting, is a perfect example;

because he was protected by local politicians (and possibly Western intelligence services) and therefore beyond the FBN's reach, agents like Knight reasoned that they might as well employ him as an informant and take out his competitors, which would still reduce the overall number of traffickers operating in the region and therefore reduce the volume of heroin reaching the United States. It was a flawed strategy, but as Americans operating on foreign soil, the agents had to take what they could get. As Joe Arpaio, a veteran of Istanbul, put it, "You either dealt with the powers that be or you didn't, and if you chose the latter path, then you might as well have packed up and gone home."[80]

District 17's primary concern was to retain access to areas of strategic importance to global counternarcotic efforts. The agents were willing to push the limits of foreign tolerance and occasionally carried out unilateral investigations behind their hosts' back, but they were on tenuous ground and knew that unsanctioned operations were a sure way to lose access. When Cusack proposed allowing the CIA to infiltrate Interpol under FBN cover, for example, he was harshly rebuked for jeopardizing the entire foreign program.[81]

The larger question is how District 17 overcame these dilemmas. Despite their apparent inability to "win" the (unwinnable) drug war, the answer seems to be that the agents were relatively effective cops, agile bureaucrats, and, when the occasion demanded it, they actually did put on spats and play diplomat. The CIA was simply one in a constellation of critical, often determinative, bureaucratic relationships.

Institutionalizing Influence

Institutional relationships were arguably the most important aspect of foreign enforcement, and they could take a variety of forms, including interpersonal and bureaucratic associations, training and equipment, and developing a rationale for U.S. intervention—all of which linger into the present.

Agents like Knight sometimes posed as travel agents, but the Bureau also played the role in all seriousness, arranging travel accommodations and serving as local guides for U.S. and foreign officials. As Siragusa reminded a colleague back in the States, "Remember, we will always try to roll out the red carpet for our friends." When foreign dignitaries visited cities like New York, the Bureau always had an agent at the airport to show them around—a gesture that built and maintained goodwill. In Europe the agents did the same for visiting officials high and low, including U.S. attorneys, judges, senators, and congressmen. Entertaining political patrons gave the agents a chance to press the FBN's virtues upon their visitors, who would then support Bureau efforts back home. With his excellent connections among European police, Manfredi provided critical assistance to Secret Service advance teams whenever Kennedy, Johnson, or Nixon visited Europe.[82]

In their dealings with foreign police officers, the agents had one final card to play: an appeal to the fraternal nature of police work. "The only difference between two policemen," Siragusa wrote, "is the language, and this barrier is easily broken down with brandy and sincerity." His account of the Abou Sayia investigation (and many others) ended with a rowdy international celebration. "We were plastered, but happy. The historic enmities were forgotten. We were friends and policemen who had just done a good job."[83]

It was this connection to foreign police services that was the real strength and ultimate legacy of District 17. In the early years, the agents were disheartened by what they perceived as backward, inefficient police organizations with little regard for drug work. Siragusa, in particular, frequently complained (this time in France), "I have given up trying to reform these policemen and convert them to our modern efficiency."[84] Faced with the absolute necessity of cooperating with foreign police, however, the Bureau stifled its exasperation and reversed course. Financial incentives helped; when Siragusa rewarded the Italian Questura for a single kilo of heroin seized in New York with a payment of six hundred thousand lire—nearly equal to the wholesale price—he reported, "I believe that this offer will spur the police to no end."[85] Eventually, however, the money ran out, and specialized training took over as a primary incentive for cooperation with the FBN. Over time District 17 launched extensive training programs in Italy, Greece, Turkey, Lebanon, and (via Garland Williams) Iran. France was the only notable exception. Another successful tactic, particularly in developing countries, was to court promising foreign officials on the assumption they would rise through the ranks and take favorable impressions of the Bureau with them.[86]

One of the interesting things about District 17 is that it had one foot squarely in the so-called First World (Italy and France) and one in the Third World (Turkey and Lebanon). This meant the Bureau dealt with both *developing* and ostensibly *developed* powers, yet it tended to judge both by the seriousness with which they confronted the dope menace. The level of any given country's commitment to drug control was taken as a direct metric of that country's standing in the civilized world, and in that regard the French were seen as little better than the Lebanese. Countries that did not share America's commitment were judged less civilized and less modern. Once District 17 was up and running, the agents tried to avoid overtly judgmental language, but countries like Turkey were frequently condemned for their backwardness and lax attitude. As Garland Williams reported during a 1949 visit to Ankara, "I have waved the flag of world opinion and talked teamwork in the community of law-abiding nations." A year later, Siragusa had a harrowing experience touring Istanbul's only addict ward. Haunted by the squalor and lack of medical care, he wrote, "I was left with the thought that civilization in this part of the world is a very slow process."[87]

Much has been written in recent years about the obligations of sovereignty and the "responsibility to protect," an idea sometimes abbreviated R2P. The theory argues that states have a basic responsibility to protect their populations from crimes like genocide and ethnic cleansing.[88] The Bureau, however, had long argued that protecting people from the ravages of addiction was a basic requirement of sovereignty, a duty owed not only to a state's citizens but to all humanity. With so much attention on the interplay between drugs, security, and sovereignty, the Bureau even anticipated the logic of the Bush Doctrine, which posits that the United States has the right to intervene in nations that harbor terrorists. Anslinger frequently argued the same was true of countries that could not or would not move against the dope menace. As he explained to one French official, "If treatment in any one of the countries concerned is lenient, that territory serves as a convenient base from which criminals may scheme and set their nefarious plans in operation" and "contaminate the population of a friendly neighbor."[89] For Anslinger, that might not be grounds for military invasion, but it was cause for international condemnation, U.S. intervention, and a permanent FBN office.

The Bureau's effort to contain addiction thus led it first to claim and then actually to achieve a tenuous kind of global jurisdiction. In 1948, Anslinger declared, "There are no national boundaries in our work. You can't afford national sovereignty when you're trying to break up the narcotics racket."[90] By 1962 the Old Man's dream was close to a reality, and the FBN was a truly global police force. The Bureau knew, however, that it couldn't do the job alone, which put it in the forefront of U.S. nation-building and modernization efforts, strategies that were used to inoculate against both radicalism and drug abuse.[91] The Bureau lacked the resources to do large-scale nation building, but it could get foreign police services up to speed and turn them into effective international partners.

In addition to training foreign police services, the Bureau assisted host nations in acquiring the latest in modern police equipment, from two-way mirrors, filing systems, surveillance and radio equipment, and navigational devices to handcuffs, blackjacks, and firearms. As historian Jeremy Kuzmarov notes in *Modernizing Repression* (2012), in many developing nations this kind of assistance was used to suppress political dissent. In most of the countries of District 17, however, the agents tended to partner with specialized departments, like the Italian Guardia di Finanza, which investigated smuggling and financial crimes but were ill-suited to widespread political oppression. Although the Bureau worked with militarized gendarme-style police forces, Turkey was the only country in which agents were directly partnered with security forces or political police.

Police training, however, was a two-way street, and the recipients ultimately decided how that training was put to use.[92] It was no different for the Bureau. Although Siragusa was able to convince the Guardia di Finanza to establish a specialized narcotic squad under Italian police captain Giuliano Oliva—and, with great difficulty, even acquired specialized navigational equipment for them—he couldn't direct their day-to-day activities and complained that, instead of hunting Mafia drug traffickers, Oliva was "up in the air, literally—in a helicopter looking for cigarette smugglers almost every day."[93] The equipment and training provided to foreign services made host nations more tolerant of the FBN presence and built a foundation for better international enforcement, but the FBN's expansion also reveals the limits of American power. No matter how far the foreign drug war reached or how many agencies were coaxed into the fight, the drug traffic remained.

The Game Remains the Same

In 1966 the Bureau's foreign drug war was stretching into its fifteenth year and showing signs of malaise. Now serving in a headquarters role as an inspector, it was Jack Cusack's turn to complain about District 17's flagging production. Noting that agents in East Asia and Latin America were closing out cases, Cusack warned that, as of June, District 17 had only three cases on the books and was "headed for its poorest annual performance to date." The Mediterranean remained a central front in the drug war, but it produced a mind-set where failure demanded only greater levels of effort and intervention rather than a reevaluation of basic strategy.[94]

Cusack also had to deal with Treasury officials who feared an international incident and were increasingly uneasy about the lack of formal guidelines governing the FBN's presence abroad. Cusack explained, "Our effectiveness in the foreign countries is only as good as our liaison with the people we work with." Questions like whether the agents could participate in arrests, testify in court, or carry guns were typically "left to the discretion of the foreign officials." It was the department's prerogative to negotiate formal terms, he acknowledged, but warned, "We would not come out very well." Ultimately, Cusack argued, "we must risk undesirable consequences for the sake of carrying out our work in foreign countries." In other words, it was actually the informal nature of the program that allowed the agents to lean on their cop-to-cop diplomacy and create the leeway necessary to fulfill their mission—a strange hybrid of soft and hard power.[95]

This was a noteworthy evolution from the early years, when the lack of formal arrangements made the FBN presence feel so precarious. A briefing memo prepared by Manfredi that same year reinforced the importance of personal relationships. At least in Western Europe, he warned, "the halycon [sic] days are fast disappearing." The Bureau could no longer count on modernization to secure its influence, and Manfredi cautioned, "Our equipment does not carry the 'magic' connotation as in the past." Above all, he counseled incoming agents, "you must be liked."[96]

While effective liaison took on greater importance in Europe, police training and modernization programs remained an effective way of securing FBN influence in the developing world. In Rome district supervisor Mike Picini observed that decolonization was offering new opportunities for American leadership and training. Bringing select officers to the States at FBN expense remained a successful method of "indoctrination." The bottom line, as Picini saw it, was that the Bureau had an obligation to "participate in the education of the various police organizations throughout this district, since all these countries having a narcotic problem can become a potential source of supply for U.S. addicts."[97] Even as the Cold War consensus was beginning to splinter under the weight of the Vietnam War, the logic of a global security perimeter lived on in the realm of drug control.

Fifteen years into the foreign drug war, narcotics remained a global threat requiring a global response. The only solution, as FBN drug warriors saw it, was to ensure that foreign nations shared the commitment and the resources to join the global drug war and contain addiction. This style of thought and policy continued more or less uninterrupted into what is more commonly identified as the start of the modern war on drugs in the early 1970s. Yet as the history of District 17's founding and expansion reveals, punitive policing, source control, modernization, and foreign intervention were the handmaidens of drug enforcement long before Nixon took up the mantle of the drug war.

By the end of the 1960s, important changes were taking place, but there were also remarkable continuities. As the narcos, dealers, and stick-up boys of David Simon's *The Wire* liked to remark, with a wry acknowledgment for the tiny roles they all played in a much larger cycle, "The game remains the same." In District 17, personnel shifted, tactics were tweaked, cases came and went, and even the FBN was eventually replaced, first by the BNDD and later by the DEA. But the drug traffic, the drug war, and the ideology of American hegemony remained.

CHAPTER 8

THE WHEEL TURNS

America's public enemy number one in the United States is drug abuse.
In order to fight and defeat this enemy, it is necessary to wage a new,
all-out offensive.

—RICHARD NIXON (1971)

Drugs are bad and we're going after them. . . . [W]e've taken down the
surrender flag and run up the battle flag. And we're going to win the war
on drugs.

—RONALD REAGAN (1982)

One of Henry Giordano's first duties as the new commissioner of narcotics was a toast. Anslinger reached mandatory retirement on his seventieth birthday in May 1962, and President Kennedy accepted his resignation in July. Giordano was confirmed as his replacement with little fuss in August, but the entire FBN hierarchy was preoccupied with the growing foreign enforcement program and preparations for a White House conference on drugs in September, so it was December before Anslinger's colleagues got around to holding a retirement dinner. That gave Giordano roughly six months to prepare a proper send-off for his influential predecessor. The American Pharmacists Association presented a medal to the outgoing Commissioner, but Giordano was the headliner and the stories he shared that night were revealing. He admitted that, as a young agent, he had once been sent to fetch the Commissioner's laundry. He also recounted the time Anslinger squeezed in a hunting trip during a visit to the Denver office and announced to the staff, "in his inimitably menacing way," that he would like to "get himself a deer." No fools, the agents trekked into the woods and dutifully staked out a young buck to turn loose for the unsuspecting Old Man. A happy Commissioner, Giordano remarked, meant a happy Bureau.[1]

Giordano played it for laughs, but he spoke to a larger truth that evening: for thirty-two critical years, Anslinger imposed his indomitable will on a fractious and controversial organization. But in hindsight, perhaps that's overstating it; maybe agents like Siragusa and Speer had staked out prize bucks of their own over the years, targets they knew Anslinger couldn't resist, like Lucky Luciano or Red China—examples of where the Bureau's commitment to drug war orthodoxy overrode the complexities of the drug trade.

Whatever the case, Giordano was no Anslinger. One colleague described him to reporters as "tough without being rough," but the new Commissioner possessed neither the force of personality nor the political acumen necessary to corral the rambunctious agency and guide it through its many crises.[2] It's also entirely possible that not even Anslinger, with all of his formidable talents, could have withstood the challenges of the middle 1960s. As Bob Dylan observed in the midst of America's cultural revolution, "The times, they are a-changing."

Much of Giordano's tenure was spent fighting a futile rearguard action against shifting American norms and increasingly lenient attitudes toward drugs. Over the course of the 1960s, the rigid and intolerant attitudes of the 1950s gave way to a generally more permissive outlook, and the American people entered one of the valleys opened up by the fracturing drug war consensus. Making matters worse, the public—driven largely by the political awakening of the baby boomers and civil rights movement—was becoming increasingly distrustful of the establishment and eager to challenge authority. For many, drug use became an act of social and political rebellion. The feds, in turn, were confronted with new problems associated with emerging recreational drugs like LSD and the abuse of pharmaceuticals like barbiturates and amphetamines. With its narrow focus on the more visceral dangers of heroin, the FBN was slow to react to the changing drug scene and resistant to additional enforcement duties, which led to the creation of rival control agencies. Together with endemic corruption, the fracturing of American drug control efforts—and the drug war consensus—hastened the FBN's demise in 1968.

Richard Nixon's drug war emerged from ashes. And after his turn leading the drug war also came apart in a welter of corruption and competing approaches, the mantle was taken up by Ronald Reagan. Whether either version marked the proper start of the "War on Drugs" or merely another turn of a larger wheel is open to interpretation, but both iterations demonstrated remarkable continuity with policies and images created by the FBN.

The drug wars of Nixon and Reagan, however, each had their own distinct characteristics. Nixon was a protean politician and approached the drug war as, to some extent, a laboratory of executive power; it offered an appealing campaign issue, a consolidating influence within the bureaucracy, and a means to project the authority of the White House. He created important pieces of infrastructure like the Drug Enforcement Administration and strengthened the legal foundations of control policy. But Nixon was also willing to entertain unorthodox stratagems and, in a sharp break from precedent, briefly experimented with a nationally coordinated treatment system in an effort to reduce demand—only to lose patience with this slow approach and turn back to a more militant strategy.

For Reagan, the drug war was part of a larger cultural shift and a corrective to the social and political ideology of the 1960s. Intent on paring back the duties and obligations of the federal government, Reagan emphasized the criminal aspects of the problem to the exclusion of all else. All nuance and complexity were boiled away, leaving only the hardest and most enduring elements: punishment and taboo. The irony is that confronting the dope menace in the name of freedom led to a massive buildup of the state police apparatus, imperiling the liberty of far more Americans than it protected, and exacerbating the drug war's many inequities and failures.

Today Nixon's brief attempt to balance U.S. drug policy and the complexities that led Reagan to abandon all complexity have been largely forgotten. Where once the drug war cycled through periods of escalation and moderation, for the past thirty-odd years it has been stuck in a model focused almost entirely on supply and predicated largely on militant policing and rhetoric—trends that began with the FBN and reached their fullest expression under Reagan and his successors. This chapter reveals how the FBN unraveled and how its legacy survived in the drug wars of Nixon and Reagan.

The End of a Beginning

To many observers, Henry Giordano seemed a strange pick for the nation's top drug cop. A pharmacist by training, he lacked Anslinger's strange charisma or the firm background in undercover work that dictated an agent's reputation among the rank and file—though he did break an important case against the Mallock brothers, a pair of Canadian middlemen working with Corsican suppliers in France and Mafia distributors in New York. In keeping with the romanticism of true-crime adventures, press coverage of his appointment played up his status as "an ace undercover operative" who came up "the hard way." In fact, most of Giordano's career was spent in administration, as the district supervisor in Minneapolis and Kansas City or as a headquarters official in Washington. Giordano enjoyed strong political ties and helped draft the 1956 Narcotic Control Act, but his chief virtue seems to have been a willingness to, as he announced upon his appointment, "continue the general policies of Mr. Anslinger" and retain the FBN's commitment to a punitive police approach.[3]

It's unclear how much influence Anslinger had over his replacement or why he decided to back Giordano over Siragusa. He was probably hoping to maintain some control over the FBN. Even at seventy, the Old Man was reluctant to leave his post and told reporters, "I'm not anxious to retire. I would not know what to do." Anslinger was allowed to keep his diplomatic portfolio, and Kennedy, Johnson, and Nixon all kept the Old Man on as the U.S. delegate to the UN Commission on Narcotic Drugs. Giordano was committed to keeping the drug war on the path set by Anslinger, but his otherwise indecisive leadership encouraged the recurrent executive-level calls to shift drug enforcement from Treasury to the Justice Department. "Privately, I am told he can't stand up to the pressure and runs away from all decisions," Anslinger confided to George White.[4]

Giordano's ascension ushered in another round of shuffling at FBN HQ and was accompanied by the abrupt departures of rivals Wayland Speer and Charles Siragusa. Shortly before Giordano's appointment, Speer tried to use the corruption issue to improve his position. During the summer of 1961, Speer visited the Manhattan office to investigate the apparent overdose of an agent. Rumor had it the agent was on the take and planning an overly ambitious graft when his confederates spiked his drink with a lethal dose of narcotics one night. Speer launched an integrity probe and was clearly on to something, but he made the mistake of questioning the agents alone in his hotel room instead of on the record and at the office. One of his targets, an African American agent named Charles McDonnell—later indicted on fourteen counts of corruption—told Senator Jacob Javits (R-NY) that Speer had exposed himself and made racist remarks. The rest of the office closed ranks, and when Speer failed to produce hard evidence of corruption, he was reprimanded by Treasury officials and sent back to the districts.[5]

With Speer's demotion, Charles Siragusa moved up to deputy commissioner, and George Gaffney, the supervisor in New York during the first French Connection cases, was brought in as assistant commissioner. Siragusa and Gaffney then set to battling it out for influence. Gaffney, however, was friends with Attorney General Robert Kennedy, dating back to their collaboration on the Senate McClellan Committee to investigate organized crime. Seeing the writing on the wall, Siragusa left in November 1963 to take charge of the Illinois State Crime Commission.[6]

Despite his reputation as a weak infighter, Giordano won some important early victories: he prevailed over several canny rivals and presided over the critical jurisdictional battle with Customs. These were noteworthy achievements, but Giordano faced two structural problems that could not easily be solved: corruption in the ranks and proliferating American drug use.

The corruption issue was kept relatively quiet until the end of the decade, as FBN and IRS inspectors slowly closed in on the suspected dirty cops. But between 1968 and 1970, the general issue of police corruption exploded with the revelations of cops like Frank Serpico. The subsequent Knapp Commission exposed an array of official abuses in the NYPD. A report by FBN inspector Ike Wurms indicated similar institutionalized corruption on the federal side, and the high-profile nature of these scandals has left the impression that it was corruption and crooked agents that killed the Bureau. In *Hep-Cats, Narcs, and Pipe Dreams* (1996), historian Jill Jonnes contends that by the end of the decade, the situation was so bad that rogue agents had actually murdered some forty to fifty informants to keep them from talking.

The Wurms Report, which remains sealed, apparently indicated that around sixty agents had gone bad and were actively colluding with heroin traffickers. Most of the corruption probes finished after the Bureau's reorganization, but the suspicion that many (perhaps most) narcotics agents were dirty did little to help the FBN's cause within the federal hierarchy.[7] Certainly, it can be said that the Bureau was born and died in the midst of corruption scandals. The fuse on the Bureau's demise, however, was already burning.

The real cause of the FBN's downfall had more to do with the changing American drug scene. New classes of drugs like barbiturates, amphetamines, and hallucinogens received a great deal of public attention but fell outside of the Bureau's traditional focus on heroin and exacerbated many of the tensions already dividing the drug control community. The first cracks in the drug war consensus appeared in the late 1950s with the rebellion of medical and legal professionals distraught with the simplistic and draconian direction of U.S. drug policy. By the time of the White House Conference on Narcotic and Drug Abuse in September 1962, the deepening fault lines were on clear display.

Both of the Kennedy brothers acknowledged the importance of law enforcement but signaled their displeasure with the rigidly punitive direction of the police approach. Realizing that the administration wanted a new approach, Treasury Secretary C. Douglas Dillon hinted to reporters that the new commissioner "might be more receptive to suggestions that narcotics addiction be treated as a disease as well as a criminal offense."[8] The Bureau, however, refused to change its stripes.

When the White House conference failed to articulate any alternatives, FBN officials convinced each other they had weathered the storm. Both of the Kennedys were "highly complimentary" of the Bureau, one agent reported, and credited the excellent work of District 17 as a justification to extend FBN operations around the world. During his own remarks at the conference, Giordano complained that there was "too much misinformation" about the Bureau and denied that the agency was only interested in locking up addicts. The FBN's highest priority, he insisted, was protecting the American people and containing the spread of addiction. FBN chief counsel Carl DeBaggio picked up this line of argument while explaining the Bureau's long-held position that every addict was a potential peddler and should be treated as such. "Our true position," DeBaggio declared, "is that a peddler who is an addict should be not be given a license to peddle just because he is an addict." In essence, FBN officials used the addict-peddler connection to dismiss any lenient treatment for users, which would only facilitate the spread of addiction. "We should attack this concept with all the vigor and force at our command," Agent Patrick O'Carroll urged in a postmortem. On that count, FBN officials felt they had prevailed.[9]

Focused on the hazard of the rehabilitative model, however, FBN officials overlooked another threat to their institutional domain: the growing abuse of licitly derived drugs like barbiturates and amphetamines, a disparate collection of psychoactive products the FBN lumped together as "dangerous drugs." Compared to opiates, barbiturates and amphetamines were relatively new as drugs of abuse, and, under Anslinger, the FBN left control of such drugs to physicians. The 1951 Durham-Humphrey Amendments to the Federal Food, Drug, and Cosmetic Act achieved a modicum of control by introducing prescription requirements. Anslinger thereafter refused to add such drugs to the FBN's portfolio and thwarted their inclusion in international control agreements, even while acknowledging their addictive potential. As the dangers of barbiturates, in particular, attracted widespread attention and the number of Americans addicted to or abusing prescription drugs eclipsed the number addicted to heroin (by a wide margin), the FBN continued to see the different classes of drugs as totally distinct from one another. Prescription drugs were generally of licit origin, came in the form of a pill, and, Agent White observed to a colleague, "lack the prima-facie physiological evils of the opiates." Although there were clear warning signs about abuse potential, the FBN simply saw pharmaceutical products as less threatening than heroin. Anslinger was also reluctant to accept new enforcement obligations that might jeopardize his cozy relationship with the pharmaceutical industry.[10]

Nevertheless, by 1962, several developments had brought fresh attention to the hazards of pharmaceuticals. News about the dangers of thalidomide—an over-the-counter sedative that caused tens of thousands of terrible birth defects in Europe and was only narrowly kept from the American market—broke that summer and breathed new life into proposed regulations of the U.S. pharmaceutical industry. A number of clinical investigations confirmed the abuse potential of barbiturates and amphetamines, and the danger was punctuated by the death of Marilyn Monroe, who was romantically linked to both Kennedy brothers and overdosed on barbiturates in August 1962.[11] At the White House conference the following month, prescription drugs were the subject of "real concern by all parties," one FBN agent reported. Yet in his remarks to the conference, Giordano insisted the FBN's purview was strictly limited to drugs of illicit origin, specifically heroin and other opiate derivatives, along with cocaine and marijuana. "We, therefore," he declared, "do not have responsibilities with regard to the so-called dangerous drugs; i.e., barbiturates and amphetamines. . . . [O]ur primary concern is with the illicit traffic which caters to the abusive use of narcotics."[12]

It took a few years for Giordano's fatal error to become apparent. Immediately following the conference, President Kennedy appointed an advisory group to study the drug problem. Dubbed the Prettyman Commission for its chairman, retired federal judge E. Barrett Prettyman, the group took an inclusive approach and quickly began to suggest a more measured response to the drug problem. "We've gone through an era of hysteria on both sides," one member commented. "We surely need a middle-road approach." The commission released its findings throughout 1963 and 1964 and recommended greater emphasis on rehabilitation, moving enforcement to the Department of Justice, and creating new mechanisms to curb the abuse of prescription drugs. By this time, however, Lyndon Baines Johnson was president and, for the time being, preferred to let Congress take the lead in carrying out the commission's suggestions.[13]

The FBN still had its supporters, but Giordano was increasingly behind the times. He flatly refused to consider widening the FBN's purview, and it began to look like he would go down with the ship. Jack Kelly, one of the agents witness to the turbulent era of the late 1960s, later wrote, "Congress asked the Bureau to take over the whole problem of hallucinogenic drugs. Giordano refused." That, Kelly recalled, was a "fatal error."[14] In response, Congress passed the Drug Abuse Control Amendments (to the Federal Food, Drug, and Cosmetic Act) in 1965, which gave new police authority to the Food and Drug Administration (FDA) in the form of the Bureau of Drug Abuse Control. Critics of the FBN's hard-line stance saw the new agency as the chance, BDAC director John Finlator observed, "to initiate a fresh approach to the national drug problem." Where the FBN's focus on the contagion of drugs led it to assume that every user was a carrier of addiction and therefore a legitimate target, BDAC's explicit mission was to police the manufacture and illicit distribution of pharmaceutical drugs but not their actual use.[15]

It was immediately apparent that the two organizations had, as Finlator put it, "diametrically opposed" philosophies. Taking a "total approach," the FDA's new police agency emphasized education and research in equal parts to law enforcement. "BDAC," Finlator wrote, "was somewhat unique . . . [and] attempted an enforcement-medical-statistical-psychological-educational approach. Consequently, it was staffed with psychologists, pharmacologists, pharmacists and mathematicians, as well as with investigative agents." Finlator previously held a high-level position with the General Services Administration and brought a collaborative management style to the job of director, which helped BDAC establish an effective rapport with the FBI and Customs.[16]

The relationship between BDAC and the FBN, however, was troubled from the start. As dealers and trafficking networks diversified into a variety of drugs, the two agencies quickly came into open conflict. Finlator and Giordano put on a show of cooperation and encouraged both agencies to display "a close spirit of cooperation," but the association was a thorny one.[17] Neither the FDA (BDAC's parent agency) nor the Department of Health, Education, and Welfare (HEW) had much experience with law enforcement, so officials naturally looked to dissatisfied FBN agents to fill BDAC's ranks. BDAC recruited about seventy former FBN agents in all, to the great ire of Treasury officials. The remaining FBN agents derided their FDA counterparts as "chicken-pluckers" (many of BDAC's officers had previously served as poultry inspectors) and assumed that all of the "jumpers" were dirty agents fleeing the ongoing integrity probes.[18]

Even worse, the new agency began to steal FBN headlines after making cases against amphetamine dealers and other pill rings. One of BDAC's biggest cases was against Augustus Owsley Stanley III, the "Acid King" of California. In 1966 the Swiss pharmaceutical company Sandoz was the only licensed manufacturer of LSD in the world and decided to hand over its entire stock to the National Institute of Mental Health. Owsley, a talented chemist and soundman for the Grateful

Dead, stepped into the breach and briefly became the world's largest producer of LSD. His arrest in 1967, however, gave BDAC new publicity, and its efforts to track shipments of lysergic acid (LSD's main precursor) led BDAC agents overseas, further encroaching on FBN prestige.[19]

In another sign of events coming full circle, the marijuana issue—always controversial and always peripheral to the Bureau's focus on heroin—brought the conflict between the two agencies fully into the open and finally sealed the FBN's fate. By the late 1960s, the merits of marijuana prohibition were under heated debate as its use increased precipitously. The Bureau's old nemesis Alfred Lindesmith resurfaced to comment, "Nobody worried very much when police sent thousands of ghetto dwellers to languish in prison for years for puffing on one joint, but now that the doctor, the lawyer, the teacher and the business executive and their children are facing the same fate, marijuana has become a cause célèbre." In retirement, former agents like George White groused about increasing marijuana use and invited friends to come "watch the wandering weed-heads strolling up and down the beach." Only half joking, White proposed posting a sign that read: "HEY MAN. ABSOLUTELY NO POT SMOKING WITHIN ONE HUNDRED YARDS OF THIS WINDOW."[20]

With the FBN's views on marijuana under public attack, Giordano dug in deeper and clung to Anslinger's increasingly antiquated positions. The Bureau continued to circulate its well-worn pamphlet *Living Death: The Truth about Drug Addiction,* which restated the gateway-drug argument. In congressional testimony, Giordano repeated his complaint that a vocal minority of marijuana advocates had distorted public perceptions, and he insisted that a large dose of pot could "cause a temporary psychosis in anybody."[21]

BDAC, on the other hand, took a very different view. Finlator dismissed the gateway-drug argument, contending, "One cannot place the blame on the drug; it is the personality itself that allows for any progression to a more debilitating drug." In an offhand remark, his boss, FDA commissioner James Goddard, also commented that marijuana was probably less dangerous than alcohol—prompting immediate calls for his resignation from drug war hard-liners in Congress. The Department of Health, Education, and Welfare, meanwhile, commissioned a secret high-level study that ultimately concluded marijuana was far less

dangerous than depicted and should be reclassified as a mild hallucinogen rather than a narcotic. Going one step further, the report recommended decriminalizing possession and transferring enforcement
duties from the FBN to BDAC. After leaving public office a few years
later, Finlator even came out for the total legalization of marijuana.[22]

When the HEW paper leaked to the media in the fall of 1967, it further exacerbated the schism between the FBN and BDAC and exposed
federal dysfunction to the American people. Controversy over the drug
problem was reaching new heights, but with enforcement functions
spread among a multitude of agencies and departments—all of which
refused to cooperate with one another—it looked like the feds were
falling down on the job. By the start of the new year, it was apparent
that an amalgamation was in the works. Despite taking a controversial stand on the marijuana issue, HEW had no appetite for the fight,
which left Treasury and Justice to battle it out. In his final year in office,
President Johnson decided to circumvent Congress (which had contributed to this fracture in the first place) and act via executive order.
Calling the present organization of police agencies and control laws "a
crazy quilt of inconsistent approaches and widely disparate criminal
sanctions," Johnson called for comprehensive new drug laws. In early
February, he announced that the FBN and BDAC would be combined
into a new agency called the Bureau of Narcotics and Dangerous Drugs
and moved to the Justice Department, following a course previously
suggested by the Prettyman Commission and several other studies on
federal organization.[23]

The Bureau of Narcotics and Dangerous Drugs

The formal transfer took place in April 1968. In public Giordano welcomed the change. On the eve of the Bureau's dissolution, he told senators, "This plan will have a great impact on the enforcement of the
Nation's drug laws. It will combine the talents and efforts of both agencies in a unified attack on the traffic." Privately, however, insiders like
Joe Arpaio recall "intrigue on a scale that would do a Greek tragedy
proud." Given the FBN's larger size and depth of experience, Giordano
likely assumed that his staff and personnel would dominate the new
organization. So he was surely disappointed when he and Finlator were

named to coequal positions as associate directors and Attorney General Ramsey Clark went outside of the hierarchy to find a new director, choosing John Ingersoll, a DOJ official and former police chief in Charlotte, North Carolina.[24]

Ingersoll represented a clean start at a time when the highest priority for Justice was to purge the BNDD of dirty agents. With corruption in the daily headlines, there was no way Giordano could lead the new agency. By December 1968, thirty-two agents had been forced out of the New York office. Attorney General Clark told reporters that few would face formal charges, but he believed a number of agents had been "illegally selling and buying drugs, retaining contraband for personal use or sale, taking money allocated for informants and failing to enforce laws." Corruption was serious enough that, in December 1970, Ingersoll asked the CIA to vet certain agents and infiltrate BNDD field offices to "monitor any illegal activities." The CIA's surveillance continued until at least the spring of 1973, when it was revealed as part of the infamous "Family Jewels" disclosure—which, it must be noted, also revealed how the CIA had enlisted noted Mafia drug traffickers Sam Giancana and Santos Trafficante in a plot to assassinate Cuban dictator Fidel Castro.[25]

Despite involving the CIA, Ingersoll strove to be nonpolitical and apply the most up-to-date techniques of public administration and criminology. In occasional correspondence with Anslinger, he acknowledged this was easier said than done, writing, "Sometimes I find it to be a disadvantage not to be political since many of my adversaries are so motivated." Ingersoll avoided overt partisanship, but he was not shy about criticizing the past direction of U.S. counternarcotic efforts. The FBN claimed to be focused on high-level traffickers, Ingersoll noted, but "what they said they were doing and what they were actually doing were often two very different things." The emphasis on retail-level dealing and quota systems reinforced the structural dependence on informants and further opened the door to corruption as agents cut corners to keep their snitches in play. In contrast, Ingersoll promised the BNDD would focus only on "major traffickers" and "operators of clandestine laboratories and the major distributors."[26]

None of this represented the break with past practices that Ingersoll or contemporary observers took it to be. The strategy was ostensibly the same as that of the FBN. The real difference was that Ingersoll was determined not to let the BNDD get distracted by retail-level policing. The agency called this new strategy "the systems approach," part of a wider vogue among governmental officials to apply large-scale analysis to bureaucratic tasks. In the case of drug enforcement, that meant the BNDD would "refrain from tracking down the individual entrepreneur" and, Finlator explained, instead "group him with other associates all of whom made up a loose system or organization."[27] In other words, the systems approach represented a shift to the more deliberate and analytical style of investigation that often proved difficult for the FBN. And that required a level of patience frequently absent from the American political system.

Nixon's Drug War

While Ingersoll tried to shift the course of U.S. drug enforcement, the American people were headed to the polls. The year 1968 was one of the most tumultuous in U.S. history and an electoral turning point. In Vietnam the Tet Offensive indicated the country was facing a major military defeat. Back home, cities all over the nation—including the capital—burned in the riots touched off by the assassination of Martin Luther King Jr. College students rose up to occupy university buildings, and the hopes of many progressives died with Robert Kennedy on a kitchen floor in a California hotel. On the Democratic side, a surging antiwar movement nearly toppled the party establishment before it was violently turned back at the Chicago convention, and the party put up Vice President Hubert Humphrey, despite his failure to win a single primary. Southern Democrats abandoned the party altogether and rallied to Alabama governor George Wallace, who promised "segregation now, segregation tomorrow, segregation forever." On the Republican side, the forces of reaction coalesced behind Richard Nixon and the suspicion that drugs and crime were somehow responsible for all of this mess. From the very start of Nixon's campaign, it was clear that "law and order" would be a central issue and an oblique way of clamping down on social unrest.

Drugs could explain how heroin- and marijuana-addled GIs were outfought by the primitive Vietcong, why violent crime had taken over America's inner cities, and why the youth were abandoning the American

way. In a policy paper released in May, Nixon described a country over-
whelmed by disorder. "Crime creates crime," he argued. Liberal enablers
had tipped the balance toward the criminal element and turned the
United States into a "lawless society." Calling organized crime a "tape-
worm" and "secret society," Nixon pledged "to wage an effective national
war against this enemy within." Three months later, while accepting his
party's nomination, Nixon renewed his promise to "open a new front
against the filth peddlers and the narcotics peddlers who are corrupting
the lives of the children of this country."[28]

Nixon won the election partly on the strength of his overtures to
southern racism and the frustrations of a "silent majority" weary of
social discord. The focus on crime and drug control was the centerpiece
of Nixon's appeal to both of those constituencies.[29] Nixon's first priorities
were détente with the USSR and China and ending the Vietnam War, but
drugs remained high on his agenda. In a July 1969 address to Congress,
Nixon claimed that drug abuse and addiction had "grown from essentially a local police problem into a serious national threat." The following day, Attorney General John Mitchell submitted draft legislation to
toughen prison sentences and grant police new authority, including the
use of wiretaps and "no-knock" warrants.[30]

Perhaps reluctant to lose any bureaucratic momentum, Nixon kept
Ingersoll as director of the BNDD, despite the fact that he was a Johnson appointee. Giordano, realizing he would never regain the top office,
resigned shortly thereafter, but he probably would have given Nixon a
more pliable partner.[31] Ingersoll was convinced that street arrests and
mass roundups explained the FBN's many failures, and he remained
stubbornly focused on the high-level international traffic. Nixon, however, needed splashy arrests to complement his political strategy. This
fundamental conflict of interests set the stage for a power struggle that
typified Nixon's approach to the presidency and the drug war.

The tension between the need to apply new strategies and demonstrate political results shaped the direction of Nixon's entire drug war,
and one of the first products of that tension was Operation Intercept.
Eager to follow up on Nixon's militant campaign rhetoric and overcome the apparent ennui of the BNDD, the White House enacted a
plan in September 1969 to dramatically increase Customs inspections
at the southern border. Ground operations were supervised by BNDD

agent Joe Arpaio, a veteran of FBN operations in Turkey, and G. Gordon Liddy, a Treasury official and zealous drug warrior. The project was, in Arpaio's words, "a full-out assault on the drug traffic right on the border." Every vehicle or person crossing the border was subject to "100 percent inspection" in an effort to prevent smuggled drugs—specifically marijuana—from reaching American consumers. Arpaio later insisted that "Operation Intercept had a real impact" and caused a spike in drug prices, but its efficacy is doubtful. One Mexican tourism official remarked at the time, "It's like trying to cure cancer with an aspirin." Despite thorough inspections, very few drugs were found. The true purpose of Operation Intercept was political: it demonstrated Nixon's commitment to the renascent drug war, and, Deputy Attorney General Richard Kleindienst hinted to reporters, it coerced Mexican cooperation by squeezing commerce. Ultimately, the operation proved so damaging to the economy on both sides of the border that it was halted after only twenty-three days. The Nixon administration, however, had made its point and received immediate assurances of future cooperation from Mexican officials, their clear irritation notwithstanding.[32]

While the BNDD focused on dismantling the French Connection, Nixon pushed for the consolidation of existing drug laws and ever more police power. The result was one of the most important pieces of legislation in the history of U.S. drug policy: the 1970 Comprehensive Drug Abuse and Prevention Act. Based on legislation submitted by the White House back in July 1969, the bill received overwhelming support when it finally reached the floor of Congress and took only a month to pass both houses. Nixon signed the act into law in October 1970 and, with the stroke of a pen, completely transformed the landscape of U.S. drug control.

The Comprehensive Drug Abuse and Prevention Act's most important effect was to replace all previous drug laws with a unitary system of regulation and shift the legal foundation from taxation to criminalization. The Harrison Narcotic Act and the Marihuana Tax Act, along with many others, were wiped out. Gone, too, was the somewhat artificial distinction between synthetic and organic drugs. In their place, the Controlled Substances Act (Title II of the omnibus bill) established a new "scheduling" system, adapted from the 1961 UN Single Convention. Under this new system, drugs were sorted into a series of "schedules" according to their potential for harm and medical value. The system was awkward and imprecise; marijuana and LSD were lumped with heroin in Schedule I as having maximum harm and no medical value, while barbiturates—despite their dangerously low threshold for toxicity— were placed in Schedule 3. But in addition to codifying new police pow- ers, the act did rationalize a previously scattershot patchwork of laws and remains the foundation of U.S. drug enforcement today.[33]

Equally important, however, the 1970 act also sought to rebalance the overly punitive direction of U.S. drug policy. Among the laws that were scrapped were the Boggs Act and Narcotic Control Act—which meant a temporary end to federal mandatory minimum sentencing. Under the new law, penalties for trafficking were pegged to the schedule system, and penalties for possession were generally capped at two years. Posses- sion of marijuana was reduced to a misdemeanor, and the act created a National Commission on Marihuana and Drug Abuse to further study the drug. Most important, the act also provided new funding to pub- lic health initiatives; for the first and only time in the nation's history, equal federal resources were devoted to policing and public health. In his remarks at the signing ceremony, Nixon was unequivocal: he didn't want to arrest addicts; he wanted to cure them. The new funding for treatment and rehabilitation, Nixon claimed, would save "hundreds of thousands of our young people who otherwise would become hooked on drugs and be physically, mentally, and morally destroyed."[34] This aspect of Nixon's drug policy was a profound change—a clear break from what came before and what was yet to come.

One of the most notorious episodes of Nixon's drug war took place shortly thereafter. Basking in the glow of his legislative victory, Nixon was preparing for the Christmas holiday when he received an unusual, uninvited visitor at the White House. Elvis Presley, in all of his come- back glory, presented himself at the front gate bearing a note—along with a Colt .45 as a gift for POTUS—that promised to "be of any ser- vice" in promoting Nixon's antidrug message to the American people. His missive landed on the desk of White House aide Egil Krogh, a fan and Nixon's point man on drug policy. Krogh convinced Nixon to take the meeting, and the picture of the two shaking hands was etched into history. Reproductions of the incongruous image remain one of the most frequently requested photographs at the National Archives today and are on prominent display in the gift shop. After bonding over their mutual distaste for hippies and the Beatles, Elvis got down to business. The King, it turned out, was an avid collector of police badges and coveted one from the BNDD. Nixon, bemused, agreed to supply one. Presley's wife, Priscilla, later revealed that Elvis had ulterior motives. With a federal narc badge, she recalled, Presley thought he "could legally enter any country both wearing guns and carrying any drugs he wished." That wasn't quite the case, and, of course, in a sad postscript, seven years later the King dropped dead from a heart attack brought on by years of prescription drug abuse—a cocktail that included barbiturates, amphetamines, and opioids and perfectly illustrated the bifurcated American drug problem.[35]

In the meantime, Nixon prepared to declare war. In June 1971, Nixon again called on Congress for more resources and again depicted a nation succumbing to crisis. Describing a "tide of drug abuse which has swept America in the last decade," Nixon warned that "the problem has assumed the dimensions of a national emergency." It was almost as if Anslinger's repeated warnings of a dope menace marauding through the underclass and pulling down mainstream America had been realized. "Not very long ago," Nixon remarked, "it was possible for Americans to persuade themselves, with some justification, that narcotic addiction was a class problem. . . . [N]ow the problem is universal." A threat on this scale required a response in kind. In his public comments, Nixon identified drug abuse as "America's public enemy number one" and declared that the country must "wage a new, all-out offensive." Though he didn't actually use the term, this is often marked as the official start of the War on Drugs.[36]

What most observers overlook, however, was Nixon's overriding emphasis on treatment and rehabilitation. "Enforcement," he argued, "must be coupled with a rational approach to the reclamation of the drug user himself." There were practical reasons for a more humane approach. "The laws of supply and demand function in the illegal drug business as in any other . . . ," Nixon explained. "As long as there is demand, there will be those willing to take the risks of meeting the demand, so we must also act to destroy the market for drugs." To that end, Nixon announced the creation of a temporary White House agency to lead the national response and coordinate treatment at the federal, state, and local levels. The new agency was called the Special Action Office of Drug Abuse Prevention (SAODAP), and Nixon installed a Chicago psychiatrist named Dr. Jerome Jaffe at its head. Nixon's first "drug czar" was a doctor.[37]

SAODAP was designed to coordinate and fund disparate treatment systems across the country, including neighborhood outreach, live-in therapeutic communities, and, most controversially, methadone maintenance. Part of the administration's unorthodox approach stemmed from the realization that, despite Nixon's campaign promises, there was little the feds could do to directly alleviate street crime. So the White House team turned to new solutions. After Marie Nyswander and Vincent Dole's pioneering work in the 1960s, methadone maintenance slowly began to gain new credibility with practitioners. The push for a nationwide treatment program came mostly from White House aides Egil Krogh and Jeffrey Donfeld, who had witnessed the potential benefits at a D.C. clinic run by psychiatrist Robert DuPont. Krogh and Donfeld were convinced that methadone could break the link between addict and peddler and therefore reduce crime by alleviating the need for addicts to resort to petty larcenies. This, in turn, led to Nixon's appointment of Jaffe, who had overseen a "mixed-modality" approach in Illinois that included methadone among a range of treatment options.

SAODAP remains noteworthy as the nation's first and only attempt at a nationally coordinated treatment system, and despite its shortcomings it remains a viable template for modern public health initiatives. It's misleading to draw too direct of a correlation, but the Nixon White House attributed a noticeable dip in the national crime rate during the first quarter of 1972 to a reduced demand for drugs—particularly in cities like Chicago, New York, and D.C. that had served as pilot projects for SAODAP's approach and saw a related decline in heroin overdoses.[38]

It's telling, however, that SAODAP's first and most successful initiative dealt not with inner-city addicts but with American GIs. By the time Nixon declared war on narcotics, heroin had become a serious concern in an actual theater of war. In April 1971, Representatives Morgan F. Murphy (D-IL) and Robert Steele (R-CT) released a report that described rising heroin addiction among U.S. servicemen in Vietnam. Noting the abundance of inexpensive, uncut heroin in the region, the congressmen estimated that some twenty-five to forty thousand troops (10–15 percent of the U.S. presence) were confirmed heroin addicts. Upon returning from a visit to the country, Steele told reporters that soldiers in Vietnam face "a far greater risk of becoming a heroin casualty than a combat casualty." That wasn't news to the Nixon team. Krogh made his own visit the year before and realized that heroin use among soldiers complicated Nixon's efforts to withdraw from the conflict. Even with the rough treatment many returning veterans received from the American public, this was not a group that could be easily demonized or blamed for their addiction.[39]

As a result, SAODAP's first order of business was a program the military promptly dubbed Operation Golden Flow—because it required all soldiers returning from Vietnam to pass urinalysis drug screening, a relatively new technology. Those who tested positive were kept in country to detox for an additional two weeks before they were allowed to return home and seek treatment from the Veterans Administration. The extent of GI heroin addiction was almost certainly overstated, but the practical effect of Nixon's solution was to decriminalize drug use in the military and shift the government response from punishment to treatment. And it worked. With a profound change in social setting—removed from both the stress of war and the ready availability of cheap narcotics—most returning veterans simply quit and did so without the aid of formal treatment.[40]

Nixon's other solutions were less progressive. One major initiative focused on Turkey, long the primary source of the Atlantic heroin trade. Police cooperation had improved since the days when George White and Charlie Siragusa prowled the streets of Istanbul, and the Turks gradually narrowed the areas where poppy could be legally cultivated, but the Anatolian peninsula remained the region's largest producer of opium. Between 1969 and 1971, the Nixon team approached the Turkish government with several proposals to preemptively buy the entire opium crop or enact a total ban on poppy cultivation in return for economic aid. Each offer was categorically refused by Prime Minister Süleyman Demirel on the grounds that opium was an important crop with a rich cultural legacy—and because Turkish officials thought regulation was more effective than prohibition. When friendly overtures failed, hard-liners in the administration threatened sanctions.

G. Gordon Liddy, now working for the White House Domestic Council, suggested sending the corpses of overdose victims to Turkish diplomats. These maneuvers only increased tension with Turkish officials, who actually had much bigger problems on their hands. In March 1971, the Demirel regime was overthrown in a bloodless coup, bringing to power yet another military government that proved more amenable to U.S. demands. In June the new authorities announced that a total ban on poppy agriculture would take effect in the fall of 1972. In an implicit quid pro quo, the White House immediately offered a thirty-five-million-dollar aid package to compensate farmers and promote alternative crop development. The Turkish people, however, interpreted the ban as a direct blow to Turkey's honor and sovereignty, and it proved so unpopular and ineffective that it was repealed after only two years.[41]

The effects of the ban as a counternarcotic measure are dubious. It inadvertently contributed to an American codeine shortage in 1974 and did little to impede the overall traffic. Poppy was unique as a winter crop, and Turkish farmers were unable to find a suitable replacement. Many kept large stockpiles, and some illicit production continued. Nixon's drug war, however, was as much about electoral politics as it was about containing addiction, and the Turkish opium ban provided a visible (if temporary) metric of Nixon's commitment. Throughout the 1972 election season, the Nixon campaign pointed to a jump in street prices (which, counter to their objectives, risked increasing crime) as proof that the ban, together with international law enforcement, had disrupted the Atlantic heroin trade. In hindsight, there's evidence to suggest that Turkey's role as a source country was already in decline, as production increased in Mexico, the Golden Triangle, and central Asia. The tumult also renewed the competition among various branches of law enforcement. Arguing for the return of a hardened border strategy, Myles Ambrose, the commissioner of Customs, reportedly commented, "The basic fact that eluded these great geniuses was that it takes only ten square miles of poppy to feed the entire American heroin market, and they grow everywhere."[42]

That fact was not totally lost on the Nixon White House. Seeing the Turkish poppy ban as merely a first step, Nixon went even further than Anslinger in deciding that poppies everywhere must be eradicated. In yet another indication of the unorthodox tactics he was willing to entertain, Nixon ordered the development of a bioengineered weevil that would devour poppy crops and perish after mating. The group, which included Krogh, Jaffe, Nixon, and Secretary of Agriculture Clifford Hardin, jokingly dubbed this mythical creature the "screw worm," and, less than a week later, Nixon secured additional congressional appropriations and private investors to fund the project. The Department of Agriculture actually began work on the poppy weevil, but shelved the project when it realized it could not guarantee the bug would not mutate or restrict its diet to poppy.[43]

Most observers are aware that Nixon's 1972 reelection campaign produced one of the most famous scandals in all of American history, but few realize just how closely Watergate was tied to the drug war. In *Agency of Fear* (1977)—a fascinating account of Nixon's drug war—journalist Edward Jay Epstein argues that the overlap between the War on Drugs and Watergate was largely a product of Nixon's efforts to consolidate power. For Nixon, power was, to some degree, its own end. But his desire to tighten the reins of government was also driven by his anger over leaks, which threatened to upend carefully laid plans. The first excerpts of the Pentagon Papers, for example, were published mere days before Nixon announced the creation of SAODAP and his "new, all-out offensive" on drugs. "In order to actually rule over government, rather than merely reigning as a figurehead," Epstein observes, "Nixon needed to control at least one federal agency with investigative powers." With such resources, Nixon could hunt down leaks within the bureaucracy, target his many political enemies, and disguise the numerous "dirty tricks" for which he was famous.[44]

Nixon's power struggle with federal law enforcement took place mostly during 1970 and 1971, as strategists like John Ehrlichman proposed a variety of schemes to bring federal police under direct White House control. A June 1970 effort to absorb domestic counterintelligence was thwarted by J. Edgar Hoover in one of his final years in office. Eugene Rossides, the Treasury Department coordinator for law enforcement (Malachi Harney's old job), similarly resisted White House efforts to commandeer the investigative resources of IRS and Customs or to have Nixon loyalist G. Gordon Liddy appointed director of the Bureau of Alcohol, Tobacco, and Firearms (ATF). Stymied in their efforts to subvert an existing law enforcement agency, in July 1971

Ehrlichman and his staff created a new executive office called the Special Investigations Unit, better known as the "Plumbers," since their job was to plug the leaks. The Plumbers were supervised by Ehrlichman's aide Egil Krogh—also Nixon's point man on drugs—with Liddy and former CIA officer E. Howard Hunt serving as deputies. All three did time for their part in the Watergate scandal. The Plumbers, however, were a temporary expedient, and, at the very same time, Liddy was busily drawing up plans for a new agency that would provide Nixon with his long-sought investigative resources. It was called the Office of Drug Abuse Law Enforcement.[45]

The creation of ODALE in January 1972 coincided with the start of Nixon's reelection campaign and signaled a sharp right turn in the drug war. ODALE, he announced, would partner local and federal officers in a campaign to drive "drug traffickers and drug pushers off the streets of America." In March, however, the first report of the National Commission on Marihuana and Drug Abuse—mandated by the 1970 Comprehensive Drug Abuse and Prevention Act—arrived and went significantly further in the direction of public health than Nixon was prepared to go. Dismissing many tenets of drug war orthodoxy, the report called for the complete decriminalization of marijuana. Nixon flatly rejected the findings. "I read it," he said, "and reading it did not change my mind." Indeed, on the eve of the report's release, Nixon traveled to New York to visit one of the first ODALE outposts and meet with Governor Nelson Rockefeller, whose eponymous 1973 drug laws led to the return of mandatory minimum sentencing. After the meeting, Nixon reiterated his opposition to decriminalization and said there would be "no sympathy whatever" for peddlers in the country's "total war" on drug addiction.[46]

ODALE, in that sense, killed two birds with one stone: it reestablished Nixon's control over the drug war and gave the White House unprecedented influence over law enforcement. Attorney General John Mitchell explained, "The past program of leaving enforcement to the localities and states has not worked. . . . We now reluctantly but with great vigor will establish a Federal presence at the local level." Over at the BNDD, Ingersoll steadily resisted White House pressure to increase arrests and refused to let politics dictate strategy. With paranoia increasingly permeating Washington, Ingersoll told reporters he was sure White House goons John Ehrlichman and H. R. Haldeman were "out to get" him. The Nixon team was also losing its patience with SAODAP. Reducing demand was a long game, and the White House wanted results in time for the election. Jaffe's management style left much to be desired, and methadone was turning out to be problematic. Many treatment centers were poorly run, supplies seeped into the illicit traffic, and community members complained that methadone clinics brought in a bad crowd and just replaced one addiction with another.[47]

ODALE thus represented a return to Nixon's "tough on crime" stance. The office essentially pioneered the "task force" approach to counternarcotics on a national scale and combined agents from the BNDD, Customs, IRS, ATF, and INS together with federal prosecutors and local police to escalate the drug war at the street level. Myles Ambrose, formerly commissioner of Customs, transferred to the Justice Department and took control of the new agency. In effect, he became the new drug czar and matched Nixon's commitment to holding the line. Unlike Ingersoll, Ambrose was fully prepared to target drugs at the retail level and told reporters, "Our task is to get as many pushers as possible off the streets . . . and to stimulate state and local police and prosecutors to attack the problem." To get around the congressional appropriations process, ODALE was financed by siphoning grants from the Law Enforcement Assistance Administration, an office intended to distribute federal funds to local police.[48]

One of ODALE's most prominent ventures was a national "heroin hotline" and advertising campaign to encourage the public to report illicit drug activity. In a bizarre turn, the only site with the infrastructure to support the new call center was in an emergency bunker deep in a Virginia mine shaft, where agents and operators were kept standing by. Of the 33,313 calls the hotline received in the first three months, about 28,000 were pranks, 5,000 were sincere but of no investigative value, and only 113 calls provided legitimate leads, producing four arrests and the seizure of two grams of heroin. From start to finish, the whole thing was little more, Ingersoll observed, than "a White House publicity stunt."[49]

The hotline was a boondoggle, but ODALE's escalation of the ground war ultimately had far more serious implications. By grouping a diverse array of federal agencies with local police, ODALE acquired unique and wide-ranging authority. It could conduct wiretaps, initiate tax audits, and make warrantless search and seizures; most controversially, it also had the legal authority to kick in any door that might hide drugs or drug users. In *Rise of the Warrior Cop* (2013), journalist Radley Balko traces many of the more alarming trends in the militarization of U.S. law enforcement to ODALE—particularly the use of military-style police raids. In its entire five-year history, Balko observes, the BNDD executed only four no-knock search warrants. ODALE, in its first six months, carried out more than one hundred; between April 1972 and May 1973, it led 1,439 paramilitary raids on America homes. The most infamous were a series of botched raids in Collinsville, Indiana, in April 1973, when ODALE troops ransacked the wrong houses and terrorized several innocent families. Ambrose was unapologetic. In widely quoted language that would have done Anslinger proud, he argued, "Drug people are the very vermin of the humanity. They are dangerous. Occasionally we must adopt their dress and tactics."[50]

Like the Plumbers, ODALE was an election-year expedient. By helping Nixon reassert his law-and-order bona fides, it probably contributed to his 1972 landslide reelection victory. Early in the start of his new term, Nixon moved to consolidate the federal drug control apparatus, and, on July 1, 1973, the Drug Enforcement Administration opened its doors. The new agency subsumed ODALE, the BNDD, the drug enforcement wing of Customs, and DOJ's Office of National Narcotics Intelligence.[51]

Finding a trustworthy captain to helm the new agency in the waning days of the Nixon administration, however, was a tall order. Most of Nixon's closest lieutenants were starting to fall to Watergate. Having already demonstrated his refusal to serve political ends, Ingersoll was obviously out and quit soon after the merger was announced. Despite his loyalty to the president and his politics, Ambrose was also untenable because of his association with the botched ODALE raids. In the end, Nixon appointed Ambrose's deputy, federal prosecutor John Bartels Jr., as the DEA's first administrator. In *Agency of Fear*, Epstein contends that Watergate actually prevented what would have amounted to an American palace coup; we can only speculate what the DEA would have looked like under the leadership of someone like G. Gordon Liddy.[52]

Due partly to the nature of its birth, the first few years of the DEA's history were tumultuous ones. Joe Arpaio worked a headquarters job for the first year and recalled that "blood was in the water." Bartels proved a poor manager and was caught between an irate public, still angry over the indiscriminate violence of the ODALE raids, and an agency paralyzed by internal rivalries. President Ford asked him to resign after less than two years. His replacement, a Justice Department lawyer named Henry Dogin, quit after only six months. Peter Bensinger, a Chicago lawyer and director of the Illinois Department of Corrections, restored a measure of order as the DEA's second official administrator, but the agency remained torn by rival factions. One unnamed DEA official told Epstein, "The bureaucrats in the drug agency simply destroy anyone who tries to control them." The turmoil, of course, also did little to alleviate the drug problem. "The heroin problem remains more or less constant," Epstein's anonymous official remarked. "There are no fewer addicts [in 1973] than there were in 1969—all that changes is the way the information about them is manipulated." Arpaio, too, later reflected that all of the reorganizations were bad for business. "Every time the government reorganizes or restructures or rearranges," he recalled, "you lose two to three years, guaranteed."[53]

As ever, U.S. drug policy was two steps forward and one step back—or perhaps it was two steps forward and two steps back. Despite notable movement toward both a public health strategy and an increasingly militarized style of policing, there was little impact on the material reality of the drug problem. Nixon's drug war ended more or less where it began: with a period of drift and drug policy lost within the deep cultural chasms dividing the American people.

The Reagan Revolution and the Return of the Drug War

After Nixon's resignation, the "long drug war" entered another down cycle, just as it had following the first collapse of the drug war consensus a decade before. With his strong appeals to stability and brief attempt to address both supply and demand, Nixon temporarily managed to restore a rough degree of accord. But it was a fragile and tenuous one. Some groups supported his "total war on addiction." As the disease concept of addiction regained traction, others pushed for decriminalization and the kind of public health strategies called for by the National Commission on Marihuana and Drug Abuse. Public officials from across the political spectrum worried about the militant turn in

U.S. law enforcement. And despite the significant increase in resources that Nixon directed to the fight, influential police leaders like NYPD commissioner Patrick Murphy said it still wasn't enough—"like pouring a glass of ice water on a forest fire."[54] With Nixon's departure, all of the divergent approaches broke once more into the open, and it took a more talented politician than either Gerald Ford or Jimmy Carter to put the drug war consensus back together again—particularly in the face of escalating use.

In a widely read essay, Tom Wolfe derided the 1970s as the "'Me' Decade." It was a fitting title for a cynical time and reflected a clear retreat from the issues that had defined the 1960s. Although a few social movements continued to limp along—most notably environmentalism and second-wave feminism—many Americans had simply grown weary of activism and turned to more individual pursuits.[55] One of those pursuits, it turned out, was drugs.

Drug statistics remain distressingly unreliable even in the modern era, but some broad generalizations are possible. After holding roughly level during the Nixon years, overall drug use climbed steadily and peaked in 1979. The only exception was heroin, as users remained around 1 percent of the population or less. Average cigarette consumption was near its peak of ten or eleven cigarettes a day (half a pack) and only just beginning to decline following a shift in emphasis from the risks assumed by the smoker to the harm inflicted by secondhand smoke. Per capita alcohol consumption climbed up to its modern peak of nearly three gallons of pure ethanol a year and slowly became repoliticized with the campaign against drunk driving. Annual marijuana use among adults ages eighteen to twenty-five rose to just past 50 percent, and increasing juvenile use provoked a strong backlash from suburban parents. And most important for the future of the drug war, cocaine came roaring back after a fifty-year absence, with around 20 percent of Americans indulging on a yearly basis.[56]

A scattered national response reflected the diverging views of the American people. At the local level, state governments moved in opposite directions. Georgia and Texas reduced penalties for possession of small amounts of marijuana to a misdemeanor. California voted down a similar ballot initiative in 1973, and Governor Ronald Reagan vetoed a second attempt from the legislature, only to have decriminalization pass immediately after his departure in 1975. Neighboring Oregon, meanwhile, decriminalized marijuana completely and without fuss. New York went in the opposite direction. In 1973 Governor Nelson Rockefeller pushed a set of laws through the Albany legislature that institutionalized a zero-tolerance approach and established state-level mandatory minimums, imposing a fifteen-year sentence for possession of one ounce of marijuana and a life sentence on peddlers of heroin, no matter how adulterated the product. A handful of other states like Michigan followed suit.[57]

The bifurcation of the American drug problem extended even into the White House. On the campaign trail in 1976 and desperate to head off a primary challenge from Reagan, Gerald Ford promised to "spare no effort to crush the menace of drug abuse" and launch "a new and more aggressive attack against this insidious enemy." Back in the West Wing, First Lady Betty Ford struggled to control her addiction to alcohol and prescription opioids.[58]

Jimmy Carter, meanwhile, offered a different approach. In August 1977, President Carter delivered his first and only major speech on drug policy. He restated the requisite commitment to source control and effective policing but, in a radical departure, advocated the complete decriminalization of marijuana. "Penalties against possession of a drug should not be more damaging to the individual than the use of the drug itself," he argued, "and where they are, they should be changed." As was often the case, Carter was prescient but ineffectual. His intended reforms went up in smoke after his drug czar, a British psychiatrist named Peter Bourne, got himself embroiled in a series of scandals—including rumored cocaine use at a NORML (the National Organization for the Reform of Marijuana Laws) Christmas party and a fraudulent Quaalude script written for a staffer. Despite no major policy shift, Carter's proposal to decriminalize marijuana combined with a host of other issues—like the battle over the Equal Rights Amendment, a stubborn economic recession, spiking energy costs, and the Iran hostage crisis—to mobilize a broad conservative groundswell that propelled Ronald Reagan into the White House.[59]

In contrast to Carter's apparent fecklessness, Reagan promised to "make America great again" by strengthening the military, rolling back social programs, deregulating, cutting taxes, and generally improving

America's standing in the world. Uniting disaffected Democrats, a newly active evangelical movement, foreign policy hawks, and corporate elites, Reagan forged a new coalition that was immediately dubbed the Reagan Revolution. His 1980 electoral victory marked the start of a new conservative era in U.S. politics and the ascendancy of the fiscal and cultural politics of the New Right.[60]

The drug war was one of the props that levered this new worldview into place—a fact that did not go unnoticed at the time. In *Smoke and Mirrors* (1996), an excellent survey of the Nixon and Reagan years, journalist Dan Baum quotes George H. W. Bush's deputy drug czar: "Between 1977 and 1992 a conservative cultural revolution occurred in America. It was called the drug war."[61] That's a mild overstatement. Drugs were one of many variables leading to the Reagan Revolution. But just as it had in previous decades, a period of proliferating drug use and diverging policy responses encouraged a renewed cycle of escalation and crackdown, accompanied by familiar drug war narratives that both mirrored and reinforced the prevailing cultural and political beliefs of the time. In many respects, the Reagan Revolution (together with his interventions in Central America) replaced the actual military conflict that had sped previous iterations of the drug war, like World War I to Prohibition, World War II to the FBN, and Vietnam to Nixon. The key factor in each was that fundamental notions of American identity seemed to be at stake, both at home and around the world.

Reagan declared war on drugs in 1982. The specific date could be accurately described as January, June, or October. In January Reagan created the South Florida Task Force to address the very real problem of escalating violence associated with the cocaine trade in Miami. Led by Vice President George H. W. Bush—former head of the CIA—the South Florida Task Force was basically a return to ODALE-style paramilitary policing, uniting every branch of federal and local law enforcement with the latest in high-tech military gear and support. In June Reagan created the Drug Abuse Policy Office and installed chemist turned culture warrior Carlton Turner as the new drug czar. In October Reagan announced that he was extending the task-force model to the rest of the nation. In a radio address announcing the policy, Reagan delivered lines he had rehearsed all summer. "Drugs are bad, and we're going after them," he declared. "We've taken down the surrender flag

and run up the battle flag. And we're going to win the war on drugs."
Reagan had used the battle-flag line back in June, but this was the first
time he publicly uttered the phrase *war on drugs*.[62]

Though it paled in comparison to what followed under George H. W.
Bush and Bill Clinton, Reagan's drug war escalated sharply thereafter.
When he took office, the DEA had just under two thousand agents and
a budget of $220 million. When Reagan left, the DEA had nearly three
thousand agents and a budget of $523 million. But that's only part of the
picture. Between 1981 and 1988, the total federal drug control budget bal-
looned from $1.5 billion to $4.6 billion. And—just as important at a time
when conservatives were trying to erase the legacy of Vietnam syndrome
and rehabilitate the use of American power—the military also had a starring role. Immediately upon taking office, the Reagan team persuaded a
compliant Congress to loosen the restrictions in the Posse Comitatus Act
and allow a greater role for the U.S. military in domestic law enforcement.
Between 1982 and 1987, the Pentagon budget for interdiction, logistics,
and counternarcotics grew from $1 million to $196 million, despite the
objections of officials like Secretary of Defense Caspar Weinberger, who
feared a detrimental blurring of civilian and military tasks.[63]

Even more important than the commitment in blood and treasure,
however, the drug war was a tool to reshape the American social contract and carry out Reagan's larger political and cultural objectives. As
far back as his 1964 speech "A Time for Choosing," delivered in the midst
of an earlier culture war, Reagan argued that the relationship between
state and citizen had become overburdened and corrupt. Weakness on
the world stage combined with excessive regulation and government
handouts to enfeeble the American people and jeopardize the country's basic freedoms.[64] One of Reagan's highest priorities upon reaching
the White House was to rebalance the social contract and empower
individual Americans by rolling back the duties and obligations of government. But that also meant holding individuals responsible for their
choices and situations, often regardless of their actual circumstances.

Ensuring that the burden of responsibility for social and economic
well-being was borne by individuals was particularly critical in the context of Reagan's economic policies. Supply-side economics, also known
as trickle-down economics or Reaganomics, rested on the premise that
cutting taxes for the rich would encourage reinvestment and boost the

economy. It did goose the economy, but not without dire consequences. Between tax cuts for the rich, curtailed government spending, back-to-back recessions, and broad urban decline, Reagan's economic policies drove millions of Americans into poverty while redistributing an ever-greater share of the national wealth to the very top of society.[65] In the face of such a profound transfer of wealth and eviscerated social safety net, Reagan had to explain why some people made it in America and some communities sank further into decline. With its myriad cultural meanings—including a historic ability to reconcile the tensions between nature and nurture and sort the worthy from the unworthy poor—the drug war offered a ready answer.

This was not a conspiracy, and Reagan was not coy about his intentions. In September 1981, he delivered a speech to the International Association of Chiefs of Police—always one of Anslinger's favorite audiences—and described crime as "an American epidemic" driven by narcotics, a flourishing criminal subculture, and permissive social norms. Repudiating the notion that regulation and "massive government spending could wipe away our social ills," Reagan described crime—and, by implication, both drug addiction and socioeconomic status—as a choice. "The truth is that today's criminals, for the most part, are not desperate people seeking bread for their families," he argued. "Crime is the way they've chosen to live."[66]

Almost exactly one year later, Reagan dusted off the same speech when he announced the creation of national task forces and declared war on drugs. Now he described the "emergence of a new privileged class in America . . . of repeat offenders and career criminals who think they have a right to victimize their fellow citizens," and he attributed the growth of this "hardened criminal class" to "misplaced government priorities and misguided social philosophy." The prevailing attitudes of the 1960s and '70s, Reagan argued, revolved around a series of "utopian presumptions" that held man as "primarily a creature of his material environment," crime as a product of inequality, and economic and political reform as the solution. But, he continued, "a new political consensus among the American people utterly [rejects] this point of view" and had begun to reassert "certain enduring truths—the belief that right and wrong do matter, that individuals are responsible for their actions, that evil is frequently a conscious choice."[67]

Here, in a nutshell, was the philosophy that underlay Reagan's entire approach to the drug war. And he wasn't altogether wrong. Evil exists and it often is a choice. Both the crime rate and drug use were at record highs, and the public demanded a response. According to Gallup, nearly half of the American people were afraid to walk alone at night.[68] Likewise, the question of choice is arguably *the* central dilemma running through the history of addiction. Honoring the capacity of individuals to act within the world demands acknowledging the existence of some element of choice, even if badly constrained. But in his effort to hold individuals to account and discredit social responsibility—thus absolving the government of any duty to redress social and economic inequality—Reagan dramatically mischaracterized the many problems facing the country. In other words, he returned to the classic reductionist view of the dope menace.

For Reagan, drugs were a moral dilemma, a matter of good versus evil. There could be no compromise, only resistance. And once again, questions of identity shaped the contest far more than any competing notions about the physiology of addiction or the pharmacology of drugs. For too long, Reagan claimed, Americans had tolerated "the illegal and highly dangerous drug traffic" and "a syndicate of organized criminals whose power is now reaching unparalleled heights." Confronting those forces was a way to reassert basic moral principles and what Reagan saw as a faltering American identity. "We live at a turning point," he claimed in his October 1982 speech, and asked, "What kind of people are we if we continue to tolerate in our midst an invisible, lawless empire? Can we honestly saw that America is a land with justice for all if we do not now exert every effort to eliminate this confederation of professional criminals, this dark, evil enemy within?"[69]

With the drug war cast in stark moral terms, counternarcotic strategy was pared down to its hardest elements: aggressive confrontation, strong cultural taboos, punitive policing, and source control. The disease concept of addiction and public health strategies were completely marginalized. The focus was entirely on supply. Efforts to address demand were a distant second, avoiding treatment altogether in favor of morally uncompromising abstinence-only education. And all of that was before anyone in the administration had ever heard of crack.

The crack epidemic was real, but it so perfectly complemented the narrative of the War on Drugs that Reagan might as well have invented it—a allegation that surfaced almost immediately and reached a crescendo following the 1996 publication of Gary Webb's "Dark Alliance" series by the *San Jose Mercury-News*. After all but vanishing in the 1920s, cocaine made a slow but steady return as an elite party drug over the course of the 1960s and '70s, initially following illicit supply channels carved out by Colombian marijuana smugglers and facilitating the rise of the Medellín and Cali Cartels. By the early 1980s, cocaine was ubiquitous. A cover story in the July 1981 issue of *Time* called it "the all-American drug" and described "a veritable blizzard of the white powder . . . blowing through the American middle class." As supply grew, enterprising dealers began to democratize cocaine in the form of crack, a cheap form of freebase cocaine that brought the drug to the masses.[70]

Pharmacologically, crack and cocaine are identical. The only significant difference between the two is their method of consumption: cocaine is snorted and absorbed through the mucus membrane of the sinuses, whereas crack is smoked and absorbed through the lungs—a more direct pathway to the brain. Strictly in terms of physiology, neither crack nor cocaine is addictive in the sense that they create physical dependency, as with heroin. Instead, cocaine hijacks the brain's reward system, flooding the brain with dopamine and causing intense feelings of euphoria followed by equally intense cravings for more. With crack, the cycle is more acute and the cravings more intense, leading to destructive patterns of compulsive binge behavior.[71]

The first indications of cocaine's metamorphosis appeared in late 1984, mostly in connection with gang competition in Los Angeles—and well after the War on Drugs was under way. By the end of the following year, the drug had arrived in several major American cities, and by the summer of 1986 the crack epidemic had arrived. On the domestic side, crack appeared like a perfect storm, tearing through inner-city neighborhoods already ravaged by poverty, pushing meager treatment services way beyond capacity, and then rebounding back up into the middle class.[72] On the international side, the apparently still-growing illicit cocaine trade encouraged the Reagan administration's increasing involvement in Central America.

The relationship—whether causal or merely correlated—between the crack epidemic and Reagan's support for the Contras lies at the root of the idea that the CIA was responsible for the crack epidemic. The full story of the Iran-Contra scandal and the many clandestine relationships therein is a long and complicated one that need not be recounted in full here. In short, the 1970s and '80s marked a period of widespread instability in Central America and saw the rise of several leftist movements—most famously the Sandinistas, who overthrew a military dictatorship and took control of Nicaragua in 1979. In response, the Reagan administration began supporting a series of right-wing militias, particularly the anti-Sandinista Contrarrevolución, or Contras. But the Contras were brutal in their methods, and between 1982 and 1984 Congress cut off their funding through a series of bills collectively known as the Boland Amendment. Eventually, this led White House staffers like Oliver North to look for covert means to continue the administration's support, most famously by funneling the proceeds of arms sales to Iran back to the Contras.

In the meantime, the twin menace of drugs and communism continued to have a synergistic effect. Reagan's support for the Contras began at precisely the same time that his administration was preparing to launch the War on Drugs at home, and in April 1986 the two became further entwined when Reagan's National Security Council raised the specter of "narcoterrorism" and formally designated the dope menace a threat to U.S. national security. One consequence of U.S. interdiction, however, was to shift an ever-greater component of the cocaine traffic from the sea and air routes leading to Miami to the overland route running through Central America and Mexico. In the long term, this empowered the Mexican cartels, whose growing influence and violent methods were foreshadowed by the gruesome murder of DEA agent Enrique "Kiki" Camarena in early 1985. In the short term, the growing volume of the overland traffic increased the participation of nearly every major actor in the region, including CIA client and Panamanian dictator Manuel Noriega and many of the same cash-strapped groups affiliated with the Contras and other right-wing militias.[73]

Indications of Contra drug running surfaced almost immediately, providing one of the threads that would ultimately unravel the larger Iran-Contra scandal. The subject was investigated by Congress, scores of journalists, and eventually the CIA itself. The controversy reached a fever pitch in late 1996, following the publication of Gary Webb's "Dark Alliance" series, which revealed that major Contra figures were only one or two degrees removed from big-time cocaine distributors in L.A., prompting outrage in the black community and demands for answers by California congresswomen Representative Maxine Waters and Senator Barbara Boxer. The idea that the CIA had knowingly allowed cocaine into the country was a bitter pill to swallow; Webb was pilloried by his colleagues and later committed suicide after struggling to repair his journalism career. But to many Americans, the idea wasn't so far-fetched in light of events like the Tuskegee experiments or the MK-ULTRA program. In 1998 the CIA tried to put the issue to rest by issuing its own report, which essentially acknowledged that the agency had turned a blind eye to the problem but forswore any direct involvement. In the end, the whole affair is probably best described as blowback rather than a conspiracy, but controversy lingers still today.[74]

In the meantime, the crack epidemic seemed to substantiate all of the worst assumptions held by Reagan's cohort of drug and culture warriors. Violence and drug abuse merely confirmed that some people—specifically people of color and marginal social status—simply refused to take responsibility for themselves and must be brought to heel, a conclusion reinforced by sensational media coverage around "crack mothers" and "crack babies" that further elaborated themes of willful disregard and social decay. Such assumptions came easy while attention remained fixed on villainous foreign traffickers and nihilistic junkies and away from the social setting against which the crack epidemic unfolded: largely inner-city communities troubled by poverty, job loss, discrimination, social immobility, and the almost total absence of social and economic services and opportunity. Seen in such light, the solution to the drug problem was escalation abroad and punishment and simplification at home.

Coming four years into the War on Drugs and on the first swells of the crack epidemic, Ronald and Nancy Reagan's "Just Say No" speech is probably one of the most famous artifacts of the drug war. Its message was disarmingly simple: just say no. "There's no middle ground," Nancy remarked at her husband's side. "Indifference is not an option." A few years later, she elaborated, "The casual user cannot morally escape responsibility for the action of drug traffickers and dealers. I'm saying that if you're a casual drug user you're an accomplice to murder." The War on Drugs was absolute, and in the "Just Say No" speech Reagan made sure the American people knew it. Calling the drug war a "national crusade" comparable to such turning points as the Civil War and the Normandy invasion, Reagan warned, "Drugs are menacing our society. They're threatening our values and undercutting our institutions. They're killing our children." It wasn't just U.S. security at stake—it was America's soul. "Drug abuse is a repudiation of everything America is," Reagan argued, and reminded his audience, "We Americans have never been morally neutral against any form of tyranny." That included the dope menace.[75]

Under Reagan the War on Drugs never deviated from this morally charged, uncompromising, and confrontational model. Soon after the "Just Say No" speech, Congress passed the Anti–Drug Abuse Act of 1986 with overwhelming bipartisan support. It was the first major piece of drug legislation since Nixon's 1970 Comprehensive Drug Abuse and Prevention Act. With the emphasis firmly on punishment and social control, the law restored federal mandatory minimum sentencing and introduced the infamous 100–1 disparity between cocaine and crack. Possession of five grams of crack or five hundred grams of cocaine netted the same penalty of five years' imprisonment without parole. Only two years later, the Anti–Drug Abuse Act of 1988 doubled down on that same punitive strategy and created the Office of National Drug Control Policy to manage the future course of American drug wars.[76]

A Broken Wheel

The rest, you might say, is history—or, more accurately, current events, as the drug war remains largely within the grooves Reagan carved into American political culture. The crack epidemic burned itself out in the 1990s, but the policies shaped to confront it set the stage for further escalation under Presidents George H. W. Bush and Bill Clinton. In the final years of the Bush and Clinton presidencies, the total U.S. drug control budget grew to $11.9 billion and $18.5 billion, respectively (Reagan finished at $4.6 billion). Most of those funds were dedicated to law enforcement, source control, and interdiction. The overwhelming focus on supply and criminalizing drug use has had devastating consequences. At the start of the new millennium, the total U.S. prison population (including local jails) was approaching two million, and the United States was jailing a significantly higher ratio of its citizens than any other nation on earth, disproportionately affecting people of color. In the year 2000, 21 percent of the state prison population was there on a drug charge. At the federal level, it was 57 percent. Between 1980 and 2014, the number of Americans serving time on a drug offense increased by more than 1,000 percent.[77] America, the land of the free, had become America, the land of mass incarceration—and the drug war was a primary agent of that change.

There are few ways to look at this. The contradiction between the U.S. obsession with order and security, on one side, and freedom and liberty, on the other, is clearly one of the recurrent tensions that define American life and history. The drug issue has consistently added to those strains, and the drug war emerged, over time and in many iterations, as a way to reconcile those same tensions. Where once U.S. drug policy swiveled between a narrow range of options that included at least some consideration of public health, after Reagan the drug war lurched irrevocably toward punishment and confrontation. Yet at the same time, all that's really changed is the scale. Most of the core assumptions guiding the drug war became entrenched during the time of the Federal Bureau of Narcotics, well before Nixon or Reagan. If we, here in the present, hope to unravel the drug war and understand the ideas and assumptions that keep it viable, we would do well to heed the lessons of the FBN's history and the cultural significance of America's drug wars.

CONCLUSION

WAGING DRUG WARS

The history of the opium fight forms a queer illustration of our National
blindness to our own faults and emphasizes our National tendency to
see, with amazing clarity, the sins of others, while remaining blind to our
own viciousness.
—DR. HAMILTON WRIGHT (1911)

What is there in the political consciousness of Americans which causes
them to engage in experiments so noble in the motive, so impotent in
the execution, so menacing in their effect?
—WALTER LIPPMANN (1931)

Drug abuse is a repudiation of everything America is.
—RONALD REAGAN (1986)

Like opiates and the panoply of uppers, downers, powders, pills, and
pot varietals that populate the American market, the drug war keeps
reappearing in new guise. Victory, America's drug warriors promise, is
always just around the corner. "The contest which the United States
has waged against the abusive use of these drugs is one of which every
American citizen has a right to feel proud," Representative Stephen G.
Porter assured fellow lawmakers in 1924, "and I am firmly convinced
that we are on the last lap of a long journey toward the suppression
of this great international sin."[1] Then as now, victories over the dope
menace—both real and imagined—have been few and far between.
Given the explosive arrival of the current opioid epidemic, it appears
we are no closer to victory today. The loss in lives and resources is, in
many respects, incalculable. But not total. Despite its many failures, the

long history of American drug wars provides insights and tools that can shape a better future.

Drugs are a complicated problem, and the United States remains one of the largest consumers of licit and illicit drugs in all the world. Crossing the boundaries between economics, politics, culture, science, biology, medicine, diplomacy, people, and states, drugs shape and influence our world at a variety of levels, from the molecular to the global, in ways seen and unseen. There is no single way to describe their importance, to study their history, or to control their use. Drug abuse represents only one of the most extreme ways that drugs touch our lives, and the true nature of addiction remains at least partly a mystery, its fundamental paradigms subject to debate.[2]

To paraphrase former secretary of defense Donald Rumsfeld, we are dealing with both known unknowns and unknown unknowns. And this, too, has been a constant. "There is no possible way of determining with any degree of accuracy the number of drug addicts in the United States," Representative Porter observed while Congress debated the merits of a dedicated enforcement agency. "They were referred to for years as drug fiends and that, naturally, made them very secretive. Some authorities say a million; some say as low as 200,000."[3] Our ability to quantify the drug problem has improved since 1930, but, sadly, this is almost as true today. The FBN began keeping a registry of known addicts in the mid-1950s, and statistical record keeping began in the 1970s with the creation of the National Institute on Drug Abuse and the Substance Abuse and Mental Health Services Administration, two agencies created from the remains of SAODAP. Prohibition and cultural taboos continue to render much of the problem invisible to the eyes of the state. The frontiers of knowledge—be it the secrets of the brain, the volume of the illicit traffic, or the number of American addicts—have been a persistent obstacle to an effective policy response.

In the face of so many unknowns, drug control has, almost from the beginning, become about *something else*. Just what that *something else* actually is has changed over time, and the drug war has taken on and shed many agendas over the years. But the continuities are remarkable, and—beyond offering insights into the drug problem itself—they can teach us something about ourselves, as a people, as a culture, and as participants in a democratic system of government.

A backward glance at the long history of American drug wars reveals a durable set of core concepts and assumptions. Whether we describe that arc as one long drug war or as a series of distinct but interrelated drug wars is, in some ways, academic. What must be appreciated is that American policymakers have struggled to craft an effective drug policy for more than one hundred years and will likely continue struggling for years to come.

Impediments are scattered across the scientific, cultural, political, and economic landscape. Addiction is a psychological and biological phenomenon; it can affect anyone, regardless of station. But the people in the most urgent need are typically not from the mainstream of society. They are frequently (but not always) the have-nots. Lacking the resources to manage their addiction, they become the most visible manifestation of the problem. Addiction strikes harder at people and communities that already face trauma, marginalization, or active discrimination in their daily lives, be it for the color of their skin, sexual preference, gender identification, socioeconomic standing, age, politics, neighborhood, or genuine mental illness. Even without drug abuse, these people are often testimony to the inequities of the American system. And addiction multiplies their ranks.

This is a real challenge from a policy perspective. Addicts don't have lobbyists. Our inability to isolate drugs and addiction from the host of socioeconomic and political tensions in which they are intertwined has introduced lasting problems into American policy. Drug control began as a set of policies intended to restrict access to a dangerous commodity and almost immediately became a tool of oppression. Drugs provided an excuse to crack down on suspect communities, but, more important, they also offered a rationale to explain why those problems persisted in the first place. In effect, drugs let government—and the rest of society— off the hook for larger structural problems and replaced those problems with a compelling enemy to confront.

The drug war is a result of those internal contradictions and unresolved dilemmas. It should thus be no surprise to find it shaped by deep-seated cultural conflicts or that the hand of the law falls disproportionately along racial and socioeconomic lines. This isn't a secret or a conspiracy; it's a reflection of the way the American people and policymakers see the world. As Nixon told, of all people, Elvis, "Those who use drugs are also those in the vanguard of anti-American protest. Violence, drug usage, dissent, protest all seem to merge in generally the same group of young people." Years later, Nixon henchman John Ehrlichman put it more nefariously. The Nixon White House, he explained, "had two enemies: the antiwar left and black people. . . . We knew we couldn't make it illegal to be either against the war or black, but by getting the public to associate the hippies with marijuana and blacks with heroin, and then criminalizing both heavily, we could disrupt those communities. We could arrest their leaders, raid their homes, break up their meetings, and vilify them night after night on the evening news."[4] Though rarely so explicit, this adversarial framework wasn't unique to Nixon, and it has consistently predisposed the state toward the hardest elements of counternarcotic strategy.

Since the dawn of the twentieth century, drugs have been something to combat, not accommodate, and there has been very little evolution in the basic meaning of the drug war. Addiction is forever caught between medical and moral interpretations and weighted with much larger debates over nature versus nurture, liberty and personal responsibility, the breadth and depth of the social safety net, and the role of the state in our everyday lives. In the American context, the most ready—and problematic—metaphor able to convey the essence of addiction was slavery, a conflation that hastened the drug war's turn toward moral confrontation and minimized the possibilities for treatment or rehabilitation or compromise.

Throughout the various phases of America's drug wars, national leaders have relied on source control, militant policing, and strong taboos as the foundation of U.S. policy. From its inception, counternarcotic strategy has focused almost exclusively on limiting the supply of drugs—an approach that immediately lent U.S. policy a global scope. Demand is typically an afterthought, and politicians have relied on deterrence instead of "soft" public health strategies like treatment and rehabilitation. The only notable departure from this framework was Nixon, the president often credited with starting the war on drugs in the first place. Just as it took Nixon the cold warrior to open relations with China, it took Nixon the drug warrior to acknowledge that demand is half of the equation.

With demand historically seen as more or less constant, U.S. law enforcement has framed the drug problem as one of exposure. As Anslinger and other drug warriors consistently argued, a citizen who lacked access to drugs could never fall victim to addiction. Yet it was impossible, they recognized, to prevent drugs from being smuggled into the country. And because the problem was not confined by national borders, the FBN swiftly concluded, neither should its response.

For the first half of the twentieth century, the country lacked the geopolitical standing or will to implement a truly global control strategy. But World War II changed everything, including U.S. global standing and the way American leaders looked at the world. The one-two punch of World War and Cold War drove home the broadening scope of American security and, even more important, threatened the future of the free world. In the 1820s, John Quincy Adams cautioned against going "abroad in search of monsters to destroy." But by the mid-twentieth century, there were monsters everywhere—among them, the dope menace. In the face of so many threats, U.S. policymakers came to believe that it was in America's interest—indeed, a historic duty—to assume the mantle of global leadership. The world had to be made safe for America, and drug control was one of those special obligations.

In effect, the global drug war turned American identity outward, and many of the drug war's most stubborn assumptions are rooted in the way the American people and policymakers think about the role of the United States on the international stage and the nature of threats in a globalized world. In retrospect, it makes sense that the drug war emerged during a period—from the early twentieth century to the dawn of the Cold War—in which the nation was reconsidering and renegotiating its place in the world. Waging a drug war helped make sense of a changing global environment and America's own internal social, cultural, and economic conflicts.

For the Bureau, drug control was primarily about security. In *The Traffic in Narcotics,* Anslinger proclaimed, "Before all else is the safeguarding of the government and its laws and its people."[5] Again, note the order in which he lists those priorities. Politics certainly influenced the way the FBN resisted public health solutions, perceived and shaped the threat of drugs, and selected targets. But in the mind of the Bureau, drug control was preventive—it was about reaching out and neutralizing a threat before it developed. By 1951 the FBN had acquired the institutional clout to begin implementing that strategy. The politics of international law enforcement required the Bureau to keep a small footprint, and the foreign drug war, introduced first in the Mediterranean and then to East Asia and Latin America, was always a comparatively small part of the Bureau's actual operations. But it was absolutely central to the FBN's global counternarcotic strategy. The agents stationed overseas were small in number, Anslinger told senators in 1955, but they were "worth 100 men here."[6]

As the FBN premised ever more of its ability to accomplish its mission on its ability to fight drugs "at the source," it provides a useful look at the development of a "politics of insecurity." As with the Cold War, the belief that foreign drugs posed a foreign threat reinforced the impulse toward hegemony and the rationale that the United States must ensure global order. But this locked the country into a classic security dilemma: the more the country engaged with the world, the more exposed it became, and the more exposed it became, the more it relied on foreign intervention and hegemony to protect itself.

The myth of Sisyphus is again instructive here. Absolute security and absolute control over drugs are impossible to achieve, yet the United States keeps pushing that boulder up the hill—and rightly so, to some extent. But the mismatch between ends, means, and unattainable goals layers in problematic tensions, between short- and long-term objectives, feelings of fear and safety, and the dubious assumption that the United States must fight its enemies abroad so it doesn't have to fight them at home. This obsession with security encourages faulty assumptions and false equivalencies—like the conflation between addict and peddler or between terrorists and fighting-age males—that further complicate the country's ability to achieve its ambitions. And despite all the expenditure of blood and treasure, the American people are essentially no more or less safe than they ever were.

As narrative framework, the war on drugs serves notable ideological functions. Americans, though loathe to admit it, thrive on war. Throughout U.S. history, opposition to foreign threats has served as a critical outlet for the expression of national identity.[7] The drug war is, in that sense, written into America's cultural DNA, and it acquired much of its specific shape and forms of expression from the intense geopolitical and ideological conflict that accompanied its development—which is to say even the drug war itself is subject to the combined influence of nature and nurture. The drug war simultaneously asserted America's identity as an international champion of morality and freedom while reducing complexity and justifying extraordinary new power and authority. It is an iteration of a story that America has been told, told itself, and will surely tell again.

A drug war is absolute. Fought to protect Americans from the slavery of addiction, the FBN's war was cast as defensive in nature, though source control and interdiction are offensive and intrusive in practice. Framed as a battle between good and evil, the drug war eliminated such ambiguity—in the minds of America's drug warriors and the public. As Hank Manfredi, an agent who split time between the FBN and the CIA, observed of the moral uncertainties of Cold War espionage: "Today you work against a Czech and tomorrow he's your friend. Then you work on a Finn, and later he's your buddy, too. But who likes a dope peddler?"[8]

Wars require enemies. This, ultimately, is where the fallacies of drug war orthodoxy have caused the most harm. Drugs don't make very good enemies by themselves; even illicit drugs are, after all, simply commodities, and—despite the FBN's alarmist portrayals—narcotics lack agency. They must be used to have an effect. This need for an enemy to confront creates a focus on criminal kingpins and foreign villains, on the one hand, and drug users, on the other. In establishing the basic parameters of the drug war and insisting that user and peddler were indistinguishable, the FBN did more than any other institution to create that dynamic. The consequences have been disastrous. In *The New Jim Crow* (2012), Michelle Alexander argues that the drug war has become a new form of racialized social control, even more nefarious and effective than segregation. David Simon, author of *The Corner* (1997) and creator of *The Wire* (2002–8), describes the war on drugs as "a genocide in slow motion," a war waged on America's poor.[9] Though never the explicit intent or design of the drug war, these have becomes its undeniable consequences, and they were apparent from the start. Even Garland Williams acknowledged, "The prisons will not hold them all."[10]

The tendency to focus on kingpins is another unfortunate product of framing drug control as a drug war. Like the war narrative itself, kingpins reduce complexity and provide a handful of high-profile targets to attack.

To borrow from former CIA director James Woolsey, it's the difference between fighting a dragon or a jungle full of poisonous snakes.[11] The recurrent appearance of various kingpins suggests the U.S. government would rather fight dragons. But the illicit drug traffic is the quintessential jungle and populated by an ever-shifting array of criminal actors and networks, many of them violent and many of them dangerous, but very few of whom approach the criminal-mastermind status invoked by the term *kingpin*. Describing law enforcement targets as drug lords and kingpins—even those who exert genuine influence—provides an illusory measure of progress; it offers a sense of accomplishment in a war with no end and no victors. A more or less straight line runs from Eli Eliopoulos to Lucky Luciano, Pablo Escobar, and—most recently—Joaquín "El Chapo" Guzmán. With El Chapo's dramatic arrest, escape, capture, escape, and recapture, all of the familiar tropes were on display, from statements about his incredible power to rosy assertions that we are finally turning a corner in the drug war. Guzmán was a powerful and dangerous criminal and his final capture should be applauded, but his downfall will do little to alter the Mexican or American drug problem or halt the flow of drugs across the border. And neither will a wall, for that matter.[12]

The villains who historically dominate popular understandings of the drug war establish a dialectic that becomes all the more critical when America goes abroad to neutralize them. In *The Murderers,* Anslinger claimed, "Evil is of one cloth" wherever it is found and must be confronted.[13] During the FBN's drug war, the imperative to stop drugs and drug traffickers justified U.S. intervention in the affairs of foreign nations across the globe and at a range of levels. The FBN never sent an army of federal agents to occupy source countries, but it developed important arguments that undercut the sovereignty of other nations. "If you want to control this traffic," Anslinger warned in 1957, "you have got to surrender some sovereign rights."[14] This argument led the Bureau to demand changes in the legal structure and political, economic, and cultural practices of other countries—which was sometimes successful and sometimes not.

The most visible manifestation of how the drug war extended U.S. dominion while eroding the sovereignty of other nations was the physical presence of American police agents. Nearly every country targeted by agents resisted intrusion into what local police saw as an entirely domestic concern. And the agents, naturally, carried their own assumptions about what it meant to work in foreign lands, many of them markedly less developed than the United States. In Turkey, for example, Agents Sal Vizzini and Joe Arpaio approached their jobs like a couple of lawmen roaming the Old West. Vizzini described Turkey as "virgin territory," where "life was cheap" and "you walked with your gun in your hand." Arpaio saw himself as "a sort of 'proto-posseman'" in "a land of mystery and intrigue," armed only with his "trusty Smith & Wesson and a pathetically small roll of flash money."[15] It's no surprise to find the memoirs of American agents operating in developing nations colored with a touch of Orientalism, but this had a very real practical effect. Depicting source countries like Turkey as an extension of the American frontier, or "virgin territory," reinforced a worldview that made intervention seem easy and natural.

FBN leadership contributed to this bleed-over effect by insisting that there was no meaningful distinction between working at home and abroad. The Bureau's claims on authority and influence were tied to the imperative of drug control and the novelty of its undercover approach, and, as Williams tried to console Agent Siragusa during his early failures in Istanbul, "The principle is the same whether it is in Turkey or New York." This was a persistent belief at FBN headquarters, where supervisors insisted that "making cases in Europe is no different from making cases in the States." In point of fact, however, it was very different. "I dont [sic] want to glamorize the work here," a wide-eyed Siragusa wrote, "but it is definitely dissimilar to narcotic law enforcement in the U.S."[16] In every country they visited, the agents had to negotiate critical—often determinative—differences in local laws, customs, languages, and power structures.

The drug war acted as a lens, focusing the American gaze inward, upon people who seemed to undermine traditional American values, and outward, upon the foreign villains who were held responsible for spreading addiction to the American people. The drug war directed the public's gaze anywhere but the mirror, to our own institutions and the social, cultural, and economic trends that facilitate excessive drug consumption. Or, as Dr. Hamilton Wright put in back in 1911, the drug issue illustrates the national "tendency to see, with amazing clarity, the sins of others, while remaining blind to our own viciousness."[17]

Today we refer to that tendency as American exceptionalism. By portraying drug control as a battle between good and evil and themselves as warriors defending freedom, the FBN developed a way of thinking about drugs that built on a long history of exceptional American identity. The FBN's insistence that America was a victim rather than a consumer of drugs essentially reversed black-market forces and elided any responsibility for underwriting global demand. Rather than address the domestic forces that created one of the world's largest drug markets, American officials preferred to look abroad for solutions. Driven by the assumption that the United States had perfected the balance between liberty, democracy, and state power, America's drug warriors convinced themselves that it was more appropriate and effective to restructure the economies, cultures, and politics of source countries than to pursue the domestic reforms necessary to reduce the American demand for drugs.

Put another way, globalization acted upon the United States by introducing foreign drugs that increased existing social problems and created new ones while threatening to undermine America's belief in its own world-historic standing. In response, the country punished its own drug users and sought to "Americanize" the rest of the world under the auspices of a war on drugs. Yet the persistence of both the drug traffic and the drug war provides a clear warning on the disconnect between the scope of American ambition and the limits of American power.

Ending the Drug War

The most fundamental problem with the war on drugs is right there in the name; it is impossible to wage war on a commodity, particularly one that remains in demand. The drug war represents such a failure of policy that it is difficult not to be harshly critical or to take its fundamental objectives seriously. As a result, critics often look to ulterior motives to explain its persistence, be it a form of social control, a war on the poor, or a component of covert operations. But the fault and the solutions lie inward and exceed the responsibility of any one person or institution. One of the greatest challenges presented by the history of American drug control is that the aim is undeniably worthy. Drugs like heroin, methamphetamine, cocaine, and marijuana—a list to which we can and should add alcohol and tobacco, and perhaps even sugar!—are all subject to abuse and absolutely require some form of control. The drug war has failed to provide that. So long as the country remains focused on punishment and reducing supply instead of demand, it will remain at war with drugs and at war with itself.

Focusing new attention on demand, however, won't solve the drug problem by itself. Ironically, proponents of legalization actually agree with drug warriors on one core assumption: demand is, to some extent, irreducible. Indiscriminate legalization would be foolish, but a careful policy of decriminalization (at the federal if not local level) would shift attention away from the impossible task of policing use and supply and move policy toward a more open and visible system of control. It would do nothing, however, to reduce the demand for drugs or help those struggling with addiction. Nearly all drug reformers agree that the single most effective step toward more effective control is to remove the stigma around addiction, regardless of how we characterize addiction itself. That is a task for society as much as it is for politicians. At the national level, we need a system of regulation that acknowledges the reality of individual outcomes and recognizes that all drugs fall within a wide spectrum of potential harm, abuse, and benefit. The shortest path to such a reality would be to dramatically revise the current drug-scheduling system with equal input from police, medical professionals, and the public. Meanwhile, we must not lose sight of the fact that law enforcement continues to play a vital role and should continue to monitor and disrupt the drug traffic at the regional and wholesale levels, particularly as the international drug trade further complicates geopolitical conflicts all over the world.

The good news is that we may be on the precipice of just such a change. The concurrent development of the marijuana legalization movement and the opioid crisis is prompting a profound shift in public thinking—most critically, that drugs are not just a problem of criminality. The fundamental injustices of mass incarceration and police misconduct are drawing increasing condemnation, and judicial and criminal reforms are among the few policy issues capable of drawing bipartisan support in a badly fractured political system. In the waning days of the Obama administration, officials from across the federal bureaucracy—from the attorney general to the surgeon general and the directors of the National Institute on Drug Abuse and Office of

National Drug Control Policy—voiced their support for a public health approach to drug control. President Obama himself remarked, "I do believe that treating this as a public-health issue, the same way we do with cigarettes or alcohol, is the much smarter way to deal with it."[18] All of this represents a massive step in the right direction.

But on the other hand, we've been here before—and the election of Donald Trump has ushered in a dramatic new round of culture war and political upheaval. One of the many challenges of the drug problem is that it tends both galvanize and get subsumed within wider cultural clashes, and when drug policy has softened in the past, as in the mid-1960s and late 1970s, it prompted a strong conservative backlash. It's entirely possible that the rise of the legal marijuana industry and efforts to revise prison sentencing, curb police authority, and confront Big Pharma could all provoke a similar counterattack and breathe new life into the drug war.

Ultimately, the drug war's end has yet to be written, and we, collectively, will be its authors. It might look like the war on terror, where the only thing that really changes is the name. But the drug war's end will probably look more like the Cold War, another conflict that seemed so pressing at the time and so perplexing, at times insane, in hindsight. The marijuana issue, the suburbanization and "whitening" of addiction, and proliferating drug use all helped put an end to the FBN, and they may now serve as the perestroika and glasnost of the drug war, where incremental reforms unleash sudden and wholesale change. Whatever new forms American drug control takes, we must act together to ensure they improve upon the clear failures of the past.

To be continued . . .

NOTES

INTRODUCTION

1. George White to Harry Anslinger, June 10, 1948, folder "George White's Reports," box 164, entry 9 (Misc. Subject Files), RG 170 (Records of the Drug Enforcement Administration), National Archives and Records Administration (hereafter NARA).
2. Frederic Sondern Jr., "Our Global War on Narcotics," *Reader's Digest,* April 1950 (condensed from *American Mercury,* March 1950); "Summary Translation, Comments of the Turkish Press," folder "George White's Reports," box 164, RG 170, NARA.
3. Alfred W. McCoy, *Policing America's Empire: The United States, the Philippines, and the Rise of the Surveillance State* (Madison: University of Wisconsin Press, 2009), 12.
4. Harry J. Anslinger and J. Dennis Gregory, *The Protectors: The Heroic Story of the Narcotics Agents, Citizens and Officials in Their Unending, Unsung Battles against Organized Crime in America and Abroad* (New York: Farrar and Straus, 1964), 79; John C. McWilliams, "Covert Connections: The FBN, the OSS, and the CIA," *Historian* 53, no. 4 (1991): 657–79; John Marks, *The Search for the "Manchurian Candidate": The CIA and Mind Control, the Secret History of the Behavioral Sciences* (New York: W. W. Norton, 1979); Douglas Valentine, *The Strength of the Wolf: The Secret History of America's War on Drugs* (London: Verso, 2004), 309–31; White, address at Stanford University Law School, Oct. 28, 1970, folder 18, box 3, George White Papers, Stanford University Libraries, Stanford, CA (hereafter White Papers).
5. White to Gottlieb, Nov. 21, 1971, folder 1, box 4, White Papers.
6. Andrew Weil, *The Natural Mind: A Revolutionary Approach to the Drug Problem,* rev. ed. (Boston: Houghton Mifflin, 2004).
7. Harold D. Lasswell, "The Garrison State," *American Journal of Sociology* 46, no. 4 (Jan. 1941): 455–68.
8. Emphasis added. Quoted in Jay Richard Kennedy, "One World—against Dope," *Sunday Star: This Week Magazine* and *Baltimore Sun,* March 7, 1948, folder 13, box 1, Harry J. Anslinger Papers, Special Collections Library, Pennsylvania State University, University Park (hereafter Anslinger Papers).

9. White to Matthew O'Connor (CA Bureau of Narcotic Enforcement), July 31, 1970, folder 1, box 4, White Papers.

10. David F. Musto, MD, *The American Disease: Origins of Narcotic Control,* 3rd ed. (New York: Oxford University Press, 1999).

11. Richard Hofstadter, *The Paranoid Style in American Politics* (New York: Vintage Books, 2008), 4–5; Robert Dallek, *The American Style of Foreign Policy: Cultural Politics and Foreign Affairs* (New York: Alfred A. Knopf, 1983); Susan L. Speaker, "'The Struggle of Mankind against Its Deadliest Foe': Themes of Counter-subversion in Anti-narcotic Campaigns, 1920–1940," *Journal of Social History* 34, no. 3 (2001): 591–610.

12. Joe Arpaio and Len Sherman, *Joe's Law: America's Toughest Sheriff Takes on Illegal Immigration, Drugs, and Everything Else That Threatens America* (New York: AMA-COM, 2008); "Full Text: Donald Trump Announces a Presidential Bid," *Washington Post,* June 16, 2015; "Inaugural Address: Trump's Full Speech," Jan. 21, 2017, www.cnn.com.

13. "Opioid Addiction, 2016 Facts & Figures," American Society of Addiction Medicine, www.asam.org; "Injury Prevention & Control: Opioid Overdose," Center for Disease Control and Prevention, www.cdc.gov; Christopher Ingrahm, "Heroin Deaths Surpass Gun Homicides for the First Time, CDC Data Shows," *Washington Post,* Dec. 8, 2016; "Drug Overdoses Killed 50,000 in U.S., More than Car Crashes," *NBC News,* Dec. 9, 2016, www.nbcnews.com; Sam Quinones, *Dreamland: The True Tale of America's Opiate Epidemic* (New York: Bloomsbury Press, 2016).

14. Richard Nixon, "Special Message to Congress on Drug Abuse Prevention and Control," June 17, 1971; Ronald Reagan, "Address to the Nation on the Campaign against Drug Abuse," Sept. 14, 1986, American Presidency Project, UC–Santa Barbara, www.presidency.ucsb.edu.

15. Andrew Preston, "Monsters Everywhere: A Genealogy of National Security," *Diplomatic History* 32, no. 3 (2014): 477–500.

16. Sondern, "Our Global War on Narcotics."

17. David T. Courtwright, *Forces of Habit: Drugs and the Making of the Modern World* (Cambridge, MA: Harvard University Press, 2001), 2.

18. Ibid., 2.

19. Paul Gootenberg, *Andean Cocaine: The Making of a Global Drug* (Chapel Hill: University of North Carolina Press, 2008), 3.

20. Jeremy Kuzmarov, *The Myth of the Addicted Army: Vietnam and the Modern War on Drugs* (Amherst: University of Massachusetts Press, 2009); Pierre-Arnaud Chouvy, *Opium: Uncovering the Politics of the Poppy* (Cambridge, MA: Harvard University Press, 2010); Daniel Weimer, *Seeing Drugs: Modernization, Counterinsurgency, and U.S. Narcotics Control in the Third World, 1969–1976* (Kent, OH: Kent State University Press, 2011); Michelle Alexander, *The New Jim Crow: Mass Incarceration in the Age of Colorblindness* (New York: New Press, 2012); Isaac Campos, *Home Grown: Marijuana and the Origins of Mexico's War on Drugs* (Chapel Hill: University of North Carolina Press, 2012); Jonathan Marshall, *The Lebanese Connection: Corruption, Civil War, and the International Drug Traffic* (Stanford, CA: Stanford University Press, 2012); Dominique A. Tobbell, *Pills, Power, and Policy: The Struggle for Drug Reform in Cold War America and Its Consequences* (Berkeley: University of California Press, 2012); Peter Andreas, *Smuggler Nation: How Illicit Trade Made America* (Oxford: Oxford University Press, 2013); Kathleen Frydl, *The*

Drug Wars in America, 1940–1973 (Cambridge: Cambridge University Press, 2013); Ryan Gingeras, *Heroin, Organized Crime, and the Making of Modern Turkey* (New York: Oxford University Press, 2014); Suzanna Reiss, *We Sell Drugs: The Alchemy of U.S. Empire* (Berkeley: University of California Press, 2014). See also William O. Walker III, ed., *Drug Control Policy: Essays in Historical and Comparative Perspective* (University Park: Pennsylvania State University Press, 1992); Paul Gootenberg, ed., *Cocaine: Global Histories* (London: Routledge, 1999); Sarah Tracy and Caroline Jean Acker, eds., *Altering American Consciousness: The History of Alcohol and Drug Use in the United States* (Amherst: University of Massachusetts Press, 2004); and Jordan Goodman, Paul E. Lovejoy, and Andrew Sherratt, eds., *Consuming Habits: Global and Historical Perspectives on How Cultures Define Drugs* (London: Routledge, 2007).

21. Alfred W. McCoy, *The Politics of Heroin: CIA Complicity in the Global Drug Trade*, rev. ed. (Chicago: Lawrence Hill Books, 2003); Gary Webb, *Dark Alliance: The CIA, the Contras, and the Crack Cocaine Explosion* (New York: Seven Stories Press, 1998); Jonathan Marshall, *Drug Wars: Corruption, Counterinsurgency and Covert Operations in the Third World* (Forestville, CA: Cohan & Cohen, 1991), 11; Peter Dale Scott, *American War Machine: Deep Politics, the CIA Global Drug Connection, and the Road to Afghanistan* (Lanham, MD: Rowan & Littlefield, 2010); Weimer, *Seeing Drugs*; Jeremy Kuzmarov, *Modernizing Repression: Police Training and Nation-Building in the American Century* (Amherst: University of Massachusetts Press, 2012).

22. John C. McWilliams, *The Protectors: Harry J. Anslinger and the Federal Bureau of Narcotics, 1930–1962* (Newark: University of Delaware Press, 1990); Valentine, *Strength of the Wolf*; Douglas Valentine, *The Strength of the Pack: The Personalities, Politics and Espionage Intrigues That Shaped the DEA* (Waltersville, OR: Trine Day, 2008); Frydl, *Drug Wars in America*; Elizabeth Hinton, *From the War on Poverty to the War on Crime: The Making of Mass Incarceration in America* (Cambridge, MA: Harvard University Press, 2016). See also various journal-length works by McWilliams, Douglas Clark Kinder, Alan Block, and Bruce Bullington.

23. Tom Carnwatch and Ian Smith, *Heroin Century* (London: Routledge, 2002), 75.

CHAPTER 1

1. House Committee on Ways and Means, *Taxation of Marihuana, H.R. 6385*, 75th Cong., 1st sess., April 27–May 4, 1937, 18–42; Senate Committee on Finance, *Taxation of Marihuana, H.R. 6906*, 75th Cong., 1st sess., July 12, 1937.

2. Anslinger, remarks at UN Commission on Narcotic Drugs, April 1953 and May 8–June 1, 1962, folder 8, box 1, Anslinger Papers; Senate Subcommittee to Investigate the Administration of the Internal Security Act and Other Internal Security Laws, *Scope of Soviet Activity in the United States*, 85th Cong., 1st sess., 1957, 3611–24; Harry J. Anslinger and William F. Tompkins, *The Traffic in Narcotics* (New York: Funk and Wagnalls, 1953), 76–99; Harry J. Anslinger and Will Oursler, *The Murderers: The Story of the Narcotics Gangs* (New York: Farrar, Straus, and Cudahy, 1961), 223.

3. Anslinger and Oursler, *Murderers*, 295; Harry J. Anslinger and J. Dennis Gregory, *The Protectors: The Heroic Story of the Narcotics Agents, Citizens and Officials in Their Unending, Unsung Battles against Organized Crime in America and Abroad*

(New York: Farrar and Straus, 1964), 223; M. L. Harney, "The Drug Menace in the United States," Oct. 8, 1952, folder 10, box 1, Anslinger Papers.

4. Matthew R. Pembleton, "The Voice of the Bureau: How Frederic Sondern and the Bureau of Narcotics Crafted a Drug War and Shaped Popular Understanding of Drugs, Addiction, and Organized Crime in the 1950s," *Journal of American Culture* 38, no. 2 (2015): 113–29.

5. Robert H. Wiebe, *The Search for Order, 1877–1920* (New York: Hill and Wang, 1967); Walter LaFeber, *The New Empire: An Interpretation of American Expansion, 1860–1898*, rev. ed. (Ithaca, NY: Cornell University Press, 1998); Nell Irvin Painter, *Standing at Armageddon: A Grassroots History of the Progressive Era* (New York: W. W. Norton, 2008).

6. Quoted in "Five Debt Accords Ratified by House," *New York Times*, Jan. 17, 1926.

7. H. Wayne Morgan, *Drugs in America: A Social History, 1800–1980* (Syracuse, NY: Syracuse University Press, 1981); David T. Courtwright, *Dark Paradise: Opiate Addiction in America before 1940* (Cambridge, MA: Harvard University Press, 1982).

8. David F. Musto, "The Origins of Heroin," and David T. Courtwright, "The Roads to H: The Emergence of the American Heroin Complex, 1898–1956," both in *One Hundred Years of Heroin,* edited by David F. Musto (Westport, CT: Auburn House, 2002), xiii–xvii, 3–19.

9. William B. McAllister, *Drug Diplomacy in the Twentieth Century: An International History* (London: Routledge, 2000), 9–39; William O. Walker III, *Opium and Foreign Policy: The Anglo-American Search for Order in Asia, 1912–1954* (Chapel Hill: University of North Carolina Press, 1991); Arnold H. Taylor, *American Diplomacy and the Narcotics Traffic, 1900–1939* (Durham, NC: Duke University Press, 1969); John Callan O'Laughlin, "Nations to Join in War on Opium," *Chicago Daily Tribune,* March 11, 1907.

10. Edward Marshall, "Uncle Sam Is the Worst Drug Fiend in the World," *New York Times,* March 12, 1911.

11. Michael A. Lerner, *Dry Manhattan: Prohibition in New York City* (Cambridge, MA: Harvard University Press, 2007), 29–39; Cassandra Tate, *Cigarette Wars: The Triumph of "the Little White Slaver"* (New York: Oxford University Press, 1999); "Congressional Debate over the Prohibition Amendment," in *Drugs in America: A Documentary History,* edited by David F. Musto (New York: New York University Press, 2002), 116.

12. "History of Narcotic Addiction in the United States," chart, folder "Flow of Illicit Narcotics from Italy," box 11, RG 170, NARA. In 1930 Representative Stephen G. Porter estimated the number of addicts at 400,000 to 450,000. House Committee on Ways and Means, *Bureau of Narcotics,* H.R. 10561, 71st Cong., 2nd sess., March 7–8, 1930, 13–15. H. Wayne Morgan argues that opiate addiction "peaked in the 1890s, and declined thereafter." Morgan, *Drugs in America,* 30.

13. "U.S. Opens War on Opium Ring," *Chicago Daily Tribune,* July 4, 1914; "War on Narcotics," *Los Angeles Times,* Jan. 9, 1923; "World War on Opium," *Los Angeles Times,* Nov. 9, 1924; "The War against Opium," *New York Times,* Mar. 11, 1926; "World War Planned on Narcotic Traffic," *New York Times,* Oct. 30, 1927; "Morgenthau Favors Tapping of Wires in Treasury Agents' War on Narcotics," *New York Times,* Oct. 16, 1934; "The War on Narcotics," *Washington Post,* Jan. 1, 1935; "Hull Praises War on Narcotics Evil," *New York Times,* April 14, 1936.

14. Ron Roizen, "How Does the Nation's 'Alcohol Problem' Change from Era to Era?,"

in *Altering American Consciousness: The History of Alcohol and Drug Use in the United States,* edited by Sarah Tracy and Caroline Jean Acker (Amherst: University of Massachusetts Press, 2004): 61–87; Lisa McGirr, *The War on Alcohol: Prohibition and the Rise of the American State* (New York: W. W. Norton, 2016); R. K. Portenoy and K. M. Foley, "Chronic Use of Opioid Analgesics in Non-malignant Pain: Report of 38 Cases," *Pain* 25, no. 2 (1986): 171–86; Sam Quinones, *Dreamland: The True Tale of America's Opiate Epidemic* (New York: Bloomsbury Press, 2016), 92–99.

15. Cong. Rec., 68th Cong., 1st sess., April 7, 1924, vol. 65, pt. 6: 5769–97; House Committee on Ways and Means, *Bureau of Narcotics, H.R. 10561,* 71st Cong., 2nd sess., March 7–8, 1930, 13–15; Cong. Rec., 71st Cong., 2nd sess. April 7, 1930, vol. 72, pt. 6: 6661–64; Cong. Rec., 71st Cong., 2nd sess., June 5, 1930, vol. 72, pt. 9: 10085.

16. *Bureau of Narcotics, H.R. 10561,* 13, 32; Anslinger and Oursler, *Murderers,* 167.

17. "Material for Radio Program, Maryland Pharmaceutical Association," Feb. 28, 1942, folder "(1690-8) Publicity, Radio, 1941–1948, #3," box 69, RG 170, NARA. See also Anslinger remarks to International Association of Chiefs of Police, Oct. 13, 1931, folder 7; Anslinger, "The Narcotic Problem: Address before the National Conference on Crime," Dec. 13, 1934, folder 10; Anslinger remarks on UN-CND (Commission on Narcotic Drugs), May 29, 1957, folder 8, box 1, Anslinger Papers; and House Committee on Ways and Means, *Taxation of Marihuana, H.R. 6385,* 75th Cong., 1st sess., 1937, 18–42.

18. Harry J. Anslinger, "Drug Addiction: A World Problem," undated, folder 8, box 1, Anslinger Papers.

19. Carl A. Trocki, *Opium, Empire and the Global Political Economy: A Study of the Asian Opium Trade, 1750–1950* (London: Routledge, 1999); Pierre-Arnaud Chouvy, *Opium: Uncovering the Politics of the Poppy* (Cambridge, MA: Harvard University Press, 2010).

20. Anslinger and Tompkins, *The Traffic in Narcotics,* 1–2; *Taxation of Marihuana, H.R. 6385,* 18–42; H. J. Anslinger and Courtney Riley Cooper, "Marijuana—Assassin of Youth," *American Magazine,* July 1937, folder 13, box 2, Anslinger Papers.

21. Harry J. Anslinger, "Narcotics in the Post-war World," *True Detective,* Feb. 1946, folder 18, box 12, Anslinger Papers.

22. *Bureau of Narcotics, H.R. 10561,* 13–15; Cong. Rec., April 7, 1930, vol. 72, pt. 6: 16.

23. David Courtwright, Herman Joseph, and Don Des Jarlais, eds., *Addicts Who Survived: An Oral History of Narcotic Use in America, 1923–1965* (Knoxville: University of Tennessee Press, 1989); Caroline Jean Acker, *Creating the American Junkie: Addiction Research in the Classic Era of Narcotic Control* (Baltimore: Johns Hopkins University Press, 2002); Morgan, *Drugs in America;* David F. Musto, MD, *The American Disease: Origins of Narcotic Control,* 3rd ed. (New York: Oxford University Press, 1999).

24. "Text of President's Message," *Washington Post,* Jan. 14, 1930; "Would Cut Output of Narcotic Drugs," *New York Times,* Feb. 21, 1931.

25. Taylor, *American Diplomacy;* McAllister, *Drug Diplomacy.*

26. Alan Block, "European Drug Traffic and Traffickers between the Wars: The Policy of Suppression and Its Consequences," *Journal of Social History* 23, no. 2 (1989): 315; Joseph F. Spillane, *Cocaine: From Medical Marvel to Modern Menace in the United States, 1884–1920* (Baltimore: Johns Hopkins University Press, 2000), 102–57.

27. Acker, *Creating the American Junkie;* Sana Loue, "The Criminalization of the Addictions: Toward a Unified Approach," *Journal of Legal Medicine* 24 (2003): 281–330.

28. Undated papers, "Common Sense Temperance" and "The American Prohibition Policy," folder 5, box 1, Anslinger Papers.

29. "Definition of Addiction," American Society of Addiction Medicine, www.asam. org.

30. Anslinger and Tompkins, *The Traffic in Narcotics*, 174–212, 223–62; Morgan, *Drugs in America*, 131–32; Acker, *Creating the American Junkie*, 132; biographical note, Lawrence Kolb Papers, U.S. National Library of Medicine, www.nlm.nih.gov; Martin Weil, "Ex-PHS Drug Aide Dies at 91," *Washington Post*, Nov. 20, 1972.

31. Anslinger and Oursler, *Murderers*, 278.

32. William S. Burroughs, *Junky: 50th Anniversary Definitive Edition* (New York: Penguin Books, 2003), 23; James H. Mulgannon, *Uncertain Glory* (New York: Vantage Press, 1972), 117; Courtwright, Joseph, and Des Jarlais, *Addicts Who Survived*; Caroline Jean Acker, "Portrait of an Addicted Family: Dynamics of Opiate Addiction in the Early Twentieth Century," in *Altering American Consciousness*, edited by Tracy and Acker, 165–81.

33. White to Gordon Pates (managing editor of the *San Francisco Chronicle*), Oct. 2, 1959, folder "(1690-10) General #6, Publicity, Publications, Nov. 1958–Dec. 1960," box 70, RG 170, NARA; Anslinger and Gregory, *Protectors*, 22.

34. Quoted from draft prepared for *American Youth Review* and provided to Assistant Treasury Secretary Nils A. Lennartson, Aug. 10, 1959, folder "(1690-10) General #6, Publicity, Publications, Nov. 1958–Dec. 1960," box 70, RG 170, NARA; Burroughs, *Junky*, xxxviii.

35. Anslinger and Tompkins, *The Traffic in Narcotics*, 293; Jack Kelly and Richard Mathison, *On the Street* (Chicago: Henry Regnery, 1974), 159–60; James Phelan, *Scandals, Scamps, and Scoundrels: The Casebook of an Investigative Reporter* (New York: Random House, 1982), 38.

36. Anslinger, "Material for Radio Program," Feb. 28, 1942, folder 8, box 1, Anslinger Papers; Anslinger and Tompkins, *The Traffic in Narcotics*, 55, 170, 302.

37. Subcommittee No. III of the House Committee on the Judiciary, *Punishment for Violation of Narcotic Laws, H.R. 6283*, 75th Cong., 1st sess., April 23, 1937, 8. The law under debate notably did not feature mandatory minimums, Treasury Dept. counsel noted, because the attorney general had forced them to drop it.

38. Anslinger and Oursler, *Murderers*, 234; Anslinger and Tompkins, *The Traffic in Narcotics*, 287.

39. Anslinger and Tompkins, *The Traffic in Narcotics*, 215–18. See also John Markert, *Hooked in Film: Substance Abuse on the Big Screen* (Lanham, MD: Scarecrow Press, 2013), ix–x.

40. Anslinger and Tompkins, *The Traffic in Narcotics*, vii, 12; Anslinger and Oursler, *Murderers*, 173, 294; Sal Vizzini, Oscar Fraley, and Marshall Smith, *Vizzini: The Secret Lives of America's Most Successful Undercover Agent* (New York: Pinnacle Books, 1972), 12, 26, 16; Joachim Joesten, *Dope, Inc.* (New York: Avon, 1953), 38, 146; Malachi Harney, "The Police and Narcotic Enforcement," Oct. 30, 1951, and "The Drug Menace in the United States," Oct. 8, 1952, folder 10, box 1, Anslinger Papers.

41. Richmond P. Hobson, "Mankind's Greatest Affliction and Gravest Menace," in *Drugs in America*, edited by Musto, 271–75; folder "Living Death," box 72, RG 170, NARA.

42. Steward Robertson, "Dope on Dope," *Family Circle*, Oct. 26, 1945; Richard Hirsch, "Freeing the Drug Slaves: An Interview with U.S. Commissioner of Narcotics Harry

J. Anslinger," *True Detective*, Oct. 1947; Anslinger, "The Treatment of Drug Addiction," *Union Signal*, June 25, 1960, folders 4, 18, and 20, box 12, Anslinger Papers; "The Necessity for the Uniform Narcotic Drug Act," folder "(1690-8) Publicity, Radio, 1941–1948, #3," box 69, RG 170.

43. Richard Hirsch, "How Treasury Agents Broke the 'Poison Sleep' Gang," *True Detective*, May 1939; "I Joined a Teen-Age Sex and Dope Gang," *Actual Romances*, Dec. 1951, folders 18 and 1, box 12, Anslinger Papers.

44. Anslinger and Tompkins, *The Traffic in Narcotics*, 295.

45. Matthew B. Robinson and Renee G. Scherlen, *Lies, Damned Lies, and Drug War Statistics: A Critical Analysis of Claims Made by the Office of National Drug Control Policy*, 2nd ed. (Albany: State University of New York Press, 2014).

46. "History of Narcotic Addiction in the United States," chart. The most up-to-date statistics are kept by the National Institute of Drug Abuse, www.drugabuse.gov, and the Substance Abuse and Mental Health Services Administration, www.samhsa. gov. See the National Survey on Drug Use and Health and "DrugFacts" series.

47. "History of Narcotic Addiction in the United States," chart.

48. Anslinger and Oursler, *The Traffic in Narcotics*, 8.

49. U.S. Treasury Dept. Press Release, Jan. 26, 1942, folder "(1690-12) Publicity, Press Release, 1938 thru 1942," box 74, RG 170, NARA.

50. Anslinger, "Narcotics in the Post-war World."

51. Ibid.

52. Michael H. Hunt, *Ideology and U.S. Foreign Policy* (New Haven, CT: Yale University Press, 1987); Tom Englehardt, *The End of Victory Culture: Cold War America and the Disillusioning of a Generation* (Amherst: University of Massachusetts Press, 1995); Melvyn P. Leffler, *For the Soul of Mankind: The United States, the Soviet Union, and the Cold War* (New York: Hill and Wang, 2007); Walter L. Hixson, *The Myth of American Diplomacy: National Identity and U.S. Foreign Policy* (New Haven, CT: Yale University Press, 2008).

53. Truman Presidential Library, www.trumanlibrary.org.

54. Harry J. Anslinger, "The Need for Narcotic Education," Feb. 24, 1936; remarks to World Narcotic Defense Association, April 13, 1936; and remarks to the International Association of Chiefs of Police, Sept. 12, 1940, folders 10, 7, and 8, box 1, Anslinger Papers.

55. Antonio Gramsci, *Selections from the Prison Notebooks*, translated by Quintin Hoare and Geoffrey Nowell Smith (New York: International, 1971); Geir Lundestad, "Empire by Invitation? The United States and Western Europe, 1945–1952," *Journal of Peace Research* 23, no. 3 (1986): 263–77; Geir Lundestad, *The United States and Western Europe since 1945: From "Empire" by Invitation to Transatlantic Drift* (Oxford: Oxford University Press, 2003); John Lewis Gaddis, *We Now Know: Rethinking the Cold War* (Oxford: Oxford University Press, 1997) and *The Cold War: A New History* (New York: Penguin Press, 2005).

56. McAllister, *Drug Diplomacy*, 156–239.

57. Charles Siragusa, Progress Report no. 45, Oct. 15, 1950, folder "Progress Reports of Charles Siragusa," box 164, RG 170, NARA.

58. Frederic Sondern Jr., "Our Global War on Narcotics," *Reader's Digest*, April 1950; Sondern, "The World War against Narcotics," *Reader's Digest*, Jan. 1956. See also Pembleton, "Voice of the Bureau."

59. For cigarettes, see National Cancer Institute, *Changes in Cigarette-Related Disease*

Risks and Their Implication for Prevention and Control, Tobacco Control Monograph Series (Bethesda, MD: National Cancer Institute, 1997), 13–14. For pharma,
see Nicolas Rasmussen, *On Speed: The Many Lives of Amphetamine* (New York: New
York University Press, 2008); Andrea Tone, *The Age of Anxiety: A History of America's Turbulent Affair with Tranquilizers* (New York: Basic Books, 2009); and Dominique A. Tobbell, *Pills, Power, and Policy: The Struggle for Drug Reform in Cold War
America and Its Consequences* (Berkeley: University of California Press, 2012). For
alcohol, see Robin A. LaVallee and Hsiao-ye Yi, *NIAAA: Surveillance Report #92,
Apparent per Capita Alcohol Consumption: National, State, and Regional Trends,
1977–2009* (Bethesda, MD: National Institutes of Health, 2011), 6.

60. "History of Narcotic Addiction in the United States," chart.

61. Courtwright, "Roads to H"; Jill Jonnes, *Hep-Cats, Narcs, and Pipe Dreams: A History of America's Romance with Illegal Drugs* (New York: Scribner, 1996); Eric C.
Schneider, *Smack: Heroin and the American City* (Philadelphia: University of Pennsylvania Press, 2008).

62. Committee on Drug Addiction and Narcotics, Minutes of Meeting, Jan. 15, 1951,
"Com on Drug Addiction & Narcotics, Meetings: 7th: Minutes, 1951 Jan," Central
File, National Academy of Sciences Archive (hereafter NAS Archive); Anslinger
and Tompkins, *The Traffic in Narcotics,* 281.

63. Anslinger and Tompkins, *The Traffic in Narcotics,* 283.

64. Kelly and Mathison, *On the Street,* 183–86.

65. "Another Problem for the Big Cities," *U.S. News and World Report,* April 6, 1959, folder
9, box 7; and "New York Forum," April 28, 1962, folder 10, box 1, Anslinger Papers. See
also Donald W. Tucker, *The Two-Edged Sword* (Indianapolis: Dog Ear, 2010).

66. Anslinger, Circular Letter no. 324, Dec. 4, 1934, folder "(0370-3) Circular Letters,
301–400," box 55, RG 170, NARA; Senator Joseph Guffey to the Assistant Secretary of State, Dec. 30, 1934, folder 5, box 3; and "Marijuana, the Weed of Folly and
Dreams," folder 8, box 1, Anslinger Papers; John C. McWilliams, *The Protectors:
Harry J. Anslinger and the Federal Bureau of Narcotics, 1930–1962* (Newark: University of Delaware Press, 1990), 84–85.

67. Report by Jack Cusack, Nov. 7, 1951, folder "(0660) France #3, 1951–1953," box 156;
Siragusa to Anslinger, July 13, 1953, folder "(1825-7) Reports Progress Dist #17, 1951–
1957 (2 of 2)," box 83; and Siragusa, Sept. 4, 1956, folder "(1825-7) Reports Progress
Dist #17, 1951–1957 (1 of 2)," box 83, RG 170, NARA. See also Anslinger and Greg-
ory, *Protectors,* 150–64; and Penny Von Eschen, *Satchmo Blows Up the World: Jazz
Ambassadors Play the Cold War* (Cambridge, MA: Harvard University Press, 2004).

68. "Drive to End Drug Traffic in Midwest Led by Woman," *Washington Post,* Dec. 8,
1934; Hirsch, "Freeing the Drug Slaves."

69. Anslinger, March 20, 1949, folder "(0370-3) Memorandum for All District Supervisors, 1936–1954," box 56, RG 170, NARA.

70. Anslinger and Oursler, *Murderers,* 175–76, 181–82; McWilliams, *Protectors,* 99.

71. "Shooting Gallery," April 9, 1950, UN-NBC Series, folder "(1690-8) Publicity, Radio,
1949 thru June 1951," box 69, RG 170, NARA.

72. Anslinger and Oursler, *Murderers,* 190–93, 20–33; Anslinger and Gregory, *Protectors,* 74.

73. Harry J. Anslinger, "The Facts about Our Teen-Age Drug Addicts," *Reader's Digest,*
Oct. 1951; and Herbert Brean, "A Short—and Horrible—Life," *Reader's Digest,* Sept.
1951, folder 1, box 7, Anslinger Papers. See also Stephen J. Gertz, *Dope Menace:*

The Sensational World of Drug Paperbacks, 1900–1975 (Port Townsend, WA: Feral House, 2008).

74. Anslinger and Tompkins, *The Traffic in Narcotics,* 226.

75. Anslinger and Oursler, *Murderers,* 77–120; Frederic Sondern Jr., *Brotherhood of Evil: The Mafia* (New York: Manor Books, 1959). See also David Brion Davis, "Some Themes of Counter-subversion: An Analysis of Anti-Masonic, Anti-Catholic, and Anti-Mormon Literature," *Mississippi Valley Historical Review* 47, no. 2 (1960): 205–24; Susan L. Speaker, "'The Struggle of Mankind against Its Deadliest Foe': Themes of Counter-subversion in Anti-narcotic Campaigns, 1920–1940," *Journal of Social History* 34, no. 3 (2001): 591–610.

76. W. H. Lawrence, "President Launches Drive on Narcotics," *New York Times,* Nov. 28, 1954; "The War on Narcotics," *New York Times,* Nov. 29, 1954; "U.S. Report Spurs Drive on Narcotics," *New York Times,* Feb. 6, 1956; "President Signs Narcotics Law," *Chicago Defender,* July 19, 1956; John Foster Dulles, State Dept. Instruction, Feb. 14, 1955, folder "(0660-A-1C) General Correspondence District #17, 1951 thru 1955," box 165, RG 170, NARA.

77. Senator Herman Welker (R-ID) is quoted in "President Signs Narcotics Law," *Chicago Defender,* July 19, 1956.

78. For 1942, see Treasury Dept. Press release, Jan. 26, 1942, folder "(1690-12) Publicity, Press Release, 1938 thru 1942," box 74, RG 170, NARA. For Mexico, see Treasury Dept. Press Service no. 37-95, Aug. 6, 1943, folder "(1690-12) Publicity, Press Release, 1943 thru 1947," box 74, RG 170, NARA; and Peter White, "Dope Inc.," *Argosy,* Feb. 1951, box 12, folder 1, Anslinger Papers. For Italy, see Charles Siragusa and Robert Wiedrich, *The Trail of the Poppy: Behind the Mask of the Mafia* (Englewood Cliffs, NJ: Prentice Hall, 1966), 83. For Europe, see monthly progress reports in box 83, RG 170, NARA. On the inconsistency of blame, see note by Siragusa affixed to memo by Wayland Speer, April 1, 1961, folder "(0660) France #4, 1954 June 1961," box 156, RG 170, NARA.

79. Ethan A. Nadelmann, *Cops across Borders: The Internationalization of U.S. Criminal Law Enforcement* (University Park: Pennsylvania State University Press, 1994); Peter Andreas and Ethan A. Nadelmann, *Policing the Globe: Criminalization and Crime Control in International Relations* (Oxford: Oxford University Press, 2006). See also Siragusa and Wiedrich, *Trail of the Poppy,* 144.

80. Daniel Weimer, *Seeing Drugs: Modernization, Counterinsurgency, and U.S. Narcotics Control in the Third World, 1969–1976* (Kent, OH: Kent State University Press, 2011); Michael E. Latham, *The Right Kind of Revolution: Modernization, Development, and U.S. Foreign Policy from the Cold War to the Present* (Ithaca, NY: Cornell University Press, 2011); Audra J. Wolfe, *Competing with the Soviets: Science, Technology, and the State in Cold War America* (Baltimore: Johns Hopkins University Press, 2013).

81. Anslinger and Tompkins, *The Traffic in Narcotics,* 192; Bruce Kuniholm, *The Origins of the Cold War in the Near East: Great Power Conflict and Diplomacy in Iran, Turkey, and Greece* (Princeton, NJ: Princeton University Press, 1980), 411; Douglas T. Stuart, *Creating the National Security State: A History of the Law That Transformed America* (Princeton, NJ: Princeton University Press, 2008), 187; Frank Ninkovich, *Modernity and Power: A History of the Domino Theory in the Twentieth Century* (Chicago: University of Chicago Press, 1994), xvii.

82. Wayland Speer to Anslinger, Jan. 10, 1961, folder "(0660) France #4, 1954–June 1961," box 156, RG 170, NARA; Anslinger and Gregory, *Protectors,* 223.

83. Anslinger, remarks on UN-CND, May 29, 1957, folder 8, box 1, Anslinger Papers.

84. Anslinger and Oursler, *Murderers,* 201, 296.

85. John F. Kennedy, "Remarks to the White House Conference on Narcotic and Drug Abuse," Sept. 27, 1962, American Presidency Project, UC–Santa Barbara, www.presidency.ucsb.edu.

86. Ibid.; Robert F. Kennedy, "Address to White House Conference on Narcotic and Drug Abuse," Sept. 28, 1962, Department of Justice, Speeches of Attorney General Robert F. Kennedy, www.justice.gov.

CHAPTER 2

1. Albert Q. Maisel, "Getting the Drop on Dope," *Liberty,* Nov. 24, 1945, folder 6, box 12, Anslinger Papers; H. Keith Weeks (Metro-Goldwyn-Mayer executive and friend) to Anslinger, Jan. 8, 1936, and April 19, 1940, folder 4, box 3 and folder 21, box 2, Anslinger Papers. Less charitably, methadone pioneer Marie Nyswander recalled him as "like a movie character of a despot." Quoted in David Courtwright, Herman Joseph, and Don Des Jarlais, eds., *Addicts Who Survived: An Oral History of Narcotic Use in America, 1923–1965* (Knoxville: University of Tennessee Press, 1989), 311.

2. Maisel, "Getting the Drop on Dope"; Jay Richard Kennedy, "One World—against Dope," *Sunday Star: This Week Magazine,* March 7, 1948, folder 13, box 1, Anslinger Papers; Will Oursler and Laurence Dwight Smith, *Narcotics: America's Peril* (Garden City, NY: Doubleday, 1952), 134.

3. Many letters held in Anslinger's papers are addressed to him at the Shoreham Hotel. For Anslinger's preference, see letter to James C. Ryan (district supervisor, New York City), April 9, 1954, folder 14, box 2, Anslinger Papers.

4. Martha Anslinger suffered from multiple sclerosis for much of her life, and Anslinger took frequent leave to care for her. John C. McWilliams, *The Protectors: Harry J. Anslinger and the Federal Bureau of Narcotics, 1930–1962* (Newark: University of Delaware Press, 1990), 10, 219n39.

5. Anslinger, remarks on UN-CND, May 29, 1957, folder 8, box 1, Anslinger Papers.

6. Howard Chappell to Douglas Valentine, July 21, 1994, folder "Chappell, Howard," box 2, the Douglas Valentine U.S. Government Drug Enforcement Collection, National Security Archives, George Washington University, Washington, DC (hereafter Valentine Collection); Jack Kelly and Richard Mathison, *On the Street* (Chicago: Henry Regnery, 1974), 93; Maisel, "Getting the Drop on Dope."

7. The "greatest living authority on dope" plaudit is from Leonard Lyall, a British narcotics expert, and listed on the jacket of Harry J. Anslinger and William F. Tompkins, *The Traffic in Narcotics* (New York: Funk and Wagnalls, 1953). See also Joseph Bransky to Nobel Prize Committee, Jan. 15, 1958, folder 9, box 2, Anslinger Papers. For VP nomination, see McWilliams, *Protectors,* 105.

8. David F. Musto, *The American Disease: Origins of Narcotic Control,* 3rd ed. (New York: Oxford University Press, 1999), 204–14; H. Wayne Morgan, *Drugs in America: A Social History, 1800–1980* (Syracuse, NY: Syracuse University Press, 1981); David T. Courtwright, *Dark Paradise: Opiate Addiction in America before 1940* (Cambridge, MA: Harvard University Press, 1982); Richard DeGrandpre, *The Cult of Pharmacology: How America Became the World's Most Troubled Drug Culture* (Durham, NC: Duke University Press, 2006).

9. Rufus King, *The Drug Hang-up: America's Fifty-Year Folly* (New York: W. W. Norton, 1972), 69; Larry Sloman, *Reefer Madness: The History of Marijuana in America* (Indianapolis: Bobbs-Merrill, 1979); *American Drug War: The Last White Hope* (film, dir. Kevin Booth, Sacred Cow Productions, 2007); Johann Hari, *Chasing the Scream: The First and Last Days of the War on Drugs* (New York: Bloomsbury, 2015).

10. McWilliams, *Protectors*, 13; Douglas Clark Kinder and William O. Walker III, "Stable Force in a Storm: Harry J. Anslinger and United States Narcotic Foreign Policy, 1930–1962," *Journal of American History* 72, no. 4 (1986): 908–27; Douglas Clark Kinder, "Bureaucratic Cold Warrior: Harry J. Anslinger and Illicit Narcotics Traffic," *Pacific Historical Review* 50, no. 2 (1981): 169–91; Rebecca Carroll, "Under the Influence: Harry Anslinger's Role in Shaping America's Drug Policy" and "The Narcotic Control Act Triggers the Great Nondebate," in *Federal Drug Control: The Evolution of Policy and Practice,* edited by Jonathan Erlen and Joseph F. Spillane (New York: Pharmaceutical Products Press, 2004), 61–99, 101–44.

11. Harry J. Anslinger and Will Oursler, *The Murderers: The Story of the Narcotics Gangs* (New York: Farrar, Straus, and Cudahy, 1961), 8.

12. Ibid., 9–10.

13. Harry J. Anslinger and J. Dennis Gregory, *The Protectors: The Heroic Story of the Narcotics Agents, Citizens and Officials in Their Unending, Unsung Battles against Organized Crime in America and Abroad* (New York: Farrar and Straus, 1964), 3–9; Anslinger and Oursler, *Murderers*, 10, 13–16; McWilliams, *Protectors*, 28–29.

14. Anslinger and Oursler, *Murderers*, 15–19; "Lt. Anslinger's Diary," March 6 and 7, 1920, folder 1, box 1; and William Phillips to "Carr," Oct. 20, 1920, folder 19, box 3, Anslinger Papers.

15. McWilliams, *Protectors*, 31; Assistant Treasury Secretary Seymour Lowman to Secretary of State, Jan. 19, 1928, folder 19, box 3; Treasury Dept. to Anslinger, Oct. 15, 1929, and memos by Anslinger and J. M. Doran (commissioner of Prohibition), Aug. 14, 1929, folder 11, box 3, Anslinger Papers.

16. "Common Sense Temperance" and "The American Prohibition Policy," folder 5, box 1, Anslinger Papers; Anslinger and Oursler, *Murderers*, 20.

17. McWilliams, *Protectors*, 37–45; Musto, *American Disease*, 206–9; Anslinger and Porter testimony before House Committee on Ways and Means, *Bureau of Narcotics, H.R. 10561*, 71st Cong., 2nd sess., March 7–8, 1930, 29–33, 13–15.

18. Anslinger and Oursler, *Murderers*, 20–22; McWilliams, *Protectors*, 37–45; Musto, *American Disease*, 206–9; "Anslinger Slated for Narcotic Post," *Washington Post*, July 1, 1930; "War on Drug Rings," *Washington Post*, Aug. 30, 1930; "Up from the Ranks," *Washington Post*, Sept. 25, 1930; "Hoover Faces Fight on Appointments," *New York Times*, Nov. 16, 1930; "Predicts Defeat for Brossard," *Baltimore Sun*, Dec. 10, 1930.

19. Jill Jonnes, *Hep-Cats, Narcs, and Pipe Dreams: A History of America's Romance with Illegal Drugs* (New York: Scribner, 1996), 104.

20. Anslinger's recollection is slightly muddled. Blease's complaints began in 1929, and most of the raids took place in April 1930 when the Porter Bill was under debate. See Anslinger and Oursler, *Murderers*, 20–24; Edmond Van Tyne, "Personalities in Law Enforcement," *True Detective*, June 1939; folder 18, box 12, Anslinger Papers; Cong. Rec., Jan. 16, 1930, H1701; "Opium Dens Honeycomb Capital, Blease Charges," *Atlanta Constitution*, Sept. 24, 1929; "Seize Opium Smokers Near Nation's Capital," *New York Times*, April 6, 1930; "Opium Dens Raided Near Capitol and 21 Chinese

Caught," *Chicago Daily Tribune,* April 6, 1930; and Alan MacDonald, "What Is a Tong War?," *Washington Post,* Aug. 31, 1930.

21. Richard Cornwall, "Undermining Washington—\$120,000,000 Worth," *Official Detective Stories,* Nov. 1954, folder 13, box 1, Anslinger Papers.

22. See records associated with the Committee on Drug Addiction and the Committee on Drug Addiction and Narcotics, 1929–1965, NAS Archive. See also Caroline Jean Acker, "Addiction and the Laboratory: The Work of the National Research Council's Committee on Drug Addiction, 1928–1939," *Isis* 86, no. 2 (1995): 167–93; and Everette L. May and Arthur E. Jacobson, "The Committee on Problems of Drug Dependence: A Legacy of the National Academy of Sciences, a Historical Account," *Drug and Alcohol Dependence* 23, no. 3 (1989): 183–218.

23. McWilliams, *Protectors,* 57, 86, 90, 106.

24. William B. McAllister, *Drug Diplomacy in the Twentieth Century: An International History* (London: Routledge, 2000), 65; Anslinger and Gregory, *Protectors,* 17–20. Constance Drexel, "Prominent Capital Woman Is Leading Fight to Eradicate World Drug Evil," *Washington Post,* Dec. 30, 1923. See also Elizabeth Wright to Anslinger, June 25, 1931, folder 9, box 3; and Anslinger to Herbert May, March 17, 1950, folder 15, box 2, Anslinger Papers.

25. McAllister, *Drug Diplomacy,* 90, 107–9; Hobson to Roosevelt, April 8, 1933; Mallinckrodt Chemical Works to Roosevelt, April 4, 1933; and T. W. Russell to Cordell Hull, April 15, 1933, folder 7, box 3, Anslinger Papers.

26. Letters from James Hill Jr. to Treasury Secretary George Humphrey and Howard B. Fonda (Burroughs Wellcome), Dec. 4, 1952; Howard B. Fonda to R. W. Albright (Distillation Products), Dec. 22, 1952; R. R. Reed (Wyeth Laboratories) to Anslinger, Jan. 5, 1953; and H. S. Howard to President Dwight D. Eisenhower, Jan. 2, 1953, folders 13 and 12, box 2, Anslinger Papers.

27. Paul Gootenberg, *Andean Cocaine: The Making of a Global Drug* (Chapel Hill: University of North Carolina Press, 2008), 198–204, 240; Ralph Hayes to R. W. Woodruff (president, Coca-Cola), Dec. 4, 1952, folder 13, box 2, Anslinger Papers.

28. Anslinger often pleaded for additional resources but was careful not to take more than he needed. See Anslinger to Representative Gordon Canfield (R-NJ), Sept. 20, 1954. Budget figures are difficult to find in FBN records. An August 14, 1953, letter from FBN official George Cunningham to George D. Riley (American Federation of Labor) cited the following annual budget and personnel numbers: 1949, \$1,542,270, 185 agents; 1950, \$1,647,000, 177 agents; 1951, \$1,850,000, 188 agents; 1952, \$2,500,000, 218 agents; 1953, \$2,790,000, 275 agents. Folder "(280-1) Bureau Operations, 1931–1954," box 48. There are numerous references to keeping expenses down. Two memos issued in 1949 (Jan. 26 and June 29) encouraged field offices to "practice every possible economy" and admonished, "Not one cent more than is absolutely necessary for the development of a good case should be expended." Folder "(0370-3) Memorandum for All District Supervisors, 1936–1954," box 56, RG 170, NARA.

29. Richard Lawrence Miller, *Drug Warriors and Their Prey: From Police Power to Police State* (Westport, CT: Praeger, 1996); Radley Balko, *Rise of the Warrior Cop: The Militarization of America's Police Forces* (New York: Public Affairs, 2013).

30. Judiciary Act of 1789, secs. 9 and 30, National Archives, www.ourdocuments.gov. For FBN lobbying, see Acting Treasury Secretary T. J. Coolidge to Vice President, June 1, 1934, and H.R. 5611, introduced May 11, 1933, folder "Narcotic Bureau, 1933–1940," box 191, entry 193 (Central Files of the Office of the Secretary of the Trea-

sury), RG 56 (General Records of the Department of the Treasury), NARA. The bill was passed on August 9, 1939, as H.R. 6556, 76th Cong., Stat. 53, Chap. 618.

31. Oursler and Smith, *Narcotics: America's Peril,* 136; Kelly and Mathison, *On the Street,* 102. A chart listing FBN auto seizures between 1954 and 1963 indicates that the Bureau confiscated between three and five hundred cars each year and provides an estimate of their value. Folder "(0280-1) Bureau Operations, 1955–1969," box 48. See also agency-wide memos by Anslinger, Jan. 9, 1950, folder "(0370-3) Memorandum for All District Supervisors, 1936–1954," and Oct. 10, 1956, folder "(0370-3) Bureau Orders, 1956–1967," box 56, RG 170, NARA.

32. McAllister, *Drug Diplomacy,* 98; McWilliams, *Protectors,* 88–89.

33. Thomas A. Reppetto, *The Blue Parade* (New York: Free Press, 1978), 287; McWilliams, *Protectors,* 89–89; Memorandum in Respect to H.R. 10586, Feb. 1, 1936, folder 4, box 3, Anslinger Papers; generally, folders "(280-1) Bureau Operations, 1931–1954" and "(0280-1) Bureau Operations, 1955–1969," box 48, RG 170, NARA.

34. Alexander Cockburn and Jeffrey St. Clair, *Whiteout: The CIA, Drugs and the Press* (London: Verso, 1998), 72; Rudolph J. Gerber, *Legalizing Marijuana: Drug Policy Reform and Prohibition Politics* (Westport, CT: Praeger, 2004); Miller, *Drug Warriors;* Sloman, *Reefer Madness.* See also Peter Guither, "Why Is Marijuana Illegal?," www.drugwarrant.com; Cheri Sicard, "The Unholy Trinity: Anslinger, Hearst, and Rockefeller," www.seniorstoner.com; "How Did 'Reefer Madness' Get Started?," www.washington-drug-defense.com.

35. Douglas Valentine, *The Strength of the Wolf: The Secret History of America's War on Drugs* (London: Verso, 2004), 21; Carroll, "Under the Influence," 70–76.

36. Anslinger to Assistant Secretary Gibbons, Feb. 3, 1936, folder 4, box 3, Anslinger Papers. Marijuana arrests jumped dramatically between 1937 and 1938, but overall arrests in 1938 and 1939 experienced only a modest increase over previous years. See Treasury Dept. press release no. 16-6, Jan. 23, 1939, and arrest figures provided by Anslinger to Treasury officials, July 10, 1939, folder "(1690-12) Publicity, Press Release, 1938 thru 1942," box 74, RG 170, NARA.

37. David F. Musto, MD, "The History of the Marihuana Tax Act of 1937," *Archives of General Psychiatry* 26 (Feb. 1972); Morgan, *Drugs in America,* 141.

38. McWilliams, *Protectors,* 54–57, 63–80; Kinder and Walker, "Stable Force in a Storm," 909; Valentine, *Strength of the Wolf,* 21; Carroll, "Under the Influence," 61.

39. Musto, "History of the Marihuana Tax Act."

40. Anslinger and Gregory, *Protectors,* 140; "Plan to Merge Federal Police Units Dropped," *Washington Post,* April 28, 1939; Aaron L. Friedberg, *In the Shadow of the Garrison State: America's Anti-statism and Its Cold War Grand Strategy* (Princeton, NJ: Princeton University Press, 2000).

41. See folders "(280-1) Bureau Operations, 1931–1954" and "(0280-1) Bureau Operations, 1955–1969," box 48, RG 170, NARA.

42. Anslinger and Gregory, *Protectors,* 71, 199.

43. Musto, *American Disease,* 121–82; Morgan, *Drugs in America,* 108–17; Jim Baumohl, "Maintaining Orthodoxy: The Depression-Era Struggle over Morphine Maintenance in California," in *Altering American Consciousness: The History of Alcohol and Drug Use in the United States,* edited by Sarah Tracy and Caroline Jean Acker (Amherst: University of Massachusetts Press, 2004), 225–66.

44. "The *Doremus* and *Webb* Decisions," in *Drugs in America: A Documentary History,* edited by David F. Musto (New York: New York University Press, 2002), 256–61;

Musto, *American Disease,* 121–82; Morgan, *Drugs in America,* 108–17; Baumohl, "Maintaining Orthodoxy."

45. Musto, *American Disease,* 204–6; Nancy D. Campbell, J. P. Olsen, and Luke Walden, *The Narcotic Farm: The Rise and Fall of America's First Prison for Drug Addicts* (New York: Abrams, 2008). For an account of the Spadra hospital in California, see Baumohl, "Maintaining Orthodoxy."

46. Campbell, Olsen, and Walden, *Narcotic Farm;* Nancy D. Campbell, "'A New Deal for the Drug Addict': The Addiction Research Center, Lexington, Kentucky," *Journal of the History of the Behavioral Sciences* 42, no. 2 (2006): 137–57; William S. Burroughs, *Junky: 50th Anniversary Definitive Edition* (New York: Penguin Books, 2003), 50–57; Nat Hentoff, *A Doctor among the Addicts* (Chicago: Rand McNally, 1968).

47. Anslinger and Gregory, *Protectors,* 141.

48. Anslinger and Tompkins, *The Traffic in Narcotics,* 185–212, 171, 231; Anslinger, "The Treatment of Drug Addiction," *Union Signal,* June 25, 1960, folder 20, box 12, Anslinger Papers.

49. Harry J. Anslinger, Broadcast over Radio Station KIRO, Seattle, July 31, 1939, folder 10, box 1, Anslinger Papers; Anslinger and Tompkins, *The Traffic in Narcotics,* 189–90; Harney quoted in Anslinger, "Treatment of Drug Addiction."

50. Herbert Raskin, "A Suggested Approach to the Problem of Drug Addiction," Appendix B, Minutes of the Committee on Drug Addiction and Narcotics (hereafter CDAN), April 8, 1960, "Com on Drug Addiction & Narcotics, Meetings: 22nd: Special: Minutes, 1960 Apr," NAS Archive.

51. Anslinger, "Treatment of Drug Addiction"; Anslinger and Tompkins, *The Traffic in Narcotics,* 186; Arnold Sagalyn, transcript of interview with Anslinger, July 9, 1971, folder "Drugs and Drug Abuse—Control of Narcotic Traffic [Research for Objective Paper], 1 of 2," box 1, Arnold Sagalyn Papers, American University, Washington, DC (hereafter Sagalyn Papers).

52. Anslinger and Tompkins, *The Traffic in Narcotics,* 191; Anslinger, "Treatment of Drug Addiction"; J. A. Buckwalter, *Merchants of Misery* (Mountain View, CA: Pacific Press, 1961), 53.

53. Anslinger to Charles Sharman (chief, Narcotics Division, Canadian Dept. of Pensions and National Health), March 28, 1940, folder 21, box 2, Anslinger Papers. See also McAllister, *Drug Diplomacy,* 94. The two men often colluded in diplomatic negotiations, and McAllister calls Sharman "Anslinger's soulmate."

54. Rufus King, *Drug Hang-up,* 39; Baumohl, "Maintaining Orthodoxy."

55. King, *Drug Hang-up,* 47–58. See also "Aspirant for Zioncheck's Seat Is Sent to Prison," *Chicago Daily Tribune,* Aug. 29, 1936; "Court Sentences Seattle Physician," *Los Angeles Times,* Aug. 29, 1936.

56. Kelly and Mathison, *On the Street,* 97.

57. Harry D. Smith to Anslinger, Nov. 13, 1930; C. R. Frazier (district supervisor, Jacksonville) to Mr. Chas. H. Nensihel and All Narcotic Officers, Nov. 3, 1930, folder "(0970) Investigations, General File (1930–1967), No. 2," box 168, RG 170, NARA.

58. Anslinger and Tompkins, *The Traffic in Narcotics,* 165. For World War II–era registrant investigations, see Joseph Bell to H. B. Westover, Nov. 4, 1944, and Harold E. Whitely to W. P. Blackwell, July 30, 1945, folder "Investigations, General File (1930–1967)," box 168, RG 170, NARA.

59. Smith to Anslinger, Aug. 9, 1940, and Anslinger to Smith, Sept. 2, 1940, folder

"(0970) Investigations, General File (1930–1967), No. 1," box 168, RG 170, NARA; Ernest Gentry to Elizabeth Bass (district supervisor, Denver), Dec. 9, 1941, folder 21, box 2, Anslinger Papers; Anslinger and Gregory, *Protectors*, 149, 83–85, 141–45.

60. Anslinger to White, Aug. 16, 1946, and White to Anslinger, Aug. 8, 1946, folder "Investigations, General File (1930–1967)," box 168, RG 170, NARA.

61. Anslinger testimony, Subcommittee on Improvement in the Federal Criminal Code, Senate Judiciary Committee, *Illicit Narcotics Traffic*, 84th Cong., 1st sess., June 2, 3, and 9, 1955: 38; George H. Gaffney to All District Supervisors, April 16, 1965, folder "(0970) Investigations, General File (1930–1967), No. 1," box 168, RG 170, NARA. See also King, *Drug Hang-up*, 43.

62. Kelly and Mathison, *On the Street*, 93–97.

63. Musto, *American Disease*, 237–39; Courtwright, Joseph, and Des Jarlais, *Addicts Who Survived*, chap. 14.

64. Kelly and Mathison, *On the Street*, 96–97.

65. McWilliams, *Protectors*, 92–95; King, *Drug Hang-up*, 63–68.

66. Folder "(1690-10) Williams, Dr. Henry Smith, MD," box 74, RG 170, NARA; King, *Drug Hang-up*, 61; Baumohl, "Maintaining Orthodoxy."

67. The La Guardia Report is available at www.drugtext.org. Anslinger's criticism may have brought the report more attention that it otherwise would have received. An evenhanded *Washington Post* editorial remarked, "We have not yet been able to obtain a copy of the report, although Mr. Anslinger insists that it is available in almost every public library." "More about Marijuana," *Washington Post*, June 24, 1951; F. H. La Guardia to Henry L. Stimson, March 18, 1931, folder 9, box 3, Anslinger Papers; King, *Drug Hang-up*, 78–85; McWilliams, *Protectors*, 102–6.

68. Caroline Jean Acker, *Creating the American Junkie: Addiction Research in the Classic Era of Narcotic Control* (Baltimore: Johns Hopkins University Press, 2002), 201–4; DeGrandpre, *Cult of Pharmacology*, 118–37.

69. John F. Galliher, David P. Keys, and Michael Elsner, "Lindesmith v. Anslinger: An Early Government Victory in the Failed War on Drugs," *Journal of Criminal Law and Criminology* 88, no. 2 (1998): 661–82. See also Acker, *Creating the American Junkie*, 204; Kinder, "Bureaucratic Cold Warrior," 175–77; King, *Drug Hang-up*, 62–63; Alfred R. Lindesmith, "'Dope Fiend' Mythology," *Journal of Criminal Law and Criminology* 31, no. 2 (1940): 199–208; Twain Michelsen, "Lindesmith's Mythology," *Journal of Criminal Law and Criminology* 31, no. 4 (1940): 375–400; and Alfred R. Lindesmith, "Handling the Opiate Problem," *Federal Probation* 12, no. 2 (1948): 23–25.

70. Acker, *Creating the American Junkie*, 202; Acker, "Addiction and the Laboratory"; Galliher, Keys, and Elsner, "Lindesmith v. Anslinger," 669. See also records associated with the Committee on Drug Addiction and the Committee on Drug Addiction and Narcotics, 1929–1965, Central File, NAS Archive.

71. Folder "Chase, Elywn F., Jr., State Dept. Special Folder," box 11, entry 10 "Classified Subject Files," RG 170, NARA.

72. John Markert, *Hooked in Film: Substance Abuse on the Big Screen* (Lanham, MD: Scarecrow Press, 2013), 24–26.

73. "Report on Drug Addiction," *Bulletin of the New York Academy of Medicine* 31, no. 8 (1955): 592–607; Jennifer M. Cameron and Ronna J. Dinnger, "Narcotic Control Act," in *Encyclopedia of Drug Policy*, edited by Mark A. R. Kleiman and James E. Hawdon (Thousand Oaks, CA: Sage, 2011), 543–45. See also CDAN Minutes, Jan.

21–22, 1955, "Com on Drug Addiction & Narcotics, Meetings: 15th: Minutes, 1955 Jan," and Jan. 20–21, 1956, "Com on Drug Addiction & Narcotics, Meetings: 17th: Minutes, 1956 Jan," NAS Archive.

74. King, *Drug Hang-up*, 120, 161–75; Galliher, Keys, and Elsner, "Lindesmith v. Anslinger"; Carroll, "Narcotic Control Act." See also CDAN Minutes, Jan. 1955 and 1956, "Com on Drug Addiction & Narcotics, Meetings: 15th: Minutes, 1955 Jan" and "Com on Drug Addiction & Narcotics, Meetings: 17th: Minutes, 1956 Jan," NAS Archive.

75. CDAN Minutes, March 29–30, 1958, "Com on Drug Addiction & Narcotics, Meeting: 19th: Minutes, 1958 Mar," Jan. 11–12, 1960, "Com on Drug Addiction & Narcotics, Meetings: 21st: Minutes, 1960 Jan." For Anslinger resignation, see "Com on Drug Addiction & Narcotics, Relationships: Bureau of Narcotics; 1959," NAS Archive.

76. King, *Drug Hang-up*, 161–75; Galliher, Keys, and Elsner, "Lindesmith v. Anslinger"; Carroll, "Narcotic Control Act."

77. Anslinger to Charles Vaille (chief, French Central Pharmacy Service), April 8, 1959, folder "(0660) France #4, 1954–June 1961," box 156, RG 170, NARA.

78. Quoted in King, *Drug Hang-up*, 176–85; Lindesmith, "'Dope Fiend' Mythology." See also Robert B. Livingston, ed., *Narcotic Drug Addiction Problems*, Public Health Service Pub. 105 (Washington, DC: Government Printing Office, 1963).

79. King, *Drug Hang-up*, 176–85; Livingston, *Narcotic Drug Addiction Problems*.

80. King, *Drug Hang-up*, 176–85; Livingston, *Narcotic Drug Addiction Problems*.

81. King, *Drug Hang-up*, 184–85.

82. CDAN Minutes, March 29–30, 1958, "Com on Drug Addiction & Narcotics, Meeting: 19th: Minutes, 1958 Mar," and Isbell to Nathan B. Eddy, July 20, 1961, "Natl Institute of Mental Health, USPHS Hospital: Lexington: Isbell H, 1961–1962," NAS Archive.

83. Morton Mintz, "Anslinger Resigns as Narcotics Chief," *Washington Post*, July 6, 1962; "Anslinger, Narcotics Chief, Resigns; Giordano Succession," *Baltimore Sun*, July 6, 1962; Richard Nixon to Anslinger, Jan. 12, 1970, folder 1, box 2, Anslinger Papers.

CHAPTER 3

1. Harry J. Anslinger and J. Dennis Gregory, *The Protectors: The Heroic Story of the Narcotics Agents, Citizens and Officials in Their Unending, Unsung Battles against Organized Crime in America and Abroad* (New York: Farrar and Straus, 1964), 13–15.

2. Williams to Anslinger, June 23, 1952, folder 12, box 2, Anslinger Papers.

3. Tom Tripodi and Joseph P. DeSario, *Crusade: Undercover against the Mafia and KGB* (Washington, DC: Brassey's, 1993), 174.

4. Douglas Valentine, *The Strength of the Wolf: The Secret History of America's War on Drugs* (London: Verso, 2004), 28–29; Eric C. Schneider, *Smack: Heroin and the American City* (Philadelphia: University of Pennsylvania Press, 2008), 1.

5. "Narcotic Shake-up Hits 11 Agents Here," *New York Times*, Nov. 18, 1936; Valentine, *Strength of the Wolf*, 28; Jill Jonnes, *Hep-Cats, Narcs, and Pipe Dreams: A History of America's Romance with Illegal Drugs* (New York: Scribner, 1996), 105.

6. United States Civil Service Commission, Personnel Form, "Garland Williams," folder "Williams, Garland," box 8, Valentine Collection. See also Anslinger and Gregory, *Protectors*, 13–15.

7. "Customs Men Join Narcotics Fight," *New York Times*, Sept. 1, 1936; "Narcotic Shake-up Hits 11 Agents Here"; Jonnes, *Hep-Cats, Narcs, and Pipe Dreams*, 106; folder "(0280), Bureau of Narcotics; Transfer of Personnel from Bureau of Prohibition," box 48, RG 170, NARA.

8. Jack Kelly and Richard Mathison, *On the Street* (Chicago: Henry Regnery, 1974), 25; Chappell to Valentine, Nov. 30, 1994, folder "Chappell, Howard," box 2, Valentine Collection.

9. Harry J. Anslinger and Will Oursler, *The Murderers: The Story of the Narcotics Gangs* (New York: Farrar, Straus, and Cudahy, 1961), 88; Anslinger and Gregory, *Protectors*, 20–21, 47.

10. Anslinger, "Material for Radio Program, Maryland Pharmaceutical Association," Feb. 28, 1942, folder "(1690-8) Publicity, Radio, 1941–1948," box 69, RG 170, NARA.

11. Anslinger, Circular Letter no. 13, Aug. 2, 1930, folder "(0370-3) Circular Letters, 1–100," box 55, RG 170, NARA.

12. James H. Mulgannon, *Uncertain Glory* (New York: Vantage Press, 1972), 52; Harry D. Smith (district supervisor, Minneapolis), undated report (ca. late 1930s or early '40s), "Narcotics," folder 9, box 10, Anslinger Papers.

13. Anslinger and Bass quoted in "U.S. Launched Nation-Wide War on Dope Traffic," *Chicago Daily Tribune*, Dec. 9, 1934, and "Drive to End Drug Traffic in Midwest Is Led by Woman," *Washington Post*, Dec. 8, 1934. See also "Full Penalty Her Formula," *Los Angeles Times*, Jan. 7, 1934; David Simon and Edward Burns, *The Corner: A Year in the Life of an Inner-City Neighborhood* (New York: Broadway Books, 1997).

14. "74 Indictments Hit at Dope Ring; New Raids Staged," *Atlanta Constitution*, Oct. 6, 1937; "74 Are Indicted in U.S. War on Huge Dope Ring," *Washington Post*, Oct. 6, 1937. For Gentile, see U.S. Treasury Department, *Mafia: The Government's Secret File on Organized Crime* (New York: Skyhorse, 2009), 794; and numerous reports in folder "(0660) Italy #4, 1951," box 159, RG 170, NARA.

15. "Raids in Big Cities Net Narcotic Ring," *New York Times*, Nov. 20, 1937; "Great Tong Linked to Opium Racket," *New York Times*, Nov. 21, 1937.

16. "Press Service No. 14-3," July 18, 1938, folder "(1690-12) Publicity, Press Release, 1938 thru 1942," box 74, entry 9, RG 170, NARA; Richard Hirsch, "How Treasury Agents Broke the 'Poison Sleep' Gang," *True Detective*, May 1939, and James Phelan, "When the Rookie Took the Tong," *True: The Men's Magazine*, Dec. 1959, folders 17 and 18, box 12, Anslinger Papers; Will Oursler and Laurence Dwight Smith, *Narcotics: America's Peril* (Garden City, NY: Doubleday, 1952), 81–89.

17. Tripodi and DeSario, *Crusade*, 31, 35; "Great Tong Linked to Opium Racket," *New York Times*, Nov. 21, 1937.

18. Anslinger to Assistant Treasury Secretary Stephen B. Gibbons, Dec. 3, 1937, folder 3 box 4, Anslinger Papers; Treasury Dept. Press Service no. 14-3, July 18, 1938, folder "(1690-12) Publicity, Press Release, 1938 thru 1942," box 74, RG 170, NARA. See also "Three Customs Men Held in Lepke Narcotics Plot," *New York Times*, Dec. 1, 1937; "Leader of Narcotics Ring Is Sentenced to Ten Years in Prison and Fined $10,000," *New York Times*, Dec. 1, 1938; "Tells How Lepke 'Cut in' on Ring," *New York Times*, Dec. 8, 1939; Oursler and Smith, *Narcotics: America's Peril*, 141–43; Andrew Tully, *Treasury Agent: The Inside Story* (New York: Simon and Schuster, 1958), 51–59; Anslinger and Oursler, *Murderers*, 43–55; Anslinger and Gregory, *Protectors*, 63–67; Malachi L. Harney and John C. Cross, *The Informer in Law Enforcement* (Springfield, IL: Charles C. Thomas, 1968), 52, 66–67; Robert A. Rockaway, *But He Was*

Good to His Mother: The Lives and Crimes of Jewish Gangsters (Jerusalem: Gefen, 2000), 24–29.

19. Associated Press, "Kansas City Drive Breaks Dope Ring," *Baltimore Sun,* April 13, 1939.

20. "3 Brothers Named in Narcotics Case," *New York Times,* Jan. 27, 1940; "3 'Newman Brothers' Sentenced to Prison," *New York Times,* April 27, 1940; Oursler and Smith, *Narcotics: America's Peril,* 120–21; Anslinger and Oursler, *Murderers,* 62–63; Anslinger to James L. Houghton (commissioner, INS), Oct. 31, 1938, folder "(0915) Immigration, 1934–1967," box 165, RG 170, NARA.

21. Anslinger, May 22, 1946, folder "(0915), Immigration, 1934–1967," box 165, RG 170, NARA; Anslinger, Aug. 16, 1951, folder 9, box 10, Anslinger Papers; Kelly and Mathison, *On the Street,* 143; Tripodi and DeSario, *Crusade,* 21.

22. Williams to Anslinger, June 23, 1952, folder 13, box 2, Anslinger Papers.

23. "Dope Peddled by Youngsters," *Los Angeles Times,* Jan. 13, 1939.

24. Ibid.; "Harlem Children Peddle Narcotics," *Baltimore Sun,* Jan. 13, 1939.

25. David Courtwright, Herman Joseph, and Don Des Jarlais, eds., *Addicts Who Survived: An Oral History of Narcotic Use in America, 1923–1965* (Knoxville: University of Tennessee Press, 1989). See "John" (132–35), "Arthur" (105–8), "West Indian Tom" (237–39), "Stick" (52–58), and "Teddy" (48–52, 249–54).

26. "Agents' Ruse Bared in Chinatown Raids," *New York Times,* March 20, 1937; Anslinger and Oursler, *Murderers,* 128.

27. "Harlem Children Peddle Narcotics," *Baltimore Sun,* Jan. 13, 1939.

28. One April 16, 1965, agency-wide memo by Deputy Commissioner George Gaffney noted the FBN had "lost more colored employees in the past year than we have been able to hire" and instructed supervisors to recruit at local schools with "a high percentage of colored students." Folder "(0370-3) Memorandum for All District Supervisors, 1955–1965," box 56. See also B. T. Mitchell to Anslinger, June 24, 1958; G. W. Cunningham to Anslinger, Sept. 30, 1933; and a series of letters between Chicago district supervisor Elizabeth Bass, G. W. Cunningham, and Anslinger re: the assignment of Agent Jaushawau Taylor in folder "(1515-9), 1932–1967," box 66, RG 170, NARA; Kelly and Mathison, *On the Street,* 243; and Donald W. Tucker, *The Two-Edged Sword* (Indianapolis: Dog Ear, 2010).

29. Anslinger and Oursler, *Murderers,* 132; "Another Problem for the Big Cities," *U.S. News and World Report,* April 6, 1959, folder 9, box 7, and "New York Forum," April 28, 1962, folder 10, box 1, Anslinger Papers.

30. "'Wildest Street' Raided for Dope," *Atlanta Constitution,* Feb. 2, 1939; Courtwright, Joseph, and Des Jarlais, *Addicts Who Survived,* 192.

31. "'Wildest Street' Raided for Dope," *Atlanta Constitution,* Feb. 2, 1939; "Narcotic Raiders Bare 'Catacombs,'" *New York Times,* Feb. 2, 1939; "30 Persons Seized in Narcotic Raids," *New York Times,* Feb. 6, 1939. See also Schneider, *Smack,* 75–97.

32. Anslinger and Gregory, *Protectors,* 76; Gary Shapiro, "Amsterdam Houses Celebrate 60 Years," *New York Sun,* July 30, 2007.

33. Simon and Burns, *Corner,* 168; Harry J. Anslinger and William F. Tompkins, *The Traffic in Narcotics* (New York: Funk and Wagnalls, 1953), 141.

34. Kelly and Mathison, *On the Street,* 13–14, 58; Mulgannon, *Uncertain Glory,* 137; Tripodi and DeSario, *Crusade,* 51; "Morgenthau Favors Tapping of Wires in Treasury Agents' War on Narcotics," *New York Times,* Oct. 16, 1934. See also *Olmstead v. United States* (1928) and *Katz v. United States* (1967).

35. Siragusa to Anslinger and All District Supervisors, Nov. 2, 1951, folder "General Correspondence District #17, 1951 thru 1955," box 165; and Siragusa, April 16, 1951, folder "(0660) Italy #4, 1951," box 159, RG 170, NARA.

36. Freedom of Information Act (FOIA) request pending for files on technical aids (boxes 147 and 149). See undated (ca. 1965) FBN briefing paper for Treasury Secretary Henry Fowler, folder "(280-17) Orientation Materials for Top Executives," box 49, RG 170, NARA. See also Jeremy Kuzmarov, *Modernizing Repression: Police Training and Nation-Building in the American Century* (Amherst: University of Massachusetts Press, 2012).

37. Most FBN accounts credit the introduction of drug dogs to Agent Earl Teets. See White to Anslinger, Jan. 9, 1970, folder 4, box 1, White Papers; Charles Siragusa and Robert Wiedrich, *The Trail of the Poppy: Behind the Mask of the Mafia* (Englewood Cliffs, NJ: Prentice Hall, 1966), 49–52; and Anslinger and Oursler, *Murderers,* 146–52.

38. Frank Morn, *"The Eye That Never Sleeps": A History of the Pinkerton National Detective Agency* (Bloomington: Indiana University Press, 1982); Tim Weiner, *Enemies: A History of the FBI* (New York: Random House, 2012).

39. Anslinger and Gregory, *Protectors,* vii–viii.

40. James Q. Wilson, *The Investigators: Managing FBI and Narcotics Agents* (New York: Basic Books, 1978), 22, 42.

41. Wilson, *Investigators,* 38; Anslinger and Gregory, *Protectors,* viii; Tom Wolfe, *The Right Stuff* (New York: Farrar, Straus, and Giroux, 1979).

42. Wilson, *Investigators,* 48; Sal Vizzini, Oscar Fraley, and Marshall Smith, *Vizzini: The Secret Lives of America's Most Successful Undercover Agent* (New York: Pinnacle Books, 1972), 15; Tripodi and DeSario, *Crusade,* 25.

43. Kelly and Mathison, *On the Street,* 21, 81; Mulgannon, *Uncertain Glory,* 177; Tripodi and DeSario, *Crusade,* 32.

44. Tripodi and DeSario, *Crusade,* 37–38; Treasury Dept. Press Service no. 18-44, Aug. 11, 1939, folder "(1690-12) Publicity, Press Release, 1938 thru 1942," box 74; folders "(0550-19) Invasion of Privacy," 1961–1967 (FOIA request pending), box 149, entry 9, and "(0515-13), Officers, Complaints Against," entry 10 (Classified Subject Files), box 11, RG 170, NARA.

45. U.S. Bureau of Narcotics, Field Manual (July 1, 1967), "Informants, Section 22," folder "(1325) Field Manual (1967)," box 66, RG 170, NARA; Tripodi and DeSario, *Crusade,* 158–59; Mulgannon, *Uncertain Glory,* 144; Kelly and Mathison, *On the Street,* 40.

46. U.S. Bureau of Narcotics, Field Manual (July 1, 1967), "Informants, Section 22"; Vizzini, Fraley, and Smith, *Vizzini,* 17–26; Mulgannon, *Uncertain Glory,* 117.

47. Vizzini, Fraley, and Smith, *Vizzini,* 17–25; Mulgannon, *Uncertain Glory,* 15–16; Anslinger and Oursler, *Murderers,* 135.

48. Siragusa and Wiedrich, *Trail of the Poppy,* 7; Vizzini, Fraley, and Smith, *Vizzini,* 10.

49. Anslinger to Assistant Treasury Secretary A. Gilmore Flues, March 16, 1959, folder "(0395) Customs #2, 1955 through December 1962," box 59, RG 170, NARA; Wilson, *Investigators,* 58.

50. Giordano to David C. Acheson (special assistant for enforcement), Oct. 15, 1965, folder "(1515-3) Officers, Complaints, October 1934 thru December 1967," box 66, RG 170, NARA.

51. Anslinger and Oursler, *Murderers,* 141; Ryan quoted in Oursler and Smith, *Narcotics: America's Peril,* 140; Harney and Cross, *Informer in Law Enforcement,* 4–5, 11, 105.

52. Anslinger, Bureau Order no. 98, June 9, 1950, folder "(0370-3) Bureau Orders, 1938–1955," and Giordano, Bureau Order no. 196, Nov. 16, 1962, folder "(0370-3) Bureau Orders, 1956–1967," box 56, RG 170, NARA. Despite the name change, Agent Vizzini deadpanned, "S.E. means special employee. Also other things, such as button man and stool pigeon, which you don't call him in an official report." Vizzini, Fraley, and Smith, *Vizzini*, 30.

53. Anslinger to supervisors, Aug. 22, 1956, folder "(0370-3) Memorandum for All District Supervisors, 1955–1965," box 56. See also undated (ca. 1965–68) briefing paper for Treasury Secretary Henry Fowler, folder "(280-17) Orientation Materials for Top Executives," box 49, RG 170, NARA; Anslinger, "Narcotics Bureau Conducts Training School for Police," *FBI Law Enforcement Bulletin* 31, no. 10 (1962), and training curriculum in folders 2 and 4, box 7, Anslinger Papers.

54. "War Is Calamity for Dope Addicts," *Baltimore Sun*, Sept. 27, 1939.

55. "M'Quillan Receives Enforcement Post," *New York Times*, Sept. 22, 1939; "Assumes New Duties as U.S. Treasury Aide," *New York Times*, Oct. 2, 1940.

56. John C. McWilliams, "Unsung Partner against Crime: Harry J. Anslinger and the Federal Bureau of Narcotics, 1930–1962," *Pennsylvania Magazine of History and Biography* 113, no. 2 (1989): 221–22; McWilliams, *Protectors*, 95–96.

57. Anslinger and Gregory, *Protectors*, 75; Oursler and Smith, *Narcotics: America's Peril*, 132–33; Douglas Clark Kinder and William O. Walker III, "Stable Force in a Storm: Harry J. Anslinger and United States Narcotic Foreign Policy, 1930–1962," *Journal of American History* 72, no. 4 (1986): 919–21; McWilliams, "Unsung Partner against Crime," 221–22; McWilliams, *Protectors*, 95–96.

58. Anslinger, June 6, 1941, folder "(280-11) Bureau Operations, 1931–1954," box 48, RG 170, NARA. Anslinger quoted in McWilliams, "Unsung Partner against Crime," 220–21.

59. Kinder and Walker, "Stable Force in a Storm," 920; Rebecca Carroll, "Under the Influence: Harry Anslinger's Role in Shaping America's Drug Policy," in *Federal Drug Control: The Evolution of Policy and Practice*, edited by Jonathan Erlen and Joseph F. Spillane (New York: Pharmaceutical Products Press, 2004), 77.

60. See the twelve files on "(0550-3) Reports to the Military" in box 13, RG 170, NARA; and Charles Schwarz (director of public relations, Treasury) to Lorene Threepersons, Sept. 6, 1943, box 189, entry 193 (Central Files of the Office of Secretary, 1933–1956), RG 56 (General Records of the Department of the Treasury), NARA.

61. Anslinger and Gregory, *Protectors*, 77; Press Service no. 14-3, July 18, 1938, folder "(1690-12) Publicity, Press Release, 1938 thru 1942," box 74, RG 170, NARA; Anslinger, memo to file, April 9, 1941, re: "Fort Eustis, Norfolk, VA," folder 21, box 2, Anslinger Papers.

62. Anslinger and Gregory, *Protectors*, 76.

63. Stimson quoted in Alfred W. McCoy, *Policing America's Empire: The United States, the Philippines, and the Rise of the Surveillance State* (Madison: University of Wisconsin Press, 2009), 319. See also Weiner, *Enemies*.

64. "Army Sergeants Get Training in M.P. Work," *Washington Post*, March 6, 1941; John Mendelsohn, ed., *Covert Warfare: The History of the Counter Intelligence Corps (CIC)*, vol. 11 (New York: Garland, 1989). For curriculum, see "Corps of Intelligence Police, Investigators Training School," folder 1756, box 161, entry 136, RG 226 (Records of the Office of Strategic Services), NARA.

65. Mendelsohn, *Covert Warfare*, 38, 50.

66. A letter from Donovan to Anslinger, dated Aug. 11, 1920 (folder 19, box 3), thanks him for passing unspecified information while a consular official. See also Morgenthau to Donovan, Dec. 23 1941, folder 21, box 2, Anslinger Papers.

67. John Whiteclay Chambers II, *OSS Training in the National Parks and Service Abroad in World War II* (Washington, DC: National Park Service, 2008), 49–50.

68. David Stafford, *Camp X* (New York: Dodd and Mead, 1986); John C. McWilliams, "Covert Connections: The FBN, the OSS, and the CIA," *Historian* 53, no. 4 (1991): 657–79; Chambers, *OSS Training,* 50–52. The "shot up the camp" rumor comes secondhand from Carl Eifler via Howard Chappell. See Chappell to Douglas Valentine, Oct. 18, 1994, folder "Chappell, Howard," box 2, Valentine Collection.

69. Chambers, *OSS Training,* 37; Anslinger and Gregory, *Protectors,* 78.

70. Chambers, *OSS Training,* 54–56; J. R. Brown to J. R. Hayden, July 7, 1942, folder 1754, box 161, entry 136, RG 226, NARA.

71. Chambers, *OSS Training,* 41–42, 54–63.

72. Ibid., 58, 41, 402; Garland Williams, "Training," folder 1754, box 161, entry 136, RG 226, NARA; Chappell to Valentine, Oct. 9, 1995, folder "Chappell, Howard," Valentine Collection.

73. Chambers, *OSS Training,* 53, 58, 41, 402; William L. Cassidy, ed., *History of the Schools and Training Branch, Office of Strategic Services* (San Francisco: Kingfisher Press, 1983), 84; Williams, "Training," folder 1754, box 161, entry 136, RG 226, NARA.

74. Major John J. McDonough to Colonel G. Edward Buxton, Nov. 24, 1943, in Cassidy, *History of the Schools and Training Branch,* 119–201.

75. Ibid.; White to McDonough, Jan. 25 and 31, 1944, folder 4, box 1, White Papers.

76. Chambers, *OSS Training,* 33, 63–68; Cassidy, *History of the Schools and Training Branch,* 3.

77. White's "experience" is quoted in Chambers, *OSS Training,* 69; Cassidy, *History of the Schools and Training Branch,* 31 32, "ahead of his time" is quoted (with added emphasis) on 35.

78. William Colby and Peter Forbath, *Honorable Men: My Life in the CIA* (New York: Simon and Schuster, 1978), 33–35; Randall Woods, *Shadow Warrior: William Egan Colby and the CIA* (New York: Basic Books, 2013), 31–36. See also Chappell to Valentine, March 23, 1994, folder "Chappell, Howard," Valentine Collection. Chappell's World War II exploits are recounted in William White, "Some Affairs of Honor," *Reader's Digest,* Dec. 1945, and OSS file, "Chappell, Howard W; INF., 01285896," box 0118, entry 224, RG 226, NARA.

79. Anslinger and Gregory, *Protectors,* 79; Siragusa and Wiedrich, *Trail of the Poppy,* 58–63; Melvin L. Hanks, *Narc: The Adventures of a Federal Agent* (New York: Hastings House, 1973), 191. See also "Siragusa, Charles," box 0715, and "Zurlo, Angelo A.," box 0865, entry 224, RG 226, NARA; and "War Diary; OSS, Berne," folder "Dyar, Charles," box 3, Valentine Collection.

80. John C. Hughes to James R. Murphy, April 29, 1944, folder 4, box 1, White Papers.

81. White to Anslinger, Jan. 6, 1943, folder "George White's Reports," box 164, RG 170, NARA; Anslinger to White, Oct. 15, 1943, folder 5, box 1, White Papers.

82. Stanley P. Lovell, *Of Spies and Stratagems* (New York: Pocket Books, 1964), 60; Anslinger and Gregory, *Protectors,* 80.

83. White to Anslinger, Oct. 10, 1944, folder 5, box 1, White Papers.

84. Anslinger's orders to White and reference to Stimson-Morgenthau communication are in letters dated March 9, 1945, and May 19, 1944, folder 5, box 1, White Papers.

85. White to Anslinger, Oct. 30, 1944, folder 5, box 1, White Papers.

86. White to Anslinger, Oct. 30, 1944, with enclosure to Major McDonough, folder 5, box 1, White Papers.

87. White to Anslinger, Oct. 1, 1945, folder 5, box 1, White Papers.

88. Anslinger to White, Feb. 6, March 3, and April 12, 1945; White to Anslinger, Oct. 1, 1945; A. F. Scharff to the Commissioner of Customs, Oct. 2, 1945; Williams to White, April 27, 1945; and Anslinger to Colonel John Murray, Oct. 26, 1945, folder 5, box 1, White Papers.

89. Anslinger and Gregory, *Protectors,* 78–79, 107; Major General R. C. Partridge to Williams, Aug. 28, 1952, folder "Williams, Garland," box 8, Valentine Collection.

90. Undated letter (ca. March 1951) from Williams to Anslinger, and Williams (on 525th Military Intelligence Service Group letterhead) to Anslinger, Oct. 12, 1951, folder 14, box 2, Anslinger Papers.

91. U.S. Treasury Dept. Press Release, Oct. 27, 1949, folder "Williams, Garland," box 8, Valentine Collection. See also reports from Williams titled "Narcotics Situation in the Near East," Jan. to Feb. 1949, folder 16, box 2, Anslinger Papers.

92. B. T. Mitchell (assistant to the commissioner) to Charles Siragusa, Sept. 22, 1953, folder "(0660-A-1C) General Correspondence District #17, 1951 thru 1955," box 165, RG 170, NARA. The "sword" remark is quoted from an undated letter to George White from "Jno," folder 1, box 4, White Papers. See also Chappell to Valentine, Nov. 30, 1994, folder "Chappell, Howard," box 2, and "Prober Resigns over Own U.S. Tax Returns," *San Diego Evening Tribune,* Nov. 23, 1953, folder "Williams, Garland," box 8, Valentine Collection.

93. Kuzmarov, *Modernizing Repression,* 1–2; Nathaniel Lee Smith, "'Cured of the Habit by Force': The United States and the Global Campaign to Punish Drug Consumers, 1898–1970" (Ph.D. diss., University of North Carolina, 2007); Civil Service and military personnel records in "Williams, Garland," box 8, and Chappell to Valentine, Nov. 30, 1994, folder "Chappell, Howard," Valentine Collection.

CHAPTER 4

1. James Phelan, "The Calculating Colonel and the Turkish Trap," *True: The Man's Magazine,* Jan. 1960, folder 7, box 1, White Papers; Edward Ranzal, "Narcotics Ace, Jailed for Silence, to Name Tipsters on Chief's Order," *New York Times,* Dec. 5, 1952; Harry J. Anslinger and J. Dennis Gregory, *The Protectors: The Heroic Story of the Narcotics Agents, Citizens and Officials in Their Unending, Unsung Battles against Organized Crime in America and Abroad* (New York: Farrar and Straus, 1964), 79.

2. Harry J. Anslinger and Will Oursler, *The Murderers: The Story of the Narcotics Gangs* (New York: Farrar, Straus, and Cudahy, 1961), 125; James H. Mulgannon, *Uncertain Glory* (New York: Vantage Press, 1972); Jack Kelly and Richard Mathison, *On the Street* (Chicago: Henry Regnery, 1974), 123; Charles Siragusa and Robert Wiedrich, *The Trail of the Poppy: Behind the Mask of the Mafia* (Englewood Cliffs, NJ: Prentice Hall, 1966), 47. See also Howard Chappell to Douglas Valentine, Dec. 20, 1995, folder "Chappell, Howard," box 2, Valentine Collection; Lovell to White, Dec. 22, 1952, folder 16, box 3; and inscription on portrait of Garland Williams given to White, box 8, White Papers.

3. Frederic Sondern Jr., *Brotherhood of Evil: The Mafia* (New York: Manor Books, 1959), 124; Derek Agnew, *Undercover Agent—Narcotics* (New York: Macfadden

Books, 1964), 90; Pierre LaFitte and James Phelan, "Tight Trap for a Top Dealer," *True: The Man's Magazine*, June 1957, folder 17, box 12, Anslinger Papers.

4. Jack Boulware, *San Francisco Bizarro: A Guide to Notorious Sights, Lusty Pursuits, and Downright Freakiness in the City by the Bay* (New York: St. Martin's Griffin, 2000), 105; Martin A. Lee and Bruce Shlain, *Acid Dreams: The Complete Social History of LSD: The CIA, the Sixties, and Beyond* (New York: Grove Press, 1994), 34; Douglas Valentine, *The Strength of the Wolf: The Secret History of America's War on Drugs* (London: Verso, 2004), 128–30.

5. The term appears to have entered the American lexicon in the 1960s. See *Online Etymology Dictionary*, s.v. "narc," www.etymonline.com; and *Urban Dictionary*, s.v. "narc," www.urbandictionary.com.

6. "Guide to the George White Papers, 1932–1970," Stanford University Library, Manuscripts Division, Stanford, CA; James Phelan, "When the Rookie Took the Tong," *True: The Man's Magazine*, Dec. 1959, folder 17, box 12, Anslinger Papers; White's unpublished autobiography, "A Diet of Danger," folder 11, box 3; and address at Stanford Law School, Oct. 28, 1970, folder 18, box 3, White Papers.

7. White, "A Diet of Danger."

8. Ibid.; address at Stanford Law School, Oct. 28, 1970.

9. Siragusa and Wiedrich, *Trail of the Poppy*, 46–49.

10. Anslinger and Gregory, *Protectors*, 79.

11. "George H. White, 37, New Anti-narcotic Chief in Chicago," *Chicago Daily Tribune*, Oct. 2, 1945; "Federal Agents Smash 'Dope' Ring," *New York Times*, Oct. 16, 1946; "Marijuana Trial Begins," *New York Times*, Dec. 3, 1946; "5 in Marijuana Ring Are Sentenced Here," *New York Times*, Dec. 5, 1946; "$53,000 Dope Seized, 3 Nabbed as Chicago Officer Trips Ring," *El Paso (TX) Herald-Post*, Oct. 5, 1946, folder 6, box 1, White Papers.

12. White to Paul Newey, July 8, 1970, folder 1, box 4, White Papers.

13. White, "A Diet of Danger," chap. 4; White to Newey, July 8, 1970, folder 1, box 4, White Papers; Newey to Valentine, Jan. 10, 1999, folder "Newey, Paul," box 5, Valentine Collection. See also Robert C. Albright, "Tight Race Puts Lucas in Danger; Majority Leader Could Lose Seat as Result of Crime Probe in Illinois," *Washington Post*, Nov. 4, 1950.

14. White to J. Spaulding Arrington, Jan. 29, 1952, folder 14, box 3, White Papers.

15. White report, Nov. 8, 1946, folder 6, box 1, White Papers.

16. Anslinger and Gregory, *Protectors*, 105–6. Anslinger mixed up some dates here and contended that White was "due for a 'vacation'" after an episode in which he accused a district attorney of associating with the mob. That was still four years off, but Anslinger was correct in remembering that the political heat was on.

17. White, address at Stanford Law School, Oct. 28, 1970.

18. White to Anslinger, May 1, 1948, folder "(0660) George White's Reports," box 164, RG 170, NARA. Under pressure from the FBN and other U.S. officials, the shah banned poppy farming in 1955 and adopted American drug enforcement models and police advisers. Ryan Gingeras, "Poppy Politics: American Agents, Iranian Addicts and Afghan Opium, 1945–80," *Iranian Studies* 45, no. 3 (2012): 315–31; Nathaniel Lee Smith, "'Cured of the Habit by Force': The United States and the Global Campaign to Punish Drug Consumers, 1898–1970" (Ph.D. diss., University of North Carolina, 2007), 216–23.

19. White to Anslinger, May 1, 1948, White reports May 29 and June 10, 1948, folder

"(0660) George White's Reports," box 164, RG 170, NARA; Anslinger to White, June 3, 1948, folder 8, box 1, White Papers. See also Douglas F. Garthoff, *Directors of Central Intelligence as Leaders of the U.S. Intelligence Community, 1946–2005* (Washington, DC: Center for the Study of Intelligence, Central Intelligence Agency, 2005), 9–47.

20. See, generally, "Progress Reports of Charles Siragusa," box 164, and "(0660) Turkey, 1951–1952," box 163, RG 170, NARA.

21. White, June 10, 1948, folder "(0660) George White's Reports," box 164, RG 170, NARA; address at Stanford Law School, Oct. 28, 1970.

22. "Summary Translation" and White, June 10, 1948, folder "(0660) George White's Reports," box 164, RG 170, NARA.

23. White, June 10, 1948, folder "(0660) George White's Reports," box 164, RG 170, NARA.

24. "Summary Translation," folder "(0660) George White's Reports," box 164. See also "United States, Turkey Join to Seize Drug Worth Million," *Baltimore Sun,* June 5, 1948; "U.S. Traps 4 in Istanbul," *New York Times,* June 5, 1948; "U.S. Agent and Turk Police Capture Dope Peddlers in Istanbul," *Chicago Daily Tribune,* June 6, 1948; Frederic Sondern Jr., "Our Global War on Narcotics," *Reader's Digest,* April 1950; Agnew, *Undercover Agent—Narcotics,* 94–96; Phelan, "Calculating Colonel"; and "The Silent Man," folder "(1690-8) Publicity, Radio, 1949 thru June 1951," box 69, RG 170, NARA.

25. Jay Richard Kennedy, "One World—against Dope," *Sunday Star: This Week Magazine,* March 7, 1948, folder 13, box 1, Anslinger Papers; Philip K. Scheuer, "'To Ends of Earth' Exciting Melodrama," *Los Angeles Times,* Jan. 30, 1948; Norbert Lusk, "Powell Opus Wins Praise," *Los Angeles Times,* Feb. 18, 1948; Donald Kirkley, "To the Ends of the Earth," *Baltimore Sun,* March 27, 1948.

26. "Summary Translation," folder "(0660) George White's Reports," box 164; report by U.S. consul C. E. Macy, Istanbul, July 13, 1948, folder "(0660) Turkey #3, 1940–1948," box 25, RG 170, NARA.

27. U.S. consul P. C. Hutton, Oct. 6, 1949, Ankara Embassy, General Records, 1949, 370.31 (box 136), RG 84 (Records of the Foreign Service Posts of the Department of State), NARA. See also Siragusa, Progress Report no. 2, July 25, 1950, folder "Progress Reports of Charles Siragusa," and Martin Pera, Report no. 2, Feb. 19, 1951, folder "(0660-A), Agent Martin F. Pera's Foreign Assignment," box 164, RG 170, NARA.

28. White and Karayel exchanged gifts (including a snub-nosed .38 revolver and ornate ceremonial sword) and correspondence for several years, suggesting some degree of sincerity. White to Karayel, Aug. 25, 1948, and Jan. 6, 1954, folder "(0660) Turkey #3, 1940–1948," box 25, and folder "(0660) Turkey #4, 1953–1955," box 163, RG 170, NARA.

29. Acting Treasury Secretary E. H. Foley to Secretary of State George Marshall, March 20 and April 25, 1950. For the Turkish government, see State Dept. telegram from Ankara Embassy, April 11, 1950, and report by Warwick Perkins (counselor), April 14, 1950, State Dept. Central Decimal File (hereafter CDF) 1950–1954, 882.53 (box 5433), RG 59 (General Records of the Department of State), NARA.

30. White reports, June 26 and July 6 to Aug. 3, 1948, and "The Enzi Syndicate," Aug. 25, 1948, folder "(0660) George White's Reports," box 164, RG 170, NARA.

31. Anslinger to White, June 17, 1948, folder 8, box 1, White Papers; White, June 10, 1948, folder "(0660) George White's Reports," box 164, RG 170, NARA.

32. "Key Witness in Dope Case Murdered," *Los Angeles Times*, March 1, 1950; "Officers Hide Second Witness after Narcotics Case Murder," *Los Angeles Times*, March 2, 1950; Chappell to Valentine, Nov. 30, 1994, folder "Chappell, Howard," box 1, Valentine Collection; White, address at Stanford Law School, Oct. 28, 1970. For Sica brothers, see U.S. Treasury Department, *Mafia: The Government's Secret File on Organized Crime* (New York: Skyhorse, 2009), 58–59.

33. White, address at Stanford Law School, Oct. 28, 1970; Memorandum Report, June 5, 1952, subject: "One Mouse, Dead, Known as 'Mike,'" and Martin Abramson, "The Mystery of the Hopped-Up Mouse," *Real Magazine*, July 1953, folder 3, box 2; and White to Warren Olney III, Nov. 24, 1952, and Dec. 23, 1953, folder 16, box 1, White Papers.

34. White to Arrington, Feb. 11, 1952, folder 14, box 3, White Papers; "Morris Still Unable to Get Inquiry Staff," *New York Times*, March 1, 1952; "Fired to Avert Cabinet Revolt, Morris Charges," *Chicago Daily Tribune*, April 11, 1952.

35. White to Olney, Nov. 24, 1952, folder 16, box 1, White Papers. For Lucchese, see U.S. Treasury Department, *Mafia*, 510; Meyer Berger, "Gangster Is Heard," *New York Times*, Nov. 15, 1952; William Fulton, "N.Y. Crime Quiz Ties High Officials to Racket Leader," *Chicago Daily Tribune*, Nov. 15, 1952; and "Lucchese New Crime Boss, Probers Told," *Washington Post*, Nov. 15, 1952. The key figure was a political fixer named Armand Chanaklian, who seems to have been Lucchese's chief political liaison and, incredibly, was assistant to U.S. Attorney Myles J. Lane, the federal prosecutor assigned to run the grand jury investigation.

36. Ranzal, "Narcotics Ace, Jailed for Silence"; "U.S. Agent Cleared in Contempt Case," *New York Times*, Dec. 9, 1952; Anslinger and Oursler, *Murderers*, 133–34. See also White to Olney, Nov. 24, 1952, folder 16, box 1, White Papers; and Ed Reid, *Mafia* (New York: Signet, 1954), 30–35, 41–44.

37. White to Olney, Nov. 24, 1952, folder 16, box 1, White Papers; Anslinger to George Morlock (State Dept.), Nov. 25, 1952, folder "(0660-A) 1949–1965," box 164, RG 170, NARA.

38. Quoted in John Marks, *The Search for the "Manchurian Candidate": The CIA and Mind Control, the Secret History of the Behavioral Sciences* (New York: W. W. Norton, 1979), 97; and John M. Crewden, "Abuses in Testing of Drugs by C.I.A. to Be Panel Focus," *New York Times*, Sept. 20, 1977.

39. Anslinger to White, Dec. 10, 1953, folder 13, box 3; and White to Olney, April 22, 1954, folder 16, box 1, White Papers; Marks, *Search for the "Manchurian Candidate,"* 95–99; John Jacobs, "The Diaries of a CIA Operative," *Washington Post*, Sept. 5, 1977.

40. Agnew, *Undercover Agent—Narcotics*, 90–94. See subsequent follow-up work in folder "(0660-A-4) Agent Levine, Foreign Tour. Assignment—Ecuador, Peru, Bolivia," box 165, RG 170, NARA.

41. Kelly and Mathison, *On the Street*, 123; Garland Roark, *The Coin of Contraband: The True Story of United States Customs Investigator Al Scharff* (Garden City, NY: Doubleday, 1964), 387–96; Valentine, *Strength of the Wolf*, 144–47; Anslinger and White correspondence, Nov. 30 and Dec. 6, 1954, folder 10, box 2, White Papers.

42. Marks, *Search for the "Manchurian Candidate"*; H. P. Albarelli Jr., *A Terrible Mistake: The Murder of Frank Olson and the CIA's Secret Cold War Experiments* (Waltersville, OR: Trine Day, 2009); Valentine, *Strength of the Wolf*, 141; Joy Rohde, *Armed with Expertise: The Militarization of American Social Research during the Cold War* (Ithaca, NY: Cornell University Press, 2013).

43. Stanley P. Lovell, *Of Spies and Stratagems* (New York: Pocket Books, 1964), 6, 29–66, 94.

44. George White, "Report on T.D.," June 2, 1943, folder 4, box 1, White Papers; Marks, *Search for the "Manchurian Candidate,"* 6–8.

45. Goldberg quoted in Marks, *Search for the "Manchurian Candidate,"* 8, and identified in Albarelli, *Terrible Mistake,* 802.

46. Lovell, *Of Spies and Stratagems,* 87.

47. Quoted in Lee and Shlain, *Acid Dreams,* 21.

48. Susan L. Carruthers, *Cold War Captives: Imprisonment, Escape and Brainwashing* (Berkeley: University of California Press, 2009), 174–216, 17–18.

49. Lee and Shlain, *Acid Dreams,* 1–2; Albert Hoffman, "d-Lysergic Acid Diethylamide," U.S. Patent no. 2,438,259, March 23, 1948.

50. Lee and Shlain, *Acid Dreams,* 90, 85, 71; "End the Ban on Psychoactive Drug Research," *Scientific American,* Feb. 1, 2014; Richard Condon, *The Manchurian Candidate* (New York: McGraw-Hill, 1959).

51. *Human Drug Testing by the CIA, 1977,* Hearings before the Subcommittee on Health and Scientific Research of the Committee on Human Resources, 95th Cong., 1st sess., Sept. 20 and 21, 1977; Jo Thomas, "C.I.A. Says It Found More Secret Papers on Behavior Control," *New York Times,* Sept. 3, 1977; Jack Anderson and Les Whitten, "CIA Love Trap Lured Diplomats," *Washington Post,* Feb. 5, 1975; numerous references in White Papers.

52. White to D. Harvey Powelson, Sept. 30, 1970, folder 18, box 3, White Papers.

53. In *A Terrible Mistake,* H. P. Albarelli Jr. contends that Olson was killed by FBN informants Jean Pierre LaFitte and François Spirito to prevent revelations about the MK-ULTRA program and an August 1951 chemical weapons experiment in Pont-St.-Esprit, France. The brainwashing element of the program is frequently used to explain Lee Harvey Oswald's role as a patsy in the JFK assassination. Leary quoted in Lee and Shlain, *Acid Dreams,* xx.

54. Marks, *Search for the "Manchurian Candidate,"* 101–10; Crewden, "Abuses in Testing of Drugs"; White, "A Diet of Danger."

55. Crewden, "Abuses in Testing of Drugs"; Marks, *Search for the "Manchurian Candidate,"* 110.

56. Quoted in Albarelli, *Terrible Mistake,* 572–73.

57. Ron Suskind, *The One Percent Doctrine: Deep Inside America's Pursuit of Its Enemies since 9/11* (New York: Simon and Schuster, 2007); Dan Froomkin, "Cheney's 'Dark Side' Is Showing," *Washington Post,* Nov. 7, 2005.

58. Marks, *Search for the "Manchurian Candidate,"* 105, 98–99; White, Address at Stanford Law School, Oct. 28, 1970.

59. White to Wolff, April 20, 1955, folder 16, box 3, White Papers; Marks, *Search for the "Manchurian Candidate,"* 35, 135–38. See also Eleazar Lipsky, *The Kiss of Death* (New York: Penguin Books, 1947), and its many film adaptations.

60. White to Gottlieb, Nov. 21, 1971, folder 1, box 4, White Papers.

61. White to Olney, Nov. 24, 1952, folder 16, box 1; and White to Malcolm Wilkey, March 12, 1955, folder 1, box 3, White Papers.

62. Hoover quoted in "White Slavery," *Time,* April 4, 1939; Harry J. Anslinger and Courtney Ryley Cooper, "Marijuana, Assassin of Youth," *American Magazine,* July 1937, and Cooper, "Double Dealers in Dope," *American Magazine,* May 1938, folder 13, and "Author Kills Self over FBI Spy Snub," *Washington Times-Herald,* Sept. 30,

1940, folder 21, box 2, Anslinger Papers; "Fifth Column Expose Failure Blamed for Cooper Suicide," *Washington Evening Star,* Sept. 30, 1940, folder "(1690-10) American Magazine, Courtney Ryley Cooper," box 70, RG 170, NARA.

63. Chappell to Valentine, Feb. 17, 1995, and June 30, 1996, folder "Chappell, Howard," box 2, Valentine Collection; George White's address book, box 7, and correspondence with Arrington, folder 14, box 3, White Papers; Anslinger to Mortimer, March 4, 1952, folder 13, box 2, Anslinger Papers; folder "(1690-10L) Lait & Mortimer," box 72, RG 170, NARA.

64. Matthew R. Pembleton, "The Voice of the Bureau: How Frederic Sondern and the Bureau of Narcotics Crafted a Drug War and Shaped Popular Understanding of Drugs, Addiction, and Organized Crime in the 1950s," *Journal of American Culture* 38, no. 2 (2015): 112–29.

65. Sondern, "Our Global War on Narcotics," *Reader's Digest,* April 1950; Frederic Sondern Jr., "The World War against Narcotics," *Reader's Digest,* Jan. 1956. See also Sondern to Anslinger, May 12, 1952; Anslinger to Representative James T. Patterson (R-CT), April 5, 1950; and Harney to Anslinger, May 1, 1959, folder "(1690-10) Reader's Digest," box 73, RG 170, NARA.

66. Sondern, *Brotherhood of Evil;* Fanny Butcher, "Author's Hope Fulfilled—the Year's Best Sellers," *Chicago Daily Tribune,* Nov. 29, 1959; folder "(1690-10) Reader's Digest," box 73, RG 170, NARA; "Congress Must Act to Stamp Out National Racketeering by Outlawing Terroristic Conspiracies," Cong. Rec., March 3, 1959, 3213–16.

67. Folders "(1690-10-H) Hyer, Richard V.," box 71, and "(1690-10) Merchants of Misery," box 72, RG 170, NARA; J. A. Buckwalter, *Merchants of Misery* (Mountain View, CA: Pacific Press, 1961).

68. Leon Siler (staff, Treasury Information Service) to Ben Pearson (Stempel-Olenick Agency), June 15, 1950; Anslinger to Fred J. Douglas (acting assistant for law enforcement), Oct. 25, 1960, folder "(1690-8A) General #3, Publicity, Television, 1959 thru 1960"; and, generally, "(1690-8A) General #4, Publicity, Television, January 1961 thru February 1963," box 69, RG 170, NARA.

69. Anslinger, Circular Letter no. 434, March 25, 1937, folder "(1690-9) Publicity, Press, 1927 thru 1946," and correspondence between White and Anslinger, Dec. 29, 1949, and Jan. 20, 1950, folder "(1690-9) Publicity, Press, 1947 thru December 1968," box 70; teletype between James C. Ryan and Malachi Harney, Dec. 18, 1951; Ryan to B. T. Mitchell, Feb. 1952; and letters from "Kayo" to "J. C." (Ryan), Feb. 14 and 21, 1952, folder "(1690-10) Saturday Evening Post," box 73, RG 170, NARA. See also Morris (Kayo) Lipsius and John Lardner, "I Put the Finger on Waxey Gordon," *Saturday Evening Post,* Feb. 23, 1952.

70. Joseph From, "Unmasking America's Monarchs of Dope," *Daring Detective,* Oct. 1938; and, generally, folder "(1690-10) From, Joseph; New York City," box 71, RG 170, NARA.

71. Williams to Anslinger, May 2, 1938, folder "(1690-9), Publicity, Press, 1927 thru 1946," box 70, RG 170, NARA.

72. Cunningham to White, July 18, 1949, folder "(1690-9), Publicity, Press, 1947 thru December 1968," box 70, RG 170, NARA.

73. "U.S. Agents Trap 36 Tong Leaders on Dope Charges," *Chicago Daily Tribune,* March 5, 1938; From, "Unmasking America's Monarchs of Dope." See also Richard Hirsch, "How Treasury Agents Broke the 'Poison Sleep' Gang," *True Detective,* May 1939, folder 18, and Pierre LaFitte and James Phelan, "'Horse' of Another Color,"

True: The Man's Magazine, March 1957, folder 17, box 12, Anslinger Papers; LaFitte and Phelan, "Tight Trap for a Top Dealer"; Phelan, "When the Rookie Took the Tong"; Phelan, "Calculating Colonel"; Anslinger and Oursler, *Murderers*, 125–31; Anslinger and Gregory, *Protectors*, 79.

74. White report, June 10, 1948, folder "(0660) George White's Reports," box 164; and "The Silent Man," folder "(1690-8) Publicity, Radio, 1949 thru June 1951, #4," box 69, RG 170, NARA.

75. Phelan, "Calculating Colonel"; Agnew, *Undercover Agent—Narcotics*, 94–96; Sondern, *Brotherhood of Evil*, 124–26.

76. Boyden Sparkes, "The Cruelest Business in the World: Narcotic Drug Smuggling, and the Relentless Warfare against It," *Elks Magazine*, Dec. 1930; Georges Corbot, "Elusive Diplomat and the King of Crime," *True Detective*, Oct. 1940; Thomas Dickson, "Glamour Girl Wrecks Reno's Dope Ring," *Special Detective Cases*, Aug. 1941; James Monahan, "Japanese Pipe Dream," *Elks Magazine*, May 1942; Harry J. Anslinger, "The Facts about Our Teen-Age Drug Addicts," *Reader's Digest*, Oct. 1951; LaFitte and Phelan, "'Horse' of Another Color." See also Herbert Brean, "A Short—and Horrible—Life," *Reader's Digest*, Sept. 1951.

77. Kansas City station KCMO, "Crime Is a Losing Game," April 18, 1949, folder "(1690-8) Publicity #4, Radio, 1949 thru June 1951," box 69, RG 170, NARA; Andrew Tully, *Treasury Agent: The Inside Story* (New York: Simon and Schuster, 1958), 133.

78. William R. Doerner and Elaine Shannon, "Latin America Flames of Anger," *Time*, Jan. 18, 1988; "Death of a Narc," *Time*, Nov. 7, 1988; Peter Dale Scott and Jonathan Marshall, *Cocaine Politics: Drugs, Armies, and the CIA in Central America* (Berkeley: University of California Press, 1991), 37–42.

79. Anslinger and Oursler, *Murderers*, 166–67, 201–6; Henry Jordan, "Crushing the Empire of the Living Dead" (pts. 2, 3, 5), *Official Detective Stories*, March, April, and June 1948, folder 9, box 12; Harry J. Anslinger, "Walk with Death," *SAGA: True Adventures for Men*, Aug. 1952, folder 11, box 1, Anslinger Papers.

80. Correspondence between White and Anslinger, Jan. 1, 1935, and Jan. 6, 1936, folder "(1690-9), Publicity, Press, 1927 thru 1946," box 70, and July 8 and 13, 1948, folder "(0660) George White's Reports," box 164, RG 170, NARA, and folder 9, box 1, White Papers. See also White to Carey McWilliams (editor of the *Nation*), Oct. 16, 1958, folder 16, box 3, White Papers.

81. Dean Jennings to White, Feb. 27, 1961, folder 7, box 3, White Papers; William J. Stevens Jr. (assistant managing editor of the *Saturday Evening Post*) to White, March 23, 1961; White to Anslinger, March 28 and April 18, 1961; Anslinger to A. Gilmore Flues (assistant secretary of the Treasury) and Dixon Donnelly (assistant for public affairs), April 4, 1961; Anslinger to Donnelly, April 25, 1961; and Anslinger to White, May 15, 1961, folder "(1690-10) Saturday Evening Post," box 73, RG 170, NARA.

82. Anslinger to White, April 14, 1965, folder 8, box 3, White Papers.

83. John Peck (Farrar, Straus, and Giroux) to Anslinger, Oct. 11, 1965; and Eugene Block to George White, Nov. 11, 1971, folder 11, box 3, White Papers.

84. "Dr. John Ferree, Aided the Blind; George H. White," *New York Times*, Oct. 26, 1975.

85. Quoted in Valentine, *Strength of the Wolf*, 61.

86. Anslinger and Oursler, *Murderers*, 282.

87. Friedrich Nietzsche, *Beyond Good and Evil: Prelude to a Philosophy of the Future*, translated by Walter Kaufman (New York: Vintage Books, 1966), epigram 146.

CHAPTER 5

1. Frederic Sondern Jr., *Brotherhood of Evil: The Mafia* (New York: Manor Books, 1959), 100–101; Sondern, "Lucky Luciano's New Empire," *Reader's Digest,* Sept. 1951; Sid Feder and Joachim Joesten, *The Luciano Story* (1954; reprint, New York: Da Capo Press, 1994), 224–29; "Luciano Taken on Ship," *New York Times,* Feb. 10, 1946; "Pardoned Luciano on His Way to Italy," *New York Times,* Feb. 11, 1946.

2. "Dewey Commutes Luciano Sentence," *New York Times,* January 4, 1946.

3. Harry J. Anslinger and Will Oursler, *The Murderers: The Story of the Narcotics Gangs* (New York: Farrar, Straus, and Cudahy, 1961), 295, 79.

4. Ronald Kessler, *The Bureau: The Secret History of the FBI* (New York: St. Martin's Paperbacks, 2003), 113; White to Warren Olney III, Nov. 24, 1952, folder 16, box 1, White Papers; Selwyn Raab, *Five Families: The Rise, Decline, and Resurgence of America's Most Powerful Mafia Empires* (New York: St. Martin's Press, 2006), 134–38.

5. Tom Tripodi and Joseph P. DeSario, *Crusade: Undercover against the Mafia and KGB* (Washington, DC: Brassey's, 1993), 63; U.S. Treasury Department, *Mafia: The Government's Secret File on Organized Crime* (New York: Skyhorse, 2009).

6. Disagreements remain around questions of timing, geography, scope, cohesion, and the causes of its rise and fall. Major works consulted include Alan A. Block, *Perspectives on Organizing Crime: Essays in Opposition* (London: Kluwer Academic, 1991; republished as *Space, Time and Organized Crime* in 1994); Lee Bernstein, *The Greatest Menace: Organized Crime in Cold War America* (Amherst: University of Massachusetts Press, 2002); Thomas A. Reppetto, *American Mafia: A History of Its Rise to Power* (New York: Henry Holt, 2004); Michael Woodiwiss, *Gangster Capitalism: The United States and the Global Rise of Organized Crime* (New York: Carroll & Graf, 2005); Thomas A. Reppetto, *Bringing Down the Mob: The War against the American Mafia* (New York: Henry Holt, 2006); Raab, *Five Families;* David Critchley, *The Origin of Organized Crime in America: The New York City Mafia, 1891–1931* (New York: Routledge, 2009); Tim Newark, *Lucky Luciano: The Real and Fake Gangster* (New York: St. Martin's Press, 2010).

7. Mel Gussow, "Mario Puzo, Author Who Made 'The Godfather' a World Addiction Is Dead at 78," *New York Times,* July 3, 1999; Matthew Flamm, "A Demimonde in Twilight," *New York Times,* June 2, 2002.

8. Harry J. Anslinger and J. Dennis Gregory, *The Protectors: The Heroic Story of the Narcotics Agents, Citizens and Officials in Their Unending, Unsung Battles against Organized Crime in America and Abroad* (New York: Farrar and Straus, 1964), 214; Charles Siragusa and Robert Wiedrich, *The Trail of the Poppy: Behind the Mask of the Mafia* (Englewood Cliffs, NJ: Prentice Hall, 1966), x, 43; Sondern, *Brotherhood of Evil,* 100–123; Ed Reid, *Mafia* (New York: Signet, 1954), 25, 38, 44–45, 60; Herbert Brean, "Men of Mafia's Infamous Web," *Life,* Feb. 1, 1960, folder 7, box 12, Anslinger Papers.

9. Sondern, *Brotherhood of Evil,* xii, 56; Reid, *Mafia,* 38, 50; Jack Lait and Lee Mortimer, *U.S.A. Confidential* (New York: Crown, 1952), 10, 12; Tripodi and DeSario, *Crusade,* 265; Brean, "Men of Mafia's Infamous Web"; David Brion Davis, "Some Themes of Counter-subversion: An Analysis of Anti-Masonic, Anti-Catholic, and Anti-Mormon Literature," *Mississippi Valley Historical Review* 47, no. 2 (1960): 205–24.

10. Anslinger and Oursler, *Murderers,* 56–73; Treasury Dept. Press Service no. 37-3, June 12, 1943, folder "(1690-12) Publicity, Press Release, 1943 thru 1947," box 74; and folder "(1690-10) Drug Barons of Europe," box 71, RG 170, NARA.

11. Anslinger and Oursler, *Murderers*, 56.

12. Sondern, *Brotherhood of Evil*, xi, 53–54; Reid, *Mafia*, 25; Reppetto, *American Mafia*, 4.

13. The murders of New Orleans police chief David Hennesy (1890), Lieutenant Joseph Petrosino of the NYPD (1909), and labor organizer Carlo Tresca (1943) are often featured. Jack Lait and Lee Mortimer, *Washington Confidential* (New York: Dell, 1951), 220; Sondern, *Brotherhood of Evil*, 58–59, 61–64, 105; Reid, *Mafia*, 9–23, 70–72, 101–2, 118–31; Siragusa and Wiedrich, *Trail of the Poppy*, 34; Anslinger and Oursler, *Murderers*, 9–10; Critchley, *Origin of Organized Crime in America*.

14. Anslinger and Oursler, *Murderers*, 7.

15. Will Oursler and Laurence Dwight Smith, *Narcotics: America's Peril* (Garden City, NY: Doubleday, 1952), 151–59; Joachim Joesten, *Dope, Inc.* (New York: Avon, 1953), 80–92; Feder and Joesten, *The Luciano Story*; Sondern, *Brotherhood of Evil*, 100–122; Anslinger and Oursler, *Murderers*, 100–109; Newark, *Lucky Luciano.*

16. Anslinger and Oursler, *Murderers*, 102; Feder and Joesten, *The Luciano Story*, 57–59; "Lucania Is Forced to Admit Crimes," *New York Times*, June 4, 1936.

17. Joesten, *Dope, Inc.*, 81; Anslinger and Oursler, *Murderers*, 102.

18. Anslinger and Gregory, *Protectors*, 74; Luciano quoted in Sal Vizzini, Oscar Fraley, and Marshall Smith, *Vizzini: The Secret Lives of America's Most Successful Undercover Agent* (New York: Pinnacle Books, 1972), 153; Oursler and Smith, *Narcotics: America's Peril*, 23–24; Sondern, *Brotherhood of Evil*, 102–7; Reppetto, *American Mafia*, 158.

19. Walter Lippmann, "The Underworld: Our Secret Servant," *Forum and Century* (Jan. 1931); Lippmann, "The Underworld: A Stultified Conscience," *Forum and Century* (Feb. 1931). See also Peter Andreas, *Smuggler Nation: How Illicit Trade Made America* (Oxford: Oxford University Press, 2013).

20. Lippmann, "Our Secret Servant" and "Stultified Conscience."

21. Anslinger and Oursler, *Murderers*, 88; Anslinger and Gregory, *Protectors*, 20–21.

22. Quoted in David Courtwright, Herman Joseph, and Don Des Jarlais, eds., *Addicts Who Survived: An Oral History of Narcotic Use in America, 1923–1965* (Knoxville: University of Tennessee Press, 1989), 88.

23. Anslinger and Gregory, *Protectors*, 74; Anslinger and Oursler, *Murderers*, 4; Lait and Mortimer, *Washington Confidential*, 225.

24. Lippmann, "Our Secret Servant." See also Reppetto, *American Mafia*, 161; Reppetto, *Bringing Down the Mob*, 20, 125; Andreas, *Smuggler Nation*, 336; and H. Richard Friman and Peter Andreas, eds., *The Illicit Global Economy and State Power* (Lanham, MD: Rowman & Littlefield, 1999), 10.

25. Stevenson quoted in Bernstein, *Greatest Menace*, 9.

26. Harry J. Anslinger, "Narcotics in the Post-war World," *True Detective*, Feb. 1946, folder 18, box 12, Anslinger Papers.

27. Justin Gilbert, "King Cobra of Crime," *True Police Cases*, Aug. 1947, and Michael Stern, "Lucky Luciano Today," *True: The Man's Magazine*, Nov. 1952, folder 19, box 12, Anslinger Papers; Joesten, *Dope, Inc.*, 80; Siragusa and Wiedrich, *Trail of the Poppy*, 69; Anslinger and Oursler, *Murderers*, 102–5, 59; Sondern, *Brotherhood of Evil*, 81.

28. Vizzini, Fraley, and Smith, *Vizzini*, 83; Siragusa and Wiedrich, *Trail of the Poppy*, ix; Tully, *Treasury Agent*, 104; Vizzini reports, Sept. 30, 1959, and Feb. 9, 1960, folder 8, box 2 and folder 8, box 4, Anslinger Papers.

29. Raab, *Five Families*, 50–57; Feder and Joesten, *The Luciano Story*, 135–66; "Luca-

nia Ruled, Vice Witness Says," *New York Times,* May 22, 1936; "Operator Identifies 'Lucky' as Vice King," *Atlanta Constitution,* May 23, 1936; "Dewey, N.Y., Prosecutor-Elect Won Fame Smashing Rackets," *Washington Post,* Nov. 3, 1937.

30. Newark, *Lucky Luciano,* 127; Anslinger and Oursler, *Murderers,* 103, 25; Joesten, *Dope, Inc.,* 39.

31. Rodney Campbell, *The Luciano Project: The Secret Wartime Collaboration of the Mafia and the U.S. Navy* (New York: McGraw-Hill, 1977). See also Newark, *Lucky Luciano,* 147–78; "Dewey Commutes Luciano Sentence," *New York Times,* Jan. 4, 1946; Emanuel Perlmutter, "Lucky Luciano's Story: Prison and Politics: Former Racket Boss, 4,000 Miles Away, Still Is a Campaign Issue," *New York Times,* Feb. 14, 1954.

32. White, Nov. 8, 1946, folder 6, box 1, White Papers.

33. Winchell appears to be the only source for the Medal of Honor claim. T. J. English, *Havana Nocturne: How the Mob Owned Cuba and Then Lost It to the Revolution* (New York: William Morrow Paperbacks, 2009); Sondern, *Brotherhood of Evil,* 115–17; Sondern, "Luciano's New Empire," *Reader's Digest,* Sept. 1951; Douglas Valentine, *The Strength of the Wolf: The Secret History of America's War on Drugs* (London: Verso, 2004), 67; Campbell, *Luciano Project,* 261.

34. Anslinger and Oursler, *Murderers,* 106; Anslinger to Sharman, March 28, 1940, folder 21, box 2, Anslinger Papers; "Luciano in Cuba; Drug Shipments Shut Off by U.S.," *Chicago Daily Tribune,* Feb. 22, 1947; "U.S. Ends Narcotic Sales to Cuba While Luciano Is Resident There," *New York Times,* Feb. 22, 1947; "Officials Deny Luciano Aided America in War," *Chicago Daily Tribune,* Feb. 23, 1947; "Luciano Called King-pin of Drug Peddlers in U.S.," *Chicago Daily Tribune,* Feb. 24, 1947; "Luciano Plot to Rule Drug Gangs Cited," *Washington Post,* Feb. 24, 1947. See also John C. McWilliams and Alan Block, "All the Commissioner's Men: The Federal Bureau of Narcotics and the Dewey-Luciano Affair, 1947–1954," *Intelligence and National Security* 5, no. 1 (1990): 178–80.

35. Williams to Anslinger, Feb. 24, 1947, folder 18, box 2, Anslinger Papers; "U.S. Narcotic Ban on Cuba Is Lifted," *New York Times,* Feb. 26, 1947; "Luciano Put on Ship," *New York Times,* March 20, 1947.

36. Reports, July 6 to Aug. 3, 1948, and "The Enzi Syndicate," Aug. 25, 1948, folder "(0660) George White's Reports," box 164, RG 170, NARA.

37. Williams to Anslinger, April 6, 1949, folder "(0660) Italy #2, 1948–1949," box 159, RG 170, NARA.

38. Williams to Anslinger, July 7, 1949, folder "(0660) Italy #2, 1948–1949," box 159, RG 170, NARA; "Rome Narcotic Raid Nets New York Man," *New York Times,* June 26, 1949; "U.S. Asks Watch on Luciano in Dope Drive," *Washington Post,* June 27, 1949; "Narcotics Charge Jails Ex-Army Deserter in Italy," *Washington Post,* Sept. 28, 1949; Siragusa and Wiedrich, *Trail of the Poppy,* 82–91.

39. Pocoroba to Anslinger, Aug. 3 and 20, 1950, folder "(0660) Italy #3, 1950," box 159; Anslinger to Giuseppe Dosi, May 24, 1950, and Harney to Siragusa, Sept. 21, 1950, folder "(0660-A) 1949–1965," box 164, RG 170; Valentine, *Strength of the Wolf,* 27, 60.

40. Edward T. Folliard, "Navy Explodes Lucky Luciano 'War Hero' Myth," *Washington Post,* April 2, 1950.

41. Anslinger to Siragusa, Aug. 22, 1950, folder "(0660-A) 1949–1965," box 164, RG 170, NARA.

42. Siragusa and Wiedrich, *Trail of the Poppy*, 33–63; Sondern, *Brotherhood of Evil*, 132; Vizzini, Fraley, and Smith, *Vizzini*, 13; Siragusa OSS file, box 715, entry 224, RG 226, NARA.

43. See, generally, folders "(o66o) Italy #3, 1950," box 159, and "Progress Reports of Charles Siragusa," box 164; and Harney to Siragusa, Sept. 21, 1950, folder "(o66o-A) 1949–1965," box 164, RG 170, NARA.

44. Reports dated Sept. 22 to Oct. 11, 1950, folder "Progress Reports of Charles Siragusa," box 164, RG 170, NARA; Siragusa and Wiedrich, *Trail of the Poppy*, 82–91.

45. Siragusa, Oct. 11 and 16, 1950, folder "Progress Reports of Charles Siragusa," box 164, RG 170, NARA.

46. Siragusa to Anslinger, Feb. 17, 1951, folder "(o66o) Italy #4, 1951," box 159, RG 170, NARA.

47. Siragusa, Oct. 21, 1950, folder "Progress Reports of Charles Siragusa," box 164; and reports dated Feb. 17, April 5, 9, and 14, 1951, folder "(o66o) Italy #4, 1951," box 159, RG 170, NARA.

48. Siragusa, Progress Report no. 6, Feb. 17, 1951; letters from Anslinger dated Feb. 19, 1951, to L. Ducloux (secretary-general, Interpol), P. Thornton (British Home Office), director of the Services de Police Judiciare (France), and B. Schneider (Federal Board of Public Health, Switzerland), folder "(o66o) Italy #4, 1951," box 159; Siragusa, Progress Report no. 24, April 5, 1951; and Siragusa to Anslinger, July 2, 1952, folder "(o66o) Italy #5, 1952–1956," box 159, RG 170, NARA.

49. Siragusa, Progress Report nos. 24–29, April 5 to April 11, 1951, folder "(o66o) Italy #4, 1951," box 159, RG 170, NARA. In retrospect, Siragusa thought the tip leading to Callaci's arrest came from a competitor. At the time, he identified the nephew as a "typical New York City Italian rackateer [*sic*]" but later described him as an innocent janitor caught up in a Mafia scheme. Siragusa and Wiedrich, *Trail of the Poppy*, 92–101. For Callaci (the elder) and Pici files, see U.S. Treasury Department, *Mafia*, 781, 828.

50. Siragusa, Progress Report nos. 28, 29, and 34, April 10, 11, and 19, 1951, folder "(o66o) Italy #4, 1951," box 159, RG 170, NARA.

51. Siragusa, Progress Report nos. 27 and 36–38, April 9 and 21–25, 1951, folder "(o66o) Italy #4, 1951," box 159, RG 170, NARA.

52. Pici's arrest was reported via State Dept. telegram, Sept. 22, 1951. See also Siragusa, Progress Report no. 38, April 25, 1951, folder "(o66o) Italy #4, 1951," box 159, RG 170, NARA.

53. Anslinger to Siragusa, Feb. 24, 1953, folder "(o66o-A-1C) General Correspondence District #17, 1951 thru 1955," box 165, RG 170, NARA.

54. Harry J. Anslinger and William F. Tompkins, *The Traffic in Narcotics* (New York: Funk and Wagnalls, 1953), 11; Michael Stern, *No Innocence Abroad* (New York: Random House, 1953), 33; Stern, "Lucky Luciano Today"; "Excerpt from Report of Proceedings Hearing held before Subcommittee on Narcotics of the Committee on the Judiciary; Illicit Narcotic Traffic, S. Res. 67," June 3, 1955, folder "(o66o) Italy #5, 1952–1956," box 159; Anslinger to Tully, March 10, 1955, folder "(1690-10 B) Bluebook Magazine," box 70; and Anslinger to Siragusa, Feb. 7, 1957, folder "(1690-10) Saturday Evening Post," box 73, RG 170, NARA.

55. Sondern, *Brotherhood of Evil*, 99; Herbert Brean, "Crooked, Cruel Traffic in Drugs," *Life*, Jan. 25, 1960, folder 7, box 12, Anslinger Papers.

56. "Sen. Kefauver Dies of Heart Ailment," *Los Angeles Times*, Aug. 11, 1963; Philip J.

Hilts, *Protecting America's Health: The FDA, Business, and One Hundred Years of Regulation* (New York: Alfred A. Knopf, 2003), 130–31; Dominique A. Tobbell, *Pills, Power, and Policy: The Struggle for Drug Reform in Cold War America and Its Consequences* (Berkeley: University of California Press, 2012), 73.

57. Bernstein, *Greatest Menace*, 62; Jack Gould, "The Crime Hearings: Television Provides Both a Lively Show and a Notable Public Service," *New York Times*, March 18, 1951.

58. Estes Kefauver, "What I Found in the Underworld," *Saturday Evening Post*, April 7, 1951; Bernstein, *Greatest Menace*, 66; Sondern, *Brotherhood of Evil*, 167–88.

59. Kefauver, "What I Found in the Underworld"; Chalmers M. Roberts, "Crime Probe to Get Gamblers' Tax Data," *Washington Post*, June 13, 1950; "Link Boyle to Racing Wire," *Chicago Daily Tribune*, Oct. 6, 1950; White, address at Stanford Law School, Oct. 28, 1970, folder 18, box 3, White Papers.

60. Siragusa to Lieutenant Colonel Vittorio Montanari, May 25, 1951, folder "(0660) Italy #4, 1951," box 159, RG 170, NARA.

61. James A. Hagerty, "Costello Defies Senators, Walks Out of Hearings Here; Faces Arrest on Contempt," *New York Times*, March 16, 1951; Campbell, *Luciano Project*, 265–69.

62. Harold B. Hinton, "Luciano Rules U.S. Narcotics from Sicily, Senators Hear," *New York Times*, June 28, 1951; "Calls Luciano King Pin of U.S. Dope Racket," *Chicago Daily Tribune*, June 28, 1951; Sondern, *Brotherhood of Evil*, 184–87; U.S. Senate, *Final Report of the Special Committee to Investigate Organized Crime in Interstate Commerce* (Washington, DC: U.S. Government Printing Office, 1951), 24–36.

63. McWilliams and Block, "All the Commissioner's Men," 180–87; Bernstein, *Greatest Menace*, 66.

64. U.S. Senate, *Final Report of the Special Committee to Investigate Organized Crime*, 1–5, 24–36.

65. Sondern, *Brotherhood of Evil*, 106; Kefauver, "What I Found in the Underworld."

66. U.S. Senate, *Final Report of the Special Committee to Investigate Organized Crime*, 1–5; Bernstein, *Greatest Menace*, 81–82.

67. Kelly and Mathison, *On the Street*, 39; Sondern, *Brotherhood of Evil*, 179–81; Bernstein, *Greatest Menace*, 61, 77–78; Larry Wolters, "Gambling Boss' Hands Betray His Fears to TV," *Chicago Daily Tribune*, March 14, 1951; "Excerpts from Third Day's Proceedings Here in Senate Committee's Inquiry into Crime," *New York Times*, March 15, 1951; James A. Hagerty, "Costello Defies Senators, Walks Out of Hearing Here; Faces Arrest on Contempt," *New York Times*, March 15, 1951.

68. Federal Bureau of Investigation, "Mafia," July 1958, FBI Electronic Reading Room, vault.fbi.gov.

69. Sondern, *Brotherhood of Evil*, 224–35; Raab, *Five Families*, 125–38; Anslinger and Gregory, *Protectors*, 213–16.

70. Siragusa, March 20, 1952, folder "(0660) Italy #5, 1952–1956," box 159; Paul Knight to Anslinger, June 28, 1955, folder "(0660-A-1C) General Correspondence District #17, 1951 thru 1955," box 165, RG 170, NARA; "Italy Halts Dope Output of Big Firm," *Washington Post*, Feb. 15, 1953; Siragusa and Weidrich, *Trail of the Poppy*, 92–101; Tully, *Treasury Agent*, 105–6; Sondern, *Brotherhood of Evil*, 130–31.

71. Chappell to Valentine, Jan. 22 and May 1, 1994, folder "Chappell, Howard," box 2, Valentine Collection; Tripodi and DeSario, *Crusade*, 267; Linda Witt, "Why Was Giancana Rubbed Out?," *People*, July 28, 1975.

72. McWilliams and Block, "All the Commissioner's Men"; Siragusa to Anslinger, July 24, 1952, folder 13, box 2, Anslinger Papers; White to John (Ehrlich, a San Francisco attorney), Jan. 25, 1955, folder 1, box 3, White Papers; Stern, "Lucky Luciano Today"; Feder and Joesten, *The Luciano Story,* 140, 163–64; Newark, *Lucky Luciano,* 133–34.

73. Reppetto, *American Mafia,* 179.

74. Campbell, *Luciano Project,* vii–ix, 1–19.

75. Vizzini, Fraley, and Smith, *Vizzini,* 84.

76. Ibid., 203–17; Newark, *Lucky Luciano,* 255–56, 261–67.

77. Reppetto, *American Mafia,* 180; Newark, *Lucky Luciano,* 213.

78. Newark, *Lucky Luciano,* xi–xii; McWilliams and Block, "All the Commissioner's Men."

79. Sondern to Anslinger, Nov. 15, 1958, folder "(1690-10) Reader's Digest," box 73, RG 170, NARA; Lait and Mortimer, *U.S.A. Confidential,* 21; Lait and Mortimer, *Washington Confidential,* 218; Anslinger and Oursler, *Murderers,* 295.

CHAPTER 6

1. Siragusa, Progress Reports 25–28, Aug. 31–Sept. 6, 1950, folder "Progress Reports of Charles Siragusa," box 164, RG 170, NARA.

2. Drug Enforcement Administration, "Foreign Office Locations," www.dea.gov.

3. Foreign enforcement work is touched on in John C. McWilliams, *The Protectors: Harry J. Anslinger and the Federal Bureau of Narcotics, 1930–1962* (Newark: University of Delaware Press, 1990); Douglas Valentine, *The Strength of the Wolf: The Secret History of America's War on Drugs* (London: Verso, 2004); Ethan Nadelmann, *Cops across Borders: The Internationalization of U.S. Criminal Law Enforcement* (University Park: Pennsylvania State University Press, 1994), 129–39; and Alan Block and John C. McWilliams, "On the Origins of American Counterintelligence: Building a Clandestine Network," *Journal of Policy History* 1, no. 4 (1989): 353–72.

4. Charles Siragusa and Robert Wiedrich, *The Trail of the Poppy: Behind the Mask of the Mafia* (Englewood Cliffs, NJ: Prentice Hall, 1966), 144.

5. Anslinger, "Narcotics in the Post-war World," *True Detective,* Feb. 1946, folder 18, box 12, Anslinger Papers.

6. Siragusa, Progress Report no. 29, Sept. 9, 1950, folder "Progress Reports of Charles Siragusa," box 164, RG 170, NARA.

7. Matthew R. Pembleton, "Imagining a Global Sovereignty: U.S. Counternarcotic Operations in Istanbul during the Early Cold War and the Origins of the Foreign 'War on Drugs,'" *Journal of Cold War Studies* 18, no. 2 (2016): 28–63; Ryan Gingeras, "Istanbul Confidential: Heroin, Espionage, and Politics in Cold War Turkey, 1945–1960," *Diplomatic History* 37, no. 4 (2013): 779–806.

8. Siragusa, Progress Report no. 29, Sept. 9, 1950, folder "Progress Reports of Charles Siragusa," box 164, RG 170, NARA.

9. Report by Bruce Kuniholm, July 21, 1948, folder "(0660) Lebanon, 1945–1953," box 160; Siragusa, Progress Report no. 29, Sept. 9, 1950, folder "Progress Reports of Charles Siragusa," box 164, RG 170, NARA; Jonathan Marshall, *The Lebanese Connection: Corruption, Civil War, and the International Drug Traffic* (Stanford, CA: Stanford University Press, 2012), 14–32; Cyrus Schayegh, "The Many Worlds of Abud Yasin; or, What Narcotics Trafficking in the Interwar Middle East Can Tell Us about Territorialization," *American Historical Review* 116, no. 2 (2011): 273–306.

10. Siragusa, Progress Report nos. 3 and 29, July 26 and Sept. 9, 1950, folder "Progress Reports of Charles Siragusa," box 164, RG 170, NARA.

11. Siragusa, Progress Report nos. 29–30, Sept. 9–12, 1950, folder "Progress Reports of Charles Siragusa," box 164, RG 170, NARA.

12. Siragusa, Progress Report nos. 29–32, Sept. 9–16, 1950, folder "Progress Reports of Charles Siragusa," box 164; and folder "(0660) Lebanon, 1945–1953," box 160, RG 170, NARA.

13. Dyar was appointed in the fall of 1947 and served until his death in August 1951. Dyar to Anslinger, Nov. 8 and 20, 1947; Anslinger to Dyer, April 1, 1947; Anslinger to Herbert May, March 17, 1950; and Francis X. Di Lucia to Anslinger, Oct. 19, 1951, folders 15 and 18, box 2, Anslinger Papers; and Anslinger to Canfield, Sept. 20, 1954, folder "(280-1) Bureau Operations, 1931–1954," box 48, RG 170, NARA.

14. Harry J. Anslinger and J. Dennis Gregory, *The Protectors: The Heroic Story of the Narcotics Agents, Citizens and Officials in Their Unending, Unsung Battles against Organized Crime in America and Abroad* (New York: Farrar and Straus, 1964), 140.

15. White, State Dept. cables to Anslinger, May 1 and 9, 1948, and report dated June 10, 1948, folder "(0660) George White's Reports," box 164, RG 170, NARA.

16. Undated letter (Feb. 1949) from Williams to White; and Williams to Anslinger, Jan. 26, Feb. 1, 4, 9 and 11, folder 7, box 1, White Papers; Williams to Anslinger, Feb. 1, 1949, folder 16, box 2, Anslinger Papers; folder "12 June 1955 letter from Knight in Paris to Siragusa in Rome," box 4, Valentine Collection.

17. Williams to Anslinger, Feb. 1, 1949, folder 16, box 2, Anslinger Papers; Anslinger and Gregory, *Protectors*, 107. A few historians have speculated that Williams participated in the 1953 coup that overthrew Prime Minister Mohammad Mossadegh—a plausible claim given his ties to military intelligence. However, there is no evidence in FBN records to indicate his involvement in the coup, which took place during his controversial appointment to the IRS, nor is there anyone fitting Williams's description in Kermit Roosevelt, *CounterCoup: The Struggle for Control of Iran* (New York: McGraw Hill, 1979); or Donald M. Wilber, Central Intelligence Agency, *Clandestine Service History: Overthrow of Premier Mossadeq of Iran November 1952–August 1953,* CS Historical Paper no. 208 (Oct. 1969).

18. Williams to Anslinger, Feb. 18, 1949, folder "(0660) Turkey #4, 1949–June 1950," box 25, RG 170, NARA; Williams to Anslinger, Oct. 12, 1951, folder 14, box 2, Anslinger Papers.

19. Williams to Manfredi, July 12, 1949, and Williams to Anslinger, April 15, 1949, folder "(0660) Italy #2, 1948–1949," box 159; Siragusa, Progress Report no. 6, Feb. 17, 1951, folder "(0660) Italy #4, 1951," box 159, and Progress Report no. 45, Oct. 16, 1950, folder "Progress Reports of Charles Siragusa," box 164; and White to Anslinger, March 14, 1951, folder "(0660) Turkey #6, 1951–1952," box 163, RG 170, NARA.

20. Anslinger to Sharman, Oct. 4, 1950, folder "(0660) Italy #3, 1950"; and Siragusa, Progress Report nos. 26 and 34, April 5–7 and 19, 1951, folder "(0660) Italy #4, 1951," box 159, RG 170, NARA; U.S. Senate, *Final Report of the Special Committee to Investigate Organized Crime in Interstate Commerce* (Washington, DC: U.S. Printing Office, 1951); Harold B. Hinton, "Luciano Rules U.S. Narcotics from Sicily, Senators Hear," *New York Times,* June 28, 1951.

21. Siragusa to Anslinger, Sept. 10, 1951, folder "(0660) Italy #4, 1951," box 159, RG 170, NARA.

22. Siragusa, Progress Report no. 6, Feb. 17, 1951, and Progress Report no. 34, April 19,

1951, folder "(0660) Italy #4, 1951," box 159. See also Siragusa to Anslinger, Feb. 5, 1945, folder "(0660) Italy #1, Sept. 1927–Dec. 1947," box 159, RG 170, NARA.

23. Siragusa to Anslinger, Sept. 10, 1951, folder "(0660) Italy #4, 1951," box 159, RG 170, NARA. Documents held in State Department records (RG 59 and 84) provide some additional insights, but Turkey was among the few countries where U.S. diplomats independently reported on American control efforts.

24. Anslinger to Siragusa, Sept. 18 and Oct. 23, 1951, folder "(0660-A-1C) General Correspondence District #17, 1951 thru 1955," box 165; and Harney to Anslinger, March 17, 1953, folder "(0660) Italy #5, 1952–1956," box 159, RG 170, NARA.

25. Anslinger to Siragusa, Oct. 10, 1951; Siragusa to Anslinger, Sept. 13, 1951; and Siragusa to Anslinger, June 20, 1952, folders "(0660) Italy #4, 1951" and "(0660) Italy #5, 1952–1956," box 159, RG 170, NARA; "U.S. Reds Said to Run Europe Drug Traffic," New York Times, Aug. 30, 1951; Frank Kelly, "Italy Shuns Ban on Narcotics Despite U.S. Deportation Drive," New York Herald Tribune, Dec. 17, 1952.

26. Siragusa to Anslinger, Sept. 17, 1951, folder "(0660) Italy #4, 1951," box 159, RG 170, NARA.

27. Frederic Sondern Jr., Brotherhood of Evil: The Mafia (New York: Manor Books, 1959), 135.

28. "Henry L. Manfredi Dies at 54; Aide to Narcotics Bureau Head," New York Times, Jan. 8, 1970; Siragusa to Anslinger, July 15, 1952, folder "(0660-A-1C) General Correspondence District #17, 1951 thru 1955," box 165, RG 170, NARA.

29. Siragusa and Wiedrich, Trail of the Poppy, 144; Sondern, Brotherhood of Evil, 135; Siragusa to Cunningham, July 29, 1955, and Anslinger to Siragusa, Sept. 18, 1951, folder "(0660-A-1C) General Correspondence District #17, 1951 thru 1955," box 165; and Siragusa to Harney, Nov. 12, 1951, folder "(0660-A) 1949–1965," box 164, RG 170, NARA.

30. Siragusa, Progress Report no. 45, Oct. 16, 1950, and Progress Report no. 3, July 26, 1950, folder "Progress Reports of Charles Siragusa," box 164; Cunningham to Siragusa, April 25, 1951, folder "(0660-A) 1949–1965," box 164; Anslinger to Siragusa, Sept. 18, 1951; and Harney to Anslinger, Sept. 20, 1954, folder "(0660-A-1C) General Correspondence District #17, 1951 thru 1955," box 165, RG 170, NARA.

31. Siragusa, Progress Report nos. 27 and 36, April 9 and 21, 1951; Siragusa to Anslinger, Sept. 10, 1951; Cunningham to Schute, June 1, 1951, folder "(0660) Italy #4, 1951," box 159; and Anslinger to Siragusa, Sept. 27, 1951, folder "(0660-A-1C) General Correspondence District #17, 1951 thru 1955," box 165, RG 170, NARA. See also William Canup to White, Oct. 21, 1948, folder 8, box 1, White Papers.

32. Siragusa to Cunningham, July 29, 1955, and Anslinger to Siragusa, Aug. 4, 1955, folder "(0660-A-1C) General Correspondence District #17, 1951 thru 1955," box 165, RG 170, NARA.

33. Anslinger to Siragusa, Oct. 4, 1957, folder "(0660-A-1C) General Correspondence District #17, 1956 thru 1958," box 165, RG 170, NARA.

34. Kelly and Mathison, On the Street, 161.

35. Harney to Mitchell, Oct. 25, 1955, folder "(0395) Customs, Dist. #17," box 59, RG 170, NARA.

36. Harney to Anslinger, July 21, 1950, folder "(0395-1) Customs Co-operation #1, 1933–1955," box 59; Anslinger to Siragusa, Sept. 24, 1951, folder "(0660-A-1C) General Correspondence District #17, 1951 thru 1955," box 165; and Siragusa to Anslinger, Oct. 12, 1951, folder "(0395-1) Customs Co-operation #1, 1933–1955," box 59, RG 170, NARA.

37. Ryan to Siragusa, June 9, 1952, and report by Agent Joseph Amato, Oct. 29, 1951, folder "(0660-A-1C) General Correspondence District #17, 1951 thru 1955," box 165, RG 170, NARA.

38. Ryan to Siragusa, June 9, 1952, folder "(0660-A-1C) General Correspondence District #17, 1951 thru 1955," box 165; and "(0660) Italy, Oil Drums," box 159, RG 170, NARA; Sondern, *Brotherhood of Evil*, 99.

39. Siragusa to Early A. Greenman (Trans World Airlines), Jan. 21, 1955; numerous references in folders "(0660-A-1C) General Correspondence District #17, 1951 thru 1955," and "(0660-A-1C) General Correspondence District # 17, 1959 thru June 1961," box 165, RG 170, NARA.

40. Clive Emsley, "Political Police and the European Nation-State in the Nineteenth Century," in *The Policing of Politics in the Twentieth Century: Historical Perspectives*, edited by Mark Mazower (Providence, NJ: Berghahn Books, 1997), 1–25.

41. Anslinger to Acting District Supervisor Andrew Tartaglino, Sept. 24, 1958; Tartaglino to Anslinger, Oct. 2, 1958, folder "(0660-A-1C) General Correspondence District #17, 1956 thru 1958," box 165; and Cusack to Knight, April 16, 1956, folder "(0660) Lebanon #3 (1955–1960)," box 160, RG 170, NARA. See conflict over recruitment of Agent Joseph Vullo: Cusack to Anslinger, March 14, 1961; and Speer to Anslinger, March 22, 1961, folder "(0660-A-1C) General Correspondence District #17, 1959 thru June 1961," box 165, RG 170, NARA.

42. Anslinger reported a 30 percent drop in U.S. narcotics arrests in September 1951, which he attributed to the work of agents in Italy and punitive jail sentences at the state level. In *Brotherhood of Evil*, Sondern reported a 40 percent drop in the illicit trafficking volume as of 1954, a figure Anslinger also gave during Senate testimony in 1955. "Narcotics Arrests Reported Off 30%," *New York Times*, Sept. 26, 1951; Sondern, *Brotherhood of Evil*, 135; "Doubts U.S. Can Halt Flow of Narcotics; Reveal 40% of Dope Blocked at Source," *Chicago Daily Tribune*, June 4, 1955. See also a report from Henry Giordano to James A. Reed (assistant Treasury secretary), March 23, 1964, including charts documenting the quantity of narcotics seized in foreign operations from 1954 to 1963. Folder "(0280-1) Bureau Operations, 1955–1969," box 48, RG 170, NARA. Seizure figures actually declined from 1955 to 1959 and then skyrocketed from 1960 to 1963.

43. Sondern, *Brotherhood of Evil*, 135.

44. Knight to Anslinger, April 26, 1954, and Siragusa to B. T. Mitchell, Nov. 21, 1955, folder "(0660-A-1C) General Correspondence District #17, 1951 thru 1955," box 165, RG 170, NARA.

45. Emphasis added. Anslinger testimony, Subcommittee on Improvements in the Federal Criminal Code, Senate Judiciary Committee, *Illicit Narcotics Traffic*, 84th Cong., 1st sess., June 2, 3, and 8, 1955, 9–63; "Doubts U.S. Can Halt Flow of Narcotics."

46. John Prados, *Safe for Democracy: The Secret Wars of the CIA* (Chicago: Ivan R. Dee, 2006); Hugh Wilford, *The Mighty Wurlitzer: How the CIA Played America* (Cambridge, MA: Harvard University Press, 2008); James Callanan, *Covert Action in the Cold War: US Policy, Intelligence and CIA Operations* (London: I. B. Tauris, 2010).

47. Siragusa to Giovanni Battista Migliori (Public Health Commissioner), Sept. 28, 1951, folder "(0660) Italy #4, 1951," box 159, RG 170, NARA.

48. Siragusa and Wiedrich, *Trail of the Poppy*, 92–101; Harry J. Anslinger and William F. Tompkins, *The Traffic in Narcotics* (New York: Funk and Wagnalls, 1953), 11, 105–12; "Italy Halts Dope Output of Big Firm," *Washington Post*, Feb. 15, 1953; Siragusa to Anslinger, March 30, 1952, and May 8, 1953, folder "(0660) Italy #5, 1952–1956,"

box 159; Knight to Anslinger, June 28, 1955, folder "(0660-A-1C) General Correspondence District #17, 1951 thru 1955," box 165; and, generally, folder "(0660-A-1C) Little Green Trunk," box 164, RG 170, NARA.

49. Siragusa and Wiedrich, *Trail of the Poppy*, 92–93; Anslinger and Tompkins, *The Traffic in Narcotics*, 11, 105–12; Siragusa to Anslinger, May 8, 1953, folder "(0660) Italy #5, 1952–1956," box 159, RG 170, NARA.

50. Siragusa to Anslinger, March 16, April 23, May 6, July 13 and 18, 1953, and Siragusa to Mr. F. Williamson (counselor, U.S. Embassy, Rome), July 24, 1953, folder "(0660) Italy #5, 1952–1956," box 159, RG 170, NARA.

51. Siragusa to Anslinger, July 30, Aug. 4, and Sept. 1, 1953, folder "(0660) Italy #5, 1952–1956," box 159, RG 170, NARA.

52. Siragusa to Anslinger, Oct. 26, 1953, and Jan. 26, 1954, folder "(0660) Italy #5, 1952–1956," box 159, RG 170, NARA.

53. Henry Jordan, "How Italy's Government Lets Heroin Flood the U.S.," *Bluebook* 101, no. 2 (1955), folder "(1690-10 B) Bluebook Magazine," box 70; and State Dept. document, July 15, 1955, folder "Foreign Reports, Dist #17, Secret File #1, Sept. 1953 thru Aug. 1955," box 13, entry 10, RG 170, NARA.

54. Siragusa to Anslinger, May 14, 1953; Siragusa to Mr. F. Williamson (counselor, U.S. Embassy, Rome), July 24, 1953; "Excerpt from Report of Proceedings Hearing held before Subcommittee on Narcotics of the Committee on the Judiciary, Illicit Narcotic Traffic, S. Res. 67," June 3, 1955, and Siragusa to Durbrow, June 24, 1955, folder "(0660) Italy #5, 1952–1956," box 159; and Siragusa to Anslinger, June 15, 1955, folder "(1690-10 B) Bluebook Magazine," box 70, RG 170, NARA.

55. Siragusa to Williamson, March 12, 1956, and Siragusa to Anslinger, March 27, 1956, folder "Foreign Reports, Dist #17, Secret File #3, Feb. 1956 thru April 1956," box 13, entry 10; and Siragusa to Anslinger, March 27 and July 12, 1956, folder "(0660) Italy #5, 1952–1956," box 159, RG 170, NARA.

56. See, generally, folder "(0660) Italy #5, 1952–1956," box 159; and Siragusa to Anslinger, March 27, 1956, folder "Foreign Reports, Dist #17, Secret File #3, Feb. 1956 thru April 1956," box 13, entry 10; and Anslinger to Siragusa, Nov. 21, 1955, folder "(0660, France) Alleged French Diversion," box 156, RG 170, NARA.

57. Harry J. Anslinger and Will Oursler, *The Murderers: The Story of the Narcotics Gangs* (New York: Farrar, Straus, and Cudahy, 1961), 220.

58. Siragusa to Anslinger, Oct. 29 and 31, 1952, folder "(0660) Lebanon, 1945–1953," box 160, RG 170, NARA; Siragusa to Anslinger, Dec. 3, 1952, folder 13, box 2, Anslinger Papers.

59. Harold Minor (U.S. ambassador, Beirut), Jan. 29, 1953; Minor to Richard Funkhouser (State Dept.), Feb. 4, 1953; and Anslinger to Malik, Feb. 10 and March 20, 1953, folder "(0660) Lebanon, 1945–1953," box 160, RG 170, NARA.

60. Siragusa to Anslinger, Nov. 3, 1953, folder "(0660) Lebanon, 1945–1953," box 160; Siragusa to Anslinger, July 15, 1952; and Siragusa to Cunningham, July 15, 1952, folder "(0660-A-1C) General Correspondence District #17, 1951 thru 1955," box 165, RG 170, NARA.

61. See correspondence between Knight and Siragusa, Dec. 7, 19 and 20, 1953, folder "(0660) Lebanon, 1945–1953," box 160, RG 170, NARA.

62. Siragusa to Knight, Jan. 29, 1954; Knight to Siragusa, March 5, 1954; and Knight to A. E. Bailleul (French Central Narcotic Office), March 29, 1954, folder "(0660) Lebanon #2 (1954 thru 1955)," box 160, RG 170, NARA.

63. Knight to Anslinger, April 12, 1954, folder "(0660) Lebanon #2 (1954 thru 1955)," box 160, RG 170, NARA.

64. See, generally, folder "(0660) Lebanon #2 (1954 thru 1955)," box 160; and Siragusa to Minor (U.S. Ambassador), Sept. 3, 1954, folder "(0660-A-1C) General Correspondence District #17, 1951 thru 1955," box 165, RG 170, NARA.

65. Siragusa to all agents, Oct. 5, 1955, folder "(0660-A-1C) General Correspondence District #17, 1951 thru 1955," box 165, RG 170, NARA; Siragusa and Wiedrich, *Trail of the Poppy,* 11.

66. Anslinger to Malik, June 18, 1954; Knight to Abraham, July 3, 1954; and Abraham to Siragusa, Oct. 30, 1954, folder "(0660) Lebanon #2 (1954 thru 1955)," box 160, RG 170, NARA.

67. Abraham to Siragusa, Sept. 18 and 21, 1954; Siragusa to Knight, Oct. 27, 1954, and Jan. 1, 1955, folders "(0660) Lebanon #2 (1954 thru 1955)," and "(0660) Lebanon #3 (1955–1960)," box 160, RG 170, NARA.

68. Siragusa to Anslinger, Dec. 16, 1954; Abraham to Siragusa, Sept. 18 and 21, 1954, folder "(0660) Lebanon #2 (1954 thru 1955)," box 160, RG 170, NARA.

69. Abraham to Siragusa, Sept. 21, 22, and 29 and Oct. 5, 1954; Siragusa to Knight, Oct. 5 and 22, 1954; Knight to Abraham, Oct. 13, 1954; and Abraham to Siragusa, Nov. 4, 1954, folder "(0660) Lebanon #2 (1954 thru 1955)," box 160, RG 170, NARA.

70. Knight to Siragusa, Nov. 20, 1954, and Abraham to Siragusa, Nov. 22, 1954, folder "(0660) Lebanon #2 (1954 thru 1955)," box 160, RG 170, NARA.

71. Knight to Siragusa, Nov. 20, 1954, folder "(0660) Lebanon #2 (1954 thru 1955)," box 160, RG 170, NARA.

72. Siragusa, Nov. 29, 1954, folders "(0660) Lebanon #2 (1954 thru 1955)," box 160, and "(0660-A-1C) General Correspondence District #17, 1951 thru 1955," box 165, RG 170, NARA. See also Siragusa and Wiedrich, *Trail of the Poppy,* 3–32; and Valentine, *Strength of the Wolf,* 122, where Dondola is identified as a Lebanese-Greek smuggler and member of the Lebanese Phalange in the occasional employ of Israeli and Arab intelligence.

73. Siragusa and Wiedrich, *Trail of the Poppy,* 3–32; Sondern, *Brotherhood of Evil,* 137–40; Frederic Sondern Jr., "The World War against Narcotics," *Reader's Digest,* Jan. 1956; Vera R. Glaser, "Traffic in Debauchery," *Western World* (June 1958), folder 20, box 12, Anslinger Papers.

74. Siragusa and Wiedrich, *Trail of the Poppy,* 3–32; Siragusa, Nov. 29, 1954, folder "(0660) Lebanon #2 (1954 thru 1955)," box 160, RG 170, NARA.

75. Siragusa and Wiedrich, *Trail of the Poppy,* 3–32; Siragusa to Anslinger, Aug. 7, 1954, folder "(0660) Lebanon #2 (1954 thru 1955)," box 160, RG 170, NARA.

76. Anslinger to Malik, Dec. 3 and 16, 1954, folder "(0660) Lebanon #2 (1954 thru 1955)," box 160, RG 170, NARA; "Doubts U.S. Can Halt Flow of Narcotics."

77. Knight to Siragusa, April 4, 1955, folder "(0660) Lebanon #3 (1955–1960)," box 160, RG 170, NARA.

78. Bailleul to Siragusa, July 2, 1954; Siragusa to Abraham, Dec. 17, 1954; Knight to Siragusa, Jan. 6 and 16, 1955; Siragusa to Anslinger, Jan. 28, 1955, folders "(0660) Lebanon #2 (1954 thru 1955)," and "(0660) Lebanon #3 (1955–1960)," box 160, RG 170, NARA; Marshall, *Lebanese Connection,* 33–48.

79. Siragusa to Anslinger, Jan. 28, 1955, folder "(0660) Lebanon #3 (1955–1960)," box 160, RG 170, NARA.

80. Azzizeh was accused of beating a suspect. Siragusa to Anslinger, March 12, 1955;

translation of article appearing in *al-Janhour al-Jadid*, March 27, 1955; Stan Swinton, "Ring Smuggling Dope into U.S. Smashed," *Buffalo Evening News*, April 5, 1955; "Rip Dope Ring in Middle East Supplying U.S.," *New York Post*, April 5, 1955, folder "(0660) Lebanon #3 (1955–1960)," box 160, RG 170, NARA.

81. Siragusa to Anslinger, March 12, 1955; report by Agent Paul Gross, Oct. 20, 1955; Siragusa to Anslinger, June 15, 1955, folder "(0660) Lebanon #3 (1955–1960)," box 160; and report by Knight, July 26, 1955, folder "Foreign Reports, Dist #17, Secret File #1, Sept. 1953 thru Aug. 1955," box 13, entry 10, RG 170, NARA. See also Marshall, *Lebanese Connection*, 33–48.

82. Knight to Siragusa, April 30, 1955; Attie to Siragusa, May 3, 1955; Siragusa to Anslinger, May 10, 1955; Mitchell to Siragusa, June 2, 1955; and Knight to Siragusa, June 10, 1955, folder "(0660) Lebanon #3 (1955–1960)," box 160, RG 170, NARA.

83. Knight, Memorandum Report, Sept. 7, 1955, folder "(0660-A-1C) General Correspondence District #17, 1951 thru 1955," box 165, RG 170, NARA.

84. Knight to Siragusa, May 26, 1955; Knight to Azzizeh, July 21, 1955; and, generally, folder "(0660) Lebanon #3 (1955–1960)," box 160. For later examples, see correspondence between Supervisor Mike Picini and Agent Dennis Dayle, Jan. 5 and March 19, 1965, folder "(0660) Lebanon #4, 1961–1967," box 160, RG 170, NARA.

85. For Azzizeh, see Knight to Siragusa, Dec. 6, 1955. For the benefits of U.S. training, see Siragusa to Knight, Feb. 17, 1956; Siragusa to Agent Joseph Salm, Sept. 25, 1957; and Salm to Siragusa, Oct. 9, 1957, folder "(0660) Lebanon #3 (1955–1960)," box 160, RG 170, NARA.

86. Siragusa to Anslinger, June 6, 1956; Anslinger to Siragusa, Oct. 12, 1956; and Siragusa to Giordano, Oct. 9, 1957, folder "(0660) Lebanon #3 (1955–1960)," box 160, RG 170, NARA.

87. Knight to Siragusa, Nov. 29, 1955; Siragusa to Salm, Sept. 25, 1957; Siragusa to M. Sicot, Nov. 16, 1956; and, generally, folder "(0660) Lebanon #3 (1955–1960)," box 160, RG 170, NARA.

88. Anslinger testimony, Subcommittee on Improvements in the Federal Criminal Code, Senate Judiciary Committee, *Illicit Narcotics Traffic*, 84th Cong., 1st sess., June 2, 3, and 8, 1955: 9–63; undated memo (ca. 1958), "Examples of Significant Cases in the Illicit Traffic"; Siragusa to Captain Mario Re (Guardia di Finanza), March 15, 1957; and Siragusa to Salm, Sept. 25, 1957, folder "(0660) Lebanon #3 (1955–1960)," box 160, RG 170, NARA.

89. Siragusa to Anslinger, May 26, 1958, folder "(0660-A-1C) General Correspondence District #17, 1956 thru 1958," box 165. Chehab was appointed ambassador to Tunisia and came under investigation by the French Sûreté; see Tartaglino to Cusack, Jan. 23, 1961, folder "Foreign Reports, Dist #17, Secret File #9, Sept. 1960 thru Sept. 1961," box 12, entry 10, RG 170, NARA. For new government, see Knight, memo reports, July 6 and Nov. 22, 1959, folder "(0660) Lebanon #3 (1955–1960)," box 160, RG 170, NARA.

90. Giordano to A. Gilmore Flues, Oct. 3, 1960, folder "(0660) Lebanon #3 (1955–1960)," box 160, RG 170, NARA.

91. Tripodi and DeSario, *Crusade*, 57. Some agents contend he was given the nickname by the Chicago press after his retirement from the Bureau. See Paul Newey to George White, Aug. 19, 1970, folder 1, box 4, White Papers. In a letter dated November 12, 1951, Siragusa tells Harney to be on the lookout for cigars sent to Washington via diplomatic pouch. Folder "(0660-A) 1949–1965," box 164, RG 170, NARA.

92. Siragusa to Colonel Vittorio Montanari (chief of staff, Guardia di Finanza), Nov. 29, 1955, folder "(0660-A-1C) General Correspondence District #17, 1951 thru 1955"; Siragusa to Anslinger, Nov. 20, 1957, folder "(0660-A-1C) General Correspondence District #17, 1956 thru 1958," box 165; and Anslinger to Siragusa, Feb. 7, 1957, folder "(1690-10) Saturday Evening Post," box 73, RG 170, NARA.

93. Siragusa and Anslinger correspondence, Dec. 5 and 6, 1956, and Feb. 11 and 23, 1957, folder "(1690-10) Saturday Evening Post," box 73, RG 170, NARA.

94. Field Information Circular no. 32, July 24, 1958, folder "(0660-A-1C) General Correspondence District #17, 1956 thru 1958"; and Cusack to Siragusa, Sept. 19, 1962, folder "(0660-A-1C) General Correspondence District #17, July 1961 thru Dec. 1962," box 165, RG 170, NARA. For CIA liaison, see Siragusa's 1977 testimony before the Subcommittee on Health and Scientific Research of the Committee on Human Resources in *Human Drug Testing by the CIA, 1977* (Washington, DC: U.S. Government Printing Office, 1977), 110–20. See also Valentine, *Strength of the Wolf,* 110; and Anslinger to White, Dec. 17, [1963], folder 18, box 3, White Papers.

95. Chappell to Douglas Valentine, Jan. 22, 1994, folder "Chappell, Howard," box 2, Valentine Collection. See also Giuliani to White, July 31, 1970, folder 1, box 4, White Papers.

96. Valentine, *Strength of the Wolf,* 106, 109–14, 227; Alan A. Block, *Perspectives on Organizing Crime: Essays in Opposition* (London: Kluwer Academic, 1991), 216; Bruce Bullington and Alan Block, "A Trojan Horse: Anti-communism and the War on Drugs," *Contemporary Crises* 14, no. 1 (1990): 39–55; *Human Drug Testing by the CIA,* 110–20; William Colby and Peter Forbath, *Honorable Men: My Life in the CIA* (New York: Simon and Schuster, 1978), 131–33; Linda Witt, "Why Was Giancana Rubbed Out?," *People,* July 28, 1975.

CHAPTER 7

1. Sal Vizzini, Oscar Fraley, and Marshall Smith, *Vizzini: The Secret Lives of America's Most Successful Undercover Agent* (New York: Pinnacle Books, 1972), 29; Jack Kelly and Richard Mathison, *On the Street* (Chicago: Henry Regnery, 1974), 38–40; Frederic Sondern Jr., *Brotherhood of Evil: The Mafia* (New York: Manor Books, 1959), 43–44.

2. Cusack to Anslinger, Sept. 15, 1960, folder "(0660) Thailand, 1957–1963," box 163. It appears a French police official or New York gangster blew Cusack's cover in 1951. See Siragusa, Dec. 3, 1951, folder "(0660-A-1C) General Correspondence District #17, 1951 thru 1955"; Cusack, Nov. 7, 1951, folder "(0660) France #3, 1951–1953," box 156; Anslinger, Field Information Circular no. 20, Jan. 28, 1958, folder "(0370-3) Field Information Circulars, 1–170," box 56; and Anslinger to M. Sicot (Interpol), Dec. 16, 1958, folder "(0660-A-1C) General Correspondence District #17, 1956 thru 1958," box 165, RG 170, NARA; and Harry J. Anslinger and J. Dennis Gregory, *The Protectors: The Heroic Story of the Narcotics Agents, Citizens and Officials in Their Unending, Unsung Battles against Organized Crime in America and Abroad* (New York: Farrar and Straus, 1964), 157–58.

3. Arthur Giuliani to George White, March 31, 1958, folder 16, box 3, White Papers; Douglas Valentine, *The Strength of the Wolf: The Secret History of America's War on Drugs* (London: Verso, 2004), 155–57.

4. Folder "(0660) Communist China, 1952–1954," box 153; "(0660-A-3) Wayland Speer's Foreign Assignment, Correspondence and General File," box 165, RG 170,

NARA; Rufus King, *The Drug Hang-up: America's Fifty-Year Folly* (New York: W. W. Norton, 1972), 121–50.

5. Anslinger, Field Information Circular no. 34, Oct. 30, 1958, folder "(0370-3) Field Information Circulars, 1–170," box 56; Tom Tripodi and Joseph P. DeSario, *Crusade: Undercover against the Mafia and KGB* (Washington, DC: Brassey's, 1993), 57–67; Siragusa to Speer, May 27, 1959, folder "(0660-A-1C) General Correspondence District #17, 1959 thru June 1961," box 165, RG 170, NARA.

6. Giordano to James A. Reed (assistant Treasury secretary), March 23, 1964, folder "(0280-1) Bureau Operations, 1955–1969," box 48; and Speer to Anslinger, March 22, 1961, folder "(0660-A-1C) General Correspondence District #17, 1959 thru June 1961," box 165, RG 170, NARA.

7. Anslinger, Field Information Circular no. 14, Oct. 7, 1957, folder "(0370-3) Field Information Circulars, 1–170," box 56, RG 170, NARA.

8. Cusack to Anslinger, March 27, 1959; Speer to Cusack, April 22, 1959; Cusack to Anslinger, Jan. 5, 1961; and, generally, folder "(0660-A-1C) General Correspondence District #17, 1959 thru June 1961," box 165, RG 170, NARA.

9. Siragusa addendum to memo from Cusack to Speer, May 27, 1959; Cusack to Giordano, July 20, 1959; Cusack to all District 17 agents, Aug. 11, 1959; Cusack to Speer, Aug. 11, 1959; Giordano to Cusack, Aug. 24, 1959; and Cusack to Anslinger, Nov. 20, 1959, folder "(0660-A-1C) General Correspondence District #17, 1959 thru June 1961," box 165, RG 170, NARA.

10. "One U.S. agency operating abroad"—the CIA—"has made a science of this technique," Cusack continued. "So far as I know, the FBI, Customs, State Department Security, I&N, ONI and the U.S. Army CID and CIC use it extensively." Cusack to Giordano, Nov. 12, 1962, folder "(0660-A-1C) General Correspondence District #17, July 1961 thru December 1962," box 165; Siragusa and Cusack, Jan. 14, 23, and 29, 1963, folder "(0660-A-1C), General Correspondence District #17, January 1963 thru September 1963," box 165, RG 170, NARA.

11. Siragusa to Anslinger, May 20, 1960 folder "(0660-A-1C) General Correspondence District #17, 1959 thru June 1961," box 165; Speer to Anslinger, May 26, 1960; folder "Foreign Reports, Dist #17, Secret File #8, April 1960 thru Aug. 1960," box 12, entry 10; and Cusack to Giordano, Oct. 15, 1962, folder "(0660-A-1C) General Correspondence District #17, July 1961 thru December 1962," box 165, RG 170, NARA.

12. Speer and Cusack, May 20 and 27, 1959, folder "(0660-A-1C) General Correspondence District #17, 1959 thru June 1961," box 165, RG 170, NARA.

13. Speer to Anslinger, Feb. 4, 1960; Cusack to Speer, May 27, 1959; and Siragusa to Anslinger, May 20, 1960, folder "(0660-A-1C) General Correspondence District #17, 1959 thru June 1961," box 165, RG 170, NARA.

14. Knight, report, March 30, 1959, folder "(0660) Turkey #9, 1957–1959," box 164; Cusack to Speer, June 18, 1959; Cusack to Anslinger, Feb. 12, 1960; and Anthony Mangiaracina, March 31, 1960, folder "(0660-A-1C) General Correspondence District #17, 1959 thru June 1961," box 165, RG 170, NARA.

15. Anslinger to Cusack, Jan. 11, 1960, folder "(0660-A-1C) General Correspondence District #17, 1959 thru June 1961," box 165, RG 170, NARA.

16. Cusack quoted in addendum to report by Agent Andrew Tartaglino, July 22, 1959, folder "(0660-A-1C) General Correspondence District #17, 1959 thru June 1961," box 165; and Speer to Anslinger, June 29, 1960, folder "Foreign Reports, Dist #17, Secret File #8, April 1960 thru Aug. 1960," box 12, entry 10, RG 170, NARA.

17. "Overseas Orientation Report; Paris, France," May 24, 1966, folder "(0280-17, Overseas) Overseas Orientation, 1963–1967," box 49, RG 170, NARA; Alfred W. McCoy, *The Politics of Heroin: CIA Complicity in the Global Drug Trade* (Chicago: Lawrence Hill Books, 2003), 46–76.

18. Tartaglino report, Oct. 18, 1960, folder "Foreign Reports, Dist #17, Secret File #9, Sept. 1960 thru Sept. 1961," box 12, entry 10; Anslinger to Morlock, April 4, 1947; and Cecil Gray to Secretary of State, Oct. 3, 1947, folder "(0660) France #2, 1945–1950," box 156, RG 170, NARA.

19. Siragusa to Anslinger, July 16, 1953; Knight to Siragusa, July 16, 1953; Siragusa to Bailleul, July 21, 1953; Siragusa to Anslinger, Dec. 23, 1953; Bailleul to White, Oct. 8, 1955; Siragusa to Anslinger, Dec. 2, 1955; and Siragusa to Anslinger, April 24, 1958, folder "(0660) France, French Police, Agent Siragusa," box 156. See also Cusack to Speer, Dec. 12, 1960, folder "Foreign Reports, Dist #17, Secret File #9, Sept. 1960 thru Sept. 1961," box 12, entry 10, RG 170, NARA.

20. Ryan to Anslinger, Nov. 17, 1955; Siragusa to Anslinger, Dec. 3, 1955; Charles Vaille (chief, Central Pharmacy Service) to Anslinger, Jan. 6, 1956; generally, folder "(0660, France) Alleged French Diversion," box 156; Cusack to Anslinger, Oct. 15, 1959, folder "(0660) France, Heroin Diversion, January 1962 thru–," box 156; and memos between Cusack, Speer, and Anslinger, July 14 and Aug. 16, 1960, folder "Foreign Reports, Dist #17, Secret File #8, April 1960 thru Aug. 1960," box 12, entry 10, RG 170, NARA.

21. Anslinger to E. H. Foley (assistant Treasury secretary), March 22, 1951, folder "(0660-A) 1949–1965," box 164; Siragusa to Anslinger, Dec. 21, 1954, folder "(0660) France, Sicot File #1, I.C.P.C. (M. Sicot), 1952 thru 1954," box 156; and, generally, folders "(0145-23A) Interpol, Region 17, 1950–1956" and "(0145-23a) Interpol, 1957–1957," box 46, RG 170, NARA; Michael Fooner, *Interpol: Issues in World Crime and International Criminal Justice* (New York: Plenum, 1989), 53–56.

22. Siragusa to Anslinger, Feb. 9, 1957, folder "(0660-A-1C) General Correspondence District #17, 1956 thru 1958," box 165; Tartaglino to Anslinger, June 10, 1959; Giordano to Cusack, June 10, 1959; and Cusack to Giordano, June 18, 1959, folder "(0620-13) Paris Branch Office," box 150, RG 170, NARA.

23. Cusack to Cemal Goktan (director general, Directorate of Public Security), June 8, 1959; Cusack to Anslinger, June 30, 1959; and Williams to Anslinger, Jan. 30, 1959, folder "(0660) Turkey #9, 1957–1959," box 164. See also, generally, folder "(0660) Turkey #10, Jan. 1960–1961," box 164, RG 170, NARA; Ryan Gingeras, "Istanbul Confidential: Heroin, Espionage, and Politics in Cold War Turkey, 1945–1960," *Diplomatic History* 37, no. 4 (2013): 779–806; and Matthew R. Pembleton, "Imagining a Global Sovereignty: U.S. Counternarcotic Operations in Istanbul during the Early Cold War and the Origins of the Foreign 'War on Drugs,'" *Journal of Cold War Studies* 18, no. 2 (2016): 28–63.

24. William B. McAllister, *Drug Diplomacy in the Twentieth Century: An International History* (London: Routledge, 2000), 196–97; Nathaniel Lee Smith, "'Cured of the Habit by Force': The United States and the Global Campaign to Punish Drug Consumers, 1898–1970" (Ph.D. diss., University of North Carolina, 2007), 216–23.

25. See margins in Cusack letter, June 30, 1959, and Siragusa to Anslinger, Feb. 16, 1959, folder "(0660) Turkey #9, 1957–1959," box 164, RG 170, NARA.

26. Vizzini reports, Jan. 26 and March 16, 1960; Cusack to Anslinger, April 14, 1960, folder "(0660) Turkey #10, Jan. 1960–1961," box 164; and Speer and Siragusa memos

to Anslinger, May 5 and May 20, 1960, folder "(0660-A-1C) General Correspondence District #17, 1959 thru June 1961," box 165, RG 170, NARA.

27. Christopher Gunn, "The 1960 Coup in Turkey: A U.S. Intelligence Failure or a Successful Intervention?," *Journal of Cold War Studies* 17, no. 2 (2015): 103–39.

28. Folder "(0660) Turkey #10, Jan. 1960–1961," box 164; and Cusack to Siragusa, July 5, 1962, folder "(0620-13) Istanbul Branch Office, 1960–1967," box 150, RG 170, NARA. See also Ryan Gingeras, "In the Hunt for the 'Sultans of Smack': Dope, Gangsters and the Construction of the Turkish Deep State," *Middle East Journal* 65, no. 3 (2011): 426–41; and Gingeras, "Istanbul Confidential." Vizzini described Eren and Labernas as "my good friends. They saved my life more than once. But I didn't tell them about my informants." Vizzini, Fraley, and Smith, *Vizzini*, 96.

29. Cusack to Anslinger, June 23, 1960, folder "(0620–13) Istanbul Branch Office, 1960–1967," box 150; Cusack to Anslinger, Sept. 22, 1960; and Cusack to Colonel Fevzi Arsin (director general, Turkish National Police), Jan. 26, 1961, folder "(0660) Turkey #10, Jan. 1960–1961," box 164. See also Cusack to Anslinger, July 15, 1960; Cusack to Vizzini, Jan. 5, 1961; Vizzini, report dated March 14, 1961; and Cusack to Anslinger, March 24, 1961, folder "(0660-A-1C) General Correspondence District #17, 1959 thru June 1961," box 165, RG 170, NARA; and Vizzini, Fraley, and Smith, *Vizzini*, 185–202.

30. Tartaglino memo, June 23, 1959, folder "(0620-13) Paris Branch Office," box 150. See also Anthony Pohl, memos dated Dec. 19, 1960, and June 25, 1961, and Speer to Anslinger, May 24, 1961, folder "(0660) France #4, 1954–June 1961," box 156; and Agent Albert Garofalo, Nov. 4, 1963, folder "(0660) France #5, July 1961 thru June 1965," box 159, RG 170, NARA.

31. Tartaglino to Cusack, July 22, 1959, cross-filed in folders "(0660) France #4, 1954–June 1961," box 156, and "(0660-A-1C) General Correspondence District #17, 1959 thru June 1961," box 165, RG 170, NARA.

32. Speer to Gaffney, April, 12, 1961, folders "(0660-A-1C) General Correspondence District #17, 1959 thru June 1961," box 165, and, generally, "(0620-13) Paris Branch Office," box 150, RG 170, NARA.

33. Speer to Cusack, Aug. 16, 1960; Speer to Anslinger, June 29, 1960; and Cusack to Speer, Dec. 12, 1960, folders "Foreign Reports, Dist #17, Secret File #8, April 1960 thru Aug. 1960" and "Foreign Reports, Dist #17, Secret File #9, Sept. 1960 thru Sept. 1961," box 12, entry 10, RG 170, NARA.

34. "Arrest Envoy in Dope Ring," *Chicago Tribune,* Oct. 4, 1960; "Guatemalan Envoy Held as Smuggler of Heroin into U.S.," *New York Times,* Oct. 6, 1960; "7 Indicted as Part of Narcotics Ring," *New York Times,* Nov. 1, 1960; Jill Jonnes, *Hep-Cats, Narcs, and Pipe Dreams: A History of America's Romance with Illegal Drugs* (New York: Scribner, 1996), 179–87; Valentine, *Strength of the Wolf,* 202–5.

35. "France, the Principal Source of Illicit Heroin in the United States," Jan. 11, 1961, and undated memo, "Comments on the Illicit Narcotic Traffic between France and the United States," folder "(0660) France #4, 1954–June 1961," box 156; and Cusack, Progress Report for Oct. 1960, folder "(1825-7) Reports Progress Dist #17, 1960," box 83, RG 170, NARA.

36. Tartaglino, Oct. 18, 1960, folder "Foreign Reports, Dist #17, Secret File #9, Sept. 1960 thru Sept. 1961," box 12, entry 10, RG 170, NARA.

37. Anslinger to Herve Alphand (French ambassador), Oct. 21, 1960; Anslinger memo, Jan. 19, 1961; undated memo, "Comments on the Illicit Narcotic Traffic between

France and the United States"; Speer to Anslinger, Jan. 10 and 31, 1961; Siragusa to Anslinger, Feb. 6, 1961; and Speer to Anslinger, Jan. 31 and Feb. 28, 1961, folder "(0660) France #4, 1954–June 1961," box 156, RG 170, NARA.

38. Anslinger provided this information to Assistant Treasury Secretary A. Gilmore Flues and requested that President Kennedy take action in a letter dated April 4, 1961. Anslinger's language was used in a letter from Treasury Secretary Douglas Dillon to Secretary of State Dean Rusk dated April 21, 1961. The American Embassy in Paris then reported presenting this information in a telegram dated May 1, 1961. See also Siragusa to Anslinger, May 23, 1961, folder "(0660) France #4, 1954–June 1961," box 156, RG 170, NARA.

39. Memos from Speer to Anslinger, May 24, 1961, folder "(0660) France #4, 1954–June 1961," box 156, RG 170, NARA.

40. Speer to Cusack, Feb. 28, 1961; and Cusack to Anslinger, March 20, 1961, folder "(0660-A-1C) General Correspondence District #17, 1959 thru June 1961," box 165, RG 170, NARA; Valentine, *Strength of the Wolf,* 275–76.

41. Siragusa, Progress Report no. 41-A, May 3, 1951, folder "(0660) France #3, 1951–1953," box 156; Speer to Anslinger, May 16, 1961; Cusack to Giordano, July 21, 1961; Pera, Oct. 17, 1961, folder "(0660-A-1C) General Correspondence District #17, 1959 thru June 1961," box 165; Cusack to Anslinger, March 21, 1961; Speer to Cusack, July 12, 1961; and Pohl reports, June 10 and 25 and July 2 and 4, 1961, folder "(0660) France #4, 1954–June 1961," box 156; and Cusack to Anslinger, July 27, 1960, folder "Foreign Reports, Dist #17, Secret File #8, April 1960 thru Aug. 1960," box 12, entry 10, RG 170, NARA.

42. Robin Moore, *The French Connection: A True Account of Cops, Narcotics, and International Conspiracy* (Guilford, CT: Lyons Press, 2003); Valentine, *Strength of the Wolf,* 263–79.

43. Cusack to Anslinger, Dec. 22, 1960, folder "(0660-A-1C) General Correspondence District #17, 1959 thru June 1961," box 165, RG 170, NARA. Perhaps it was no coincidence that in 1961, Garland Williams was reassigned to sub-Saharan Africa, where he served out the remainder of his government service until 1963. U.S. Civil Service Commission, Personnel Form, "Garland Williams," folder "Williams, Garland," box 8, Valentine Collection.

44. Philip Nichols Jr. (commissioner of Customs) to James A. Reed (assistant Treasury secretary), Aug. 6, 1962, folder "(0280-18) Bureau Overseas Operation, Consolidation of Treasury Enforcement Program, June 1962 thru December 1963," box 49, RG 170, NARA.

45. State Dept. cable from FBN to Siragusa, Sept. 21, 1956, State Dept. CDF, 1955–1959, 102.14, RG 59, NARA; Tartaglino, Oct. 18, 1960, folder "Foreign Reports, Dist #17, Secret File #9, Sept. 1960 thru Sept. 1961," box 12, entry 10; and Nichols to Reed, Aug. 6, 1962, folder "(0280-18) Bureau Overseas Operation, Consolidation of Treasury Enforcement Program, June 1962 thru December 1963," box 49, RG 170, NARA.

46. Cusack to Giordano, Aug. 28, 1962; and Siragusa to Giordano, Gaffney, and DeBaggio, Sept. 7, 1962, folder "(0280-18) Bureau Overseas Operation, Consolidation of Treasury Enforcement Program, June 1962 thru December 1963," box 49, RG 170, NARA.

47. Anslinger to Flues (assistant Treasury secretary), Dec. 13, 1961, folder "Foreign Reports, Dist #17, Secret File #10, Oct. 1961 thru Dec. 1963," entry 10, box 12, RG 170, NARA.

48. B. T. Mitchell to Ernest Gentry, May 20, 1953, folder "(0660) Communist China, 1952–1954," box 153, RG 170, NARA.

49. Harry J. Anslinger and William F. Tompkins, *The Traffic in Narcotics* (New York: Funk and Wagnalls, 1953), 54–56; McCoy, *Politics of Heroin.*

50. Anslinger frequently cited Deverall's pamphlet *Mao Tze-tung: Stop This Dirty Opium Business* as "a good piece of work" and sent copies to officials at Radio Free Europe (letter to Philip Gould, June 30, 1954), influential journalists like Victor Riesel (letter from Reisel, March 11, 1955), and concerned citizens (letters to John J. Iago and Eugene Doorman, Aug. 31 and Nov. 30, 1954). Folders "(0660) Communist China, 1952–1954" and "(0660) Communist China, 1955–1958," box 153, RG 170, NARA.

51. Correspondence between Anslinger and Ed Reid, Jan. 22 and 26, 1954, folder "(0660) Communist China, 1952–1954," box 153; and numerous items between Anslinger and Committee of One Million member Marvin Liebman, folder "(0660) Communist China, 1955–1958," box 153, RG 170, NARA. See also Valentine, *Strength of the Wolf,* 68–70, 76–79; and Jonathan Marshall, "Cooking the Books: The Federal Bureau of Narcotics, the China Lobby and Cold War Propaganda, 1950–1962," *Asia-Pacific Journal: Japan Focus* 11, no. 37 (2013).

52. Don T. Christensen (consul), State Dept. report, Dec. 14, 1963, folder "(0660) Burma, 1960–1967," box 152; U.S. Army intelligence report, Feb. 17, 1957, folder "(0660) Thailand, Safe #1, thru Dec. 1963," box 10, entry 10, RG 170, NARA.

53. White to Anslinger, Aug. 28 and Sept. 1, 1944, folder "(0660) Burma, 1937–1954," box 152, RG 170, NARA.

54. Speer to Anslinger, April 16, 1952, and July 4, 1954, folder "(0660) Communist China, 1952–1954," box 153; Speer to Anslinger, July 15, 1954, folder "(0660) Thailand, 1949–1956," box 163; Speer to Anslinger, July 28, 1954, folder "(0660) Burma, 1937–1954," box 152; and, generally, folder "(0660-A-3) Wayland Speer's Foreign Assignment, Correspondence and General File," box 165, RG 170, NARA.

55. Speer to Anslinger, July 17, 1954, folder "(0660) Thailand, 1949–1956," box 163, RG 170, NARA. The "former OSS man" was Jim Thompson, a.k.a. the "Silk King of Thailand."

56. Speer to Anslinger, July 16 and 20, 1954, folder "(0660) Thailand, 1949–1956," box 163, RG 170, NARA; Denis D. Gray, "America's OSS Agents: Thai 'Students' Remember Daring World War II Exploits," *Los Angeles Times,* Nov. 29, 1987.

57. Speer to Anslinger, July 16–24, 1954, and, generally, folder "(0660) Thailand, 1949–1956," box 163, RG 170, NARA.

58. State Dept. reports by Vice-Consul Eric V. Youngquist, June 29 and July 25, 1955, and Economic Officer Harry Conover, April 23, 1956. See also Anslinger to Vaille, Sept. 14, 1955, folder "(0660) Thailand, 1949–1956," box 163; State Dept. cable, Dec. 15, 1958; Williams to Leonard Unger (American Embassy, Bangkok), Sept. 23, 1959, folder "(0660) Thailand, 1957–1963," box 163; and report by Thai police, "The Narcotic Aspect in Thailand," forwarded to Giordano by Treasury Dept. official Arnold Sagalyn, Feb. 18, 1964, folder "(0660) Thailand, 1964–1965," box 163, RG 170, NARA.

59. Cusack to Anslinger, Oct. 28, 1961, folder "(0660) Communist China, 1959–1961," box 153; Cusack reports, Feb. 23, 1962, folder "(0660) Thailand, 1957–1963," box 163; March 2, 1962, folder "(0660) Communist China, 1962–1963," box 153; and Nov. 30, 1961, folder "Foreign Reports, Dist #17, Secret File #10, Oct. 1961 thru Dec. 1963," box 12, entry 10, RG 170, NARA. See also Jonathan Kwitny, *The Crimes of Patriots: A*

True Tale of Dope, Dirty Money, and the CIA (New York: Simon and Schuster, 1987), 211–13; and Thomas Fuller, "William Young, Who Helped U.S. Organize Secret War in Laos, Is Dead at 76," *New York Times,* April 3, 2011.

60. Vizzini, Fraley, and Smith, *Vizzini,* 220–22.
61. Folder "(0660) Thailand, 1957–1963," box 163, and folder "Dist 16, Confidential #1," box 12, entry 10, RG 170; State Dept. telegram, Oct. 13, 1962, State Dept. CDF, 1960–1963, 102.14, RG 59, NARA; Leslie H. Whitten, "Ton of Raw Opium Seized by Agents," *Washington Post,* Oct. 19, 1962.
62. See, generally, folder "(0280-18) Bureau Overseas Operation, Consolidation of Treasury Enforcement Program, June 1962 thru December 1963," box 49, RG 170; and State Dept. telegrams, Aug. 1 and 8, 1962, State Dept. CDF, 1960–1963, 102.1402, RG 59, NARA.
63. John F. Kennedy, "Remarks to the White House Conference on Narcotic and Drug Abuse," Sept. 27, 1962, American Presidency Project, UC–Santa Barbara, www.presidency.ucsb.edu.
64. Cusack to all agents of District 17, Nov. 27, 1962, folder "(0660-A-1C) General Correspondence District #17, July 1961 thru December 1962," box 165. For a list of foreign offices and FBN districts, see Siragusa to CIA Deputy Director of Plans, May 6, 1963, folder "(0280-18) Bureau Overseas Operation, Consolidation of Treasury Enforcement Program, June 1962 thru December 1963." Generally, see also folder "(0280-17, Overseas) Overseas Orientation, 1963–1967," box 49, RG 170, NARA.
65. Reed to Giordano, Oct. 22, 1962, folder "(0280-18) Bureau Overseas Operation, Consolidation of Treasury Enforcement Program, June 1962 thru December 1963," box 49, RG 170, NARA.
66. Vizzini, Fraley, and Smith, *Vizzini,* 227–39, 310; Vizzini to Giordano, Oct. 8, 1962, Siragusa to Bangkok Embassy, Oct. 8, 1962; and James P. Hendrick (Treasury) to Henry L. Koren (State Dept.), Jan. 21, 1963, folder "Dist 16, Confidential #1," box 12, entry 10, RG 170, NARA.
67. Patrick O'Carroll to Giordano, Dec. 10, 1963, folder "(0660) Thailand, 1957–1963," box 163; and State Dept. cable, Dec. 29, 1962, folder "Dist 16, Confidential #1," box 12, entry 10, RG 170, NARA.
68. Gaffney (deputy commissioner) to Michal F. Cross (Treasury), Jan. 26, 1967, folder "(0660) Communist China, 1964–1967," box 153, RG 170, NARA.
69. McAllister, *Drug Diplomacy in the Twentieth Century,* 185–211.
70. Anslinger to Charles Vaille (French police official), July 11, 1955, folder "(0660) France #4, 1954–June 1961," box 156, RG 170, NARA.
71. McCoy, *Politics of Heroin;* Jonathan Marshall, *The Lebanese Connection: Corruption, Civil War, and the International Drug Traffic* (Stanford, CA: Stanford University Press, 2012); Valentine, *Strength of the Wolf;* Douglas Valentine, *The Strength of the Pack: The Personalities, Politics and Espionage Intrigues That Shaped the DEA* (Waltersville, OR: Trine Day, 2008); H. P. Albarelli Jr., *A Terrible Mistake: The Murder of Frank Olson and the CIA's Secret Cold War Experiments* (Waltersville, OR: Trine Day, 2009); Gingeras, "Istanbul Confidential"; Alan Block and John C. McWilliams, "On the Origins of American Counterintelligence: Building a Clandestine Network," *Journal of Policy History* 1, no. 4 (1989): 353–72; John C. McWilliams, "Covert Connections: The FBN, the OSS, and the CIA," *Historian* 53, no. 4 (1991): 657–79.
72. Sidney Gottlieb to Anslinger, Sept. 7, 1961, folder "(4004-A) Confidential," box 164, RG 170, NARA.

73. Anslinger to Assistant Treasury Secretary Rose, Oct. 29, 1953, folder "(0660) Lebanon, 1945–1953," box 160; Siragusa to Deputy Director of Plans (CIA), May 6, 1963, folder "(0280-18) Bureau Overseas Operation, Consolidation of Treasury Enforcement Program, June 1962 thru December 1963," box 49. In a report dated May 20, 1960, Siragusa describes "2 long talks" with Manfredi and a CIA official in Rome regarding a "diplomat who wishes to defect" and information furnished by Siragusa to the CIA: folder "(0660-A-1C) General Correspondence District #17, 1959 thru June 1961," box 165. See also folder "Foreign Reports, Dist #17, Secret File #9, Sept. 1960 thru Sept. 1961," box 12, entry 10, RG 170, NARA.
74. William Colby and Peter Forbath, *Honorable Men: My Life in the CIA* (New York: Simon and Schuster, 1978), 131–33; Tripodi and DeSario, *Crusade;* Vizzini, Fraley, and Smith, *Vizzini,* 166–84, 241–42; Valentine, *Strength of the Wolf,* 190–205. See also Arthur Giuliani to George White, March 31, 1958, folder 16, box 3, White Papers.
75. Siragusa to Anslinger, June 29, 1956, and Feb. 15 and May 29, 1957; and Cunningham to Siragusa, June 7, 1957. A July 15, 1960, memo from Cusack to Anslinger similarly reports, "Agent Manfredi will continue to do Mafia research as well as concentrate on several highly classified special investigations." Folders "(0660-A-1C) General Correspondence District #17, 1956 thru 1958" and "(0660-A-1C) General Correspondence District #17, 1959 thru June 1961," box 165, RG 170, NARA. See also Valentine, *Strength of the Wolf,* 113. Vizzini identified Manfredi as a CIA officer who investigated but did not run Luciano. Vizzini, Fraley, and Smith, *Vizzini,* 145.
76. Bruce Bullington and Alan Block, "A Trojan Horse: Anti-communism and the War on Drugs," *Contemporary Crises* 14, no. 1 (1990): 39–55; Jonathan Marshall, *Drug Wars: Corruption, Counterinsurgency and Covert Operations in the Third World* (Forestville, CA: Cohan & Cohen, 1991).
77. Knight, July 16, 1953, "(0660) France, French Police, Agent Siragusa," box 156; and Knight to Siragusa, Nov. 29, 1955, folder "(0660) Lebanon #3 (1955–1960)," box 160, RG 170, NARA.
78. Mark Philip Bradley, "The Ambiguities of Sovereignty: The United States and the Global Human Rights Cases of the 1940s and 1950s," in *The State of Sovereignty: Territories, Laws, Populations,* edited by Douglas Howland and Luise White (Bloomington: Indiana University Press, 2009).
79. Frederick T. Merrill, Foreign Service Despatch, Sept. 15, 1952, State Dept. CDF, 1950–1954, 882.53 (box 5433), RG 59, NARA.
80. Joe Arpaio and Len Sherman, *Joe's Law: America's Toughest Sheriff Takes on Illegal Immigration, Drugs, and Everything Else That Threatens America* (New York: AMACOM, 2008), 189.
81. Cusack to Anslinger, March 27, 1959; and Giordano to Cusack, April 2, 1959, folder "(0145-23a) Interpol, 1957–1957," box 46, RG 170, NARA.
82. Siragusa to Ross Ellis (district supervisor, Detroit), Oct. 5, 1955, folder "(0660-A-1C) General Correspondence District #17, 1951 thru 1955," box 165, RG 170, NARA. Countless examples of travel arrangements can be found throughout the General Correspondence files for District 17. See also "Henry L. Manfredi Dies at 54; Aide to Narcotics Bureau Head," *New York Times,* Jan. 8, 1970.
83. Charles Siragusa and Robert Wiedrich, *The Trail of the Poppy: Behind the Mask of the Mafia* (Englewood Cliffs, NJ: Prentice Hall, 1966), 5, 32.
84. Siragusa to Anslinger, Progress Report no. 43, May 5, 1951, folder "(0660) France #3,

1951–1953," box 156. See also Siragusa, Progress Report no. 45, Oct. 16, 1950, folder "Progress Reports of Charles Siragusa," box 164, RG 170, NARA.

85. Siragusa to Anslinger, Oct. 4, 1951, folder "(0660-A-1C) General Correspondence District #17, 1951 thru 1955," box 165, RG 170, NARA.

86. Siragusa comments on Greek official Gerasimos Liarommatis (of the Abou Sayia case), folder "(0660-A-1C) General Correspondence District #17, 1951 thru 1955," box 165; and Manfredi to Giordano, Jan. 24, 1962, folder "(0280-17, Overseas) Overseas Orientation, 1963–1967," box 49, RG 170, NARA.

87. Williams to Anslinger, Feb. 18, 1949, folder "(0660) Turkey #4, 1949–June 1950," box 25; and Siragusa, Progress Report no. 14, Aug. 17, 1950, folder "Progress Reports of Charles Siragusa," box 164, RG 170, NARA.

88. "International Coalition for the Responsibility to Protect," www.responsibilityto protect.org.

89. Anslinger to Jacques Boudoin, May 29, 1951, folder "(0660) France #3, 1951–1953," box 156, RG 170, NARA.

90. Jay Richard Kennedy, "One World—against Dope," *Sunday Star: This Week Magazine,* March 7, 1948, folder 13, box 1, Anslinger Papers.

91. Michael E. Latham, *The Right Kind of Revolution: Modernization, Development, and U.S. Foreign Policy from the Cold War to the Present* (Ithaca, NY: Cornell University Press, 2011); Daniel Weimer, *Seeing Drugs: Modernization, Counterinsurgency, and U.S. Narcotics Control in the Third World, 1969–1976* (Kent, OH: Kent State University Press, 2011).

92. Alfred W. McCoy and Francisco A. Scarano, eds., *Colonial Crucible: Empire in the Making of the Modern American State* (Madison: University of Wisconsin Press, 2009).

93. Siragusa to Anslinger, Feb. 28, 1954, and July 28, 1955, folder "(0660) Italy #5, 1952–1956," box 159; and, generally, folders "(0660-A-1C) General Correspondence District #17, 1951 thru 1955" and "(0660-A-1C) General Correspondence District #17, 1956 thru 1958," box 165, RG 170, NARA.

94. Cusack to John Enright (assistant to the commissioner), June 30, 1966, folder "(0280-18 #2) Bureau Overseas Operation, Consolidation of Treasury Enforcement Program, January 1964 thru December 31, 1967," box 49, RG 170, NARA.

95. Unsigned memo (from Cusack) to Giordano, July 19, 1966, folder "(0280-18 #2) Bureau Overseas Operation, Consolidation of Treasury Enforcement Program, January 1964 thru December 31, 1967," box 49, RG 170, NARA.

96. Manfredi, "Liaison Training Paper," May 6, 1966, folder "(0280-17, Overseas) Overseas Orientation, 1963–1967," box 49, RG 170, NARA.

97. Picini to Giordano, March 16, 1966, folder "(0280-17, Overseas) Overseas Orientation, 1963–1967," box 49, RG 170, NARA.

CHAPTER 8

1. Henry L. Giordano, "Harry Anslinger, the First United States Narcotic Commissioner," 1962 Remington Medal Dinner, Dec. 4, 1962, folder 14, box 1, Anslinger Papers.

2. "Tough Narcotics Chief, Henry Luke Giordano," *New York Times,* July 9, 1962.

3. Morton Mintz, "Anslinger Resigns as Narcotics Chief," *Washington Post,* July 6, 1962; "Tough Narcotics Chief, Henry Luke Giordano"; Wolfgang Saxon, "Henry

Giordano, 89, Head of Narcotics Bureau in 60's," *New York Times,* Oct. 10, 2003. Giordano's pharmaceutical background was probably decisive, and Anslinger tipped executive James G. Flanagan (president of S. B. Penick) to his impending appointment in a letter dated April 29, 1962, folder 5, box 2, Anslinger Papers.

4. Mintz, "Anslinger Resigns as Narcotics Chief"; Nixon to Anslinger, Jan. 12, 1970, folder 1, box 2, Anslinger Papers; and Anslinger to White, Dec. 17, 1963, folder 18, box 3, White Papers; Douglas Valentine, *The Strength of the Wolf: The Secret History of America's War on Drugs* (London: Verso, 2004), 281.

5. Valentine, *Strength of the Wolf,* 216–18; Jill Jonnes, *Hep-Cats, Narcs, and Pipe Dreams: A History of America's Romance with Illegal Drugs* (New York: Scribner, 1996), 193–94; Theodore W. Hendricks, "Former U.S. Narcotics Official Here Faces 14-Count Indictment," *Baltimore Sun,* July 11, 1968.

6. Anslinger, Field Information Circular no. 103, Jan. 16, 1962; and Giordano, Field Information Circular no. 112, Sept. 13, 1962, folder "(0370-3) Field Information Circulars, 1–170," box 56, RG 170, NARA; Anslinger to White, Dec. 17, [1963], folder 18, box 3, White Papers; "Siragusa Gets State Crime Job; Tells Plan," *Chicago Tribune,* Nov. 14, 1963; Valentine, *Strength of the Wolf,* 281.

7. See, generally, folder "(1515-13) Officers, Complaints against, thru May 31, 1967," box 11, entry 10 (Classified Subject Files), RG 170, NARA. See also Hendricks, "Former U.S. Narcotics Official Here Faces 14-Count Indictment"; "Probe of U.S. Narcotics Unite near End; Arrests Expected," *Baltimore Sun,* Dec. 14, 1968; "32 U.S. Narcotics Agents Resign in Corruption Investigation Here," *New York Times,* Dec. 14, 1968; David Burnham, "Graft Study Finds Inaction by Police in 72 Drug Cases," *New York Times,* Aug. 14, 1972; Jonnes, *Hep-Cats, Narcs, and Pipe Dreams,* 191–201; T. J. English, *The Savage City: Race, Murder, and a Generation on the Edge* (New York: HarperCollins, 2011).

8. John F. Kennedy, "Remarks to the White House Conference on Narcotic and Drug Abuse," Sept. 27, 1962; and Robert F. Kennedy, "Address to White House Conference on Narcotic and Drug Abuse," Sept. 28, 1962, Department of Justice, Speeches of Attorney General Robert F. Kennedy, www.justice.gov; "Dillon Swears in Giordano as Narcotics Bureau Head," *New York Times,* Aug. 18, 1962.

9. Giordano, Field Information Circular no. 123, Dec. 17, 1962, including O'Carroll's summary and statements by Giordano and DeBaggio, folder "(0370-3) Field Information Circulars, 1–170," box 56, RG 170, NARA.

10. Charles Grutzner, "Grave Peril Seen in Sleeping Pills," *New York Times,* Dec. 16, 1951; White to Harney, Feb. 24, 1971, folder 18, box 3, White Papers; Anslinger, remarks at UN-CND, May 29, 1957, folder 8, box 1; and Austin Smith, MD (Pharmaceutical Manufacturers Association), to James G. Flanagan (S. B. Penick), May 31, 1962, folder 6, box 2, Anslinger Papers.

11. "Barbiturates Held More Dangerous than Dope," *Washington Post,* Oct. 15, 1955; "Illegal Barbiturates Held Threat to Youth," *Los Angeles Times,* Aug. 10, 1961; Howard Hertel and Don Neff, "Marilyn Monroe Found Dead, Sleeping Pill Overdose Blamed," *Los Angeles Times,* Aug. 6, 1962; Gene Sherman, "White House Parley to Study Barbiturates," *Los Angeles Times,* Sept. 23, 1962; Andrea Tone, *The Age of Anxiety: A History of America's Turbulent Affair with Tranquilizers* (New York: Basic Books, 2009); Dominique A. Tobbell, *Pills, Power, and Policy: The Struggle for Drug Reform in Cold War America and Its Consequences* (Berkeley: University of California Press, 2012).

12. Giordano, Field Information Circular no. 123, Dec. 17, 1962, folder "(0370-3) Field Information Circulars, 1–170," box 56, RG 170, NARA.

13. "Narcotics Study Unit Named by President," *Washington Post,* Jan. 17, 1963; Dr. Roger O. Egeberg quoted in Gene Sherman, "New U.S. Narcotics Policy Heralded in Panel's Findings," *Los Angeles Times,* Feb. 10, 1963; "Narcotics Law Report Stresses Rehabilitation," *Washington Post,* Jan. 20, 1964; William Knighton, "Antidope Drive Begun," *Baltimore Sun,* July 16, 1964; Louis Cassels, "Estimate 60,000 Americans Are Narcotics Habit Victims," *Chicago Daily Defender,* April 8, 1965.

14. Jack Kelly and Richard Mathison, *On the Street* (Chicago: Henry Regnery, 1974), 203.

15. John Finlator, *The Drugged Nation: A "Narc's" Story* (New York: Simon and Schuster, 1973), 22–23. See also "Act of July 15, 1965" (Drug Abuse Control Amendments of 1965), Public Law 89-74, 79 STAT 226.

16. Finlator, *Drugged Nation,* 22–55.

17. Memo dated Oct. 10, 1966, folder "(1685-4 #1) Public Health—Department of Health, Education and Welfare, Bureau of Drug Abuse Control, May 1966 thru July 31, 1967," box 69, RG 170, NARA.

18. Kelly and Mathison, *On the Street,* 203; Finlator, *Drugged Nation,* 22–55; Valentine, *Strength of the Wolf,* 380–84; Tom Tripodi and Joseph P. DeSario, *Crusade: Undercover against the Mafia and KGB* (Washington, DC: Brassey's, 1993), 155.

19. Fred Black, "New Federal Agency Aided in Pep Pill Raid," *Washington Post,* Jan. 27, 1967; "Reported 'Mr. LSD,' and Four Others Seized," *Los Angeles Times,* Dec. 22, 1967; Robert Wiedrich, "2 Million in Drugs Seized in U.S. Raid," *Chicago Tribune,* Jan. 28, 1968; Finlator, *Drugged Nation,* 22–55.

20. Lindesmith is quoted in Lee Berton, "Marijuana at Issue, Harsh Laws Challenged in Courts, Criticized within the Government," *Wall Street Journal,* Nov. 20, 1967; White to Paul Newey (former FBN agent) and Matthew O'Connor (CA Bureau Narcotic Enforcement), July 8 and 31, 1970, folder 1, box 4, White Papers.

21. Folder "Living Death," box 72; Giordano, statement before Senate Subcommittee to Investigate Juvenile Delinquency, March 5, 1968, folder "(1690-5) Giordano #8, Speeches, January 1968 thru January 1969," box 69, RG 170, NARA.

22. "Probe of Pot in Progress, HEW Admits," *Chicago Tribune,* Oct. 15, 1967; Berton, "Marijuana at Issue"; Finlator, *Drugged Nation,* 53–55, 179–221.

23. "Johnson Widens Narcotics Fight," *New York Times,* Feb. 8, 1968; "Drug Unit Is Approved by House," *Washington Post,* April 3, 1968; Finlator, *Drugged Nation,* 52–55.

24. "Notification of Transfer," April 8, 1968, folder "Manfredi, Hank," box 5, Valentine Collection; Giordano, statement before Senate Subcommittee to Investigate Juvenile Delinquency, March 5, 1968, folder "(1690-5) Giordano #8, Speeches, Jan. 1968 thru January 1969," box 69, RG 170, NARA; "Former Police Chief to Head U.S. Dope Unit," *Chicago Tribune,* July 13, 1968; "Ex-Police Chief Heads New U.S. Drug Bureau," *New York Times,* July 13, 1968; Joe Arpaio and Len Sherman, *Joe's Law: America's Toughest Sheriff Takes on Illegal Immigration, Drugs, and Everything Else That Threatens America* (New York: AMACOM, 2008), 179.

25. "32 U.S. Narcotics Agents Resign"; James Markham, "Narcotics Corruption Appears Easy and Common," *New York Times,* Dec. 23, 1972; Central Intelligence Agency, "Family Jewels," May 16, 1973, Central Intelligence Agency, Freedom of Information Electronic Reading Room, www.foia.cia.gov. See also Trafficante and Giancana

entries in U.S. Treasury Department, *Mafia: The Government's Secret File on Organized Crime* (New York: Skyhorse, 2009), 118, 144.

26. Ingersoll to Anslinger, July 11, 1969, folder 1, box 2, Anslinger Papers; "Narcotics Chief Says U.S. 'Failed Miserably' in Curbs," *New York Times,* Feb. 12, 1969; "U.S. to Switch Drug Tactics, Director Says," *Los Angeles Times,* March 26, 1969; David Burnham, "Police Setup on Vice Deplored as Making Corruption Easy," *New York Times,* Nov. 11, 1968.

27. Finlator, *Drugged Nation,* 85.

28. "Nixon: 'Toward Freedom from Fear,'" *Washington Post,* May 12, 1968; Nixon, address accepting the presidential nomination at the Republican National Convention, American Presidency Project, UC–Santa Barbara, www.presidency.ucsb.edu.

29. Analyzing Nixon's 1968 victory in an August 24, 1970, memo, Pat Buchanan argued, "Presidential elections in the coming decade will turn on the 'Social Issue,' . . . drugs, demonstrations, pornography, disruptions, 'kidlash,' permissiveness, violence, riots, crime. The voters will not tolerate a 'liberal,' on these issues." Campaign of 1970, box 6, President's Personal File, Richard Nixon Presidential Library and Museum, NARA. Special thanks to Sarah Thelen for this document.

30. Stuart Loory, "President Urges Tough New Laws on Illicit Drugs," *Los Angeles Times,* July 15, 1969; William Robbins, "Congress Gets Nixon's Bill to Curb Drug Abuses," *New York Times,* July 16, 1969; Drug Enforcement Administration, DEA History, "1970–1975," www.dea.gov.

31. "Head of Narcotics Bureau Will Stay on under Nixon," *New York Times,* Feb. 27, 1969; "Giordano Retires as Aide of U.S. Narcotics Bureau," *New York Times,* March 1, 1969.

32. Dial Torgerson, "Border Narcotics Check Backs Autos 3 1/2 Miles into Tijuana," *Los Angeles Times,* Sept. 19, 1963; A. D. Horne, "U.S. Halts Operation Intercept," *Washington Post,* Oct. 11, 1969; Arpaio and Sherman, *Joe's Law,* 45–47; Edward Jay Epstein, *Agency of Fear: Opiates and Political Power in America* (New York: G. P. Putnam's Sons, 1977), 46–53, 81–85.

33. U.S. Congress, Public Law 91-513, "Comprehensive Drub Abuse Prevention and Control Act of 1970," Oct. 27, 1970; Steven R. Belenko, ed., *Drugs and Drug Policy in America: A Documentary History* (Westport, CT: Greenwood Press, 2000), 276–84, 292–99.

34. U.S. Congress, Public Law 91-513, "Comprehensive Drub Abuse Prevention and Control Act of 1970"; Richard Nixon, "Remarks on Singing the Comprehensive Drug Abuse Prevention and Control Act of 1970," Oct. 27, 1970, American Presidency Project; Kathleen Frydl, *The Drug Wars in America, 1940–1973* (Cambridge: Cambridge University Press, 2013), 353–61; Belenko, *Drugs and Drug Policy,* 276–84.

35. Peter Carlson, "When Elvis Met Nixon," *Smithsonian Magazine,* Dec. 2010; "When Nixon Met Elvis," Nixon Presidential Materials, NARA; Ellen Fried, "From Pearl Harbor to Elvis: Images That Endure," *Prologue* (Winter 2004).

36. Richard Nixon, "Remarks about an Intensified Program for Drug Abuse Prevention and Control" and "Special Message to the Congress on Drug Abuse Prevention and Control," June 17, 1971, American Presidency Project; Robert Young, "Nixon Declares War on Narcotics Use in U.S.," *Chicago Tribune,* June 18, 1971; Dan Baum, *Smoke and Mirrors: The War on Drugs and the Politics of Failure* (Boston: Little and Brown, 1996).

37. Nixon, "Remarks about Intensified Program" and "Special Message to Congress," June 17, 1971.

38. Mathea Falco and John Pekkanen, "The Abuse of Drug Abuse," *Washington Post*, Sept. 8, 1974; Epstein, *Agency of Fear*, 72–78, 123–32; Michael Massing, *The Fix* (Berkeley: University of California Press, 1998), 102, 128–29.

39. "GI Heroin Epidemic Reported in Vietnam," *Los Angeles Times*, April 20, 1971; Michael Getler, "U.S. Vows Crackdown on Heroin Flows to GIs," *Washington Post*, May 28, 1971; Tom Buckley, "It's Always a Dead End on 'Scag Alley,'" *New York Times*, June 6, 1971; Epstein, *Agency of Fear*, 121–22; Massing, *The Fix*, 107–12.

40. Dana Adams Schmidt, "Addiction in Vietnam Spurs Nixon and Congress to Take Drastic New Steps," *New York Times*, June 16, 1971; Nixon, "Special Message to the Congress," June 17, 1971; Jeremy Kuzmarov, *The Myth of the Addicted Army: Vietnam and the Modern War on Drugs* (Amherst: University of Massachusetts Press, 2009); Eric C. Schneider, *Smack: Heroin and the American City* (Philadelphia: University of Pennsylvania Press, 2008), 159–81; Massing, *The Fix*, 113–20; Baum, *Smoke and Mirrors*, 48–58.

41. Epstein, *Agency of Fear*, 86–92; Joseph L. Zentner, "The 1972 Turkish Opium Ban: Needle in the Haystack Diplomacy?," *World Affairs* 136, no. 1 (1973): 36–47; Nasuh Uslu, *The Turkish-American Relationship between 1947 and 2003: The History of a Distinctive Alliance* (New York: Nova Science, 2003), 219–51.

42. Uslu, *Turkish-American Relationship*, 241–43; Epstein, *Agency of Fear*, 88, 242–45.

43. Epstein, *Agency of Fear*, 147–51.

44. Ibid., 194.

45. Ibid., 193–207.

46. "Nixon Sets Up Agency to Fight Drug Pushers," *Los Angeles Times*, Jan. 28, 1972; Felix Belair Jr., "President Opens Narcotics Drive," *New York Times*, Jan. 29, 1972; James M. Markham, "President Calls for 'Total War' on U.S. Addiction," *New York Times*, March 21, 1972; Aldo Beckham, "Legalized Pot Opposed by Nixon," *Chicago Tribune*, March 21, 1972; David Kraslow, "President Vows to Act unless Food Prices Fall," *Los Angeles Times*, March 25, 1972; Baum, *Smoke and Mirrors*, 71–72; Massing, *The Fix*, 136. The National Commission on Marihuana and Drug Abuse report *Marihuana: A Signal of Misunderstanding* is available at the Shaffer Library of Drug Policy, www.druglibrary.org.

47. Mitchell quoted in Belair, "President Opens Narcotic Drive." See also "Drug Official Quits, Hits Ex-Nixon Aides," *Los Angeles Times*, June 30, 1973; "Drug Agency Head Quits, Assails White House," *Baltimore Sun*, June 30, 1973; Mathea Falco and John Pekkanen, "The Abuse of Drug Abuse," *Washington Post*, Sept. 8, 1974; Epstein, *Agency of Fear*, 246–50.

48. "Drug Law Enforcer: Myles Joseph Ambrose," *New York Times*, Jan. 29, 1972; Dana Adams Schmidt, "Ambrose Sets Up Drug Drive Bases," *New York Times*, Feb. 19, 1972; Drug Enforcement Administration, DEA History, "1970–1975," Epstein, *Agency of Fear*, 208–20.

49. Epstein, *Agency of Fear*, 221–24.

50. Tom Wicker, "Gooks, Slopes and Vermin," *New York Times*, May 4, 1973; "Wrong Number, Wrong Tactics," *Chicago Tribune*, May 7, 1973; Andrew H. Malcolm, "Violent Raids against the Innocent Found Widespread," *New York Times*, June 25, 1973; Curt Matthews, "Indicted U.S. Drug Agents Blame 'Vacuum of Leadership,'" *Washington Post*, Sept. 1, 1973; Radley Balko, *Rise of the Warrior Cop*, 105–22.

51. Drug Enforcement Administration, DEA History, "1970–1975"; Finlator, *Drugged Nation*, 295–323.

52. "Drug Official Quits, Hits Ex-Nixon Aides," *Los Angeles Times,* June 30, 1973; "Drug Agency Chief Quits and Charges White House Interference," *New York Times,* June 30, 1973; Drug Enforcement Administration, DEA History, "1970–1975"; Epstein, *Agency of Fear,* 2, 229–41.

53. Epstein, *Agency of Fear,* 255–56; Arpaio and Sherman, *Joe's Law,* 93, 67; Douglas Valentine, *The Strength of the Pack: The Personalities, Politics and Espionage Intrigues That Shaped the DEA* (Waltersville, OR: Trine Day, 2008).

54. Linda Charlton, "Murphy Attacks U.S. Drug Efforts," *New York Times,* Feb. 23, 1972; "Total War on Drug Addiction," *Chicago Tribune,* March 22, 1972; "Drug Experts Praise Recommendation to Decriminalize Pot," *Chicago Daily Defender,* Aug. 19, 1972; Warren Weaver, "U.S. Drug Study Stresses Treatment, Not Penalties," *New York Times,* March 23, 1973; Charles H. Percy, "Surprise Raids a 'National Disgrace,'" *Los Angeles Times,* Dec. 4, 1973.

55. Tom Wolfe, "The 'Me' Decade and the Third Great Awakening," *New York,* Aug. 23, 1976.

56. See the National Survey on Drug Use and Health and "DrugFacts" series at the National Institute of Drug Abuse (www.drugabuse.gov) and the Substance Abuse and Mental Health Services Administration (www.samhsa.gov). A composite of the relevant years can be found in Lana D. Harrison, Michael Backenheimer, and James A. Inciardi, "Cannabis Use in the United States: Implications for Policy," in *Cannabisbeleid in Duitsland, Frankrijk en de Verenigde Staten,* edited by Peter Cohen and Arjan Sas (Amsterdam: Centrum voor Drugsonderzoek, Universiteit van Amsterdam, 1996), 210. See also National Cancer Institute, *Changes in Cigarette-Related Disease Risks and Their Implication for Prevention and Control,* Tobacco Control Monograph Series (Bethesda, MD: National Cancer Institute, 1997), 13–14; Robin A. LaVallee and Hsiao-ye Yi, *NIAAA: Surveillance Report #92, Apparent per Capita Alcohol Consumption: National, State, and Regional Trends, 1977–2009* (Bethesda, MD: National Institutes of Health, 2011), 6; Baum, *Smoke and Mirrors,* 76–103.

57. Belenko, *Drugs and Drug Policy,* 117–19; Baum, *Smoke and Mirrors,* 76–103.

58. Rudy Abramson, "Ford Says He'll Seek Mandatory Prison Terms for Traffickers in Hard Drugs," *Los Angeles Times,* April 10, 1976; Gilbert A. Lewthwaite, "Ford Keys Texas Campaign Speech to War on Drugs, Courts' 'Laxity,'" *Baltimore Sun,* April 10, 1976; "Betty Ford's 'Overmedication' Problem Ascribed to Taking Combination of Drugs," *Baltimore Sun,* April 12, 1978.

59. Jimmy Carter, "Drug Abuse Message to the Congress," Aug. 2, 1977, American Presidency Project; Baum, *Smoke and Mirrors,* 104–36.

60. William C. Berman, *America's Right Turn: From Nixon to Clinton* (Baltimore: Johns Hopkins University Press, 2001); Lisa McGirr, *Suburban Warriors: The Origins of the New American Right* (Princeton, NJ: Princeton University Press, 2001); Allan J. Lichtman, *White Protestant Nation: The Rise of the American Conservative Movement* (New York: Atlantic Monthly Press, 2008), 330–435.

61. Baum, *Smoke and Mirrors,* 104.

62. Herbert H. Denton, "President Forms Drug Abuse Task Force," *Washington Post,* June 25, 1982; "Reagan Vows War on Dope Trade," *Washington Post,* Oct. 3, 1982; Ronald Reagan, "Radio Address to the Nation on Federal Drug Policy," Oct. 2, 1982, and "Remarks Announcing Federal Initiatives against Drug Trafficking and Organized Crime," Oct. 14, 1982, American Presidency Project; Baum, *Smoke and Mirrors,* 162–76.

63. Drug Enforcement Administration, "DEA Staffing & Budget," www.dea.gov; *National Drug Control Strategy, Budget Summary* (Washington, DC: White House, 1994), 2; Bill Billiter, "Military to Get into War on Drugs," *Los Angeles Times,* Feb. 14, 1982; Baum, *Smoke and Mirrors,* 168.

64. Ronald Reagan, "A Time for Choosing," Oct. 27, 1964, Ronald Reagan Presidential Library & Museum, www.reaganlibrary.gov.

65. U.S. Census Bureau, *Income, Poverty, and Health Insurance Coverage in the United States, 2011* (Washington, DC: U.S. Government Printing Office, 2012), 13; Economic Policy Institute, "When Income Grows, Who Gains?," www.stateofworkingamerica. org.

66. "Excerpts from President's Address on Program for Fighting Crime in U.S.," *New York Times,* Sept. 29, 1981.

67. Reagan, "Remarks Announcing Federal Initiatives."

68. "Crime Rate United States," *Data 360,* www.data360.org; Lydia Saad, "Most Americans Believe Crime in U.S. Is Worsening," *Gallup,* Oct. 31, 2011.

69. Reagan, "Remarks Announcing Federal Initiatives."

70. Michael Demarest et al., "Cocaine: Middle Class High," *Time,* July 6, 1981; Gary Webb, *Dark Alliance: The CIA, the Contras, and the Crack Cocaine Explosion* (New York: Seven Stories Press, 1998); Craig Delaval, "Cocaine, Conspiracy Theories & the C.I.A. in Central America," *Frontline: Drugwars,* Oct. 9–10, 2000, www.pbs.org.

71. National Institute on Drug Abuse, "DrugFacts: Cocaine" and "The Reward Circuit: How the Brain Responds to Cocaine," www.drugabuse.gov.

72. Andy Furillo, "Cocaine Syndicate War Blamed for 25 Murders," *Los Angeles Times,* Oct. 20, 1984; Furillo, "South-Central Cocaine Sales Explode into $25 'Rocks,'" *Los Angeles Times,* Nov. 25, 1984; Jane Gross, "A New, Purified Form of Cocaine Causes Alarm as Abuse Increases," *New York Times,* Nov. 29, 1984; Peter Kerr, "Drug Treatment in City Is Strained by Crack, a Potent New Cocaine," *New York Times,* May 16, 1985; "New York Police Fight 'Crack' Epidemic," *Baltimore Afro-American,* May 31, 1986; Kerr, "Crack Addiction Spreads among the Middle Class," *New York Times,* June 8, 1986; John J. Goldman, "New York City Being Swamped by 'Crack,'" *Los Angeles Times,* Aug. 1, 1986; "Crack Wars," *Baltimore Afro-American,* Aug. 30, 1986.

73. Delaval, "Cocaine, Conspiracy Theories & the C.I.A."; National Security Council, "National Security Decision Directive Number 221: Narcotics and National Security," April 8, 1986, Federation of American Scientists, Intelligence Resource Program, www.fas.org; Ioan Grillo, *El Narco: Inside Mexico's Criminal Insurgency* (New York: Bloomsbury Press, 2011), 55–72.

74. Robert Parry and Brian Barger, "Contras Deal Drugs for Cause," *Chicago Tribune,* Dec. 21, 1985; "Come Contras Linked to Drugs, U.S. Admits," *Chicago Tribune,* Aug. 27, 1986; David S. Hilzenrath, "2 Hill Panels Probing Alleged Links between Contras and Drug Trafficking," *Washington Post,* Aug. 8, 1987; Alexander Cockburn and Jeffrey St. Clair, *Whiteout: The CIA, Drugs and the Press* (London: Verso, 1998), 1–94; Frederick Hitz, "Report of Investigation Concerning Allegations of Connections between the CIA and the Contras in Cocaine Trafficking to the United States," Jan. 29, 1998, Central Intelligence Agency, Office of Inspector General, www.cia.gov.

75. Ronald and Nancy Reagan, "Address to the Nation on the Campaign against Drug Abuse," Sept. 14, 1986, and "Remarks at a Meeting of the White House Conference for a Drug Free America," Feb. 29, 1988, American Presidency Project.

76. Belenko, *Drugs and Drug Policy,* 306–22.

77. *National Drug Control Strategy*, 2, 187; *National Drug Control Strategy, Budget Summary, February 2000* (Washington, DC: U.S. Government Printing Office, 2000), 2, 7; Allen J. Beck and Page M. Harrison, "Prisoners in 2000," *Bureau of Justice Statistics Bulletin* (Aug. 2001); Sentencing Project, "Fact Sheet: Trends in U.S. Corrections," Dec. 2015, www.sentencingproject.org; Roy Walmsley, "World Prison Population List, 11th Edition," *Institute for Criminal Policy Research* (Oct. 2015).

CONCLUSION

1. Cong. Rec., 68th Cong., 1st sess., April 7, 1924, vol. 65, pt. 6: 5768–69.

2. Gabor Maté, MD, *In the Realm of Hungry Ghosts: Close Encounters with Addiction* (Berkeley, CA: North Atlantic Books, 2010); Marc Lewis, *The Biology of Desire: Why Addiction Is Not a Disease* (New York: Public Affairs, 2015).

3. *Bureau of Narcotics, H.R. 10561,* Hearings before the House Committee on Ways and Means, 71st Cong., 2nd sess., March 7–8, 1930, 13–15; Donald Rumsfeld, Department of Defense News Briefing, Feb. 12, 2002, archive.defense.gov.

4. Egil Krogh, "Meeting with Elvis Presley," Dec. 21, 1970, Nixon Presidential Materials, NARA; Dan Baum, "Legalize It All: How to Win the War on Drugs," *Harper's Magazine,* April 2016.

5. Harry J. Anslinger and William F. Tompkins, *The Traffic in Narcotics* (New York: Funk and Wagnalls, 1953), 293.

6. Anslinger quoted in "Doubts U.S. Can Halt Flow of Narcotics; Reveal 40% of Dope Blocked at Source," *Chicago Daily Tribune,* June 4, 1955.

7. Michael H. Hunt, *Ideology and U.S. Foreign Policy* (New Haven, CT: Yale University Press, 1987); Tom Englehardt, *The End of Victory Culture: Cold War America and the Disillusioning of a Generation* (Amherst: University of Massachusetts Press, 1995); Walter L. Hixson, *The Myth of American Diplomacy: National Identity and U.S. Foreign Policy* (New Haven, CT: Yale University Press, 2008).

8. Quoted in Tom Tripodi and Joseph P. DeSario, *Crusade: Undercover against the Mafia and KGB* (Washington, DC: Brassey's, 1993), 154.

9. Michelle Alexander, *The New Jim Crow: Mass Incarceration in the Age of Colorblindness* (New York: New Press, 2012); Simon is quoted in *The House I Live In* (dir. Eugene Jarecki, al-Jazeera Documentary Channel, BBC, 2012). See also David Simon and Edward Burns, *The Corner: A Year in the Life of an Inner-City Neighborhood* (New York: Broadway Books, 1997). In *Drug Warriors and Their Prey: From Police Power to Police State* (Westport, CT: Praeger, 1996), Richard Lawrence Miller also equates the drug war with genocide.

10. Williams to Anslinger, June 23, 1952, folder 12, box 2, Anslinger Papers.

11. Douglas F. Garthoff, *Directors of Central Intelligence as Leaders of the U.S. Intelligence Community, 1946–2005* (Washington, DC: Center for the Study of Intelligence, Central Intelligence Agency, 2005), 221.

12. Ioan Grillo, *El Narco: Inside Mexico's Criminal Insurgency* (New York: Bloomsbury Press, 2011).

13. Harry J. Anslinger and Will Oursler, *The Murderers: The Story of the Narcotics Gangs* (New York: Farrar, Straus, and Cudahy, 1961), 201.

14. Anslinger, remarks UN-CND, May 29, 1957, folder 8, box 1, Anslinger Papers.

15. Sal Vizzini, Oscar Fraley, and Marshall Smith, *Vizzini: The Secret Lives of America's Most Successful Undercover Agent* (New York: Pinnacle Books, 1972), 87–107;

Joe Arpaio and Len Sherman, *Joe's Law: America's Toughest Sheriff Takes on Illegal Immigration, Drugs, and Everything Else That Threatens America* (New York: AMACOM, 2008), 113, 152–53.

16. Williams to Siragusa, Aug. 11, 1950, folder "(0660) Turkey #5, July 1950–Dec. 1950," box 25; Speer to Anslinger, Feb. 4, 1960, folder "(0660-A-1C) General Correspondence District # 17, 1959 thru June 1961," box 165; and Siragusa, Progress Report no. 8, Aug. 2, 1950, folder "Progress Reports of Charles Siragusa," box 164, RG 170, NARA.

17. Quoted in Edward Marshall, "Uncle Sam Is the Worst Drug Fiend in the World," *New York Times,* March 12, 1911.

18. For an overview of the late Obama administration's approach, see "Addiction in America," *Washington Post Live,* May 4, 2016; and Jann S. Wenner, "A Conversation with President Obama," *Rolling Stone,* Dec. 15–29, 2016.

ARCHIVAL SOURCES

National Archives and Records Administration, College Park, MD

RG 56, General Records of the Department of the Treasury
    Entry 193, Central Files of the Office of Secretary, 1933–1956
    Entry 198, Office Files of Secretaries, Under Secretaries, and Assistant Secretaries, 1932–1965

RG 59, Department of State, Central Files
    Central Decimal Files: 1950–1954, 1955–1959, 1960–1963

RG 84, Records of the Foreign Service Posts of the Department of State
    France (Paris, Marseille); Italy (Rome); Lebanon (Beirut); Turkey (Ankara, Istanbul)

RG 170, Records of the Drug Enforcement Administration
    Entry 9, General Subject Files
    Entry 10, Classified Subject Files

RG 226, Records of the Office of Strategic Services
    Entry 136, Washington and Field Station Files
    Entry 224, Personnel Files

Harry J. Anslinger Papers

Special Collections Library, Historical Collections and Labor Archives, Pennsylvania State University, University Park

National Academy of Sciences

Committee on Drug Addiction (1929–39); Committee on Drug Addiction, Advisory (1939–46); Committee on Drug Addiction and Narcotics (CDAN, 1947–65)

Arnold Sagalyn Papers

Special Collections, American University, Washington, DC

Douglas Valentine U.S. Government Drug Enforcement Collection

National Security Archives, George Washington University, Washington, DC

George White Papers

M1111, Department of Special Collections, Stanford University Libraries, Stanford, CA

Newspapers and Periodicals

Baltimore Sun
Chicago Defender
Chicago Tribune
Los Angeles Times
New York Times
Reader's Digest
Saturday Evening Post
Wall Street Journal
Washington Post

INDEX

truth drug. *See* drug(s): truth drug;
MK-ULTRA
Tully, Andrew, 158, 175
Turkey, 1–2, 41, 52, 114, 134–39, 156–57,
183, 198, 202–3, 205–7, 211, 226–29,
238, 245–49, 252, 261, 265, 267–69,
286, 290–91, 316. *See also* District 17;
Istanbul
Turner, Carlton, 299

Uniform State Narcotic Laws, 70
United Nations, 40, 43, 126, 160, 179,
208, 218–20, 222, 229, 246, 254,
257, 261–62, 275. *See also* drug(s):
diplomacy
U.S. Army's Criminal Investigation
Command (CID), 125
U.S. Commissioner of Narcotics, 58,
63, 258, 275. *See also* Anslinger,
Harry J.; Giordano, Henry
U.S. Congress, 14, 28–29, 48, 63–4, 70, 79,
82, 85–86, 149–53, 186, 192, 205, 220,
229, 233, 240, 279, 282, 300, 304–5
U.S. Customs, 54, 94–95, 101, 111, 122,
143, 155, 212–13, 238, 240, 250–54,
258–60, 280, 285–86
U.S. Department of Health, Education,
and Welfare (HEW), 279–81
U.S. Department of Justice, 56, 68, 86,
165, 275, 279, 282–83, 294, 282
U.S. Department of State, 43, 47, 61–62,
68, 84, 107, 127, 202–4, 208–12, 219,
232, 251, 254–60
U.S. Department of Treasury, 40, 43, 58,
62–63, 68–73, 77, 96, 110–14, 126, 138,
153–54, 159, 205, 212–13, 232, 250–51,
259–60, 270, 282, 292; Law Enforcement Officers Training School,
113, 232. *See also* Federal Bureau of
Narcotics: training programs of
U.S. Public Health Service, 34, 73–74, 82
U.S. Supreme Court, 73; decisions of,
55, 73, 107

Valachi, Joseph, 165, 192
Valentine, Douglas, 15, 129, 193, 236, 264
Vandenberg, Hoyt, 135
Van Hee, Julius A., 61
Venezuela, 62
Versailles, Treaty of, 25

Vietnam War, 40, 53, 72, 115, 124, 284,
289–90, 299
Vizzini, Sal, 109–11, 160, 172, 175, 181,
194–95, 239, 248, 258–60, 263, 316
Volstead Act of 1919, 63
Voutsinas, Anastasio, 199–200, 203

Walker, T. J., 158
War on Drugs, ix–x, 12, 271, 274, 288, 292,
299–306, 311, 313–19. *See also* drug
war; Reagan, Ronald: drug war of
Washington, D.C., 45, 60, 64–65
Watergate, 151, 292–95
Waters, Maxine, 305
Webb, Gary, 15, 303–5
Wentworth, Thomas Russell, 66
White, George H., 1–5, 34, 43, 79, 99–
100, 118–25, 128–62, 165, 168, 174,
178–80, 188–89, 194, 202–8, 221, 234–
35, 239, 245, 255, 275, 278, 281, 290
White House Conference on Narcotic
and Drug Abuse, 55, 259, 272, 277–79
"white slavery." *See under* slavery
Williams, Garland, 93–107, 112–22, 129,
131, 134, 140, 142, 155, 178–80, 202,
205–7, 221, 234, 247, 257, 267–68,
314, 316
Williams brothers, E. H. and Henry,
82–84
Wilson, James Q., 108–12
Winchell, Walter, 100, 178
wiretaps, 107, 110, 294
Wolfe, Tom, 109, 297
Wolff, Harold, 150
Woolsey, James, 315
Woman's Home Companion, 49
World War I, 26, 59, 61, 78, 115–16, 299
World War II, 4, 39–40, 44, 113–25, 131–
32, 143–44, 164, 177, 205, 207, 213,
255, 299, 312
Wright, Elizabeth Washburn, 63–66
Wright, Hamilton, 25–26, 28, 63, 316
Wurms, Ike, 276–277

Young family, Harold, Gordon, and
William, 257–58
Yugoslavia, 114, 181–82

Zurlo, Angelo, 122
Zweier, Arthur G., 132

MATTHEW R. PEMBLETON is a writer and historian based in the Washington, DC region. A longtime Maryland resident, Matt completed his doctorate in History at American University in 2014 and occasionally teaches college history courses on various subjects in U.S. history. He also works as a consultant and Postdoctoral Research Fellow at the National Academies of Sciences, Engineering, and Medicine, where he supports a project on the history of the Academy complex and its place in national affairs. You can follow his work at www.mattpembleton.com.